Book of the Gods and Rites
and
The Ancient Calendar

The Civilization of the American Indian Series

The founding of Mexico-Tenochtitlan in 1325. The Aztecs found an eagle perched on a nopal cactus on an island in Lake Tetzcoco, which they took as the sign of their future metropolis. On either side of the eagle are Aztec chieftains. Above the eagle appear a shield and arrows, symbols of Tenochtitlan's mission as conqueror of the world.

BOOK OF THE GODS AND RITES
and
THE ANCIENT CALENDAR

**by
Fray Diego Durán**

Translated and edited by
Fernando Horcasitas
and
Doris Heyden

Foreword by Miguel León-Portilla

University of Oklahoma Press
Norman

By Fernando Horcasitas and Doris Heyden (translators)

The Aztecs: The History of the Indies of New Spain, by Fray Diego Durán (New York, 1964)
The Olmec World, by Ignacio Bernal (Berkeley, 1967)
Book of the Gods and Rites and The Ancient Calendar, by Fray Diego Durán (Norman, 1971)

By Fernando Horcasitas

De Porfirio Díaz a Zapata (Mexico City, 1968)

By Doris Heyden

La idumentaria de Oaxaca antiqua (Mexico City, 1970)

International Standard Book Number: 0–8061–0889–4

International Library of Congress Catalog Card Number: 73–88147

Book of the Gods and Rites and *The Ancient Calendar* is Volume 102 in *The Civilization of the American Indian Series*.

FOREWORD

THIS translation of two classic works of the sixteenth-century Dominican friar Diego Durán will be welcomed by ethnohistorians and students of ancient Mexico. Fernando Horcasitas and Doris Heyden, who based their translation on the original manuscript, have performed a valuable service to the English-reading public. Credit is also due the University of Oklahoma Press, which presents this important source in its distinguished Civilization of the American Indian Series.

The history of Durán's writings is a remarkable paradox. The first scholar to mention him was a brother Dominican, the chronicler Agustín Dávila Padilla. In his *Historia de la fundación y discurso de la Provincia de Santiago de México* (1596), Dávila Padilla tells us that Diego Durán "wrote two books on the Mexican Indians: one on their history and one about their ancient customs." Then, writing of what I have called the paradox of Durán's work, he affirms that it is "the finest account ever written in this field," adding that, unfortunately, Durán's writings "brought him little renown." The latter statement is amply confirmed by the fact that

v

Durán's books were not published in his lifetime and that he did not foresee the fate that was to befall them. Others were to gather information from them—for example, his kinsman the Jesuit Juan de Tovar. Another Jesuit, however, was to be even more fortunate: Joseph de Acosta used part of Durán's chronicle in his popular *Historia natural y moral de las Indias* (1590).

Though Durán's books remained unpublished for many years, his reputation as a great scholar was never completely forgotten. In 1639 the renowned bibliographer León Pinelo stated that in his opinion Durán's treatises were "remarkable books." More than a century later Juan José Eguiara y Eguren, in his *Biblioteca Mexicana* (1755), and still later José Mariano Beristáin y Souza, in his *Biblioteca Hispanoamericana Septentrional* (1816–20), praised the chronicler, though they had never seen his manuscript.

For almost three hundred years, however, Dávila Padilla's comment that Durán's writings "brought him little renown" held true. But exceptionally creative things seldom fall into permanent oblivion. From Ramírez's pioneer edition of Durán's works (1867–80) to that of the scholar Angel María Garibay K. (1967), the writings of the Dominican friar have emerged to take their place among the most valuable and most widely quoted works on ancient Mexico.

Now Fernando Horcasitas and Doris Heyden (who in 1964 translated and edited an English edition of Durán's *Historia de las Indias de Nueva España y Islas de Tierra Firme*) present the first English version of the *Book of the Gods and Rites* and *The Ancient Calendar*, a rich mine of ethnographic and calendrical material stemming from pre-Conquest times.

It is not my intention in these preliminary words to analyze the contents of the works or to evaluate the eyewitness sources which served Durán. Suffice it to say that the following pages contain remarkable sixteenth-century accounts of the religious world of the Aztecs, their gods and rituals, their ceremonies and feasts, and such fundamental and fascinating features as the calendar, the market places, and the games of these ancient people.

The works contain a bounty of data, different from yet in some ways comparable in scope to those obtained by the indefatigable Fray Bernardino de Sahagún. It has been no easy task to translate Durán's archaic Spanish, dotted with Aztec terms, into English. The reader will surely agree that the translators have produced a flowing and lucid text and that the works of Fray Diego Durán are still "highly pleasing" and, as Dávila Padilla wrote, "the finest account ever written in this field."

MIGUEL LEÓN-PORTILLA

Director
Instituto de Investigaciones Historicas
Universidad Nacional Autónoma de México

Mexico City
January 1, 1971

CONTENTS

Contents

ILLUSTRATIONS

Black and White Plates

Book of the Gods and Rites

MAP

BIBLIOGRAPHICAL NOTE

IT IS probable that only one copy of the three works by Fray Diego Durán was penned in the author's own hand. That manuscript was sent from Mexico to Spain, possibly to the library of a Dominican monastery, sometime between 1581 and 1821. Later, probably after the secularization of church property in Spain under Isabella II, the manuscript was deposited in the National Library of Madrid.

After Durán's death in 1588, he was all but forgotten for almost three hundred years. One reference to his writings appears in Dávila Padilla (1596):

> Fray Diego wrote two books, one a history and the other on the ancient customs of the Mexican Indians, the finest account ever written in this field. He was a very sick man, and his works brought him little renown, though a section of them has been printed in the *Historia natural y moral*, by Father Joseph de Acosta, who received it from Father Juan de Tovar. [Dávila Padilla, 653]

Dávila Padilla was referring to a résumé of some fifty pages of

Durán's chronicle, which had appeared as Book VII of Acosta's *Historia natural y moral de las Indias* (1590). Durán's work is also mentioned and praised in a letter from the scholar Juan de Tovar to the Jesuit Acosta (Bernal, 1964, *xxi*).

In the ensuing centuries Fray Diego was mentioned by a number of scholars: Antonio de León Pinelo (1629, 101), Juan José Eguiara y Eguren (1755), José Mariano Beristáin y Souza (1816–21), Alonso Franco (1900, 196), and Francisco Javier Clavijero, S.J. (1944, I:39). It is unlikely, however, that any of these historians and bibliographers were able to consult the original manuscript. For almost three hundred years Durán's large, beautifully illustrated work lay hidden from the world. It was not until the early 1850's that a renowned Mexican scholar, José Fernando Ramírez, discovered it in the National Library of Madrid. It has remained there to this day, except for a period in 1964, when it was taken to the United States for exhibit at the Spanish pavilion of the New York World's Fair.

The Codex Durán, the original manuscript, forms one corpus of 344 sheets of European paper, written in a clear script on both sides of each sheet and numbered only on the right-hand folio. Each page is made up of two columns averaging thirty-six lines each. The Spanish spelling would have been considered atrocious even in its time, and virtually no effort was made to lighten the reader's task by means of punctuation. The work is illustrated with 127 colored drawings, 70 in the *History*, 36 in *Book of the Gods and Rites*, and 21 in *The Ancient Calendar*. The drawings can be compared to some of the hand-drawn miniatures in medieval religious books. The artist is unknown.

In the original manuscript the *History* appears first, though it was written after the other two works. The *History* contains seventy-eight chapters, numbered with Roman numerals, and appears on folios 1 to 226. The *Book of the Gods and Rites* appears on folios 226 to 316 and is divided into twenty-three chapters. Though the nineteenth-century edition numbers the chapters of the *History* and the *Book of the Gods and Rites* consecutively, the present translation reverts to the chapter numeration of the original manuscript. *The Ancient Calendar* appears on folios 316 to 344 and is subdivided into an epistle, three chapters on the calendar, a section for each of the eighteen Aztec months, and an appendix on the five unlucky days.

By the time Ramírez discovered the manuscript, it had suffered serious mutilations. The title page had been ripped off (as a consequence of which the original name of the combined works is unknown), and in its place had been inscribed "Historia de las Indias DN. Y Yslas y tierra firme." At the end of the *Book of the Gods and Rites* three lines had been blotted out with heavy black ink. A friend of Ramírez, Francisco González de Vera, the librarian of the Ministry of War in Madrid, held the page against the light and concluded that the lines read "by Father Diego Durán, friar of the Order of Preachers." It is to be suspected that someone wished Fray Diego's name to fall into oblivion and perhaps tried to plagiarize his work.

Mysterious alterations had also been made in the manuscript. An anonymous hand, spurred by motives unknown, had scratched out a number of passages. One such mutilation, of eleven lines, occurs immediately following a description of the Spaniards' violation of the "hidden chambers of the maidens who served the gods" (fol. 211). Another obliteration appears after the lines describing the hanging of Cuauhtemoc by Cortés (fol. 220).

The Madrid manuscript was bound during the nineteenth century. The binder is scarcely to be praised for his work. Large parts of the colored illustrations were cut off, and on some pages, in spite of the wide margins, the written lines also lost a few letters.

Despite the abuses the manuscript had suffered, Ramírez realized the significance of his discovery. With the help of González de Vera, he engaged a scribe to copy the manuscript and a highly skilled artist to reproduce the illustrations. According to an annotation in pencil on the inside of the cover, the scribe was paid three hundred pesos for his work. The copy was completed in Madrid on April 1, 1854. The copyist produced an accurate text, 513 pages long, in flowing script, to which Ramírez added an index. The artist responsible for copying the illustrations, a man of great talent and sensitivity, reproduced the original drawings on separate sheets of paper and later pasted them in their proper places in the new manuscript. It is those reproductions which appear in this book. The Ramírez copy was sent to Mexico and is preserved today in the Historical Archives of the Library of the National Museum of Anthropology (No. 556 [15585]).

Ramírez decided to publish Durán's works in a two-volume edition, together with a slim *Atlas*, which was to contain the illustrations. Unfortunately for the fate of Durán's chronicle, the 1850's and 1860's were chaotic years in Mexico. The type for the first volume was set, however, and engravings were made of the illustrations. Volume I, containing the first sixty-eight chapters of the *History*, appeared early in 1867. Almost immediately afterward, Maximilian of Hapsburg was overthrown, and Ramírez, a supporter of Maximilian, was forced into exile. After the fall of the Second Empire the Durán copy and the illustration plates were preserved in the School of Mines in Mexico City. Although their rediscoverer is unknown, in 1873 a publisher, Eduardo Gallo, issued a work entitled *Hombres ilustres mexicanos*, in which eight of the Durán illustrations appeared, somewhat altered, but certainly taken from the Ramírez copy. Seven years later Gumesindo Mendoza, director of the National Museum of Mexico, urged two officials of the Mexican government, Protasio P. Tagle and Ignacio Mariscal, to co-operate in publishing the second volume of the Ramírez edition and the *Atlas*. These books, which appeared in 1880, contained the last portion of the *History*, the *Book of the Gods and Rites*, *The Ancient Calendar*, and the *Atlas*. A monograph by Alfredo Chavero was appended to the work. A facsimile edition of the 1867–80 work was printed in 1951.

The 1967 edition of the complete works of Fray Diego Durán, by Angel María Garibay K., is the most recent version of the original Spanish manuscript.

Durán never identifies the artist or artists who drew the illustrations for his work. The friar collected copies of pictorial documents while he was writing his books, as he himself mentions in Chapter I of the *Book of the Gods and Rites*:

I found this painting as old, as ancient, as the first, as can be seen on the adjoining sheet, together with a picture of Topiltzin. In order to lend me this, the Indian from Chiauhtla made me swear that I would return it to him. When I had given him my word that when I had copied it I would return it, he finally loaned it to me with so much ceremony and elaborate talk and in such great secrecy, that I was astonished at the value he placed upon it. And I will affirm my belief that he stayed tenaciously with the artist until the picture was done.[1]

The draftsman who painted the final version of the illustrations may have been a Spanish Dominican friar or an Indian trained in the monastery. In either case, the illustrations are probably the work of one man, who used earlier pictorial documents as references.

Of the Durán illustrations Donald Robertson, art historian of Tulane University has written:

> Until now, publication of the illustrations has been essentially based upon the lithographs made by a draughtsman for Ramírez. These are published as the *Atlas de Durán*; since this was not a photographic edition our knowledge of the illustrations has been somewhat limited. Furthermore, in the *Atlas*, lithographs of the many vignettes scattered throughout the text are gathered together so that their relation to the text is not precisely determinable. It is because of this inadequate publication history that the physical composition of the illustrations has not been noted in the literature.
>
> During March of 1965 I was able to examine the original codex at some length and discovered peculiarities in some of the illustrations of the document. In many instances the illustrations of the Madrid codex are cut from an older manuscript and pasted onto their present positions. In some instances the "cut-out" illustrations have a fragment of Spanish on their reverse. This older prose as of now has not been collated with the text of the *Codex Durán* because the fragmentary prose is only preserved on the reverse face of the paste-overs where they are attached to the present codex. [Robertson, personal communication, 1967]

The pasted illustrations referred to by Robertson may have

[1] See pp. 15–16.

been clipped from a first draft written by Durán. Robertson states, however:

> There is a remote possibility that the Durán paste-overs come from a distinct and lost account, not strictly related to the Madrid codex. This question can only be resolved by a study and collation of the fragments of prose on the reverse of the paste-overs with the text of the Durán codex. I had neither the time nor the technical facilities to make such a detailed study in Madrid.

> The style of the illustrations ranges from rather close adherence to native conventions surviving in the later sixteenth century to illustrations abreast of contemporary European artistic trends. Illustrations or vignettes with a more predominantly native cast include the "Temple and Skull Rack" (Chapter II), the genre scene of folio 300v (Chapter XX), the "Round Dance and Musicians" (Chapter XXI), the "Patolli Game" (Chapter XXII), and the "Ball Court Scene" (Chapter XXIII), all having suggestions of the style used in passages of Sahagún's *Florentine Codex* and all being paste-overs.

> These particular illustrations are characterized by a rather strict two-dimensionality. The figures exist in a world where space does not extend backward and forward into the picture space but things further in depth are shown above things nearer to the viewer. In the "Patolli Game" and the "Ball Court Scene" important forms are shown in plan, although the human figures appear in elevation. In the "Round Dance and Musicians" the dancers are shown flattened into a ring radiating from the center, a center where the drums and drummers are shown in elevation. These particular vignettes are also those with the least interest in landscape and its dominant elements—sky, clouds, and vegetation.

> By and large, the remaining illustrations rely heavily on elements of landscape to create three-dimensional spatial settings for human activities. European principles of perspective also give to the actors in the scenes the visualized space of nature, or at least a space suggesting the space of a stage.

> The Renaissance flavor of the Durán illustrations, however, is carried in large part by detail in the elaborate framing elements omitted in the *Atlas* engravings. It is in these framing elements that one finds the vocabulary of form reminiscent of German and Netherlandish design books: strap-work, swags with boucraines, and the

constant use of leaf forms suggesting the classic acanthus. They remind us of classic forms to be seen in the Augustinian church of Ixmiquilpan and the paintings in the patio of the Hospital de Jesús in Mexico City.

Round arches supported by columns, both with details from Spanish Plateresque architecture, echo the forms and shapes to be found in sixteenth century Mexican colonial buildings. Painted versions of similar architecture can still be seen in the frescoes of monasteries such as Acolman and are common in the *Florentine Codex* and other Mexican manuscripts of the same period. [Robertson, 1968, 340–48]

The translation that follows was prepared from the second volume of the Ramírez edition, which was printed in 1880 under the direction of Gumesindo Mendoza in Mexico. Subsequently, having obtained a microfilm of the original sixteenth-century manuscript through the kindness of Raúl Noriega, we checked the entire text for fidelity. Although Ramírez's text is generally faithful to the original Madrid manuscript, we found it necessary to check all Nahuatl names. We discovered the 1880 edition to be plagued with errors; for example, Tec Calli (House of Lords) appears as Teuccalli (Temple); Mimixcoa (Cloud Serpent) was transformed into Nuinixcoa; Amiztequihuaque became Huitztequilmaque; Miztoncaltecuhtli was changed to Huitztoncatecutly; and Mixcoateocalli became Mixcoatcocally. The Nahuatl used in the present translation is faithful to the original manuscript in Madrid.

In this translation punctuation and capitalization have been modernized, and words and phrases have been inserted in brackets to clarify obscure expressions or to supply lacunae. We have divided overlong paragraphs into shorter ones for easier reading. The translation tends to the literal rather than the free, with the occasional sacrifice of good prose in favor of accuracy.

We wish to express our gratitude to Savoie Lottinville, Director Emeritus of the University of Oklahoma Press, and to the staff of the Press, for their patience and encouragement in working with us. We are also grateful to Antonio Pompa y Pompa, Director of the Library of the National Museum of Mexico, for facilitating our consultation of manuscripts; to Raúl Noriega, who lent us the microfilm copy of the original Durán manuscript in Madrid; to Donald Robertson, for his comments on the illustrations; and to Father Victorino Aranda, curate of Zacualpan and Hueyapan, Morelos, who assisted us in our examination of the archives of his two parishes.

FERNANDO HORCASITAS
DORIS HEYDEN

Mexico City
January 1, 1971

Book of the Gods and Rites

and

The Ancient Calendar

¶ A GUIDE TO NAHUATL PRONUNCIATION

All Nahuatl words are stressed on the penultimate syllable.

The *a* is pronounced as in *wad*.

The *e* is pronounced as in *set*.

The *i* is pronounced as in *elite*.

The *o* is pronounced as in *orb*; in some local forms of the language it took on the sound of the *o* in *foot*. Hence the varying forms *Tetzcoco* and *Tetzcuco*.

The *c* is pronounced like the *c* in *cow*. When followed by *i* or *e* it has the sound of *s* in *song*.

The *qu* when followed by *e* or *i* is pronounced like the *c* in *cow*.

The *z* is always pronounced like the *s* in *song*.

The *hu* is pronounced like the *w* in *will*.

The *tl* is considered an independent sound in Nahuatl, similar to the *tl* in *rattler* but with a stronger sound.

The *h* is pronounced as in *hot*.

The *x* is pronounced like *sh* as in *shoot*.

The rest of the consonants are pronounced in Nahuatl approximately as they are in English.

FRAY DIEGO DURÁN: HIS LIFE AND WORKS

BY FERNANDO HORCASITAS

AND

DORIS HEYDEN

I. Diego, Child of Seville and Tetzcoco

W HEN an inconspicuous Dominican friar, Diego Durán, died in Mexico in 1588 (Dávila Padilla, 653), his passing was largely unnoticed by the world. Today even the place of his burial is unknown. Among his meager possessions, however, he bequeathed to civilization a manuscript, which was later to find its way to the National Library of Madrid, Spain. It was rediscovered there in the nineteenth century by the Mexican scholar José Fernando Ramírez (Durán, 1951, I:*vi*). When the text was published, historians and anthropologists realized that this sheaf of papers revealed Durán to be one of the dozen or so most articulate ethnographers who wrote about the pre-Columbian New World.

Durán has never been the subject of a biography in the true sense of the word, though various studies have mentioned the date and place of his birth and half a dozen events in his life and have provided commentaries (some of them excellent) on his works. In these pages we have attempted a reconstruction of the friar's life from internal evidence, basing our work upon a careful scrutiny of Durán's writings (Durán, 1951; Durán, 1581). After arranging

3

hundreds of autobiographical details scattered throughout Durán's works (sometimes in the most unexpected passages), we have tried to approach Durán in a new way, unveiling him as a puzzled human being and a scholar rather than as simply an obscure author of dusty chronicles.

It was not until 1925 that the scholar Francisco Fernández del Castillo discovered, among the papers of the Inquisition in the Archivo General de la Nación in Mexico City, a document in which Durán himself states that he was born in Seville (Fernández del Castillo, 1925, 223–29). Like many other Spanish immigrants in Mexico, Fray Diego was an Andalusian. Nothing is known about his parents except through indirect references in his writings. His family did not belong to the original group of conquerors who came with Cortés, and they were not encomenderos, or holders of fiefs in New Spain. We may assume that his parents were people of humble station, his father possibly a petty official in the Spanish government, or perhaps a small trader or farmer.

When Durán was very small, he and his parents migrated from Seville to New Spain and lived for some time in the city of Tetzcoco (Texcoco), near Mexico City. "Some will think that I am being partial to my background in praising Tetzcoco so inordinately; although my teeth were not born there, it was there that my second teeth came out" (Durán, 1967, II:23). This comment would place his birth date around 1537.

Tetzcoco had been a place of splendor in pre-Columbian times, the veritable "Athens of the Western World" (Prescott, 132). Its privileged position on the shore of Lake Tetzcoco permitted a bountiful agriculture and the creation of elaborately designed groves and gardens. A few miles to the east rose the Hill of Tetzcotzinco, the marvelous garden of the Tetzcocan kings, a rival of the Alhambra or the terraced gardens of Babylon. There royalty had taken pleasure in the carved-stone baths, fountains, flower gardens, and harems. Beyond Tetzcotzinco loomed the misty heights of the Mountain of Tlaloc, God of Rain, the holiest mountain of pagan Mexico.

Tetzcoco was a great metropolis until the Spanish Conquest.

It was governed by King Nezahualcoyotl, the Fasting Coyote (1402–72)—poet; astronomer; lawgiver; engineer and builder of palaces, temples, and aqueducts; founder of the library of Tetzcoco; one of the greatest scholars of pre-Christian Mexico. He was succeeded by his son, Nezahualpilli, who reigned from 1472 to 1516. Nezahualpilli was the Fasting Prince, a seer, a brilliant astronomer, a man who—according to the reminiscences of the people—was the very incarnation of the perfect prince, the epitome of all the refinements admired by the people in pre-Spanish days.

How beautiful the Nahuatl language sounded in Tetzcoco! Men claimed that it was more elegant and polished than that of Mexico and other cities. No doubt by the age of six Diego had become fluent in the Tetzcocan way of speaking.

After the Spanish Conquest, Tetzcoco had ceased to be the Athens of America. Day by day it had ceded its power to Mexico City. Its temple had been razed, its library had disappeared, and the *tlamatinime*, "scholars," had perished or gone into hiding. The pleasure gardens of Tetzcotzinco were falling into ruins, and Don Carlos, the last representative of the ancient Tetzcocan dynasty, had been tried and executed for performing human sacrifice.

In the Tetzcoco of Diego's boyhood Christianity was taking roots. Northeast of the city, in Tepetlaoztoc, lived a Dominican hermit, Fray Domingo de Betanzos. It is possible that during his early years Diego visited the holy man at his hermitage, a contact which may have influenced him to enter the Dominican order.

II. The Mexico of the 1550's—Diego's Formative Years

After some years in Tetzcoco, Diego and his family moved to Mexico City. He may have been ten or twelve years old when the family moved—his writings do not give specific dates. He was now living in the capital of New Spain:

> *Mexico-Tenochtitlan,*
> *Among the reeds and the rushes;*
> *The place of the prickly pear cactus*
> *Standing in the midst of the waters.*

Where the eagle rises,
Where the eagle screams,
Where the eagle opens its wings!

(Alvarado Tezozómoc, 3)

But what had been the heart of the Aztec world before the Spanish Conquest was by 1547 a skeleton of ruins among mounds on which Christian churches were beginning to rise. Some Spanish settlers and a few surviving conquerors or their descendants were trying to adapt themselves to life on this chaotic field where two cultures had met.

Durán did not discuss his education, but it is probable that he first attended the Franciscan school of Tetzcoco, founded by Fray Pedro de Gante in 1523. In the City of Mexico several schools educated Spanish, Indian, and mestizo children. One school throve in the Monastery of San Francisco el Grande. Others were the School of San Juan de Letrán, the school conducted by the Augustinians, and the College of Santa Cruz of Tlatelolco (Ricard, Chaps. VI–VII). We do not know whether Diego attended one of those establishments or was taught at home. To judge from the rough style of his writing, it is doubtful that he was influenced by the polished prose and poetry of Spain's Golden Age.

Besides their studies, boys found unending sources of wonder in the city. Perhaps Diego was once sent to deliver a message to His Excellency the Archbishop of Mexico and was surprised to find that, up a flight of steps on the Calle de Moneda, the Christian prelate ruled supreme upon the remains of the temple where hearts had once been offered to Tezcatlipoca. (Names like Tezcatlipoca presented no difficulty for Diego, though the boys in Mexico City may have poked fun at his Tetzcocan accent—his voicing of *ô* slightly like *ū*, a variant that was considered a refined pronunciation.)

On Sundays he doubtless accompanied his parents to mass in the cathedral, a rather plain, single-naved church built by the Franciscans thirty years before, which also stood near the ruins of the Great Temple of Mexico. After mass he may have strolled with his father and mother to Santo Domingo, the church and

6

monastery of the Dominicans, a somewhat rustic establishment three blocks north of the cathedral. The church had been built in 1526, the year of the Dominicans' arrival in New Spain. There lived the friars, garbed in black and white, the most learned men— so Diego had heard—in New Spain.

Like other boys, he feared yet was attracted to the *casa del diablo*, the home of the "heathen goddess," the haunted house of Mexico. It stood halfway between Santo Domingo and the cathedral. Sometimes Diego and his schoolfellows would dare one another to explore the ruins of this house of gloom, where, according to legend, Cihuacoatl, the Snake Woman, and the stone idols that attended her were still buried in the debris.

Diego and his young Indian and Creole friends occasionally wandered to the four ancient barrios of Mexico City, by 1550 known as San Juan Moyotlan, Santa María Cuepopan, San Sebastián Atzacualco, and San Pablo Zoquipan. Chapels now stood upon the ruins of the temple pyramids of these ancient wards, symbols of the fourfold founding of Mexico in 1325.

In one of the four wards, San Pablo Zoquipan, Diego came across a school of gymnasts and dancers, a survival of ancient Mexica sport. It was thrilling to watch as groups of three men stood upon one another's shoulders, jumped, and performed extraordinary acrobatics. It was not, thought the boy, the work of the devil, as some murmured, but the agility of a conquered race still exhibiting its prowess.

The Franciscan monastery lay toward the west, at the site of Moteczoma's zoo. Now a gigantic wooden cross, two hundred feet high (McAndrew, 247–48), carved from immense ahuehuete trees of Moteczoma's Chapultepec, rose as a reminder of the triumph of the New Faith. Later Durán was to compare its height with that of the Great Temple of Mexico.

Another walk led to the Street of Tacuba. On the way Diego passed the Shrine of the Martyrs (today the Church of San Hipólito, the patron saint of Mexico City). At this historical spot Cortés had been caught while fleeing the city in the middle of the night, and most of his men—Spaniards and Tlaxcalans overloaded with

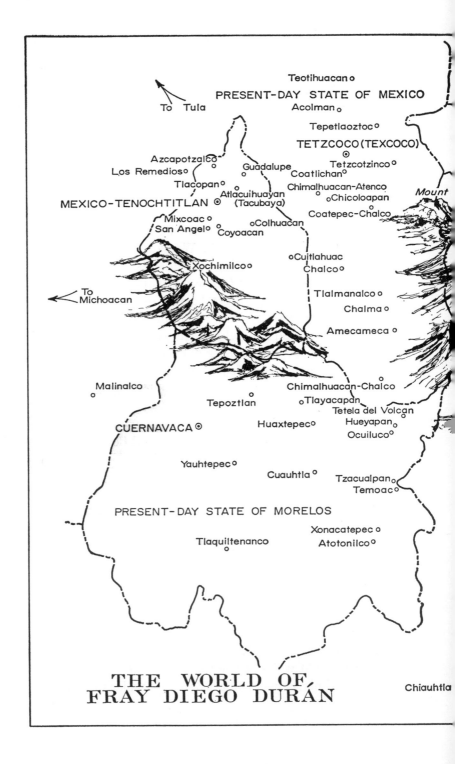

Teotihuacan ○

PRESENT–DAY STATE OF MEXICO

Acolman ○

Tepetlaoztoc ○

TETZCOCO (TEXCOCO)
◎

Azcapotzalco ○
Guadalupe ○   Tetzcotzinco ○
Los Remedios ○   Coatlichan ○

Tlacopan ○   Chimalhuacan-Atenco ○
Atlacuihuayan   ○ Chicoloapan
(Tacubaya)

MEXICO–TENOCHTITLAN ◎   Coatepec-Chalco ○

Mixcoac ○   ○ Colhuacan
San Angel ○ Coyoacan

○ Cuitlahuac
Chalco ○

Xochimilco ○   Tlalmanalco ○

To   Chalma ○
Michoacan

Amecameca ○

Mount

Malinalco   Chimalhuacan-Chalco ○
○

Tepoztlan ○   ○ Tlayacapan

Tetela del Volcan
CUERNAVACA ◎   Huaxtepec ○   Hueyapan ○

Ocuiluco ○

Yauhtepec ○

Cuauhtla ○   Tzacualpan ○
Temoac ○

PRESENT–DAY STATE OF MORELOS

Xonacatepec ○

Tlaquiltenanco ○   Atotonilco ○

THE WORLD OF
FRAY DIEGO DURÁN

Chiauhtla

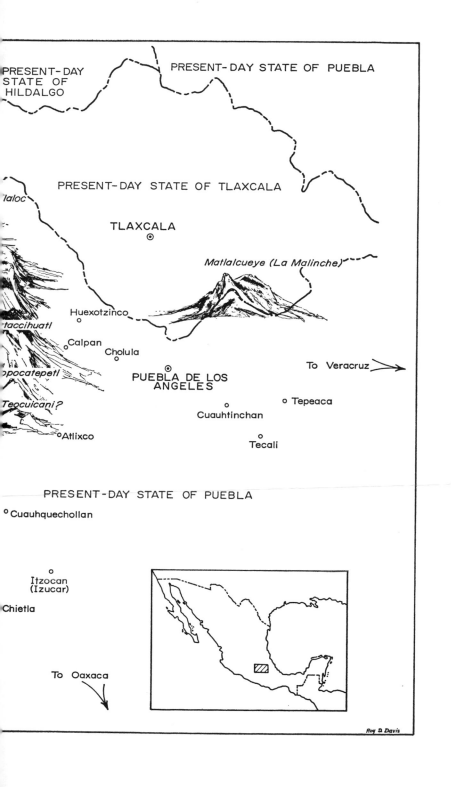

PRESENT-DAY
STATE OF
HILDALGO

PRESENT-DAY STATE OF PUEBLA

PRESENT-DAY STATE OF TLAXCALA

TLAXCALA
◎

Matlalcueye (La Malinche)

laloc

Huexotzinco
○

taccihuatl

Calpan
○
Cholula
○

◎
PUEBLA DE LOS
ANGELES

To Veracruz ➤

popocatepetl

○ Tepeaca

Cuauhtinchan
○

Teocuicani?

○
Tecali

○Atlixco

PRESENT-DAY STATE OF PUEBLA

○ Cuauhquechollan

○
Itzocan
(Izucar)

Chietla

To Oaxaca

Roy D. Davis

gold—had died there. Many years later Durán was to speak of the *noche triste* in his *History*.

At Santiago Tlatelolco, almost a mile north of the cathedral, stood the ruins of several pre-Hispanic temples. Occasionally Diego saw Mexica boys, grandsons of the highest Aztec nobility, entering the College of Santa Cruz of Tlatelolco. It was said that a certain Franciscan monk, Fray Bernardino de Sahagún, taught them Latin and Spanish, meanwhile learning Nahuatl from them and preparing an extensive work on the pagan past of the Aztec nation.

To the south, beyond the mountains of Ajusco, lay the Tierra Caliente—the Hot Country—also called the Marquesado, largely the private property of the heirs of Cortés, who had conquered the area for Spain. On the way to the mountains were the ruins of a shrine—Tocititlan, the Place of Our Grandmother—where Cortés had met and first conversed with the Angry Lord in 1519. The ruins stood near the Hospital de Jesús, where Cortés's remains lie today.

To the north was a small shrine where the goddess Tonantzin had been worshiped in earlier times and where Mother Guadalupe was revered in Diego's time. Going west, the schoolboy climbed to the top of Los Remedios, the hill where Cortés was said to have rested in his darkest hour. In the center of the city Diego often passed the monumental Aztec sacrificial stones standing between the cathedral and the viceregal dwelling.[1]

All these sights and sounds, the relics and descendants of a vanished empire, fired Diego's mind with lifelong passion for the history of his adopted country. Later he was to observe that this land was the finest and most delightful in the world (Durán, 1967, II:23).

At times Diego's wanderings led him eastward along the banks of the canals which flowed to the center of the city—today the Merced Market. Thousands of canoes crowded the water, filled with produce of all kinds: maize of many colors, red and green tomatoes, tons of string beans and dried beans, flowers of a hundred varieties—sun-colored marigolds ("flowers of the dead"), dahlias,

[1] See p. 80. Page references at the bottoms of pages refer to the translation in subsequent pages of this book.

red poinsettias—ducks, quail, partridges, fish, *ahuauhtli* ("mosquito eggs"), turkeys, pigeons, frogs, lake shrimp, doves, green amaranth, pumpkins, tender squash, and great sacks of the native delicacy, pumpkin seeds. Scarcely a word of Spanish could be heard in the hum created by merchants and market women, the latter dressed in clothing almost identical to pre-Hispanic garb. These people were the descendants of the Aztecs, the sculptors of the mighty stones in the city. Few coins circulated among the vendors and buyers; the ancient cacao bean was still the standard currency.

The society of young Durán's Mexico City was an unstable and motley one—two religions, two political systems, two races, two languages—in sum, two conflicting societies struggling to adapt to one another in a painful cultural, social, religious, and racial accommodation. In the royal palace ruled His Excellency Antonio de Mendoza, viceroy and personal representative of His Sacred and Caesarean Majesty, the Roman Emperor Charles V. A few blocks northeast of the palace ruled another "majesty," His Highness Diego Tehuetzqui, a puppet of the Spanish government, the grandson of Emperor Tizoc, who had ruled Mexico from 1481 to 1486.

The city teemed with Spaniards: gaunt Franciscans; Augustinian and Dominican monks; ruffians, adventurers, gamblers; a few old conquerors who had long and dubious yarns to tell about Cortés and Moteczoma; women of doubtful virtue; a few dispossessed descendants of the men who had risked their lives to capture one of the richest jewels in the crown of the emperor; a few settlers, petty officials, and shopkeepers. There were thousands of halfbloods, nearly all of whom were illegitimate offspring of Spaniards and Indian women. A growing colony of enslaved Negroes from Africa further confused the racial picture. Diego was to describe the former superb social organization of the Aztec city and to lament that in his own times "one can barely tell who is the knight, who the muleteer, who the squire, who the sailor."[2] He was to recall with disgust witnessing brutal fights among the Negroes, sponsored and wagered upon by the Spaniards. The matches took place upon the Aztec sacrificial stones.[3]

[2] See p. 195. [3] See pp. 180–81.

11

But the Indians still made up the largest numbers of this metropolis of seventy thousand inhabitants (Gibson, 387). Though crushed and humiliated, the Aztecs were not completely broken:

> Like a plant caught beneath the ruins of a building that has collapsed, which—after a painful struggle—manages to push its leaves through the ruins, thus the mind of the vanquished Indians was pierced to its innermost depth, but did not die: it accepted that which it could and that which it desired from the invaders, and continued to live its own life. [Garibay, 1953–54, II:8]

One day, on a visit to the home of relatives, Durán was aghast to see the old marks of branding irons (like those used on cattle) on the flesh of the servants, a survival from the times when Indians had been slaves (Durán, 1967, II:574). Such stains on the history of Spain in the New World—reminders of the war against slavery waged by the Dominican Bartolomé de las Casas—disturbed Diego profoundly, though, as he was to report later, the slaves were freed under Mendoza, viceroy from 1535 to 1550.

III. Diego Enters the Dominican Order

We do not know under what circumstances Diego became a monk, but we do know that he became a novice at the Monastery of Santo Domingo in Mexico City on May 8, 1556, around the age of nineteen (Beristáin y Souza, I:442). That he was accepted into the Dominican order is further evidence of his Spanish birth, for the admission of native-born boys was discouraged (Sandoval, 54).

The views and aims of the Dominicans, the second religious order to arrive in New Spain, were more inclined toward theology and social and political philosophy than were those of the earlier Franciscans. The vigor of the Dominican order was evidenced by the intellectual strife on the nature of the American Indian waged between Bartolomé de las Casas and the greatest Spanish socioreligious thinkers of the day. The Dominican establishment in Mexico City was of considerable importance by the time Diego joined it (see Part IV below).

Diego's new home, the church and monastery of Santo Domingo, faced west. A great atrium with a small chapel in each of the four corners led to the church itself, behind which were several cloisters and four dormitories. The monks and priests dined in a large refectory. As a novice, Diego was probably not given a private cell but slept in one of the dormitories. Every day the students were obliged to rise early, take part in the pious acts of the community, learn the fundamental rules of the order, and study Latin, the Scriptures, theology, and philosophy.

By September, 1559, Diego had become a deacon (Sandoval, 54), and not long afterward he was ordained a priest by the archbishop, probably in the old cathedral. As Diego left the building in the company of other new priests, he passed the carved Aztec stones which stood near the Puerta del Perdón, the northern entrance, mute reminders of the ancient peoples who had stirred his childhood curiosity.

In 1561, Durán was apparently sent with other missionaries to the Province of Oaxaca (Sandoval, 85n.12). But, as Bernal notes, "The length of his stay in that region is unknown; he is never mentioned among Dominicans who labored in Oaxaca at that time. Durán himself never speaks of his stay in that province. I believe that he must have remained there a short time, and it is probable that ill health prevented him from gaining fame there" (Bernal, 1964, *xxiii*). Durán's writings show that he was not familiar with the region.

For more than twenty-five years Durán's wanderings took him from monastery to monastery. The area covered by his extensive travels becomes easier to define when one studies the direct and indirect references scattered throughout the body of his work. The tenor of the writing also suggests that he did not make a return visit to Spain.

IV. **The Dominican Empire**

Within the area described by Durán, Dominican activities were never more intense than they were in the last half of the sixteenth century. Frenzied building activity was producing a chain of magnificent churches and monasteries, rich with land and tribute, reaching from Mexico City to Peru. The churches were elaborately carved and turreted like castles on the outside, and the interiors shone with gold and silver. A Dominican empire was being forged, causing alarm to kings and viceroys and later leading Durán to try to justify the lavishness of its churches. The temple of the false god Huitzilopochtli, Durán wrote, had been a rival of that of Solomon. "Yet in our own times there are those who say that a small, squat adobe church is good enough for our God!"[4]

In the Mexico City region a number of other Dominican establishments besides Santo Domingo were thriving or would soon be erected. In Azcapotzalco, the ancient capital of the Tecpanecs, was the church and monastery of San Felipe y Santiago (built in 1554). Southward, in Tacubaya (a city today largely encompassed by Mexico City), the cloister of La Purificación would be constructed before 1578. By 1562 there would be another Santo Domingo in Mixcoac, a church which the Dominicans are thought to have wrested from the Franciscans. San Juan Bautista of Coyoacan was built after 1560. In 1599, after Durán's death, another Dominican church, San Jacinto, would rise in what is now San Angel. Still farther south, San Pedro y San Pablo in Cuitlahuac had been ceded by the Franciscans to the friars of Santo Domingo in 1554.

Toward the east, in what is now the State of Mexico, was Santa María Magdalena at Tepetlaoztoc (founded around 1529), home of the saintly hermit Domingo de Betanzos. Southbound travelers came upon Santo Domingo of Chimalhuacan-Atenco (founded in 1559) and San Vicente Chimalhuacan-Chalco (founded before 1528). San Juan Bautista at Tenango-Chalco would be founded in 1575. On the border of the Marquesado stood La Asunción de Amecameca (founded about 1537), about the time of Durán's birth). Then came La Natividad de Nuestra Señora Coatepec-Chalco (ceded by the Franciscans to the Dominicans around 1559).

Farther south lay the Marquesado (today the State of More-

4 See p. 75.

los), the rich semitropical domain given to Cortés by Charles V, the region Durán was to love. George Kubler (1948) has given us a brilliant picture of the Dominican churches and monasteries in the region, among them La Natividad de Nuestra Señora in Tepoztlan (founded about 1559), Santo Domingo Huaxtepec (founded after 1561), Asunción Yautepec (founded between 1554 and 1567), and Santo Domingo Tlaquiltenango (to be ceded by the Franciscans in 1570). On the east, forming a circle around Popocatepetl, were Santo Domingo Hueyapan, taken from the secular clergy in 1563; San Juan Bautista Tetela (built between 1562 and 1581), which also originally belonged to the secular clergy; Santo Domingo Izúcar (to be built before 1597); Santo Domingo Atlixco (founded in 1562); and, finally, Santo Domingo de Puebla de los Angeles (founded in 1534), today one of the most elaborate of all Mexican churches.

Outside Durán's territory, farther south in what are now the states of Oaxaca and Chiapas, as well as in Guatemala, other splendid Dominican churches and monasteries were beginning to flourish.

V. Fray Diego as a Missionary: His Searching Years

Let us return to the territory of which Durán speaks most frequently: the Marquesado. Before the coming of the Spaniards, it had been the land of the Tlalhuicas, who with six other groups, including the Aztecs, had migrated from the north in the thirteenth century. According to Durán, the Tlalhuicas were coarse, barbarous people, and when they spoke Nahuatl, their accent left much to be desired, unlike that of the people of Tetzcoco, with their "beautiful language, elegant and polished" (Durán, 1967, II:23). When Fray Diego arrived in the Marquesado, he was enchanted. As he later described it:

> This is certainly one of the most beautiful lands in the world, and if it were not for the great heat it would be another Garden of Eden. There are delightful springs, wide rivers full of fish, the freshest of woods, and orchards of many kinds of fruits, many of them native

to Mexico and others to Spain, which supply all the neighboring cities with fruit. It is full of a thousand different fragrant flowers. This place is very rich in cotton and the commerce in this product is carried on here by people from all over the country. [Durán, 1964, 11]

Fray Diego had heard conflicting explanations for the luxuriance of the region, one being that the springs of the Marquesado were fed by the waters of Lake Tetzcoco.[5]

Though Durán gives no information about the Dominican house to which he was sent, we know that he resided in several monasteries in the Marquesado. His trips occasionally led him to the stronghold of the Franciscans, the Valley of Puebla, where he probably visited monasteries at Calpan, Tecali, Atlixco, Huexotzinco, Tlaxcala, and Cholula. It was at the last-named town, the Mecca of the ancient peoples, that he recorded in Nahuatl a story told to him by an aged survivor of pre-Conquest times, the powerful cosmogonical myth he was later to record in Chapter I of his *History* (Durán, 1964, 4–5).

Though it is impossible to place Durán's travels in chronological order, a few examples of what he learned on those journeys will give an idea of the environment in which the future historian found himself:

Here is a story I was told about a woman who accompanied the army of Cortés and who later was married to Martín Partidor. As Cortés was leaving Huaxtepec after having subdued the entire hot country, he passed through Ocuituco where he was received in peace. After this he ascended to a town called Tetela [del Volcán] where the Indians were lined up in order to fight, having much confidence in the rugged nature of the place. Other Indians from Hueyapan, which faced the town across a deep ravine, also appeared in a warlike fashion. When Cortés saw these forces he ordered his men to prepare themselves. But this Spanish woman, advised by certain soldiers, mounted a horse, took a lance and a leather shield and asked the Spanish captain for permission to attack the Indians and demonstrate her personal valor. Cortés granted her this, whereupon she

[5] See p. 166.

16

came forth and, spurring on the horse, she attacked the enemy, yelling, "Saint James, and at them!" The infantry then followed her and when the Indians saw them coming, some fled and others fell into the ravine. The town was taken and all the chieftains with their hands crossed came to surrender to Cortés. When the latter realized the bravery of the woman, he granted her the two towns of Tetela and Hueyapan in the name of His Majesty. [Durán, 1964, 321–22]

The snowy slopes of the Smoking Mountain still guarded mysteries—as they do to this day. In Temoac, Zacualpan, Tetela, and Hueyapan the natives told stories about a sacred mountain called Teocuicani, the Divine Singer, where stood the House of Mist, originally built for human sacrifice. Until the Conquest pilgrims had gone there to worship a divinity of jade "as tall as an eight-year-old boy." The statue, it was said, "disappeared" with the coming of the Faith.[6]

We do not know whether Durán visited the House of Mist, but it is almost certain that he climbed to the top of Mount Tlaloc, "the highest peak of the high peaks and mountain ranges, . . . lofty and shady, . . . whose beauty cannot be expressed in words" (Muñoz Camargo, 40). There stood the temple of the God of the Water, its remains still visible today. Durán was to rival modern archaeologists and ethnographers in his careful description of the site and of the religious ceremonies performed there.

One frosty November day Durán left the monastery in which he was staying, bound for the City of Mexico. As he was leaving the village (perhaps Coatepec), he met a half-naked Indian, shivering with cold, bearing a huge load of firewood to sell in a nearby market. Sorry for him, Fray Diego paid the native the full price of the load, asking him to keep the wood and warm himself with it at home. Later the missionary turned to see the Indian walking behind him, still bearing his burden. When Durán expressed his surprise, the native responded that he must go to the market and that Durán could have his money back if he wished. Greatly upset by the Indian's lack of "common sense," the good father, suspecting that

[6] See p. 258.

the man's trip to the market was part of ancient ritual obligations, upbraided him for his heathenism. The Indian bowed his head humbly, saying that the practice was not due to ancient belief but was simply his people's way of doing things.[7] The social and economic mores of Spain were certainly different from those of Mexico—two worlds separated by thirty thousand years of evolution and consequently having widely differing values.

Durán had ample opportunity to observe those values. For example, in a town not far from the City of Mexico he became acquainted with a crone, over ninety years old, who always excused herself from attending mass because of her advanced age. Although she was drawn to every market in the area, she had to be all but dragged to confession. One day as she was returning from well-spent hours (probably dedicated to friends, some ripe gossip, and a few sociable jugs of pulque), she fell dead of sunstroke on the road, her pitiful pack containing a few ears of green corn falling by her side. Her body was brought to the church, but the consensus of the village vendors was that the proper place to bury her was not in the churchyard but in the market place, so that "the place which had served her well in life and which she so loved, in death would not be denied her."[8]

Among the contrasts in the meeting of the New World with the Old, food played an important part. In ancient times the *itzcuintli*, or hairless Mexican dog, had been fattened and cooked for the table, a repulsive food to the European. Fray Diego heard reports that at a village near the Augustinian Monastery of Acolman, northeast of Mexico City, dogs were still being sold as food. To satisfy his curiosity, he visited the town on a market day, to find more than four hundred dogs, large and small, some already purchased, others waiting to be bought. He was not comforted by the comment of a Spanish settler who happened to be standing nearby that fewer dogs than usual had been put up for sale that day. When he questioned a buyer, Durán was told that the animals were the main delicacy at fiestas, weddings, and baptisms. This revelation deeply

7 See p. 277.
8 See p. 275.

18

grieved Fray Diego, for he knew that in heathen times dogs had been sacrificed to the gods and afterward eaten. He was also amazed to discover that in the village butcher shops dog meat, though considerably more expensive than beef, was preferred. Mistaking cultural patterns for religion, Durán wondered why the people were allowed to eat such "unclean things."[9]

Durán's affairs occasionally took him back to the Mexican capital. Let us try to reconstruct one such journey, made by water around 1575. Skimming over the lake in a canoe, Fray Diego passed a place called Pantitlan, where many skeleton-like tree trunks still stood erect in the water. Durán asked what they signified. The boatman glibly explained that they were merely the remains of trees which had once grown in the shallow lake waters. Durán well knew that each tree trunk was a decaying marker that had been set up in earlier times as witness to the yearly sacrifice of a young girl, representing Chalchiuhtlicue, Goddess of Water. Fray Diego remembered hearing that near the tree trunks great quantities of gold, precious stones, and jewelry had been cast into a whirlpool every year as an offering to the water deity. (Present-day stories of Moteczoma's undiscovered treasure are not necessarily fiction.)

In 1575 the central part of the City of Mexico had not greatly changed in appearance since Durán's days as a seminarian there twenty years before. The primitive cathedral was still standing, though work on a new structure had been inaugurated in 1573 with the setting of the cornerstone of what is now the Cathedral of Mexico City. Another change had taken place: on the east side of the cathedral, the site of the former Palace of Moteczoma (where Cortés built his home after the Conquest), stood the Royal Palace, where His Excellency Martín Enríquez de Almanza reigned as representative of the king of Spain. Fray Diego also noted two new establishments—the Inquisition and the Jesuit Foundation—both of which were to have a strong impact upon Mexico during the next two centuries.

The home to which the Cortés family had been reduced stood on the site of the ancient Palace of Axayacatl (today the National

[9] See p. 278.

Pawn Shop). Durán may have walked past the Puerta del Marqués on the Street of Tacuba and thought of the suicidal flight of the Spanish invaders in 1520. Durán's adopted city was filled with reminders of the past.

VI. Durán Fights the Devil and the Secular Clergy

Back in the Marquesado, another reminder of the past greeted him in Huaxtepec, a once-wealthy town which still boasted the pleasure gardens of Moteczoma I, who ruled from 1440 to 1469. A stone image of Ometochtli, Two Rabbit, God of Pulque, had recently been carried from the town of Tepoztlan to Huaxtepec to be buried in the foundations of the church.

The old pagan gods (or loathsome devils, as Durán thought of them) were still alive, brazenly showing their faces on cornerstones, clearly visible in the walls of shrines, standing in niches. Perhaps more terrifying, these images lived on, invisible to the spectator, hidden within Christian structures, such as in walls of the Cathedral of Mexico and in the church at Huaxtepec. The demons undoubtedly still wielded their baleful influence upon the natives. These idols reflected the customs of a people who, after fifty years of contact with Spanish priests, persisted in their ways.

One day Fray Diego discovered that a couple he had joined in marriage with full Catholic rites had been led away after the ceremony by pagan priests to be married again according to pre-Hispanic ritual.[10] On another occasion Durán was called to hear the confession of an old woman at the point of death. Before anointing her, he noticed her large head covering and suspected something unusual. On removing the cloth, he saw that her hair had been shorn according to ancient religious custom. A thousand other survivals, perhaps the work of the devil, disturbed him. Children's heads were feathered with the plumes of wild birds, and liquid rubber, or "divine pitch," was smeared on their heads. These children continued to run away when they saw a missionary approaching them, "scarcely knowing where to hide; though we have been

10 See p. 123.

here fifty-five years, [the Indians] flee from us as they did on the first day."[11]

Once Fray Diego had a sharp exchange of words with an aged woman who had been a priestess in the times of Moteczoma. She informed him that Easter and Christmas were nothing new to the Indians, nor was Corpus Christi, or the other feasts of the Catholic calendar, since all had been celebrated in Mexico long before the Conquest. Enraged, the Dominican exclaimed, "Evil old woman, . . . the devil has plotted and has sown tares with the wheat so that you will never learn the truth!"[12]

When Indians became ill, superstition took an even firmer grip on them. Then reappeared the heathen incense, the liquid rubber, the tamales and tortillas, the magic papers, the necklaces of many colors, and the snake bones.[13] Even worse, the natives would offer heathen foods and incense to the images of Christian saints.[14] In despair Durán exclaimed, "And if you don't believe the pot was broken, behold its fragments!" Durán learned to despise Christians who were willing to close their eyes to this rampant idolatry. (Were he to return to Mexico four centuries later, he would find the situation virtually unchanged among the indigenous groups.)

But, of course, reasoned Durán, the natives were not to be held responsible for their idolatry. The guilt lay with the Christian churchmen. Later he was to dedicate page after page to denunciations of the *ministros*, or secular clergy, and the religious orders, not excluding the Dominicans. References to clerical indifference and ignorance of the native languages, way of life, and pre-Hispanic history appear repeatedly in his works. One day he entered an Indian church where a fellow Dominican was about to preach. "Refulsit sol in clipeos aureos!" the priest exclaimed, as he announced the theme of his sermon, translating the biblical quotation for his Indian flock as, "The sun shone upon the golden shields."

[11] See p. 126.
[12] See p. 417.
[13] See p. 118.
[14] See p. 235.

The priest expounded in fair Nahuatl upon the Divine Splendor and the Divine Persons. The friar, carried away by his theological arguments, rambled on for some time. But interest lagged among the native listeners. Fray Diego turned his eyes toward some of his Indian fellow worshipers, to observe them scratching lines on the floor and counting pebbles. They were playing *patolli*, the Aztec pachisi, in the house of God! When the mass ended, Durán left the church, disappointed and troubled. "How little we, the preachers, have grasped the real needs of the Indians."[15]

The future historian was also disturbed by the clergy's lack of interest in preserving the ancient records of the Indians. In mistaken zeal some of the early missionaries had destroyed a storehouse of knowledge which could have illuminated the missionaries' path toward an understanding of pagan ways. The Franciscan Juan de Zumárraga was reputed to have burned a number of painted manuscripts.

No one could seriously doubt that the Franciscans had been giants in "zeal, filled with spirit and divine fervor" (Durán, 1964, 321). They had truly been the incarnation of the Twelve Apostles. But had they not been too lenient in permitting a superficial conversion to Christianity?[16] Did not the Franciscans go from door to door begging for food, in the manner of the Aztec priests?[17] Whenever the Indians were caught chanting pagan hymns, did they not abruptly switch their theme to Saint Francis of Assisi, adding a hallelujah or two to the beat of the drum and the plaintive notes of the flutes?[18] And if the holy Franciscan monks were lax, what could be said of the secular clergy? In a disturbing contrast to the ancient religious discipline, the Indians were now usually late to mass and indifferent during services. Occasionally, just as the sermon was about to begin, the people suddenly remembered other duties, such as sowing or reaping, and departed, leaving the church empty and the minister dubious about the strength of their faith.[19] Yes, the Christian clergy had failed in many ways.

[15] See p. 219.
[16] See pp. 125–26.
[17] See p. 428.
[18] See p. 207.
[19] See p. 397.

The missionaries were indifferent and faulty in their knowledge of the native languages. They ate, drank, and slept comfortably, their consciences undisturbed. "For the love of Christ crucified," exclaimed Durán, "let them wake up to their responsibility in the things they have undertaken!" The Nahuatl vocabulary of many of the ministers was limited to such rudimentary expressions as, "How do you say this?" Fray Diego was reminded of the coarseness of the first Spanish conquerors, who had tried to pick up dirty words from the natives, only to be laughed at. There was no doubt in Durán's mind: most Spanish priests in Mexico were no better than tourists.[20]

VII. Quetzalcoatl or Saint Thomas?
Fray Diego as a Diffusionist

Another subject troubled Durán. As time passed, he became deeply puzzled by similarities between personages, rites, and events in the Old Testament and those in the religious life of the Aztecs. He also found parallels between Christianity and the native religion. During vigils in his monastery, with the peaks of Popocatepetl and Iztaccihuatl visible from his cell, Durán may well have wondered about Topiltzin-Quetzalcoatl, the generous preacher of a gentle way of life, the beloved teacher, who had departed across those mountains in his flight toward the east, toward the Old World. Had not the Lord stated categorically that the apostles were to preach the Gospel to *all* nations? Had the Apostles failed to carry out the Divine Teacher's command: "Go ye into all the world, and preach the gospel to every creature"?

Durán had few persons with whom to discuss such questions, and no books but the Bible and Aztec picture writings to enlighten him. He sought answers to the questions alone. Both Hebrews and Mexicans believed that "in the beginning God created the heaven and the earth." The Old World had its Tower of Babel, and New Spain its lofty Pyramid of Cholula (Durán, 1967, II:16–17). The pagan priests of Huexotzinco kept an ark containing holy relics, a

[20] See p. 171.

treasure held in as much awe as the Ark of the Covenant of the Jews.[21] The culture hero Topiltzin had touched the sea with his rod, and the waters had parted, allowing his persecuted people to pass through the gap unharmed while their pursuers were drowned.[22] Both Jews and Aztecs had been fed on their pilgrimages by manna from heaven (Durán, 1967, II:16). On occasion, when the Aztecs prayed, they lifted their eyes fervently to the image of a bird placed on top of a pole, much as the sons of Israel had worshiped a serpent set upon a pole during their wanderings in the wilderness.[23]

Some of the food regulations in the Aztec temple reminded Durán of the priestly customs mentioned in Leviticus.[24] Some Old Testament personages and practices even made Durán look upon his Aztec proselytes as descendants of the Jews. There was the traitor Abimelech of the biblical account who had drunk human blood, an act parallel to the bloody sacrifices of the Mexicans.[25] The Indians purified themselves by bathing, a ceremony similar to the Jews' rite of purification.[26] The Aztecs were subject to strict prohibitions regarding some foods. In the Old Testament, Fray Diego read, the Jews had observed certain dietary prohibitions.[27] Aztec servers in the Great Temple of Mexico carried out offices similar to those described in Deuteronomy.[28] The ancient Mexicans offered quail to their deity, sprinkling the altar with the bird's blood, in a manner similar to the burnt offering of turtle doves described in Leviticus.[29]

In Mexico foods were brought to the shrines, just as lambs, calves, and goats were offered in the Temple of Jerusalem.[30] Leviticus stated that the sacrificial animals of the Hebrews were

21 See p. 143.
22 See p. 62.
23 See pp. 205–206.
24 See p. 105.
25 See p. 451.
26 See p. 244.
27 See p. 94
28 See p. 85.
29 See p. 104.
30 See pp. 104, 121.

24

to be without blemish; among the Aztecs, the same unblemished quality was required of human victims.[31] Similarities existed between the Indian priests and those described in Deuteronomy: sacerdotal functions were inherited from father to son within certain lineages.[32] At a low point in their religious history the chosen people of Jehovah had offered human sacrifices, including their own children, to idols, as recorded in Psalm 106 (Durán, 1967, II:18).

As in the case of Moses and his followers, when four men carried the Ark of the Covenant, the chosen people of Huitzilopochtli in their exodus designated four men to carry images of the tribal deities, the supreme god being borne within an ark of rushes (Durán, 1967, II:26). While the Aztecs ended their calendrical cycle every fifty-two years, Hebrew law as set forth in Leviticus ordained that after every forty-nine-year cycle the fiftieth was to be a jubilee, a hallowed occasion, a year of rest.[33] Above all, Hebrews and Aztecs shared one striking similarity: both, as chosen people of God, had endured rigorous pilgrimages in the wilderness until they had reached their respective promised lands—Canaan and the Valley of Mexico (Durán, 1967, II: 21–22). By the time Durán wrote his two ethnographic works he believed it possible that the Mexican natives were of Jewish origin. A few years later, when he wrote his *History*, practically no doubts were left in his mind.

Then rose the question of pre-Conquest influences in Mexico. If the Apostles had gone forth to preach to all nations, which of the Twelve had reached these shores? Had it been Saint Thomas, the apostle associated with India and the Indians? Had the saintly Topiltzin-Quetzalcoatl been Saint Thomas?

To Durán, certain details suggested that conclusion. Topiltzin had performed miracles; he had been honored and revered as a holy person; his hair had been long and straight and his beard red, streaked with white; he had spent much of his time praying in a

[31] See p. 131.
[32] See p. 85.
[33] See p. 389.

cell, where he had lived chastely and performed acts of penance; he had abstained from meat and fasted; he had built altars and shrines and knelt before them; he had been followed by disciples whom he taught to pray and to preach; he had come from foreign parts; he had been persecuted during his stay in Mexico; disappointed with the meager fruits of his preaching, he had departed from the land in the direction of the eastern sea.[34]

As though in confirmation of these stories, one day Fray Diego heard rumors of a mysterious document kept by the Indians of Ocuituco, at the foot of Popocatepetl in the Marquesado. The natives claimed that the document had been bequeathed to them by Topiltzin himself when he passed through the village. The painted manuscript was said to be about one foot long and covered with characters. Eager to examine the book, the Dominican friar journeyed to Ocuituco and begged the Indians to show it to him. The natives, however, swore that they had burned it six years earlier, fearing it would cause them trouble. Durán was also told that the book had been destroyed because the Indians had been unable to read the script, which was different from European writing. Fray Diego was discouraged by the news, feeling that the book might have settled the questions troubling him. It could well have been "the Holy Gospel in Hebrew." Having scolded those who had destroyed the document, Durán left the village in disappointment. The disappearance of the "Hebrew" text only served to whet his curiosity, however.

Another trip, into the mountainous area between the Valley of Mexico and Puebla, proved more fruitful. There a wise old Indian from Coatepec produced a pictorial manuscript painted in strange characters. It portrayed the life of Topiltzin and his disciples. The native told Durán the story of the holy man. Fray Diego was shown a picture of the "saint" wearing a headdress "very much like" the miter worn by Christian bishops.[35]

Doubts assailed him, however, when he returned to his monastery and pondered what he had seen and heard. Had the holy man

[34] See pp. 61, 68.
[35] See pp. 65–66.

indeed been Saint Thomas? Legends were plentiful about a great man who with his rod had opened a path in the sea for his followers. Could Moses have been the protagonist of an epic migration which brought Hebrew culture to the New World? There were other possibilities. A widespread medieval legend recounted how Saint Raymond of Peñafort, a thirteenth-century Catalonian, had sailed from Majorca to Barcelona using his cloak as a vessel. Durán had heard a similar story about the great Topiltzin.[36] One thing seemed certain: someone, at some time, had come to the New World and had preached the Bible to the natives.

Other parallels had to be considered before conclusions could be reached about the origin of the Mexicans. The austere lives led by Aztec seminarians were reminiscent of the lives of postulants in Christian countries.[37] Any inclination toward the priesthood was encouraged and given an opportunity to develop. Seminarians passed through a series of grades before attaining the priesthood.[38] Catholic and Aztec priests had much in common: they offered incense, offered a divine sacrifice in their rites, chanted, did penance, wore elaborate robes, fasted, made vows of celibacy, lived in communities, observed holy days, exhorted the people to do penance for their sins, and wore their hair in a tonsure.[39] Aztec youths aided the priests in the service of the temple in Mexico, much as altar boys served in Christian churches. Among the Aztecs there were cloistered nuns, girls about twelve or thirteen years old, who lived chastely, their only occupation that of serving the gods. These girls were directed by older women much like Christian abbesses or prioresses.[40]

After washing away their sins[41] and fasting,[42] the Aztecs then offered unleavened bread to Huitzilopochtli. The oblation consisted of a cake of *huauhtli*, made of *tzoalli*, or amaranth-seed

[36] See p. 62.
[37] See pp. 82–83, 111.
[38] See p. 112.
[39] See pp. 81–82.
[40] See pp. 83–84.
[41] See p. 245.
[42] See p. 94.

dough, "the flesh and bones of the god Huitzilopochtli."[43] A ceremonial washing took place before the *tzoalli* was consecrated and consumed.[44] The consecrated bread was carried to the sick on certain occasions.[45] The sacrificial victims were constantly renewed before the image of Tezcatlipoca, much as the Host is reserved and renewed in the tabernacles of Catholic churches.[46] The flower decorations of the Feast of Tezcatlipoca reminded Fray Diego of the flowery altars set up in Christian churches for the reserving of the Host on Maundy Thursday.[47]

Counterparts of the other sacraments also existed in Mexico: penance or confession and a rite similar to baptism.[48] The symbolism and apparel of pre-Hispanic heathens and of European Christians were similar: the cross could be compared to the Xocotl, the Sacred Pole, and the vestments of both priesthoods had much in common.[49] The burning of incense was to be compared with the burning of candles.[50] Double feasts were common in both cultures.[51] The Aztec priests rose to pray at the same hour that monks said matins.[52] Native priests blessed children. The Indians honored relics much as Catholics venerated the *Agnus Dei*.[53] The drums of ancient Mexico and the bells of Christendom had much the same function.[54]

An Aztec "Lent" comparable to the Lent of Christian countries had undoubtedly existed. The same could be said about Easter, which in some ways resembled the holy day of Tlacaxipehualiztli.[55] The Feast of Toxcatl could be compared to the Rogation days.

43 See pp. 88–90.
44 See p. 245.
45 See pp. 453, 95.
46 See p. 126.
47 See p. 104.
48 See pp. 54–55, 102, 245, 266.
49 See p. 443.
50 See p. 235.
51 See p. 229.
52 See p. 119.
53 See p. 209.
54 See p. 134.
55 See pp. 225, 417.

Heathen pleas for rain were similar to the Catholic litanies.[56] Pentecost had parallels to the Feast of Tezcatlipoca. The Aztec dramatic representations performed in the Month of Toxcatl often coincided with Corpus Christi, when religious dramas were staged in Spain.[57] People bathed on the Feast of Ochpaniztli, as Christians did on the day of Saint John the Baptist.[58] The natives quickly accepted the practice of offering ears of corn and strings of chilis and flowers on the Feast of the Nativity of Our Lady on September 8, remembering the ceremonies of the goddess Chicomecoatl, which had been held about the same day. The Aztecs had celebrated a feast in honor of their dead children and another for deceased adults—celebrations similar to All Saints' Day and All Souls' Day.[59] One day after Christmas the Aztecs celebrated the descent of Huitzilopochtli to earth and indicated his presence by the impression of a child's foot upon a ball of dough.[60]

Biblical personages had parallels in the Aztec pantheon. Topiltzin could be compared to Christ, Saint Thomas, Saint Raymond, and Moses. "Giants" had also lived in Mexico; some of them had attempted to build a "Tower of Babel" in Cholula (Durán, 1964, 5). A trinity was worshiped: the Aztecs "revered the Father, the Son, and the Holy Ghost, calling them Tota, Topiltzin, and Yolometl. These words mean Our Father, Our Son, and the Heart of Both, honoring each one separately and all three as a unit."[61] The Trinity was also revered as Totec, Xipe, and Tlatlauhquitezcatl. Totec meant Awesome and Terrible Lord Who Fills One with Dread; Xipe meant Man Who Has Been Flayed and Ill-treated; Tlatlauhquitezcatl meant Mirror of Fiery Brightness.[62]

One goddess had three names. One was Chalchiuhcihuatl, "which means Precious Stone or Emerald, because she was chosen from among all women," a name that doubtless reminded Durán

---

[56] See p. 102.
[57] See p. 426.
[58] See p. 449.
[59] See p. 442.
[60] See pp. 241, 461–62.
[61] See p. 161.
[62] See p. 174.

of the Virgin Mary. The same goddess was also called Chicome-coatl, or Seven Snake, "because the natives believed that she had prevailed against seven serpents, or sins." That name undoubtedly called to mind Mary Magdalene, from whom the Lord ejected seven evil spirits. The third name, Xilonen, meant She Who Always Walked and Remained as Fresh and Tender as a Young Ear of Corn.[63] The Sacred Pole, Xocotl, had functioned as the patron and guardian of Coyoacan. After the Conquest the guardianship of the town was given to Saint John the Baptist.[64] Nahui Ollin, Four Motion, the calendrical name for the solar god, had been the patron of Aztec warriors, just as Saint James was the patron of Spanish warriors.[65]

Durán also meditated on the moral code of the native peoples. How had these people received commandments almost identical to the Mosaic laws?[66] The sermons of the Aztec priests extolled a peaceful life filled with reverence, modesty, good breeding, obedience, and charity toward the poor and toward strangers. These sermons, delivered in elegant language, filled with rhetoric and metaphor, often referred to the lowly state of man in relation to his creator.[67] In Aztec theology the wicked were to suffer in the underworld for sins committed in this life, but pardon for sins could be obtained during the jubilee held every four years.[68]

During all his years of research among his native friends in the villages, Durán was tormented by these parallels. He wavered, he vacillated; at one moment he was convinced that preachers of the Hebrew religion had been in the New World; at the next, that Christian preachers had visited Mexico.

Then, of course, there was a third and overwhelming element to consider: Satan, the Evil One, always trying to disguise his own wicked plans against mankind in the garb of the True Religion. Perhaps Satan *had* been in Mexico, teaching the natives evils that

63 See p. 437.
64 See p. 445.
65 See p. 186.
66 See p. 95.
67 See p. 184.
68 See p. 97.

were reflected in their bloody sacrifices. In this process the devil had managed to mix Christian symbolism with paganism and thus hindered the work of the missionaries in bringing Christianity to the people. Durán was to refer to the parable of the tares and the wheat, which were to grow side by side until the tares could be uprooted and cast into the fire.[69]

Modern-day archaeologists, of course, place no credence in Durán's diffusionist theories. Scientists generally agree that New World Indian cultures were the result of a long evolution of Mongolian peoples who migrated from northeastern Asia many thousands of years before the time of Moses or of Saint Thomas the Apostle.

VIII. Durán Meets the Penitent Conqueror

For a time Fray Diego resided in the Dominican monastery at Huaxtepec, in what is now Morelos. There, he was to write, "I lived with a most honest priest, a man who was jealous of the glory of God and of His doctrines."[70] That priest was Fray Francisco de Aguilar, who had as much to tell Durán about the Conquest from the Spanish point of view as any man alive, since he had been a soldier under Cortés.[71] The former warrior, more than ninety years old when Durán knew him, was in poor health, having suffered from gout for thirty years. His hands and feet were paralyzed and every movement—sitting, standing, or lying down—caused him excruciating pain (Dávila Padilla, Chap. XXXVIII). As Aguilar lay in his cell at Huaxtepec, he unfolded before Fray Diego his version of what he now considered a sinful conquest and his atonement.

Aguilar left Cuba with Cortés at the end of 1518, when Moteczoma and the people of the Mexican capital were already trembling with fear at omens and rumors of the return of Topiltzin. Aguilar was present at the fierce Battle of Tecoac and later was one of the few hundred Europeans privileged to see Mexico-Tenochtitlan in its pre-Hispanic splendor.

[69] See p. 125.
[70] See pp. 409–10.
[71] See p. 75.

31

According to the account Durán received from Aguilar and other members of the conquering army:

> . . . the day they entered the City of Mexico, when they saw the height and grandeur of the temples, they thought them castellated fortresses, splendid monuments and defenses of the city, or castles or royal dwelling places, crowned with turrets and watchtowers. Such were the glorious heights which could be seen from afar! Thus the eight or nine temples in the city were all close to one another within a large enclosure. . . . How marvelous it was to gaze upon them— some taller than others, some more lavish than others, some with their entrances facing the east, others the west, others the north, others the south! All stuccoed, carved, and crowned with different types of merlons, painted with animals, [covered] with stone figures, strengthened by great, wide buttresses! How [the temples] gave luster to the city! How they gave it dignity . . .![72]

The ancient monk could add a personal touch to his narration. He had been a guardian of the Emperor Moteczoma while the latter was held prisoner in the Palace of Axayacatl, and he recalled the massacre of the flower of Tenochtitlan in 1520. After the Conquest he had been rewarded with lands and Indians and at the age of fifty had relinquished those treasures to become a Dominican monk.

It can be assumed that Fray Diego listened eagerly to the narrative of the dying man. It may well have been the turning point in his life—the point at which he became a historian. Intimate contact with a man who had seen pre-Conquest Tenochtitlan and had known Moteczoma, Cortés, Cuauhtemoc, and Malintzin at the floodtide of their destinies probably served as a catalyst.

During one of their conversations at Huaxtepec, Aguilar may have shown Fray Diego passages of a text he had been obliged to dictate to a scribe on the unwelcome orders of the Dominicans in Mexico: the story of his experiences as a soldier of Cortés. Nearly four centuries later the manuscript was published as the *Historia de la Nueva España de Fray Francisco de Aguilar*. Aguilar's chronicle was not the only one being prepared at the time. In 1577, Philip II ordered one of the most ambitious programs of census taking in

[72] See pp. 75–76.

history: the *relaciones* of the Indies, which of course included Mexico. A questionnaire containing fifty inquiries was prepared, to be answered by each of the townships of Spanish America. Among the topics covered were geography, politics, and tribute. The questions that dealt with the life of the pre-Columbian peoples are of special interest to anthropologists: Which gods had the Indians worshiped? What rites had been performed? What medicines had cured their ailments? Who had been their local sovereigns? How had the natives dressed? What had been their social patterns?

Between 1577 and 1583 most of the officials in Mexico attempted to answer His Majesty's questions, with uneven results. Authorities formerly indifferent to native culture suddenly found themselves functioning as amateur anthropologists. The *relaciones* produced by Spanish officials, Aguilar's chronicle, the encyclopedic work being prepared by Sahagún and his Indian informants at Tlatelolco, and the need to tell the world about the fruitlessness of missionary efforts—all these influences led Fray Diego to commence his chronicle, destined to be one of the greatest ethnographic accounts of aboriginal America.

IX. The Plague

It was at about this time, in 1576, that catastrophe struck. The Black Death had reached New Spain and within six years had wiped out at least one-fourth of the population. By 1600 plague-ridden Mexico had suffered a population decrease of 90 per cent or more (Gibson, 138). Durán wondered whether the Almighty was punishing the natives for their heathenism or visiting his wrath upon the parasitic clergy. Was God weary of men disobedient to his commandments, ridden with superstition, filled with lust and sensuality? The Franciscan Motolinía associated epidemics with socioeconomic evils: "God smote and chastised this land and those who dwelt in it, both natives and foreigners, with ten harsh plagues" (Motolinía, 15–22). Those plagues he listed as smallpox, massacres, famine, exploitation, toilsome tribute, the adoration of gold, forced labor in the rebuilding of Mexico City, slavery, the heavy

33

burden of the mines, and social upheaval resulting from quarrels among the Spaniards.

Bubonic plague swept over the land, destroying rich and poor, Christians and heathens, witch doctors, Catholic priests, monks, royal officials, native informants who had become good and trustworthy friends—many disappeared in this "latest chastisement" of New Spain.[73] Death was a regular visitor to every family. In the cataclysm there were revivals of paganism, idolatry, astrology, and strange cults, some of a diabolical nature. The economy of the country was shaken; manual labor became scarce, causing a shortage of food and a rise in prices. Remains of half-finished Dominican monasteries, among them the splendid basilica church and monastery at Cuilapan, Oaxaca, stand today as testimony to want of hands and spirit.

Another ailment, an ecclesiastical one, troubled the Dominicans. Some of the mendicant foundations were gradually being taken over by the secular priests, whose backgrounds were inadequate for the work. By and large they were strangers, unfamiliar with the language, customs, and psychology of their flocks. Was the spiritual conquest that had just begun to bear fruit to be lost forever? In this twilight of the monks and the Indians, Durán began writing his chronicle, conceived in bitterness.

X. Durán's Aims

One passage from Durán's *Ancient Calendar* is sufficient to illustrate his principal aim in recording what he had learned of the Aztecs:

> Not only today but in the past we have known of old men who were proselytizers, soothsayers, wise in the old law, who taught and still teach the young folk, who are now being educated. They instruct them in the count of the days, and of the years, and of the ceremonies and ancient rites; [they tell them] about the fabulous and false miracles of the old gods. Owing to this suspicion I was encouraged to produce this work, moved only by the zeal of informing and illumi-

73 See p. 150.

34

nating our ministers so that their task may not be in vain, worthless. In some places their labor [has been in vain]. The ministers, workers in this divine task of the conversion of the natives, should know about these things, if their aim is to be effective and fruitful in their doctrine. In all of this we are concerned with the salvation of the soul or the perdition of both the teacher and the disciple. In order to administer the sacraments, one needs more knowledge of the language, customs, and weaknesses of these people than most think. Let not the servant of God who wishes to bring forth fruit in this vineyard of the Lord be content in saying that he can understand confession [in the native language] and that is enough. We need a great deal more than that in order to explain the mysteries of our Faith and the benefit and necessity of the sacraments in which they abound. Let the minister beware lest he endeavor to preach the truth and he preach falsehood and lies. For this will be to the detriment of our brethren. . . .[74]

Fray Diego asked God to forgive him for having called the Indians unrepentant heathens and the Spanish priests dolts. He states that he will be willing to do penance for his slander—if such it was.[75] These promises must be taken with a grain of salt. Durán was as certain of the natives' paganism and the missionaries' ignorance as he was of his own breathing.

The natives possessed good discipline, a well-structured social order, keen intelligence, ability, and breeding. In other areas, however, they displayed strange bestiality and blindness. How little the Spanish world understood these strengths and failings! Durán could well have described his aim in the words used to introduce the journal *Tlalocan* in 1942: "What we are after are materials which will contribute to an understanding and appreciation of the Indian peoples who have been so often libeled, grotesquely romanticized, or ignored by even their own ashamed descendants" (Barlow and Smisor, 1–2). Durán not only desired these goals but also, being human, wished to exhibit his knowledge and experience in a field in which both Indians and Spaniards were confused. As a child of both worlds, he felt he possessed a deeper perception of

[74] See p. 386.
[75] See pp. 219, 387, 411.

their cultures than any of the other scholars of New Spain. Why should his store of knowledge remain hidden when it could be brought to light to honor God, benefit mankind, and incidentally demonstrate his ability as a historian and religious reformer?

From the outset Fray Diego was convinced that his writings would arouse interest among his readers. Ever since the time of Columbus, Iberian Spaniards had been avid to learn about life in the New World. Exotic descriptions were hungrily received by a people whose popular literature was still confined to *novelas de caballería*, rambling and fantastic stories of knight-errantry. In his descriptions of the wonders of Mexico, Durán often echoed the conqueror Bernal Díaz del Castillo: "I have gained nothing of value to leave to my children and descendants but this my true story, and they will presently find out what a wonderful story it is" (Díaz del Castillo, 1928, 41).

It was Durán's destiny that his works would become part of the remarkable cycle of chronicles of New Spain, beginning with the letters of Cortés and continuing with the histories of Francisco López de Gómara, the Anonymous Conqueror, Sahagún, Gerónimo de Mendieta, Díaz del Castillo, Alvarado Tezozómoc, Alva Ixtlilxochitl, and Chimalpahin, the cycle closing with Torquemada around 1620. All these works were the forerunners of modern-day Mesoamerican ethnography.

Durán referred to his work as "pleasant and gratifying" and expressed confidence that it would please his readers or those to whom it was read aloud.[76] Thus he had a second goal in mind: he would not only guide the Catholic ministers but also give pleasure to others.

Finally, to judge from Durán's own comments, he was commissioned to undertake the work by one or more superiors of his order, or in any event was encouraged by them to do so (Durán, 1967, II; 575). It is probable that he worked on the project in one of the Dominican monasteries at the foot of Popocatepetl, possibly in Hueyapan.

[76] See pp. 140, 154.

XI. **Durán's Sources**

Fray Diego Durán produced three ambitious works: the *Book of the Gods and Rites,* a remarkably detailed description of the life of a vanished civilization; *The Ancient Calendar,* one of the main guides to the intricate Mesoamerican system of counting time; and *The History of the Indies of New Spain,* which follows the Aztec people from their obscure beginnings in the ninth century (according to Durán's Indian sources) to their fall in 1521. More than seven centuries of uninterrupted history are covered in Durán's work.

Volumes so rich in information are not produced solely through memories of childhood experiences, though certainly many of Durán's passages are based on recollections dating back to the 1540's, barely thirty years after the Conquest. His books bear witness to long and painstaking consultation of reliable sources, both written materials and converse with living informants. The chronicler was conscientious in his efforts to validate his information, particularly when confronted with contradictions. On occasion he traveled many miles to ascertain a single fact.[77]

The text of the three books contains no evidence that Durán had access to contemporary printed works, such as those by Cortés, Las Casas, and Gómara. There is, however, a wealth of evidence that he consulted works in manuscript. One source, the value of which cannot be overestimated, is a document in Nahuatl (referred to by Fray Diego as the *History*), which he translated and used as the basis for his last work, *The History of the Indies.* This important historical document, nameless and of anonymous authorship, has come to be called Crónica X. It has been commented upon at length by Barlow (1945), Bernal (1964), Sandoval, O'Gorman, García Martínez, and Leal.

Durán did not use Crónica X in writing his two earlier works, the *Book of the Gods and Rites* and *The Ancient Calendar.* For those books he relied on other "written" documents, the pre-Columbian books now known as codices. They had been executed in hieroglyphic writing on fiber paper or deerskin, folded in the

[77] See p. 63.

37

form of screens. Their contents ranged from records of tax collection and history to ritual and calendrical matters. Those works, of which fewer than two dozen are extant today, were scarce even in Durán's time, the remnants of the once great Aztec libraries destroyed by overzealous Europeans. The surviving manuscripts had been hidden away by natives who wished to keep alive the old traditions.

Over the years Fray Diego had been allowed to look at a few of the books. But the Indians were understandably difficult to deal with, hiding and denying the existence of calendars, almanacs, genealogies, and so on.[78] But Durán's background, his obvious interest in Aztec culture, and his knowledge of the language permitted him to overcome these barriers. Two incidents Durán mentioned may be cited as examples. A chapel was being built in an Indian village, and the people were asked whom they preferred as its patron, Saint Paul or Saint Augustine. The Indians insisted that they wanted neither saint but rather Saint Luke as their patron. Their insistence made Fray Diego suspicious. At the time he had in his possession a Tonalamatl, or Book of Days. On consulting it, he found that the Feast of Saint Luke fell under the sign *calli*, the birth sign of the chief of the town. Durán's ability to co-ordinate a Christian holy day with an Aztec date by means of a complex calendrical document was no small feat and demonstrates the depth of his knowledge of the aboriginal time count.[79] Earlier Fray Diego mentioned that he had identified the year of Cortés's arrival in the native calendar.[80]

In his works the chronicler frequently mentions having consulted pre-Hispanic manuscripts and paintings. An Indian from the town of Chiautla reluctantly lent him a painted document depicting the fabled Topiltzin.[81] In Tetzcoco a chieftain exhibited a document showing Moteczoma in chains (Durán, 1967, II:541–42). At Tlatelolco, Fray Diego admired still another codex showing events

[78] See p. 63.
[79] See p. 410.
[80] See p. 319.
[81] See p. 64.

and structures which dated from some three hundred years before the Conquest. Durán may have been reminded of the vestiges of ancient buildings which dotted the landscape of his adopted country (Durán, 1964, 15). He was deeply regretful that so many of the Aztec works had been destroyed: "Those who with fervent zeal (though with little prudence) in the beginning burned and destroyed all the ancient Indian pictographic documents were mistaken. They left us without a light to guide us."[82] "These writings would have enlightened us considerably had not ignorant zeal destroyed them. Ignorant men ordered them burned, believing them idols, while actually they were history books worthy of being preserved."[83]

In addition to Crónica X and a few pre-Hispanic documents, other written material was available to Durán. One was an enigmatic Book of Spells, handwritten in Nahuatl, containing incantations. There were several copies of the book, which may have been the basis for Hernando Ruiz de Alarcón's *Tratado de las supersticiones y costumbres gentílicas* (1892). Durán seems to have made little use of the book, however, and wrote of it somewhat scornfully.[84]

Besides written sources and paintings, Durán consulted a number of Indian informants. In the Mexico of Durán's time thousands of men and women were still living who had been young in the days before the Conquest. Fray Diego spent hours listening to stories, historical anecdotes, gossip, fables, traditions—and undoubtedly lies. Before writing his works, he sifted his material, making every effort to eliminate the improbable or contradictory.

One of Durán's informants was a wise old man from Cholula. Durán judged him to be about one hundred years old. Questioned about ancient traditions, the ancient one commenced, "In the beginning, before light or sun had been created, this world lay in darkness and shadows" (Durán, 1967, II:17). By the time the elder had finished his origin myth, the Bible-oriented priest was

[82] See p. 55.
[83] See p. 396.
[84] See p. 152.

convinced that he had encountered the history of the native people at its very roots. Others told Durán about the first rising of the sun or the birth of modern mankind—which had taken place at Teotihuacan, according to certain sources.[85] When he asked why beans were sown so late in a certain year, an old man referred him to the intricacies of the native calendar.[86] When he asked where the people had obtained the ability to foretell events and fates, he received the frustrating response that it had been bequeathed to them by their ancestors. Fascinating indeed must have been an interview he held with a group of pagan priests regarding astrology.[87] Another elder told the Dominican a legend of a pagan priest who had dreamed of a century plant with face and hands and had popularized the cult of the maguey god.[88]

The ancient metropolis of Mexico provoked an extraordinary interest in Durán. From dozens of informants he gathered information that was to appear throughout his works. Curiosity led him to question a number of persons about a gruesome spectacle in the center of the city, the skull rack: "I asked whether [the skulls] were set up flesh and all?"[89] He also tried to discover what the Indians believed was the real cause of Moteczoma's death (Durán, 1964, 302–303). Certain old men remembered with awe a Spaniard who had dared to enter the holy of holies of the Great Temple and cast down the blessed image of the supreme divinity, Huitzilopochtli.[90] Durán's native informants must have numbered hundreds.

Durán's most reliable Spanish informant, Fray Francisco de Aguilar, has already been mentioned. Although Durán admits that most of the conquerors were given to falsehood and exaggeration and therefore not to be trusted (Durán, 1967, II:542), he occasionally consulted them and their descendants. His descriptions of

[85] See p. 78.
[86] See p. 397.
[87] See p. 404.
[88] See p. 218.
[89] See p. 79.
[90] See p. 213.

Mexico are partly derived from those of Spanish eyewitnesses.[91] He also learned how a conqueror named Montaño had heroically climbed to the very crater of Popocatepetl to obtain sulphur for Cortés's gunpowder—a story confirmed by Montaño's children.[92] Other Spaniards were of help in describing regions of the country unfamiliar to him.[93] Alonso de Ávila confirmed the Aztec's story about the Spaniard—his father, as it happened—who had entered the Great Temple and sent the hideous idol of the god Huitzilopochtli rolling down the steps.[94] "Blessed image" or "hideous idol," Fray Diego was fortunate to hear both sides of the story.

XII. Durán's Works Completed—and Forgotten

Durán's works were written in the following order: *Book of the Gods and Rites* (ca. 1576–79), *The Ancient Calendar* (1579), and *The History of the Indies* (1580?–81) (Durán, 1967, II:575).[95] To these works may be added an earlier draft or notebook which is no longer extant.[96]

Durán clearly meant his works to be printed. "Once my book is published," he wrote, "no one will be able to feign ignorance [about the idolatry of the natives]."[97] His first draft of the *Book of the Gods and Rites* was circulated among a few friends, probably Dominicans, who offered criticisms and suggestions. One critic accused him of being "too succinct and concise."[98] Later, in *The*

[91] See pp. 75–76.

[92] See p. 254.

[93] See p. 63.

[94] See p. 213.

[95] See pp. 126, 240, 383, 389. Although Garibay dates the *Book of the Gods and Rites* as 1570 (Durán, 1967, I:xvii), Durán himself states in Chapter V of the book, "We [the Spaniards] have been here fifty-five years." If Fray Diego is referring to the arrival of Cortés (1519), the date of the writing of the book would be 1574. If he is referring to the consummation of the Conquest of Mexico (1521), the date would be 1576. He cannot be referring to the arrival of the Dominicans in Mexico (1526), for the date would then be 1581, and we know that the second book, *The Ancient Calendar*, was finished in 1579. We believe that the *Book of the Gods and Rites* is certainly no earlier than 1574–76.

[96] See pp. 70–71.

[97] See p. 269.

[98] See p. 140.

Ancient Calendar, he commented that others were fearful that his work would "revive the ancient customs and rites among the Indians." His response to such objections was that the Indians had been so careful about preserving the ancient traditions that they needed no instruction.[99] "It has not been my purpose," wrote Durán, "to tell fables and ancient customs but to warn with Christian zeal the ministers of God who with such fervor practice the ministry which God gave them and for which they were chosen [to fulfill] their blessed works. Let them search out, let them uproot the tares which grow among the wheat. Let them be ripped out so that they not grow side by side with the divine law and doctrine."[100]

To judge from such statements, the *Book of the Gods and Rites* was intended primarily for Spaniards in Mexico, both clerics and laymen, and undoubtedly many read it in manuscript. A Jesuit, José de Acosta, included a large portion of Durán's material in his *Historia natural y moral de las Indias*, published in 1591, three years after Durán's death. Why, then, were the friar's works condemned to oblivion for several centuries? It must be remembered that by the time Fray Diego finished his third book Spain was ending its pioneer days in the Americas and was about to enter the seventeenth century, that great century of consolidation. Politically, New Spain was stable. Superficially at least, the Indians were good Catholics, and Indo-Christian churches and chapels dotted the countryside. A number of dioceses had been established, each with its cathedral and bishop, and the religious orders had found a *modus vivendi* with the secular clergy and appeared to be under the control of the civil authorities. The fighting spirit of the first Franciscans had largely disappeared, and the economic status of the clergy was infinitely better. The Indian peoples were submissive, paid tribute regularly, and were loyal subjects of Philip II.

In Madrid, His Majesty himself had enough local and international problems to keep him from worrying excessively about possible pagan survivals in his overseas dominions. England was a constant threat; Drake and other English privateers were assault-

99 See p. 411.
100 See p. 125.

ing Spanish pride in a variety of ways. Another threat to Philip II's world was Protestantism, a danger much greater than the remnants of paganism surviving among the conquered and humiliated natives of the New World. The prosperous second-generation Spaniards in Mexico were for the most part interested in mines, encomiendas, and important positions within the army, church, and state. Except for some who preserved the crusading spirit, they considered the Indians a means of achieving their aims rather than men to be molded into devout Christians.

Who was willing to lose sleep because the flowery staffs of Tezcatlipoca were used in Christian processions in Indian Mexico?[101] Who, besides a few monkish scholars, cared whether Topiltzin had been Moses or Saint Thomas? Who was disturbed because the natives of Mexico still hung ears of corn from their rafters, a custom dating from heathen times?[102] Writing in a time and under conditions different from those of the earlier Las Casas, anyone who bemoaned minute pagan survivals was no longer interesting or welcome. Moreover, Fray Diego had branded the secular priests as tourists and foreigners. He had repeatedly said that, from a religious point of view, Spain was making grave mistakes in the New World. These criticisms were undoubtedly valid, but times had changed, and the "last angry man" of his generation was no longer needed.

XIII. A New Project: **The Treatise on Things Past**

In 1581, upon finishing his *History*, Durán wrote, "I am commanded to write a new treatise on things past, from that date [1521] until these sorry and unhappy times" (Durán, 1964, 323). This statement is vague. What material was his new book to cover? No *Treatise on Things Past* has survived—and possibly was never written—and we can only speculate about it. Possibly it was to be a continuation of his previous works, made up of comments on the conquerors, the secular clergy, and the negative relationship be-

101 See p. 103.
102 See p. 176.

tween Europeans and Indians. It may be that Durán was planning a work in which his own life (seldom referred to in his extant books) played a prominent role. Was he to write a history of the activities of the Dominicans in New Spain, a prototype of Dávila Padilla's *Historia*?

It seems likely that the projected work was to include all these themes, as well as some critical comment about Spanish activities in the New World during the first sixty years after the Conquest. This conjecture is strengthened by the two mutilated and partly illegible passages in the original manuscript of the *History*. One deals with the invasion of Moteczoma's harem by the Spanish conquerors; the other, with the execution of Cuauhtemoc by Cortés. While the first obliteration may have been the result of a censor's prudishness, the second passage was undoubtedly destroyed because it contained material dangerous to the conquerors' reputations. If indeed Fray Diego did complete his treatise, it may have proved so explosive that it had to be destroyed. If it does survive, lying unknown in some Spanish or Mexican archive, it will be a rewarding discovery for some ethnohistorian of the future.

XIV. Fray Diego Durán as an Ethnographer

Those persons unfamiliar with the difficulties facing the ethnographer in field work may not realize the problems Durán encountered in his researches. To obtain authentic material from an informant alien to one's culture is no easy task. One must contend with reticence, omissions, contradictions, half-truths, and outright lies; suspicion of the ethnographer's motives; and fear of the consequences of revealing the occult aspects of the indigenous religion. These problems are oftentimes coupled with a language barrier.

When the ethnographer has managed to overcome these difficulties (though always only in part), he finds himself with a collection of notes, some repetitious, others incomplete, many untrustworthy. He sifts his material, laboriously checks again with his informants, and prepares his first draft, which he hopes to convert into a coherent whole. This procedure is no easy task today, and Fray Diego was burdened with even greater handicaps. He was dealing with a conquered people who had a natural distrust of their masters. Indians who recalled the pre-Conquest culture were reluctant informants. One wonders how many of them were willing to talk about their shattered social and political world.

Since he overcame these difficulties, Durán must be accorded the rank of genuine ethnohistorian. Many of his descriptions of pre-Hispanic Mexico are unique, not to be found in any other source. The accuracy of his ethnographic material is confirmed by comparison with the facts known to modern archaeology and ethnography. In spite of his rambling Spanish prose and his numerous repetitions, his presentation is usually vivid and dramatic. And his thoroughness in dealing with native religious rites is at times unrivaled even by Sahagún.

XV. Durán's Last Years

Durán's final comment as an ethnographer was made in 1581, when he drew his *History* to a close: "From the period of the plague to the unhappy present, this most fertile and rich land together with its capital, Mexico, has suffered many calamities and has declined with the loss of its grandeur and excellence and the great men who once inhabited it" (Durán, 1964, 323). Nothing is known of his life from 1581 to 1585. According to a contemporary account, he was in Mexico City in 1586, when he was called upon by the Inquisition to act as interpreter for a Nahuatl-speaking woman (Fernández del Castillo, 1925, 224). It is probable that he lived in Mexico City from about 1585 until his death in 1588. His last years were burdened by very poor health (Dávila Padilla, 653).

In the last year of his life Durán carried his criticisms of the clergy one step beyond his writings. In a manuscript dated July 14, 1587, now in the Papers of the Inquisition in the Archivo General de la Nación in Mexico, appears the following report (presented below in summary form):

> Fray Diego accuses, in his own handwriting, a fellow Dominican Fray Andrés Ubilla, of grave misdeeds:

45

1) Ubilla refused to give alms to the poor and preached against almsgiving.

2) Ubilla wrested sacred books from other Dominicans. In this he resembled Luther, who had destroyed books belonging to the True Faith.

3) Ubilla removed ornaments and images from certain churches and had cast them away to lie indecorously among old pieces of wood and mats.

4) Ubilla stole gold and silver reliquaries and relics. He could have kept the metal and returned the relics, but he gave both away to laymen and worthless women.

5) Ubilla caused scandal by his frivolous talks with younger men.

6) Ubilla said mass without having confessed these sins.

7) Ubilla held private conversations with Satan and possessed a *familiar* [a companion demon] who advised him. He is also reported to have been heard talking to certain phantoms. [Fernández del Castillo, 224–27]

This document, of a distinctly medieval flavor, was signed by Durán. Nothing more is known of the accusations or of the outcome. We do know, however, that Ubilla was a *definidor*, a member of the council of the Dominican Province of Mexico, and that after Durán's death he was appointed bishop of Chiapa, a see which dated to the time of Las Casas.

XVI. Epilogue[103]

In one year, Pentecost fell on the same day as the Aztec Feast of Tezcatlipoca, a coincidence unknown to most of the Spanish clergy. In the atrium of a Dominican church near Popocatepetl the friars prepared to lead a large group of Indians in procession.

Standing aside, Durán looked upon the throngs congregated in the churchyard. In lieu of candles the Aztecs carried in their hands the flowered staffs of Tezcatlipoca, the Smoking Mirror. The

---

[103] The following scene, as reconstructed by the translators, is based upon evidence appearing throughout Durán's works. The subject is mentioned specifically in Chapter IV of the *Book of the Gods and Rites*.

priests, confident in the faith of their flock, prepared to intone a chant in Latin.

The procession began to move, the priests intoning the Veni Creator, the Indians behind recalling the Smoking Mirror.

Wearily, Fray Diego picked up one of the flowered staffs of Tezcatlipoca and joined the procession.

"I see these things," he thought, "but I am silent."

Fortunately for us who live in a world that strives to understand each man within his own culture, Fray Diego Durán was not silent. In his outspokenness—which was to prove his own undoing —he produced a vigorous account of a vanished civilization, together with the story of his anguish as an eyewitness to the birth pangs of another.

Book of the Gods and Rites

Book of the Gods and Rites

I am moved, O Christian reader, to begin the task of [writing this work] with the realization that we who have been chosen to instruct the Indians will never reveal the True God to them until the heathen ceremonies and false cults of their counterfeit deities are extinguished, erased. Here I shall set down a written account of the ancient idolatries and false religion with which the devil was worshiped until the Holy Gospel was brought to this land. Fields of grain and fruit trees do not prosper on uncultivated rocky soil, covered with brambles and brush, unless all roots and stumps are eradicated.

This becomes clear when we study the characteristics of our Catholic Faith. Since it is one, one Church, adoring one True God, it cannot coexist with any other religion or belief in other gods. Any other human belief opposed to the Faith loses the quality of the Faith itself, and though this [individual] believes in the Catholic Faith, he is deceived inasmuch as his belief is based not on Christian but on human faith. Perhaps he was influenced by hearsay. Thus the Moslem believes in his religion, and the Jew in his. We should take [their condition] into consideration: since idolatry has not been totally erased from their minds, they mix the Christian Faith with heathen beliefs. Thus the Faith among them is superficial; though they come to confession and believe in the One God, they would accept ten if someone came around telling them there are ten.

Among the causes [of this situation] is the lack of a firm basis in the Catholic Faith. To these people it is only a "human" faith; and though this may not be blamed on their unpreparedness and uncouthness, the latter may be partly responsible for their laxity in the Faith. Let us consider, however, that in Spain there are people as uncouth and coarse, or almost so—for example, the people of some parts of Castile, toward Sayago, Las Batuecas, and other corners of provinces where men's minds are extraordinarily brutish and rude (especially in matters of religious instruction), much more so than these natives. At least the latter are taught catechism every Sunday and holy day, and receive the Gospel. The former, though in many villages, never hear a sermon in their lives. You may encounter one (who has spent his entire life in the country) who finds it impossible to distinguish or know anything about the size of a star. He will say, "It is like a nut," and, "The moon is like a cheese." Nevertheless, in spite of his coarseness, this man will allow himself to be torn to pieces defending a single article of the Faith. If you ask him, "Why is God One and also a Trinity?" he will answer, "Because that is the way it is." And if you ask him, "Why are there Three Persons in the Trinity and not four?" he will answer, "Why not?" And these two answers, "That is the way it is," and, "why not?" satisfy all their doubts and questions regarding the Faith, since they believe firmly what their parents taught them and what is believed and sustained by our Holy Mother the Church.

By this I argue that [the Spaniards] hold the Faith and its foundations firmly and that these [Indians] are easily swayed, prone to doubts, and will believe any doctrine. If a thousand dogmas were preached, they would believe all of them. By this I also argue that the foundations of the Faith [in Mexico] are not firm, and it behooves us to enlighten the people. Every year we hear their confessions during Lent, and again they learn through the priests; then they go away, forgetting it immediately.

What I have said about religious belief makes it clear that he who believes in a false deity does not believe in God; this can be said about men of all the nations of the world. But the case of the Indians is a special one, more so than of the other nations, since these people are poorer in spirit and the least prone to abandon their way of life and rites. Though some may feel and realize that what they believed in pagan times was false, natural fear and cowardice impede them from giving up these things. I affirm this for I see that not only in the Divine Cult but in earthly things [the Indians] are cowardly and fearful. Instead of hiring themselves out to a Spaniard, earning three reals a week, they prefer to go from market to market, trading things which are hardly worth twenty cacao beans. They will offer the Spaniard four reals to be given their liberty in order to return to their little houses or huts. Occasionally they will work four days of the week, and on Friday, or even Saturday, in order to escape from the Spaniard, they will flee, leaving their pay behind. I have observed these things for a long time and have wondered how to explain them. From long experience in observing the toil and afflictions [of the Indians], I find a common and universal cause: their spirit has been so hurt, so crippled, that they live in fear. They look upon everything unfamiliar or unknown as something harmful and fearful to them. They are like wild animals which, when hunted, are intimidated by everything and forced into flight.

This may be the result of their inborn wretchedness and the lowly condition nature gave them or of their gloomy, melancholy, and earthy constitution or the result of social conditions under which they lived. In part these people were well organized and polished, but on the other hand they were tyrannical and cruel, filled with the shadows of retributions and death. They were seldom loyal to one another for fear of punishment. And after the Faith arrived, the shadows grew beyond measure. From that time on [these people] have been afflicted with nothing but death, toil,

53

trouble, and anguish. All these things helped to break their spirit, to intimidate them to the point that they distrust us, do not believe us. They will not tell us things they knew about the lives of their ancestors. Regarding the worship of God and the receiving of the Sacraments, they dare not listen to God himself or seek the salvation of their souls because of their fears. Thus many of them never go to confession, afraid that the confessor will scold; others fear to receive the Eucharist, afraid of the obligations which will be imposed upon them to sin no longer. This is their condition in spite of the commands [of our priests].

And these are my conclusions: [the Indians] will never find God until the roots have been torn out, together with that which smacks of the ancestral religion. Thus the practice of the Faith is corrupted where there remain survivals of the cult and faith in another god. These people are reluctant to abandon things familiar to them. While the memory [of the old religion] lasts, they will turn to it, like those who find themselves ill or in need. While they call on God, they also seek out sorcerers, shamans who laugh at [Christianity], and then return to the superstitions, idolatries, and omens of their forebears. I have seen these things; I understand them. If we are trying earnestly to remove the memory of Amalech, we shall never succeed until we fully understand the ancient religion. In my humble judgment, therefore, I believe there is nothing in the world so barren as a man who lives out his entire life attempting to grasp something he does not understand, who feels no need of penetrating the roots of heathen beliefs of ancient times, who vainly strives to prevent these frail and weak people from mixing their old and superstitious rites with our Divine Law and Christian Religion. The ancient beliefs are still so numerous, so complex, so similar to our own in many cases that one overlaps the other. Occasionally we suspect that they are playing, adoring idols, casting lots regarding future events in our very presence—yet we do not fully understand these things. We believe they do [Christian] penance and practice certain absentions. But [they] always had their own sacraments and a divine cult which in many ways coincides with our own religion, as we shall see during the course of this work.

Those who with fervent zeal (though with little prudence) in the beginning burned and destroyed all the ancient Indian pictographic documents were mistaken. They left us without a light to guide us—to the point that the Indians worship idols in our presence, and we understand nothing of what goes on in their dances, in their market places, in their bathhouses, in the songs they chant (when they lament their ancient gods and lords), in their repasts and banquets; these things mean nothing to us. Heathenism and idolatry arc present everywhere: in sowing, in reaping, in storing grain, even in plowing the earth and in building houses; in wakes and funerals, in weddings and births (especially if the child is the offspring of a nobleman, when complex rites are performed).

The most elaborate rites were found in the celebration of the feasts. And everything was associated with heathenism and idolatry, even bathing in the river. Elders were often offended with the community if certain acts were not accompanied by ceremonial.

All these things are concealed from us, kept as a tightly guarded secret. The task of discovering and making them known is overwhelming. He who attempts [to do so] will soon discover this, and of a thousand other customs [he will be lucky if he discovers] one half.

Let our priests who toil in missionary work take note of the grave error in ignoring these things; the Indians will make mockery of the Faith, and the minister will remain in the dark. I have experienced some of these things in recent times. I have discovered a number of sly tricks which no one had paid any attention to.

He who wishes to read this book will find an account of all the main gods worshiped in ancient times by these ignorant and blind people, with the rites and ceremonies performed in the entire land and in the Province of Mexico. He will find the count of the days, months, weeks, and years and the manner and dates on which the festivals were celebrated. All this is meant as an instruction which the curious reader will discover in this book, written with that aim. If the fruits [of my work] are meager, my intention and zeal in presenting it are not.

☐☐☐☐☐☐☐☐☐☐☐☐☐☐☐☐☐☐☐☐☐☐☐☐☐☐☐
☐☐☐☐☐☐☐☐☐☐☐☐☐☐☐☐☐☐☐☐☐☐☐☐☐☐☐

CHAPTER I

¶Which treats of what is known of a great man who dwelt
in this land. His name was Topiltzin, our Lord, also
known as Papa, High Priest, known to the Aztecs as
Hueymac, who lived in Tula.[1]

B EFORE we begin to speak of the individual gods and of the rites
and ceremonies with which they were honored, I wish to tell of a
great man who once came to this land. I shall describe his religious
life and the cult taught by him, causing the Mexicas to invent ceremonies and rites, adore idols, build altars and temples, and offer
sacrifice, when they knew of him [in later times].

Topiltzin, called Papa by the Indians, was a venerable and
devout person, held in deference, honored and revered as one would
a holy man. Much is known regarding him. I saw a picture of him
(as he is portrayed in the accompanying illustration) [Plate 1] on
an ancient paper which was shown to me in the City of Mexico.
This document showed Topiltzin with a venerable appearance: as
an old man with a long red beard turning white. His nose was some-

[1] In Durán's time there was utter confusion about Topiltzin-Quetzalcoatl, the
great Toltec priest-king and holy man who sinned and was banished by the Toltec
people. The mystery of this man has not been completely clarified in our own times;
there are controversial theories about his identity, history, and birth and death dates.

Archaeological work carried out since 1940 in the ancient city of Tula, in the
State of Hidalgo, north of Mexico City, confirms Durán's statement that Tula was the

57

what long with blotches on it, and somewhat wasted. A tall man, with long, straight hair, sitting in great dignity.

He spent all his time praying in his cell; seldom was he seen. He fasted and abstained. He lived chastely; he lived doing penance. He built altars and oratories in all the wards of the city, and he set up images on the walls and on altars. He knelt down before these images, worshiped them, and kissed the earth, at times with his mouth, at times with his hand. His entire life was occupied in constant prayer. This priest always slept upon the floor where stood the altar he had built. There his disciples came, and there he taught them to pray and preach. These disciples were known as Toltecs, which means Masters, or Men Wise in Some Craft.[2]

The great deeds and wondrous acts of Topiltzin, his heroic

---

city of Quetzalcoatl, ruler of the Toltecs. Historical studies by Wigberto Jiménez Moreno, of the Mexican National Institute of Anthropology, based on sixteenth-century native and missionary chronicles, also indicate that Tula was the metropolis of Topiltzin-Quetzalcoatl. Jiménez Moreno has reconstructed the historical account as follows:

Topiltzin-Quetzalcoatl was a son of Mixcoatl, Cloud Serpent, king of the Toltec-Chichimec people in the early period of Toltec history, between the ninth and tenth centuries A.D. (*chichimec* means "nomad" or "barbarian"). Mixcoatl was murdered by a usurper, and Topiltzin's mother, Chimalman, Shield Hand, died when he was born. The boy was brought up by his maternal grandparents in Tepoztlan, south of Mexico City (now in the State of Morelos), the center of the cult of Quetzalcoatl, the Plumed Serpent (originally a water deity and later God of the Wind). When the youth became a man, he was made high priest of this cult and adopted the name of the god. He spent most of his life in the city of Tula, or Tollan, where he acquired fame as a holy man. He dedicated himself to penance and fasting.

Despite the reverence in which he was held, a conflict between two rival religious sects—one of which urged him to offer human sacrifice—led to a plot against him. Certain sorcerers offered him strong wine, made him drunk, and led him to commit incest with his sister. Disgraced, the priest abandoned Tula and went eastward toward present-day Veracruz. Before his final departure, however, he left various signs of his passing throughout the countryside and promised to return one day. In later times the Aztecs were to take Cortés for Topiltzin-Quetzalcoatl. Jiménez Moreno, 24–34.

[2] We now know through archaeological discoveries that the Toltecs formed a great civilization which reached its peak in central Mexico around the year A.D. 1000. This group, like the Aztecs of a later period, originated in northwestern Mexico and spoke the Nahuatl language. The Toltecs introduced metallurgy in the central highlands of Mexico and left us the impressive ruins of Tula.

acts, are famed among the Indians. These deeds are of such renown and remind one so much of miracles that I dare not make any statement or write of them. In all I subject myself to the correction of the Holy Catholic Church. But even though I wish to adhere to the Holy Gospel of Saint Mark, who states that God sent the Holy Apostles to all parts of the world to preach the gospel to His creatures, promising eternal life to all baptized believers, I would not dare affirm that Topiltzin was one of the blessed Apostles. Nevertheless, the story of his life has impressed me greatly and has led me and others to believe that, since the natives were also God's creatures, rational and capable of salvation,[3] He cannot have left them without a preacher of the Gospel. And if this is true, that preacher was Topiltzin, who came to this land. According to the story, he was a sculptor who carved admirable images in stone. We read that the glorious apostle Saint Thomas was a master craftsman in the same art. We also know that this apostle was a preacher to the Indians but that, having become discouraged there, he asked Christ (when the Lord appeared to him at a fair) to send him wherever He wished except to the Indians.[4] I am not surprised that the Holy Apostles were reluctant to deal with these natives—rude, inconsistent, rough, and slow in understanding the things of their salvation. They are fickle and inclined to believe in the most fabu-

---

[3] At this point Durán is clearly a Dominican in his defense of the rationality of the Indians. Only two generations had passed since the Dominican Antonio de Montesinos had first preached in the city of Santo Domingo the Indians' rights to be treated as human beings. And the struggle between Las Casas' "noble Indian" theory and Gonzalo Fernández de Oviedo's "dirty dog" theory was still fresh in the minds of the European colonists. It is not surprising, therefore, that Durán should stress this point, which was one of the fundamental controversies in the sixteenth century.

[4] Durán's insistence upon Christian missionary work in the Americas before 1492 should be considered part of the thinking of his time. The biblical texts were generally accepted in a literal manner. Thus the Twelve Apostles, as obedient servants of the Lord, could not have disobeyed the divine command to go forth to preach to all the peoples of the earth. It is understandable that Durán, in his quest for an ancient Christian preacher in the Americas, would have chosen Saint Thomas, who, according to legend, preached the gospel in Goa, India. In the mind of the average European of the period the names India and the Indies (that is, the New World) were connected if not synonymous. Today, of course, we know that there was little contact between one hemisphere and another for tens of thousands of years.

lous omens without any true basis or facts. Is there a man of average intelligence in our Spanish nation willing to believe that by sucking the hair of the head with the mouth a headache will disappear? Who will believe that on rubbing a sore spot stones, pebbles, or chips of blades will come out? Yet their own fakirs convinced them of these things. It was also believed that the health of children depended upon shearing their hair in one way or another. All of this is of the lowest, poorest, and most abominable human judgment. It has been difficult to persuade these people not to shave a child's head, leaving bunches of hair, and to remove the crosses they wore on their heads. Their faith in such things is so great that when these things are removed they go about pale and in mortal fear, dreading that their children will die. I am not surprised that we who deal with them become exasperated and flee from them, since the Apostles themselves, sanctified and filled with grace, begged not to be sent to Indian peoples. Nevertheless, this should not daunt us, since most of the ancient beliefs have been discarded.

To return to our subject: Topiltzin was a man who had come from a foreign country. This indicates that he appeared in this land [as a newcomer], since I can find no account of his homeland. However, it is well known, that after he arrived in this country he began to gather disciples and to build churches and altars. He and his disciples went out to preach in the villages; they went up to the hills to preach, and their voices would carry two or three leagues like the sounding of trumpets. They preached in the valleys and performed wondrous things which must have been miracles. Astonished, the people called these men Toltecs. It is also true that they performed heroic deeds with their hands. Today I have had the experience of asking, "Who made the cleft in this hill?" "Who created this spring?" "Who opened this cave?" or "Who constructed this building?" [The natives] have always answered that it was the Toltec disciples of the High Priest, Papa. Thus we can probably deduce that this man was an apostle whom God sent to this land and that the rest of them, the master craftsmen or wise men, were his disciples. They proved his preachings by their miracles in their attempts to convert these people to the Evangelical

Law. But, having seen the roughness and hardness of the natives' worldly hearts, the Toltecs abandoned this country and returned to their place of origin, where they could obtain some fruit from their labor and preaching. Great was the stubbornness of the natives in their cursed and evil law. Those of us who live among them today have found this out. Those who originally possessed some true knowledge are now very few. The natives were as obstinate in their old childlike beliefs as they are in giving them up. Now that they have the Faith, they may be reprehended for having believed in such low and unfounded things as their ancient rites and ceremonies.

I heard it affirmed that a great persecution arose against Topiltzin and his disciples and that a bitter war was waged against them, since the number of people who had accepted the New Law was great, and many were those who followed the preachings and example of that holy man and of his disciples. They say that the leader of this persecution was Tezcatlipoca, who pretended to have come down from heaven for that purpose. He also feigned miracles; he gathered disciples and wicked people to molest those honest men and to banish them from the land. The Toltecs were not allowed to settle in any town. They were forced to go back and forth until Topiltzin made his home in Tula, where he reposed for some years, until the persecution began anew. Finally, weary of being harassed, he and his followers decided to give in to their persecutors and to depart.

Having come to this decision, Topiltzin called together the people of Tula and all his disciples. He thanked them for having allowed him to live among them and then bade them farewell. Sorry to see him depart, the people of Tula asked him the reason for his going. Topiltzin replied that the cause had been the persecution of those wicked men. Speaking to them lengthily, he prophesied the arrival of strangers who would come to this land from the east. They wore unusual and multicolored clothing from head to foot. They used head coverings. This was the punishment which God was to send them in return for the ill-treatment which Topiltzin had received and for the shame of his banishment. In this chastisement young and old were to perish. No one was to escape from the hands of his sons who were to come to destroy them. Even if the people hid in caves and in the caverns of the earth, from there they would be brought forth; they would be persecuted and slain.

In their books the people of Tula then painted pictures of the men whom the High Priest had prophesied. They did so in order to remember and await the event. This was later to be confirmed with the coming of the Spaniards. Topiltzin also told them that the arrival of the strangers would not be witnessed by them or by their children or by their grandchildren, but would be seen by the fourth or fifth generation. "These will be your masters! These you will serve. They will mistreat you and will take your lands away, just as you have done to me!" Turning to his disciples and to other followers who went along weeping, he said, "Yea, brethren! Let us depart from this place where we are not loved and go where we may find rest!"

So it was that Topiltzin began to walk, passing through most of the towns in this country. He gave every village and every hill its name, each one appropriate to the appearance of the town or hill. A number of people followed him from each place. He set out for the sea, and there merely by speaking to it he opened a great hill and disappeared within. Others say that he cast his mantle upon the sea, making a sign upon it with his hand, and, seating himself on the mantle, he then moved over the waters, never to be seen again. When I asked another aged Indian what he knew about the departure of Topiltzin, he narrated to me Chapter Fourteen of Exodus, stating that the Papa had reached the sea with a number of followers and that he had stricken the water with his staff. The waters then dried up, and a road appeared. Topiltzin and his men had managed to pass, but his pursuers, who went after him, were swallowed up when the waters returned to their place and were never heard of again. When I realized that [the Indian] had been reading what I know and I recognized the path he was following, I ceased interrogating him in order to stop this repetition of Exodus. I suspected that he was acquainted with this book. The Indian was so well informed that he ended by relating the punishment of the snakes suffered by the children of Israel owing to the complaints against God and Moses.

Topiltzin passed through all the towns that I have named, and it is stated that he carved crosses and effigies upon the rocks. I asked the natives where I could see some of these in order to know the truth of the story, whereupon they referred me to certain places where these things could be seen. One of them was in the Zapotec region.[5] Therefore, I questioned a Spaniard who had been in this place regarding the truth of the native account, and he swore to me that he had seen a crucifix carved upon a rock in a ravine. An old Indian also told me that when the Papa passed through Ocuituco he left a large book there, four fingers in height and written in characters. I was extremely moved to possess this book and thus went to Ocuituco, where I begged the Indians in the most polite way to show it to me. But they swore that six years before they had burned it since they could not understand the writing. The latter was not similar to ours, and since they feared that it might bring harm to them, they destroyed it. I was sorry to hear this, because the manuscript could have shed light on our suspicion that it might have been the Holy Gospel in Hebrew. Vehemently I reprehended those who had had the book burned.[6]

The disciples of this saintly man wore long tunics which came down to the feet. On their heads they used coverings made of cloth or hats. When the Indians tried to paint these headdresses or hats which were [worn by the disciples of Topiltzin], they depicted sea snails. The tunics were of many colors. Some of them wore their hair long, and these hair styles were to be called by the Indians in

---

[5] The theme "Quetzalcoatl was here" was so common in pre-Conquest times that Durán's reference to Topiltzin's stay in the Zapotec region and, a few lines below, to events in Ocuituco, a town southwest of Popocatepetl, is simply a repetition of ancient stories found in many parts of Mesoamerica. A surprising number of those stories, however, appear to come from the region around Popocatepetl, Smoking Mountain, and Iztaccihuatl, Mountain of the White Woman.

[6] Just as the Mayas of Yucatán kept their Books of Chilam Balam—books of history and fortunetelling—so each Nahuatl-speaking town of the Mexican highlands employed a special scribe to keep its books and almanacs for consultation regarding omens, calendrical information, genealogy, land boundaries, and business accounts. It is probable that the book was a *tonalamatl*, a calendrical book of days.

later times *papa*. I found this painting as old, as ancient, as the first, as can be seen on the adjoining sheet [Plate 2], together with a picture of Topiltzin. In order to lend me this, the Indian from Chiautla made me swear that I would return it to him.[7] When I had given him my word that when I had copied it I would return it, he finally loaned it to me with so much ceremony and elaborate talk, and in such great secrecy, that I was astonished at the value he placed upon it. And I will affirm my belief that he stayed tenaciously with the artist until the picture was done. I tried to find out something about this, and the Indian narrated all of what I just said. However, he added material in telling me that all the ceremonies and rites, building temples and altars and placing idols in them, fasting, going nude and sleeping on the floor, climbing mountains to preach the law there, kissing the earth, eating it with one's fingers, and blowing trumpets and conch shells and flutes on the great feast days—all these things imitated the ways of that holy man.[8] He offered incense at the altars and ordered that musical instruments be played in the temples which he had built.

I was desirous of finding out whether these things were true. Therefore, I questioned an Indian advanced in years, from Coatepec,[9] who was considered a wise man in his town. This man

[7] The implication is that the picture was another relic left by Quetzalcoatl—again in a town not far from Popocatepetl, the present-day Chiautla de Tapia.

[8] Among the Aztecs the greatest reverence that could be shown to a god or a sovereign was to place the middle finger of one hand on the earth and then suck the earth which had adhered to it. This action indicated one's humility, and may well have been associated with the deity Tlazolteotl, Eater of Filth, who devoured the blemishes of mankind.

[9] Further association of the town of Coatepec with the conquerors is found in this story from Durán's *History*: "A peasant who was a native of Coatepec in the province of Texcoco was plowing his fields calmly when a mighty eagle descended upon him, took him by the hair with its claws and carried him into the heights until he was lost from the sight of those who had been with him. The peasant was carried to a high mountain where he was taken into a dark cave. There he heard the eagle say, 'O powerful lord, I have complied with your wishes; here is the peasant you ordered me to bring.' The farmer heard a voice saying, 'Bring him here. Welcome!' The man was taken by the hand into a lighted place and there he saw Moteczoma asleep or perhaps unconscious. The peasant was made to sit next to the sleeping king. He was given flowers and tobacco to smoke and he was told, 'Take these things, be at ease, and behold that wretch Moteczoma, unconscious, drunk with his pride and

died of the great plague.[10] I begged him to tell me whether what was written and painted there was true, but the Indians find it difficult to give explanations unless they can consult the book of their village. So he went to his home and brought back a painted manuscript, but the characters impressed me more as representations of magical things than history. Within this document was to be found in almost unintelligible signs the entire life of Papa and his disciples. This native narrated the life of Topiltzin to me as I had known it but in a better manner than I had heard before. I was highly pleased with all this, since this man gave me so much more information. He showed me the picture of Topiltzin celebrating feasts, wearing the feathered crown we saw in the painting. It

haughtiness! He feels nothing but scorn for everyone and if you wish to see how his pride has blinded him, burn him in the thigh with the tobacco you carry and you will see that he does not feel it.' The man was afraid to do this but he was told, 'Burn him, do not fear.' The peasant then touched him with the fiery tobacco and Moteczoma did not stir or feel the burn.

" 'Do you see,' asked the voice, 'how he is unaware of everything? Do you see how drunk he is? Know that for this reason you have been brought here. Return to the place from which you were brought and go tell Moteczoma what you have seen. That he may know what you say is the truth tell him to show you his thigh and point out the place where you scorched him. There he will find the sign of fire. Also tell him that the God of All Created Things is angered and that he himself has sought the evils that are to come upon him. His reign is coming to an end. Let him enjoy what remains of it! Let him be patient since he has been the cause of his own ruin!'

"The eagle was told to transport the peasant back to his field. The man was then picked up by the hair and deposited in the place where he had been found. The eagle said, 'Behold, peasant and common man that you are, do not fear! Go with spirit and a strong heart and do what the Lord has commanded. Do not forget any of the words that you are to say!' With this the eagle disappeared again into the heavens.

"The poor peasant seemed to be awakening from a dream, frightened as he was by what he had seen. However, with his digging stick still in his hand he came before Moteczoma and told him of the strange events, and the king remembered that the night before he had dreamed that a common man had wounded him in the thigh with burning tobacco. He then looked at his thigh and felt such pain that he dared not touch the burned flesh. Without asking the peasant any other questions, Moteczoma called his jailers and ordered that the man be thrown into jail and starved to death. The Indian was then cast into prison and forgotten there" (Durán, 1964, 255–56).

[10] According to Gibson (138), "In the late sixteenth and early seventeenth centuries it was common to speak of a total decrease of 90 per cent or more in the Aztec population in the intervening years since the Conquest. This decrease was due largely to smallpox and other epidemics." Durán's Coatepec informant undoubtedly succumbed to the plague of 1576–81.

looked very much like the miter that bishops wear on their heads when they say mass. This is an illustration of his disciples [Plate 2].

These illustrations show the disciples whom Papa brought with him. These were called Toltecs and Children of the Sun. Much could be told about their great feats and memorable deeds. Their main city was Cholula,[11] though they were to be found in all the

[11] Cholula, possibly the largest archaeological site in the world, according to Ignacio Marquina, of the Mexican Institute of Anthropology, has also been one of the longest-lived cities. Settled in pre-Classic times, many centuries before the Christian era, Cholula received a strong impact from Teotihuacan during the Classic period (ca. A.D. 300–800) and after the fall of the latter city continued its existence as the same type of temple site, pilgrimage destination, and market center that had formerly characterized Teotihuacan and that later was to be typical of the great Mexico-Tenochtitlan (but without the dominating militaristic and imperial elements found in the Mexica capital). During the post-Classic period Cholula was occupied by the Historic Olmecs (A.D. 800–1300), people of Popoloca-Mixtec origin but Nahuatlized. During this period Cholula extended its influence to northwestern Mexico, south to Oaxaca, and east to Veracruz. The splendid Mixtec-Cholula polychrome pottery, introduced by the Historic Olmecs, dates from that period.

At the fall of the Classic world, about A.D. 900, a Nahua group, the Toltecs, invaded central Mexico and eventually were found in many centers, including Cholula. Actually they went south to that region after the collapse of the Toltec capital, Tula, in the twelfth century. Firsthand historical sources which speak of Cholula state that the priest-king Topiltzin-Quetzalcoatl, a refugee from Tula, arrived at and resided in Cholula for some years. The Toltecs, under Olmec tyranny for some time in that city, finally rebelled and took possession of the area in 1292. Less than two centuries later the region, except for the Tlaxcala "republic," came under the control of the Aztecs.

At the time of the Spanish Conquest, Cholula was still a bustling metropolis of markets and shrines, the cultural and economic crossroads of the Aztec empire. It connected the Gulf Coast with the Valley of Mexico, the rich cities of the Puebla-Tlaxcala area with Oaxaca, the Soconusco region, and Central America. The grandiose proportions of Cholula and its great pyramid caused sixteenth-century chroniclers to claim that the region had been inhabited by giants, an idea strengthened by the discovery of mammoth bones. The colonial Church of Our Lady of Los Remedios now stands on the summit of Tlachiualtepetl, Man-made Hill, whose base covers almost 525,000 square feet, making it the largest pyramidal structure in the world. This pyramid was formed of various structures superimposed on earlier ones in different periods.

Long-term excavations, as well as anthropological and historical studies of the region, are being carried out in Cholula by the Mexican National Institute of Anthropology and History, the German-Mexican Puebla-Tlaxcala Project, and the University of the Americas. Among recent findings are mural paintings on a pyramid wall that date from the fifth century A.D. and a statue of the god Quetzalcoatl, the deity of Cholula.

After the Spanish Conquest the Indians replaced their numerous shrines with

land. They lived in that place before the Cholulans settled there. They were preachers to the mountaineers of Tlaxcala, the latter known as Chichimecs and Giants.[12] They were clothed in colored tunics, which the Indians called *xicolli*. Because of their headdresses they were also called *cuateccise*, which means "heads with snails."

The lords of this place begged the holy man Hueymac[13] to wed. He responded that he had already decided to marry, but not until the oak gave apples, the sun rose from the west, the sea could be walked upon with dry feet, and the nightingales grew beards like those of men.

In a painting I saw Hueymac depicted wearing a long gown and a large hat upon his head, together with an inscription which read "Father of the Children of the Clouds."[14]

Christian churches (in a letter to Charles V, Cortés reported having seen 400 temples). It is also said that there are 365 churches, one for each day of the year, but actually the number is smaller. About 50 have been counted in the city of Cholula, and more on the periphery, totaling perhaps 100.

[12] In Mesoamerican chronicles the Giants are often mentioned in relation to the Classic period (A.D. 300–800). The legend of the Giants is a favorite one in many parts of Mexico. It is a product of the discovery of gigantic bones of Pleistocene animals such as the mammoth, *Bison antiquus*, and a type of elephant, which were earlier mistaken for human bones. Before the Conquest so many of the immense bones had been disinterred in the Valley of Teotihuacan that the people named a site near the pyramids Acolman (from *acolli*, "tall" or "broad-shouldered," and *mani*, "where there are"). Furthermore, who but men-greater-than-men, giants or gods, could have constructed pyramids of such extraordinary proportions in Teotihuacan, Place of Gods? The legend applies to Cholula not only because remains of the same type were found there but also because the Teotihuacan civilization influenced the development of the city. Mammoth bones were objects of curiosity to the Spaniards as well as to the Indians. Sahagún himself mentioned that Giants or Quinametin built Teotihuacan as well as Cholula. Fossilized bones were sent to Spain during the sixteenth century—perhaps the first Mexican curios. Francisco Hernández, commissioned to investigate many natural phenomena of the New World, judged the Giants to be more than sixteen feet tall, basing his estimate on the size of the mammoth bones. The Museum of Prehistory at Tepexpan in the Valley of Teotihuacan has a comprehensive exhibit of gigantic animal bones discovered there and elsewhere.

[13] Modern historians identify Hueymac as the last Toltec ruler during whose reign the great Tula collapsed. Early chronicles state that he committed suicide at Chapultepec Hill near Mexico City around A.D. 1200.

[14] The historian here refers to the Mixtec people, a highly civilized group of nations lying southeast of Cholula, in Oaxaca. They were remarkable artisans and metalworkers, and most of the authentic pre-Spanish books extant today were pro-

I was still curious and wished to press the Indian to give more information, so that—one word here and another there—I could complete my book. Again I asked him the reason for the departure of the holy man from this land. He answered that the persecution by Quetzalcoatl and Tezcatlipoca (both of them wizards and magicians, who could change their forms as they wished) had been the reason.[15]

I questioned the native regarding the unhappy causes which obliged the holy man to flee. He responded that, while Hueymac was absent from his rooms, the wizards had secretly introduced a harlot called Xochiquetzal, who lived a whorish life in those times. When Topiltzin returned to his cell, ignorant of the harlot's presence, the evil wizards spread rumors about Xochiquetzal, who was lying in the cell of Topiltzin. This they did in order to spoil the priest's reputation and that of his disciples. Since Topiltzin was chaste and lived a life of purity, this insult wounded him deeply, and he immediately decided to depart from this country.

I asked the Indian whether he knew or had heard where the priest had gone. Although he told me some incredible things, he confirmed my idea that Topiltzin had gone toward the seacoast. He was never heard from again, nor is it known where he went. The only thing known is that he went to inform the Spaniards, his sons, about this country and that he brought them for the sake of vengeance. So it is that the Indians, having been told of the ancient prophecy of the coming of strangers, were always anticipating it. Thus, when news came to Moteczoma of the arrival of the Euro-

---

duced by the Mixtecs. They were said to have been born of the clouds, hence the name Durán gives them: Hijos de las Nubes. Durán's association of the Mixtecs and the Toltecs of Quetzalcoatl is somewhat confirmed by the fact that when the Aztec warriors conquered northern Oaxaca toward the middle of the fifteenth century they found a great ruler called Atonal, head of the powerful state known as Coixtlahuaca, who still thought of himself as king of the Toltecs.

[15] Nahualism, the ability to transform oneself into an animal at will, was a basic aspect of the ancient religion. The gods themselves were believed to become werejaguars, eagles, or snakes when it suited their purposes. Tezcatlipoca, Smoking Mirror, who embodied a spirit of mischief, was one of the Supreme deities of the Aztec pantheon. In this reference the names Quetzalcoatl and Tezcatlipoca probably signify the rival sects whose intrigues forced Topiltzin into disgrace and flight.

peans at San Juan de Ulúa and Coatzacualco, he already knew of their dress and their customs.[16] Moteczoma examined the ancient paintings and books and realized that they were the sons of Topiltzin, whose arrival had already been announced to him. So he sent them a splendid present consisting of jewels, feathers, gold, and precious stones. In fear of what had come upon him, [Moteczoma] sent a message asking the newcomer to depart, since he did not wish to see him. He knew through his prophecies that the strangers had not come to bring good, but rather evil and harm.

When the Spaniards arrived at the port, Moteczoma's lookouts saw them and spread the news, saying that the sons of Hueymac had arrived. Moteczoma answered: "Those men have come to seek the treasure that Hueymac abandoned here when he departed and which he had gathered in order to build a temple. Let them take it away! Let them not come here!" All this was shown to me in a painted manuscript which represented the life and deeds of Moteczoma.

[16] San Juan de Ulúa is the fortress near the port of Veracruz. Cortés first visited Coatzacoalco to the south and reached Ulúa in April, 1519. Upon his arrival the Aztec dignitaries declared that Topiltzin-Quetzalcoatl had returned.

CHAPTER II

¶Which treats of the great god of the Mexicas, named Huitzilopochtli, and of the rites and ceremonies with which he was honored.

THE god shown in the picture [Plate 3] is he whom the Mexicas adored as the greatest divinity of all and in whom they held the greatest trust. It was said that he set men's hearts on fire and gave them courage for war. Believing these same things, the pagans venerated the god Mars and carried the statue of this deity to war. In the history [of the Mexica god of war] we shall deal with some remarkable and curious things which will serve as a lesson for the clergy; for the layman it will make pleasant [reading].[1]

The most solemn and celebrated feast in all the land (especially among the Tetzcocans and the Mexicas) was that of the god called Huitzilopochtli. Much is remarkable about this feast and its rites since it was a mixture of diverse ceremonies. Some resemble those of our Christian religion; others, things of the Old Testament; and still others, diabolical and satanical, were invented [by the Indians]. I feel certain that I was not confused by different versions I obtained from several sources. My aim was the truth, and

[1] In the sixteenth-century manuscript this paragraph is found at the end of Chapter I, but it was undoubtedly meant to appear at the beginning of Chapter II.

this desire fired me to make more inquiries than were necessary. Of the many things written in the first draft, however, I removed the Indian wordiness in telling fables and irrelevant matters (when anyone is willing to listen to them, they go on forever). I will set down here all the things on which I found my informants agreed.

And so that the truth of my story is from witnesses (some by ear, others by eye) in agreement, I shall speak of that which is essential and necessary for the instruction of the clergy. This is our principal aim: to warn them of the confusion that may exist between our own feasts and those [of the Indians]. These, pretending to celebrate the festivities of our God and of the Saints, insert, mix, and celebrate those of their gods when they fall on the same day. And they introduce their ancient rites in our ceremonies. It should not surprise us if this happens today, for our movable feasts and their ancient and most important ones often coincide and at other times fall close to one another. [The people] will honor their idol; then they will observe the solemnities of the feast, take pleasure, dance, and sing! They are merrier than when [the feasts] fall on different days, for when they coincide they celebrate with more freedom, feigning that the merriment is in honor of God —though the object is the [pagan] deity. I would not dare make such a rash assertion were I not so sure and did not have under my protection some who strive for their salvation and who trust in God. We are now less blind and ignorant than we were in former times. Let our ministers take warning; let them realize it is a great evil if an Indian garbs himself in the attire of his [ancient god]. This would be a great deceit: to celebrate [the god], to sing chants extolling his false excellency and grandeur, to wear different garments and ornaments; to use new rhythms and chants for every occasion. This is evil and idolatrous, since all formerly performed according to the characteristics of each pagan god. Let the reader, so that he realize I am speaking the truth, observe the following when he attends a fiesta: if he sees a couple of men in front of the others wearing different adornments and dancing different steps, going and coming in the direction of those who lead the dance, creating a merry din occasionally, ending with a whistle or pronouncing unintelligible words—let him be aware that these men represent gods, that the feast is for them, with both secret and public dancing. This is probably going on today as it did before.

The god we have described was feared and revered so intensely in the land that he was the only one called Lord of Created Things and The Almighty. To him were offered the greatest and most important sacrifices. His temple was the most outstanding in this land: the largest, most solemn, and most sumptuous. I constantly heard the conquerors tell of its excellence, height, and beauty, of its ornate structure and its solidity. The residence of Alonso de Avila now stands upon the site, but today this is a rubbish heap. I shall speak of the temple later, in the proper place.[2]

Huitzilopochtli was a wooden statue carved in the image of a man seated upon a blue wooden bench in the fashion of a litter; from each corner there emerged a serpent-headed pole, long enough for a man to bear on his shoulder. This bench was sky blue, indicating that Huitzilopochtli's abode was in the heavens. The god's forehead was blue, and above his nose ran a blue band which reached from ear to ear. On his head he wore a rich headdress in the shape of a bird's beak. These birds were called *huitzitzilin*. We also call them *zunzones* ["hummingbirds"], and they are green and blue. In Michoacan [today] religious images are made with the feathers of this bird. The beaks of these small birds are long and black, and the feathers are shiny. But before I go on, I wish to tell an excellent and wondrous thing in honor and praise of Him who created this bird. For six months of the year it is dead, and for six it is alive. And, as I have said, when it feels that winter is coming, it goes to a perennial, leafy tree and with its natural instinct seeks out a crack. It stands upon a twig next to that crack, pushes its

[2] In introducing the Great Temple of Mexico, Durán sets the stage for a large number of the religious acts he is to describe in succeeding pages. The temple was an enormous enclosure covering about 500,000 square feet, in the center of Mexico-Tenochtitlan. According to Sahagún, this city within a city contained more than seventy-two temples, monasteries, nunneries, colleges, and seminaries, as well as artificial ponds, ball courts, botanical gardens, skull racks, and a special dwelling place for the Foreign Gods. Though most of this great religious complex now lies under downtown Mexico City, a few exposed remains near the present-day cathedral give some idea of the splendor of the ancient setting.

beak into it as far as possible, and stays there six months of the year—the entire duration of the winter—nourishing itself with the essence of the tree. It appears to be dead, but at the advent of spring, when the tree acquires new life and gives forth new leaves, the little bird, with the aid of the tree's life, is reborn. It goes from there to breed, and consequently the Indians say that it dies and is reborn. And with my own eyes I have seen this bird in winter with its beak thrust into the crack of a cypress, holding onto a branch as if it were dead, motionless. Having marked the spot, I returned in the spring when the trees had budded and become leafy, and I could not find it. I feel secure in writing this here, and I believe what the Indians told me. I praise the Almighty Omnipotent God, capable of performing even greater wonders![3]

The beak which supported the headdress of the god [Huitzilopochtli] was of brilliant gold wrought in imitation of the bird I have described. The feathers of the headdress, extremely beautiful and plentiful, came from green birds. [The idol] wore a green mantle and over this mantle, hanging from the neck, an apron or covering made of rich green feathers, adorned with gold. When he was seated upon his bench, [the apron] covered him to the feet. In his left hand he carried a white shield with five tufts of white feathers placed in the form of a cross. From these hung yellow feathers as a sort of border; from the top [of the shield], a golden banner. Extending from the handle were four arrows. These were the insignia sent from heaven to the Mexicas, and it was through these symbols that these valorous people won great victories in their ancient wars, as I narrate in another book. In his right hand the god held a staff carved in the form of a snake, all blue and undulating. He was girded, [and from the belt rose] a shining gold banner set against his back. On his wrists he wore golden bracelets. He was shod in blue sandals. Each of these ornaments had its significance and connection with pagan beliefs.

[3] There is reason to accept Durán's story about the hibernation of the hummingbird. Evidence of a hibernating bird was found by Edmund C. Jaeger, in this case the small poorwill of the western United States, which sleeps in rocky clefts for three months of the winter (Jaeger, 1953, 273–80).

Thus garbed and adorned, the idol always stood upon a tall altar within a small chamber hung with numerous pieces of cloth, decorated with jewels, gold ornaments, and feather shields—the most splendid and finely wrought objects with which the people could adorn it. A curtain was always hung before it, indicating reverence and veneration. Next to this room stood a second room, no less richly decorated, the home of an idol called Tlaloc. These chambers were at the summit of the temple, and in order to ascend there were one hundred twenty steps. To give me an idea of the height [of these rooms], I was told that they were about as tall as a cross which exists in the courtyard of [the Monastery of] San Francisco in the City of Mexico. Both these chambers were finely carved, all the figures [sculptured] in the round. These images and beasts are now placed at the corner of the royal palace, under the city clock. Some of these figures were utilized as lintels, others as cornerstones, others as torch or light stands. In sum, both rooms were replete with carved figures and beasts of different types, in homage to and to the glory of these idols.[4]

[4] Among the pre-Hispanic peoples of Mexico, the Olmecs and the Mexicas were the great sculptors, the former flourishing in Tabasco and Veracruz between 1500 B.C. and A.D. 100, the latter on the temperate central plateau between the thirteenth and sixteenth centuries. Characteristic of Mexica sculpture is its masterful technique and variety of materials (basalt, volcanic stone, obsidian, rock crystal, jade, turquoise, pyrite, alabaster, serpentine, carnelian, diorite, shell, and many others), combined with an austere style which exemplifies the "heart of jade" idealized by the Aztecs. Their sculpture, all of it dramatic, ranged from highly stylized monumental pieces (such as Coatlicue) to representations of small animals and insects. There is no doubt that many of these sculptures functioned as a "celestial court" to the gods. Many stood for calendrical signs—the dog, eagle, ocelot, serpent, death's head, rabbit. The whole world of the Mexicas was built around the calendar cycle; therefore, it was natural that these representations were symbols of the all-important day count, each with its magico-religious characteristics.

Apparently in Durán's time certain pre-Hispanic sculptures were still exhibited on the façades and corners of private and public buildings. In later times most of them were removed. As late as 1794, however, the *Indio Triste*, a squatting man carved in stone, a standard-bearer, could be seen on the Street of El Indio Triste, now the corner of Carmen and Guatemala streets. Others to be seen today are the "sun" at the corner of Madero and Motolinía streets; a small Tlaloc on the exterior of the apse in the Church of Santiago Tlatelolco; and a superb plumed serpent which serves as a cornerstone of the Mansion of the Counts of Santiago de Calimaya, now the Museum of the City of Mexico, at the corner of Pino Suárez and El Salvador streets.

These two gods were always meant to be together, since they were considered companions of equal power.

Facing the two rooms of these gods was a square space, forty feet on each side, plastered smoothly with stucco. In the center, in front of the two shrines, stood a pointed green stone about as high as a [man's waist]. When a man was thrown upon it, on his back, the form of [the stone] bent his body. Men were sacrificed upon this stone in a way which we will see elsewhere, and, since there are so many remarkable things in the details of this temple, after I have shown an illustration, I wish to make special mention of each thing. This will not fail to interest and please when it is heard and read about and when we realize the fine craftsmanship with which these people built temples to their deities and how they adorned and polished them. Yet in our own times there are those who say that a small, squat adobe church is enough for our God!

Having described the decoration of the god, let us hear of the notable and beauteous things of his temples. [This time] I shall begin not with the account I have received from my Indian informants but with that of a friar who was one of the first conquerors to arrive in this land. He called himself Fray Francisco de Aguilar. He was highly venerated, a person of great authority in the order of our glorious Father, Saint Dominic. I obtained from him and from other trustworthy and reliable conquerors [the following account]. They assured me that the day they entered the City of Mexico, when they saw the height and grandeur of the temples, they thought them castellated fortresses, splendid monuments and defenses of the city, or castles or royal dwelling places, crowned with turrets and watchtowers. Such were the glorious heights which could be seen from afar! Thus the eight or nine temples in the city were all close to one another within a large enclosure. Within this compound they all stood together, though each had its own staircase, its special courtyard, its chambers, and its sleeping quarters for the priests of the temples. All of this took up much ground and space. How marvelous it was to gaze upon them—some taller than others, some more lavish than others, some with their entrances facing the east, others the west, others the north, others the south! All stuccoed, carved, and crowned with different types of merlons, painted with animals, [covered] with stone figures, strengthened by great, wide buttresses! How [the temples] gave luster to the city! How they gave it dignity, to the point that there was little else to see!

Since the god we refer to was the principal deity, his temple was the most sumptuous and magnificent of all. Its own private courtyard was surrounded by a great wall, built of large carved stones in the manner of serpents joined to one another. He who wishes to see these stones may go to the Cathedral of the City of Mexico. There he will observe them, serving as pedestals and bases of the columns.[5] These stones, today used as bases, formed the wall of the Temple of Huitzilopochtli. This wall was called Coatepantli, Snake Wall. Above the chambers or shrines [of the temple] where the idol was kept was a beautiful battlement of small black stones like jet;[6] all were placed in perfect order and pattern, the entire frame stuccoed in white with red paint, shining splendidly. Above the battlement stood some beautifully carved merlons like snails. The balustrades alongside the stairway ended at the top with two seated stone men holding standards in their hands. From these standards emerged a kind of net bag crowned with rich yellow and green feathers, [and hanging from them] were long tufts of the same. This courtyard contained many rooms and apartments belonging to friars and nuns, aside from other [chambers] on the top for priests and ministers who served the god. The courtyard was so large that during a feast it held eight to ten thousand men, and this will not sound fanciful when I narrate a true happening, told [to me] by someone who with his own hands murdered many natives within [this courtyard].

[5] As the visitor to the National Museum of Anthropology in Mexico City ends his tour of the Mexica Hall, he comes face to face with a fitting symbol of the climax and end of the Aztec culture: a stone column from the ruins of the primitive cathedral. The entire base is carved with an elaborate representation of Tlaltecuhtli, God of the Earth. This "stone of the two cultures," dramatically depicting the fusion of Christianity with the native religion, is a perfect illustration of the syncretism which forms the core of Durán's work.

[6] Probably obsidian, a volcanic glass common in Mexico.

When the [Marqués] Cortés entered the City of Mexico with his men, the Indians were celebrating the feast of their supreme god. When the marqués discovered this, he begged Moteczoma, monarch of the land (since the feast of their god was taking place), to give orders to all the lords, braves, and captains to appear, to celebrate and perform the usual dance, for he wished to take pleasure in the magnificence of the kingdom. This wretched king was already a prisoner, kept under guard, and in order to please [Cortés], in order to demonstrate the wealth and grandeur of his kingdom, he gave orders to all the noblemen of [the City of] Mexico and the entire region to gather, bringing their wealth and splendid ornaments which they possessed in jewels, stones, and feathers. Nothing was to be lacking in giving pleasure to the Teotl. Cortés and the other Spaniards were called thus; it means Gods, since at the beginning the [natives] believed firmly that they were divine, with unfortunate results, to judge by what happened later. Thus all the flower of Mexico appeared for the dance—great, valiant, brave men. In a painted picture I calculated them to be eight thousand six hundred men—all of high birth or captains of great valor. They not only came from [the City of] Mexico but had been called from nearby cities and towns.

Once they were in the courtyard celebrating their feast, the doors leading to the square were taken [by the Spaniards], and all the natives were knifed to death without a single exception. They were stripped of their jewelry and wealth, which they had worn to show their splendor and also to please. May our Lord restrain my hand and pen so that I not protest too strongly against this atrocious, wicked deed—comparable to all the cruelties of Nero. The result of this massacre was a rebellion and war against the Spaniards and the death of Moteczoma, king and lord of the land. His own vassals rose against him, accusing him of complicity with the Spaniards in that deed, giving orders that [the natives] gather to be slain. Because of this they denied him their obedience and elected as king a nephew named Cuauhtemoc.[7]

[7] According to reliable sources on the history of the Conquest, Durán is incorrect in placing Cortés in Mexico City at the time of this tragic event of 1520. These

I have brought up this story to give a clear idea of the magnitude of the courtyard of the temple. It must have been immense, for it accommodated eight thousand six hundred men, dancing in a circle. This courtyard had four doors or entrances, one on the east, another on the west, one on the south, and another on the north. From each one of these began one of the four causeways: one to Tlacopan (today we call it the Street of Tacuba); another toward Guadalupe; another toward Coyoacan; and yet another toward the lake and the canoe dock. The four main temples had entrances facing the directions I have mentioned, and the four gods standing in them also faced the same directions. Even though the reason given for this [plan] be fictitious, I shall not refrain from narrating it so that this arrangement is comprehensible.

The ancients believed that before the sun rose or had been created the gods discussed lengthily among themselves, each insisting stubbornly on the direction he thought appropriate for the rising of the sun, which had to be determined before its creation. One, desirous of having his own way, said it was necessary that the sun rise in the north; another contradicted him, saying the south was better; another said no, that it should appear in the west; still another said that the east was most convenient for its rising. The last had his way. He turned his face [toward the direction] in which he wanted the sun to appear, and the rest turned their faces toward the directions they had chosen. These four doors [of the square] existed for this reason. And so they spoke of the door of such and such a god, and of others, each door being named for its god.

In front of the main door of the Temple of Huitzilopochtli there were thirty long steps about one hundred eighty feet in length. These were separated from the courtyard wall by a passage. On top [of the platform] was a walk thirty feet wide and as long

---

sources clearly indicate that Cortés was absent at the time of the massacre and that Captain Pedro de Alvarado was responsible for it. See the works of Bernal Díaz del Castillo, Francisco de Aguilar, Cortés, El Conquistador Anónimo, Andrés de Tapia, Fernando Alvarado Tezozómoc, Bartolomé de las Casas, and Antonio de Herrera y Tordesillas and the anonymous *Anales de Tlatelolco*.

as the steps. The passage was plastered, and its steps were finely worked. Along the center of this ample and long walk stood a finely carved palisade as tall as a great tree. Poles were set in a row, about six feet apart. All these thick poles were drilled with small holes, and the holes were so numerous that there was scarcely a foot and a half between them. These holes reached to the top of the tall, thick poles. From pole to pole, through the holes, stretched thin rods strung with numerous human heads pierced through the temple. Each rod held twenty heads. These horizontal rows of skulls rose to the height of the poles of the palisade and filled it from end to end [Plate 4]. One of the conquerors assured me that they were so numerous they were impossible to count, so close together that they caused fright and wonder. These skulls were all that remained of those who had been sacrificed.

After the latter were dead and their flesh had been eaten, the skulls were delivered to the ministers of the temple, who strung them there. When I asked if they were changed or removed at any time, I was given a negative answer. When [the skulls] became old and deteriorated, they fell in pieces. When the palisade became old, however, it was renovated, and on its removal many [skulls] broke. Others were removed to make room for more, so that there would be a place for those who were to be killed later.[8] I asked whether they were set up flesh and all, and everyone said no; after the flesh had been eaten, only the skull was brought to the temple. Some were left with their hair on, and thus they remained until the hair fell off. I also asked what was done with the other bones. The [people] told me that the owner of the native who had been sacri-

[8] The team of archaeologists working in the Plaza de las Tres Culturas at Tlatelolco, Mexico City, from 1960 to 1965 discovered various deposits totaling more than one hundred skulls which had once been strung on a skull rack such as Durán describes. In the opinion of the archaeologist Eduardo Contreras, of the Mexican Institute of Anthropology, the hair, brains, eyes, tongues, and other fleshy parts were probably removed from the craniums before they were perforated and placed on the *tzompantli* pole for exhibition (personal communication, 1967). The skulls found at Tlatelolco had been severed from the body without vertebrae (with the occasional exception of a cervical vertebra) and had large perforations in both temples. The holes were about three inches in diameter. They were strung by passing a rod through the holes.

ficed placed them in the courtyard of his home on long sticks as trophies of his glorious deeds and to show that [the remains had belonged] to a prisoner of his, captured in a good war. All of this was to his own honor and vainglory.

A strange ceremony was performed with those who were to be sacrificed. All the victims were placed in a row at the foot of this palisade, at the top of the stairs. While they stood there, accompanied by guards who surrounded them, a priest appeared. He was garbed in a short tunic edged at the bottom with a fringe of tufts. He descended from the summit of the temple carrying a dough image made of *tzoalli* dough, which is made of amaranth seeds and maize and kneaded with honey.[9] The priest brought down an idol made of this dough. Its eyes were small green beads, and its teeth were grains of corn. [The priest] descended the steps of the temple as swiftly as possible and climbed to the top of a great stone set in a high open space in the middle of the courtyard. This stone was called *cuauhxicalli*, and I saw it at the door of the Cathedral some days ago.

The priest went up one small staircase and came down another on the opposite side. Still embracing the image, he ascended to the place where those who were to be sacrificed stood, and from one end to the other he went along showing the figure to each one saying, "Behold your god!"

After exhibiting this, he descended. Thereupon all those who were to die followed him in a procession to the place where they were to be sacrificed. There the butchers, the ministers of Satan,

---

9 *Alegría*, the present-day survival of the ancient communion bread described here, is a yellowish-brown cake made of toasted amaranth seeds (*Passus Amaranthus hypocondriacus, A.*) mixed with honey or sugar and covered on one side with a paper-thin wafer colored bright pink. It is eaten as a sweet and is usually sold by itinerant Indian vendors at fairs, on pilgrimages, and in front of churches on holy days. According to informants from Xalitla, Guerrero, *alegría* in that region is made by placing a small amount of water in a pot and bringing it to a boil. *Panela*, brown sugar in cake form, is added to the water, and when the sugar has melted and formed a thick sirup, the pot is removed from the fire, and the amaranth seeds (or sesame seeds, which are used in that area) are stirred in. The mixture is then poured into a rectangular form, allowed to cool, and cut into squares. The sirup must be thick enough so that it will harden and sufficiently cool before the seeds are added so that they do not burn.

stood prepared. They sacrificed the victims, opening their chests, taking out their hearts, and—still half alive—[the victims] were sent rolling down the steps of the temple, and the steps were bathed in blood. This was the ceremony performed on the feast of this god with the sacrificial victims, as shown in the painted picture.

As I have said, within the wall surrounding this temple stood two monasteries, one for seclusion for boys between eighteen and twenty years of age. These were called monks, and they wore the hair of their head in the form of a friar's tonsure, though the hair was somewhat longer since it reached to any point between the middle part of the ear and the nape of the neck, [the lock] being four fingers wide. The hair was allowed to grow to the shoulder and was knotted like a braid. At times certain discrepancies were evident in the account [given me by these natives]. Some say that in Mexico the tonsure was not worn and that [the young monks] were not tonsured but were completely shaved with a razor, that the tonsure was used only by the monks in the temple of the province of Chalco and in that of Huexotzinco. Pictures of these things can be seen on the corresponding sheet [Plate 5].

These illustrations show the youths who served in the temple of Huitzilopochtli in seclusion, who lived in chastity, poverty, and obedience. They served as deacons, ministering to the priests and hierarchs of the temple. [Their life was devoted to] the incense burner, the fire, the vestments; they swept the sacred places; they brought firewood to keep the flame eternal in the divine brazier—which was like an ever-burning lamp.

Other youths were like altar boys who served in this temple. They did manual work. They set up branches and decorated the temples with flowers and rushes,[10] served the priests, took care of

[10] In mentioning flowers and rushes, Durán introduces an element characteristic of the Aztec ceremonial he is to present so vividly. These people, enamored of "flower and song," decorated their holy places gloriously, each branch, bud, flower, seed, and twig having its own religious significance. Luxuriant plants and flowers, branches of pine, cedar, spruce, and the heavy leaves of the maguey plant were interwoven with prickly-pear leaves, wild-cherry leaves, *tejocote* leaves, yucca, *cucharilla*, leaves of the yucca bulb, rattan, leaves of ahuehuetes, palms, amaranths, cornstalks, avocados, and the reeds and rushes of the lake. The practice is still common in ritual observances in modern Mexico.

the small blades which were used for self-sacrifice, accompanied those who went to beg alms in order to bring back the offering. All these were under the care of captains or superiors. [The superiors] were called *telpochtlatoque*, which means "directors of young men." All lived with such chastity and modesty that when they came out into public places where there were women they kept their heads low and their eyes on the ground without daring to raise [their eyes to the women's faces]. Their dress consisted of short net mantles.

These youths who lived in seclusion were called *elocuate-comame*. When this name is explained in our language, it almost sounds nonsensical [since it refers to] the *tecomate*,[11] which is smooth and was used in referring to their shaved heads. And to indicate that their heads were tonsured, the word *elotl* ["ear of corn"] was employed. People called this tonsure "a smooth head like a gourd with a round rim like that of an ear of corn," for that is what *elocuatecomatl* means. From this stems the present-day heathen custom of placing wreaths on the heads of children. Let this no longer be permitted, for it means that the mothers and the fathers who do this are allowed to commit idolatry. Let those who are in charge of the Indians forbid this [custom], even though they may not be aware of it because they do not understand the natives. Let this be a warning to [the ministers] so that they oppose it, since it is a form of idolatry.

The youths who dwelt in seclusion had permission to go out into the city in groups of four or six, humbly seeking their alms throughout the wards. They had permission (though this may not have been given them expressly) to enter the cornfields and pick as many ears of corn as they needed, and the owner dared not reprimand or stop them; nor did he have a right to say, "Well done," or, "Wrongly done." They possessed this liberty because they lived in poverty—they had no income, no food supply except that which they begged as alms or picked from the cornfields for their daily nourishment. They also lived in chastity and austerity.

11 The *tecomate* is a spherical gourd or bowl with a rimless mouth, called by archaeologists a neckless olla.

There were no more than fifty of these penitents. Their labor consisted of keeping the everlasting fire of the temple burning; bringing the wood which was to be burned; arranging branches and adorning the temple; rising at midnight to blow shell trumpets to awaken the people; watching over the idol in his rooms at night so that the fire would not go out; taking care of the incense with which the priests honored the god at midnight, at dawn, and at sunset. This incense ceremony was called *tlenemactli*. These [youths] were firmly controlled by their superiors and were very obedient. They never strayed in the slightest from the rules. At the time they had finished their burning of incense, at the ordained hour of the night, they went to a special place, where they pricked the fleshy parts of their arms. The blood they drew was smeared from their temple to the lower part of the ear. When the bloodletting had ended, they immediately went to wash in a lagoon (I will later speak about this [ceremony] when we deal with the priests of the temples). These youths did not paint themselves with cinnabar or smear pitch on their heads or bodies. Their garments were rough white mantles of maguey fabric. This penance and exercise lasted a full year, which was spent entirely in seclusion, mortification, and fasts and strange penitences.

The second house or apartment I have mentioned stood on the other side of the courtyard, in front of the first. This was a cloister for nuns, who lived in seclusion, all of them virgins between twelve and thirteen years of age. They were called Maidens of Penitence, and their life was exactly like that of the males. They lived in chastity and seclusion as maidens who had been assigned to the service of the god. Their only work was sweeping and sprinkling the temple and cooking the daily food for the idol and for the ministers of the temple, using the things that had been collected as alms. Viands prepared for the god were small tortillas fashioned in the manner of hands and feet; others were twisted like taffy. The latter type of food was called *macpaltlaxcalli* and *cocoltlaxcalli*, which means "bread with hands," "[bread] with feet," or "twisted [bread]." Together with these breads some chili stews were prepared and placed before the idol; this was done every day. When these girls entered [the convent, they had] cropped hair, but from the time they went in their hair was allowed to grow; they can be seen on the reverse of this sheet [Plate 6].

The present illustration shows the way of life of the cloistered maidens who served in the Temple of Huitzilopochtli. They lived in the same retirement and seclusion (just as nuns do today) for a certain length of time—in continence and chastity. They swept and watered the sacred places; they made food for the gods, the priests, and the hierarchs of the temples. On certain festive occasions they feathered their legs and arms and painted their cheeks with color. They rose at midnight to praise the gods, doing this constantly. They performed the same exercises as the males. Duennas like abbesses and prioresses [watched over them], keeping them busy making cloth in different manners for the adornment of the gods and of the temples and doing many other things peculiar to the service and ministry of the gods.

[The maidens] were always dressed in white without embroidery or color. They spent one year in the convent, like the boys. When the year of their service and penitence was completed, they left the place in order to marry, both males and females. As soon as they had departed, others entered, vows having been made by themselves or by their parents to serve the temple one year in penance. At midnight, at the very hour the boys pricked their fleshy parts, at that same time the girls cut the upper parts of their ears. The blood drawn was smeared on their cheeks—in the place where women apply paint. These young women possessed a pool in their cloister where they washed after bloodletting. Their cloister was large. They lived with great decorum, and the strictness in which they were kept was so great that if some [maidens] or some [young men] were discovered in any transgression against chastity, no matter how slight, they were slain, without any mercy, accused of having offended their god and great lord. Regarding this, it was believed that because both youths and maidens lived there, although their lack of constancy and great weaknesses were known, they were supposed to live with restraint and discipline. When a mouse or bat was seen to enter or leave the shrine of the god—or if a

84

cloth belonging to the temple had been gnawed or was found with a mouse hole in the material—the priests immediately stated that some sin had been committed. Some offense had been done to their god, inasmuch as the mouse or bat or some other animal had dared to insult the deity. They became very watchful then, endeavoring to find out who was the cause of such a profanation and irreverence. Once the culprit had been discovered (no matter his rank), he was immediately slain. Thus was avenged the insult to their god. The word for insult was *tetlazolmictiliztli*.

These youths and maidens had to come from six wards which had been appointed for this purpose. [They] could not belong to any other ward.

Both youths and maidens served in the temple one year, from one feast to the time the same was celebrated on the next year. After completing their penance and seclusion, they departed from the place. The lords and chieftains of the wards I have mentioned had, by this time, made ready those who were to enter for that new year. They were to begin their service to the gods and exercises with as much modesty and penance as those who had gone before. They were turned over to the priests and old men of the living quarters (so they were called), to be instructed in the ceremonies— both young men and women who were to serve for one year. This always occurred, without fail; from those wards [were sent] youths and maidens dedicated exclusively to the service of this god. This is in agreement with that which God ordained to the priests and the ministers of the temple according to Deuteronomy: they were to come from the tribe of Levi and from the seed of Aaron. As inheritance, God granted them the right to eat of the oblations and sacrifices offered to God himself. He commanded them not to take part in the inheritance of their brethren but in the inheritance of God alone. He was to be their only patrimony. Thus did the priests and ministers of this country observe these things. As I have said, they lived in poverty, they ate only of the alms, offerings, and oblations which the temples received—by the alms which were given to them. They possessed no rents, no lands, no patrimony. They possessed only such goods as they had and the calling that was their inheritance and patrimony. And so they never lacked food or any other necessary thing; [offerings were brought to them] so regularly, in such abundance, that the leftovers were given away to the needy and the poor.

The cloistered virgins of this temple (two days before the feast of the god we are dealing with) ground a great quantity of amaranth seeds, called *huauhtli*, together with toasted maize. When this had been ground, it was mixed with black maguey sirup.[12] After it was kneaded, an idol was made of that dough—exactly like and as large as the wooden one I have described. Green, blue, or white beads were inlaid as his eyes, and his teeth were grains of corn. His feet and hands [were also formed]. He was in a sitting position, as we saw him in the painted picture [Plate 3]. When the [idol] had been finished, all the lords came, bringing a finely worked, rich costume which was just like the dress of the god I have described. The dough was dressed in the form of the idol. On it was placed the bird's beak of shining, burnished gold; the feather headdress on his head; his apron of plumes; his shield, staff, bracelets, and anklets, his splendid sandals; and his breechcloth, a magnificent piece of needlework and feathers. When he had been thus finely garbed and adorned, he was set upon a blue bench, similar to a litter, to which four handles were attached. In this fashion was the dough idol adorned and placed upon this bench or litter. On the morning of the feast, an hour before dawn, all the girls came out dressed in white, wearing new shirts and skirts. On that day they were called the Sisters of Huitzilopochtli, that is to say, Ipilhuan Huitzilopochtli.[13]

They came along crowned with garlands of toasted, burst corn, called *momochitl*. They wore thick garlands of this corn, and around their necks were big necklaces of the same, hanging under the left arm. Thus adorned, their red paint placed upon their cheeks, their arms feathered with red parrot plumes from the elbow

12 Maguey sirup, still prepared by modern-day indigenous groups, is made by boiling the *aguamiel*, or "honey water," exuded by the century plant until it thickens into a sirup.

13 Ipilhuan Huitzilopochtli is more accurately translated as Children or Daughters of Huitzilopochtli.

to the wrist, they placed the litter upon their shoulders and carried it to the courtyard.

The young men stood outside. All of them were covered with beautifully worked net mantles and fine breechcloths embroidered with feathers, crowned with the maize garlands described and necklaces of the same around their necks. And as soon as the maidens appeared with the idol upon their shoulders, [the youths] approached with great reverence and set [the litter] upon their own. They carried it to the foot of the temple steps, whereupon all the people made a profound obeisance, touching earth on the ground and carrying it to their mouths. This ceremony was very common among these people at the main feasts to their divinities. After this rite had been performed, all the people formed in procession and with great swiftness made their way to the Hill of Chapultepec. There they made a stop and offered sacrifice, and from this place they continued with the same pace toward Tacubaya.[14] There a second station was made. From Atlacuilhuayan [Tacubaya] they went on to Coyoacan and, without pausing, returned to the City of Mexico. This journey was accomplished in three or four hours. The procession was called Ipaina Huitzilopochtli, which means the Swift, the Fleet Path of Huitzilopochtli.[15] Some [made the journey not] on the same date but on its commemoration twenty days later. Nevertheless, whether on the same day or a score of days later, these things were performed in honor of this god, as has been stated. I believe, however, that it was performed on its main feast and not on its commemoration.

When they reached the steps of the temple, the litter was set down. [Then] they took thick ropes and tied them to the handles of the litter. With much care and reverence, some pulling from above, others helping from below, the litter with the idol was carried up to the pinnacle of the temple, in the midst of the sounding of trumpets and flutes, to the din of the shells and drums. The litter was carried up in this [cautious] way because the temple steps

[14] A section of Mexico City just south of Chapultepec Park.

[15] According to Alonso de Molina (1944), a literal translation would be He Who Runs Swiftly for Huitzilopochtli (*painani* is "*el que corra ligeramente*").

were extremely steep and narrow and the staircase long. They could not ascend with this [litter] on their shoulders without [the risk] of falling, and thus they chose this manner to go up. While they were ascending, all the people stood below in the courtyard with great reverence and awe. Once they had reached the top and had placed [the idol] in a flower-decked shelter made in the form of a bower, the youths then scattered flowers of many hues and kinds and covered the entire place with them, all the steps and overflowing [into the courtyard].

After these things had been done, the maidens appeared in the finery I have described. From their convent they brought out some pieces of amaranth-seed dough (the same as that used in the making of the idol) in the form of large bones. These bones were given to the young men, who in turn carried them up and placed them at the feet of the god and [filled] the place with them until there was no room for more; according to their account there were four hundred dough bones.[16] This dough shaped like bones was called "the bones and flesh of Huitzilopochtli." It is worth remembering that there were two ceremonies here which should not be forgotten.

After these cloistered virgins had brought out the bones which they had made, they delivered them to the cloistered youths (for the boys were not permitted in any way or at any time to enter the women's convent). [The young men] received [the bones] from their hands and carried them up, placing them before the idol. Never was a woman permitted to enter the presence of the god or to make offerings before him, or even to ascend the steps. Any transgression of this type was regarded as a sacrilege or crime (*laesus majestatis*), and truly it was so in their code. When the bones had been placed there, the elders of the temple came out—priests, deacons, and all the other ministers and sacrificers according to their seniority (for they had excellent discipline and order regarding their names and titles, as will be explained in its place).

16 In Nahuatl the word *centzontli* ("four hundred") is also often used to mean "many," much as we say "thousands," without meaning an exact count. The Aztec count, based on the vigesimal system, counted by fives up to twenty (*cempoalli*, "one count") Twenty counts added up to four hundred (*centzontli*, "a head of hair" or "many").

They came in a procession, wearing their multicolored, embroidered net mantles, according to their rank and office, with garlands on their heads and around their necks. Behind them emerged the gods and goddesses, [or rather] their impersonators, dressed in the proper garb of each deity. In an orderly fashion they formed around the pieces of dough. They performed a ceremony of chanting and dancing upon them. With this, [the dough] was considered blessed and consecrated as the flesh and bones of the god Huitzilopochtli. Then the sacrificers known as *chachalmeca* made ready [for sacrifice]. These were high-ranking men possessing great honors, whose ways, office, and activities will be seen in the next chapter.

CHAPTER III

¶Regarding the manner in which men were sacrificed during the ceremonies.

W<small>E</small> have already related some things told to us about the god Huitzilopochtli. But before our narration of the many ceremonies that are still to come (since everything must be in the correct order), I wish to tell of the way in which the natives sacrificed. I have dedicated a special chapter to this because there is much to tell regarding both the sacrifice itself and the special ministers appointed to perform it.

So ended the ceremony of the blessing of the pieces of dough in the form of the bones and the flesh of the god. They were revered and honored in the name of Huitzilopochtli with all the respectful veneration that we ourselves hold for the Divine Sacrament of the Altar. To exalt the occasion further, the sacrificers of men were also present. They had been appointed for this high position on the festive occasion. There were six of them: four for the feet and hands, another for the throat, and yet another to cut open the chest to extract the heart of the sacrificial victim as an offering to the devil. Five of these men were called *chachalmeca*, which in Spanish means "a priest or minister of divine or sacred things." It was a high-ranking position among the Indians, much revered, and was passed down from father to son like our own primogeniture. Sons succeeded their fathers in the cruel, bloody, and diabolical office. The sixth priest, whose task it was to slay, was regarded with awe, as if he were a high priest or pontiff. His title varied according to the times and feasts during which he performed sacrifice. The pontifical vestments adorning him also varied when he appeared to fulfill his fearsome, supreme calling on the feast of the god we are describing. His priestly title was Topiltzin [Our Lord], and under this name he dressed himself in garments which honored the great man called Topiltzin, already described in a previous chapter. These were his garments: a red mantle similar to a dalmatic, fringed in green; a headdress of splendid green and yellow feathers; in his ears, golden earplugs inlaid with green jade; in his lower lip, a labret of blue stone.

Smeared with black, the six sacrificers appeared. Five of them wore their hair crisply curled and encircled with leather bands which went around the forehead. Before them they carried tiny paper shields painted in different colors. These men were clad in white dalmatics embroidered in black; these were called *papalo-cuachtli* and bore the very figure of the demon on them. Seeing them come out with their ghastly aspect filled all the people with dread and terrible fear! The high priest carried in one hand a large stone knife, sharp and wide. Another carried a wooden yoke carved in the form of a snake. They humbled themselves before the idol and then stood in order next to a pointed stone, which stood in front of the door of the idol's chamber. The stone was so high that it reached one's waist. And it was so sharp that when the sacrificial victim had been stretched across it on his back he was bent in such a way that if the knife was dropped upon his chest it split open with the ease of a pomegranate.

These butchers stood in order. They wore upon them the frightful aspect of the demon whom they represented on that day: a white circle around the mouth which, painted as it was on black, was a hellish thing to see.

All the prisoners of war who were to be sacrificed upon this feast were then brought forth. Perforce they were to come from Tepeaca, Calpan, Tecali, Cuauhtinchan, Cuauhquecholan, and Atotonilco, and from no other nation. This god was not to be served with victims from any other state but those which have been named, others not being desirable to him. Surrounded by guards (as has been described in the last chapter), the victims were forced to ascend to the long platform at the foot of the skull rack—all of them totally nude. A hierarch delegated for this task then came down from the temple. In his arms he carried a small idol which he showed to those who were to die, and, having passed by the entire line of prisoners, he descended from the platform, followed by all. Then he went up to the place where the satanical priests were ready. They seized the victims one by one, one by one foot, another by the other, one priest by one hand, and another by the other hand. The victim was thrown on his back, upon the pointed stone, where the wretch was grabbed by the fifth priest, who placed the yoke upon his throat. The high priest then opened the chest and with amazing swiftness tore out the heart, ripping it out with his own hands. Thus steaming, the heart was lifted toward the sun, and the fumes were offered up to the sun. The priest then turned toward the idol and cast the heart in its face. After the heart had been extracted, the body was allowed to roll down the steps of the pyramid. Between the sacrificial stone and the beginning of the steps there was a distance of no more than two feet.

All the prisoners and captives of war brought from the towns we have mentioned were sacrificed in this manner, until none were left. After they had been slain and cast down, their owners—those who had captured them—retrieved the bodies. They were carried away, distributed, and eaten, in order to celebrate the feast. There were at least forty or fifty captives, depending upon the skill which the men had shown in seizing and capturing men in war. The same sacrifice was practiced by the men of Tlaxcala, Huexotzinco, Calpan, Tepeaca, Tecali, Atotonilco, and Cuauhquecholan with men from the region of Mexico they had captured. The same feast, the same rites, were performed in front of their god, just as was done in Mexico. All the provinces of the land practiced the same ceremonies. It was a universal festival and was named Coailhuitl, which means Feast Which Belonged to One and All. Every town sacrificed the prisoners taken by their own captains and soldiers. Thus it is possible for us to calculate the number of men sacrificed on that day in the entire land. While I am reluctant to give inexact information, I believe I was told that more than a thousand men died in this land on that day, all to be carried off by the devil!

And because it pertains to our theme, I wish to mention here the purpose of the wars between Mexico and Tlaxcala and the Tlaxcalans, for many times we have heard that with the greatest of ease the Mexicans vanquished Tlaxcala, Huexotzinco, Tepeaca, Tecali, Calpan, Cuauhtinchan, Acatzinco, Cuauhquecholan, and Atlixco; they had subjected that region just as they had subjected the rest of the land. But the people of Mexico did not wish to do this for the two reasons which were given by their kings. The first one, the main one, was that they desired those enemies as food, delicious, tasty, and hot for the gods, since that flesh was sweet and pleasant to them. The second reason was the continual training of the valiant men of Mexico, in order to determine the worth of each. So it was that the wars which took place between the City of Mexico and Tlaxcala truly had as their sole object the capturing of men on both sides, to sacrifice them in the manner I shall describe.

When a festive occasion was drawing near on which a sacrifice was to take place (there were few which did not include it), the priests approached the rulers, telling them that the gods were famished and wished to be remembered. Then the rulers made provisions, consulted among themselves regarding the hunger of the gods, and prepared their men for an appointed day. Messengers were sent to the Province of Tlaxcala, telling the Tlaxcalans to make ready for war. When the men were placed in formation and the troops set in order, the squadrons departed toward the plains of Tepepulco, where the armies met. The whole contest, the entire battle, was a struggle whose aim it was to capture prisoners for sacrifice. Therefore, the town (on either side) which could excel by sending a very large number of men to battle did so to bring back as many captives as possible for sacrifice. In this way the object of the battle or encounter was more to capture than to kill. This was their goal: to seize yet not to slay; to do no harm to man or woman, to a home or cornfield, but to feed the idol! To feed human flesh to the accursed and famished butchers!

We have described the manner in which sacrifice took place, and an illustration of it appears at the beginning of the chapter [Plate 7]. I show it in a picture for clarity and as a sign of the cruelty with which sacrifice was practiced.

I wish now to finish my description of the ceremonies performed on the feast of Huitzilopochtli. The sacrifice ended when all the victims had been slain. Their blood was sprinkled generously upon the image of dough and upon the pieces of dough which represented the flesh and the bones of the god. All were now consecrated with human blood. And the lintels of the temples and the chambers of the gods were smeared with this, as were the faces of the idols. It was then that all the young men and the maidens adorned (as I have stated above) with garlands and necklaces of burst grains of corn came out in an orderly fashion, in lines which faced one another. They danced and sang to the beat of a drum, while singers chanted songs in praise of the god and his feast. All the lords, elders, and nobles answered [the songs]. Dancing, they formed a circle, just as they do today, leaving the youths and maidens in the middle. This performance was attended by the entire city.

On the same day it was a solemn rule in all the land that no one eat anything but *tzoalli* with honey; this was the dough with which the idol was formed; it had to be eaten at dawn. No one was to taste water or any other food until afternoon. It was considered an ill omen, a sacrilege, to drink anything after having eaten that food, until the ceremonies and sacrifices had terminated. Because of this, water was hidden from the children. Young people who had reached the age of reason were told: "Do not drink, for you have eaten *tzoalli*. The wrath of the god might fall upon you and you would die!" This rule was kept as rigorously as that of the Jews in not eating the flesh of pork.

After these ceremonies, dances, sacrifices, farces, and games had ended—all performed for the gods—the actors, priests, and dignitaries of the temple took the image of dough and stripped it of its ornaments. Then this and the parts which represented its bones and flesh were broken up into small fragments. Beginning with the elders, everyone received communion with this [*tzoalli*]—old and young, men and women, old men and children. All received it with such reverence, awe, and joy that truly it was a thing of wonder! The people claimed that they had eaten the flesh and the bones of the gods, though they were unworthy. Those who had sick ones at home begged for a piece and carried it away with reverence and veneration. All those who received the communion were obliged to give tithes of the same seed which had formed the dough of the flesh and the bones of the god.

Let the reader note how cleverly this diabolical rite imitates that of our Holy Church, which orders us to receive the True Body and Blood of our Lord Jesus Christ, True God and True Man, at Eastertide. Furthermore, another thing is remarkable: this feast fell on the tenth of April, that is, around Easter, which usually comes at this time. Though it is a movable feast, sometimes [Easter] falls eight or ten days before; sometimes it falls the same number of days after. From these things two observations can be made: either (as I have stated) our Holy Christian Religion was known in this land or the devil, our cursed adversary, forced the Indians to imitate the ceremonies of the Christian Catholic religion in his own service and cult, being thus adored and served.

All of this will be noted in many other passages especially referring to this same day and feast.

Once the solemn rites had terminated, an elder with high authority, one of the dignitaries of the temple, arose. In a resonant voice he then preached words regarding the law and ritual, similar to the Ten Commandments which we are obliged to keep:

Thou shalt fear, honor, and love the gods.

The gods were so honored and revered by the natives that any offense against them was paid for with one's life. They held the gods in more fear and reverence than we show to our own God.

Thou shalt not use the names of the gods on thy tongue or in thy talk, at any time.

Thou shalt honor the feast days.

The natives, with a terrible rigor, fulfilled all these ceremonies and rites with fasts and vigils, without exception.

Thou shalt honor thy father and thy mother, thy kinsmen, priests, and elders.

No nation on earth has held its elders in such fear and reverence as these people. The old father or mother was held in reverence under pain of death. Above all else these people charged their children to revere elders of any rank or social position. So it was that the priests of the law were esteemed, respected, by old and young, lord and peasant, rich and poor. Old people, in our own wretched times, are no longer honored; they are held in contempt and are scorned.

Thou shalt not kill.

Homicide was strictly prohibited, but it was not punished by physical death. It was paid for with a civil death. The murderer was turned over to the widow or to the relatives of the deceased, [to be] forever a slave. He was to serve them and to earn a living for the children of the deceased.

Thou shalt not commit adultery.

Adultery and fornication were also condemned, to the point that if a man was caught in adultery a rope was thrown about his neck, he was stoned, and [he was] then dragged throughout the entire city. After this the body was cast out of the city to be eaten by wild beasts.

Thou shalt not steal.

This commandment was kept in a more rigorous way than it

is today, since the thief was either slain or sold for the price of the theft.

Thou shalt not bear false witness.

These people condemned false witness. They punished those caught lying.

Those who had committed these sins and broken the law went about constantly filled with fear, imploring mercy of the gods, asking not to be discovered. Pardon for these sins was granted every four years on the jubilee; their remission took place on the Feast of Tezcatlipoca.

The feast ⌊we have been referring to⌋ was celebrated with many more rites than the previous one. I will describe these in another chapter, as briefly and in as much detail as possible. Even though I would like to be brief, the great diversity of the rites and ceremonies of these people does not permit me to be so; moreover, the style of my Indian informants varies greatly in some things and is verbose in others. Because of these reasons I have not been able to be as brief in my chapters as I would have desired; but if I do not follow the manner in which these things were told, my plans in writing this work would end in utter confusion. Therefore, I ask that no one accuse me of being tedious and wordy. My desires are to shed light through this account and to please my gentle reader.

CHAPTER IV

¶Which treats of the god known as Tezcatlipoca and of the manner in which he was honored.

THE most important and solemn feast, in which the most splendid ceremonies took place (except those we have just dealt with) was that of the god known as Tezcatlipoca [Plate 8]. These superstitious people commemorated it with such varied rites and sacrifices that it was a wondrous thing. In this they showed their reverence for the deity, since his feast was placed on the same level as that of Huitzilopochtli. The commemoration was known as the Feast of Toxcatl, one of many in the native calendar. Therefore, two festivities were held: one, Toxcatl, of calendrical significance; and the other, that of the idol Tezcatlipoca.

The form of this idol in the City of Mexico was the following: it was made of a shining stone, black as jet, the same stone of which sharp blades and knives are fashioned. In other cities the figure was of wood, carved in the form of a man, completely black from his temples down. His forehead, nose, and mouth were of the natural color of an Indian. He was dressed in splendid native garments. The earplugs were of gold, occasionally of silver; from his lower lip hung a labret of crystalline beryl into which was inserted a green

98

or blue feather, which, emerging from it, shone like an emerald or a ruby. The labret was about a palm's length. His hair hung in a queue. His head was encircled with a band of burnished gold, ending in a golden ear painted with fumes or puffs of smoke. This meant that he listened to the prayers and requests of wretches and sinners.[1]

From between the ear and the band appeared a large, thick bundle of aigrettes and heron feathers. From his neck hung a golden jewel so large that it covered his entire chest. On his arms he wore two golden bracelets. In his navel was encrusted a fine green stone. In his left hand he carried a fan of precious feathers, blue, green, and yellow. These emerged from a round plate of gold, shining and brilliant, polished like a mirror. This [mirror] indicated that Tezcatlipoca could see all that took place in the world with that reflection. In the native language it was called Itlachiayaque, which means Place from Which He Watches. In his right hand he bore four arrows, which signify the punishment for sin inflicted upon evil men. So it was that the people were deeply afraid that this idol would make known their sins. On his ankles the idol wore twenty golden bells, called foot rattles. Tied to his right foot was a deer hoof, which denoted his swiftness, agility, and might in all his works. A net mantle hung from his shoulders; it was beautifully worked, black and white, with a border running around it adorned with white, black, and red flowers, all decorated with plumes. The shoes upon his feet were in the Indian manner, richly worked. Tezcatlipoca was always attired in this manner.

On his feast, which took place every four years, there was a general remission of sins, and an impersonator of the god was slain.

The temple in which the idol of Tezcatlipoca stood was lofty and magnificently built. Eighty steps led to a landing twelve or fourteen feet wide. Beyond it stood a wide, long chamber the size of a great hall. The door was wide and low, as is customary in Indian buildings. The hall was hung with splendidly worked cloth in the

[1] Although the name Tezcatlipoca implies smoke, in the illustration (Plate 8) the "fumes" closely resemble the scrolls used by Nahuatl scribes to indicate speech. These volutes appear to characterize Tezcatlipoca as a listener.

Indian manner in different colors and designs, all covered with feathers, so favored by these people on their decorations and garments. The door of this chamber was always hung with a veil or with a finely worked door covering. In this way the chamber was kept closed off and dark, and the idol hidden. No one dared enter this place, with the sole exception of the priests appointed to serve in the cult of the god.

Inside, next to the wall, facing the door of this room, stood an altar. It was as tall as a man, and upon it was a wooden pedestal the width of one hand, and on this stood the idol. The altar itself was similar to those used by our Holy Christian religion and the Catholic Church. It was covered with the most elegant, most finely wrought, richest mantles ever woven or embroidered. These people had no silk; therefore, their cloth was of cotton, but finely worked and beautifully woven in different patterns. These mantles served as frontals. The beams of this chamber were painted in a crude manner. On its head the idol wore a dust cover adorned with featherwork, insignia, devices, and weapons. It was something to see, together with different forms of featherwork, decorated with gold and jewels.

The feast of this divinity took place on the nineteenth of May by our own calendar, while by the native one it was the fourth feast, which is called Toxcatl. It was celebrated in such a magnificent manner that it rivaled the previous feast. On the vigil of this day the lords came to the temple carrying a new attire (like the one we have described) and gave it to the priests so that the idol might be clad in it. Once it had been received, the ministers went into the shrine and dressed him, having first removed the garments he already wore. The latter were stored in some wicker boxes even more reverently than we put away sacerdotal vestments. Many precious things were kept in those boxes—jewels, bracelets, and feathers, so carefully stored that they served no other purpose than that of being adored as if they had been the god himself. Aside from the customary attire with which the god was dressed, on this day special ornaments were added, such as featherwork, bracelets, sunshades—all the best that could be given to him. When he had

been dressed in the most meticulous way, the door covering or
curtain was removed so that Tezcatlipoca might be seen by all.
When the door was cleared, a hierarch of the temple, entitled
Titlacahuan, came out. He was dressed in the same clothes as the
idol, carrying flowers in his hands and a small clay flute which gave
forth a shrill sound. Turning to the east, the priest played the flute,
and, turning respectively to the west, north, and south, he did the
same. After he had played the flute in the direction of the four parts
of the world, all those present and those who were absent but who
could hear him, placed a finger on the ground, smearing it with
earth, whereupon they placed it within their mouths and ate the
earth which had stuck to their fingers. Then all prostrated themselves, weeping, invoking the darkness of the night and the wind,
begging not to be forsaken, forgotten, or killed, begging that the
labors of this life be alleviated.

On hearing the notes of the flute, thieves, fornicators, murderers, and all other sinners were filled with fear and sadness. Some
were so abashed that they could not conceal their having sinned
and during all those days prayed that their transgressions remain
unrevealed. In the midst of tearful and strange confusion and
repentance they offered large quantities of incense to placate the
god. On hearing the flute that day, brave and courageous men, all
the old soldiers, implored the gods, in rare anguish and devotion, to
be given victory against their enemies and strength to bring back
many captives from war. These men prayed to the God of All
Created Things, to the Lord by Whom We Live, to the Sun, to
Quetzalcoatl, to Tezcatlipoca, to Huitzilopochtli, and to Cihuacoatl
—all of the principal divinities adored by the natives.

This ceremony was performed ten days before the feast. During these days the man with the flute blew it in the four directions
so that all would perform the rite of eating the earth and of begging
the gods for the things they coveted. They prayed, lifting their eyes
toward the heavens, sighing and moaning like people who are truly
sorrowful for their faults and sins. Nevertheless, their sorrow was,
in truth, simply because of fear of worldly punishment to be
administered to them, and not of chastisement after death, since

they disclaimed knowledge of the perils of the afterlife. So it was that these people faced death without sorrow or fear. This is proved by the fact that on this day they prayed that their sins not be exposed.

Today the natives continue with their fears of admitting or revealing their sins, even in confession. They are afraid that if they admit the truth they will receive some earthly harm or punishment, ignoring the afterlife as if it did not exist. Therefore, our priests do wrong when they become rough or angry at the weak Indians in confession, threatening them or menacing them with gestures. They well know the weakness of these people; they should know that it is imperative to show kindness, patience, and love in the act of confession, so as to avoid sacrileges resulting from an exhibition of severity. The faults [of our clergy] that I have described should be judged as cases for the Inquisition, and ministers who behave in this manner should be suspended perpetually.

When the festivities of Tezcatlipoca arrived, all the people of the city gathered in the courtyard of the temple[2] to celebrate the Feast of Toxcatl, which means Something Dry. It must be noted that the aim of the celebration was to petition rain, much like our own pleas and litanies which usually fall in the month of May. The natives also held the feast in May, as I have explained. The festivities began on the ninth of that month and ended on the nineteenth.

Early on this solemn day the ministers of the temple brought out a bier richly adorned with cloth of many colors—yellow, green,

2 Today in many religious processions in modern Mexico the sacred image is not allowed to leave the church atrium, the floor of which is purified and ritually swept and then covered with pine needles, petals, grass, and leaves. The bearers do not allow the sacred effigy to touch the ground, and their own feet do not touch the earth but tread upon the floral covering. In many villages in Mexico, particularly Huamantla Tlaxcala, Ixtapalapa, Tlahuac, and Xochimilco, huge flower carpets, arches, wreaths, crowns, and other floral adornments are made in honor of the favorite holy images—saints, the Virgins, Christ—for a multitude of shrines, such as Guadalupe, Chalma, Los Remedios, San Juan de los Lagos, Our Lady of Tlaltenango, and the Sacromonte at Amecameca. The spectacular flower arrangements at these modern Catholic sites are living reminders of the ancient artistic patterns. Thus the ancient ceremonial use of flowers is still evident in modern Mexican life, from the golden *cempoalxochitl* (marigold) used on the Feast of the Dead to the ornately decorated boats rented to tourists on the canals of Xochimilco.

blue, and red. To this litter were attached as many handles as there were priests to carry it. These men were all smeared with black, and their hair was long. Some say that they wore wigs; others say that they let the hair grow long for this purpose like the Nazareos [penitents in Holy Week], half [of the hair] braided with white ribbons. The priests wore the same type of clothing as that worn by the idol. Upon the litter was carried the representative of the god, whom they called Likeness of the Divine Tezcatlipoca. There are two opinions regarding this matter: some say that it was the original wooden idol which usually stood upon the altar, while others believe that it was a live man who represented the deity upon the bier.

Having placed the litter on their shoulders, the priests brought it out to the steps of the temple. The youths and maidens who lived in seclusion were then brought forth, carrying a thick, twisted cord of toasted corn, with which they adorned the bier. Then they threw a string of this toasted corn around the neck of the idol and placed a garland of the same material upon its head. This string was called *toxcatl* and indicated the barrenness and dryness of the season. The boys appeared smeared with soot; they wore net mantles, strings of toasted maize about their necks, and garlands of the same. The girls appeared in fine new dresses—skirts, *huipils*, with strings of toasted maize about their necks, and on their heads tiaras made of twigs covered with the same maize. Their arms and legs were feathered with red plumes, and their cheeks were painted. Many necklaces of corn were then brought forth and were placed around the necks and on the heads of the noblemen. Instead of candles they carried flowers in their hands, just as they do today on some feasts, especially on the Day of the Ascension and on Pentecost (which falls around May) and on other festivals which correspond to the ancient ones. I see these things, but I am silent, since I realize that everyone feigns ignorance. So I pick up my staff of flowers like the rest and walk along, thinking of our gross ignorance, for great evils may be concealed under these customs.

After the idol had been placed upon the litter, the ground was covered with the maguey leaves instead of sedge, and down the steps, now covered with these leaves, came the litter carried on the shoulders of the priests. The procession made its way about the courtyard, led by two priests who carried clay incense burners. These priests went back and forth to the idol constantly, offering it incense, and every time the incense was burned, each raised his arm as high as he could. This ceremony was in honor of the god and of the sun, who were asked to grant that all these prayers and pleas rise to heaven, just as the perfumed smoke rose. The rest of the people remained standing in the center of the courtyard, turning toward the god each time he passed. These people carried new hemp ropes about six feet long with a knot at the end, with which they flagellated themselves furiously on their backs, just as nowadays we do penance. All around the courtyard and on its crenellated roofs hung ornaments of branches and flowers, so beautifully arranged, so fresh, that it warmed one's heart to gaze upon the festive decorations. When the procession ended, the idol was returned to his place and seat [in his chamber]. After this had been done great crowds of people came in, to cover the room and the entire courtyard with flower arrangements done in the native way, in different forms and in many colors. It looked like the monument [we set up for the Sacrament on Holy Thursday]. These flowers had been brought to the priests from youths who were outside the chamber, and the priests adorned the place with their own hands, and the curtain was not drawn for one day.

When the ceremonies had been performed, as was customary, there were offerings of lengths of cloth, precious stones, and incense. The last was offered in large quantities. Other gifts were pine torches, bunches of ears of corn, quail—all these things brought because of vows and promises people had made during the year to give something on that special feast. When they offered the quail, a native ceremony took place similar to one we have read about in the Old Testament. The poor brought quail as an offering, delivering them to the priest, who took each quail in his hand and, having wrenched its head, cast it bleeding at the foot of the altar. The same was done with all the other quail. This same ceremony is found in the first chapter of Leviticus.

Other offerings consisted of food given by each according to his means. All these things became the property of the ministers of the temple, who put them away in the chambers and rooms which existed there. Having made these offerings, the people returned to their homes in the villages to eat, and the ceremony was left pending until they had dined. But this refers only to the common people, because in the temple the maidens I have mentioned continued the rites. They appeared richly clad in their blouses and skirts, covered with strings of toasted corn, crowns of maize on their heads, paint on their faces, and feathers on their arms and legs. The youths were smeared with soot; they were adorned with their net mantles, necklaces, and garlands of toasted corn, and wore heron feathers and false labrets. It was the task of these young people to serve the god his food. This was cooked by certain women who had made a solemn promise to be cooks for the idol on this day and to serve him only in the temple and not outside. Thus at dawn all the women who had made the vow arrived and offered their services to the dignitaries and priests of the temple. They explained that they had come to fulfill the vow they had made: that of giving food to Tezcatlipoca. Then they prepared the food neatly and with great care—an amazing variety of rich dishes and different breads!

The food having been prepared and the noon mealtime having arrived, the virgins of whom I have spoken came forth. [They walked] in lines, [each] with a small basket of breads in one hand, and in the other a plate filled with stew, of which there were many varieties. All these young women had been painted with a black circle around the mouth. In front of these maidens strode an elder who served as a steward to the god and as leader of these girls. He wore a white surplice adorned with a tufted border which reached his calves. Over this surplice he wore a sleeveless jacket of red leather similar to a penitent's garment. Instead of sleeves he wore what looked like wings with other long ornaments hanging in similar fashion. From these wings hung wide ribbons from which was suspended, in the middle of the back, a medium-sized gourd. The gourd was perforated with holes, and in each one of these had been placed a flower. It was also adorned with little balls of tobacco and soot. This gourd was called Iyetecon [His Little Gourd]. Humble and contrite, his head lowered, the old man led the procession, and, when they had reached the first steps, he made signs of obeisance. Then he stepped to one side as the girls began to arrive with the food. Little by little they placed it in orderly rows, each bringing an offering in her turn. Once the food had been placed there, the old man became their guide again, and then all the maidens returned to their cloisters.

When they had departed, the youths and priests of the temple emerged to gather the food. This was taken to the apartments of those called Calmeca teteuctin, who were the dignitaries of the temple. The priests and the ministers who had fasted five days in a row, who had eaten only once a day, who had lived separate from their wives during those five days, who had not left the temple, who had been flogging themselves with the ropes we have mentioned—they were the ones who had bled themselves and made themselves martyrs to the devil! Then was brought in the food that by this time was as eagerly desired as salvation itself. The men gorged themselves with that "divine nourishment," as it was called. No one was permitted to partake of this food except these dignitaries; this rule was observed with such rigor and fear that no one dared eat even though he saw the food there, even though he was famished. All of this will be found by the reader in the Book of Leviticus, where we find similar divine laws transmitted by Moses to Aaron, to his sons, and to the priests and the attendants of the temple—that is, to all the males of that lineage and generation.

The meal having ended, the people of the city gathered once more in the courtyard of the temple to observe and celebrate the end of the feast. When everyone was present, a male slave was brought forth. This man had represented the god for one year, and was clothed, adorned, and honored as the deity himself. High reverence was paid to him, and then he was delivered to the sacrificers who appeared at the same time, decorated and dressed as I have already described. Four of the sacrificers seized the victim by the feet and the hands while the priest opened his chest and extracted his heart, raising it with his hand as high as he could, offering its steam to the sun. After a moment, about [the length of] an Ave Maria (during which it was held on high), the heart was thrown toward the idol, and the cadaver was rolled down the steps.

Tezcatlipoca was now dead. The people then went to a place called Ixhuacan, consecrated to that purpose, and the youths and maidens, wearing the ornaments I have described, appeared, playing music. The dignitaries of the temple danced and sang, standing in an orderly fashion around the drum. And all the lords danced in a circle. Their garments and decorations were the same as those of the young people. They wore tiaras on their heads like those worn by the maidens, which was an ornament intertwined with the string of toasted corn, called, as we said, Toxcatl, to whom the second solemn feast was dedicated. No one but this man was sacrificed on this day. It was only every four years that others died with him, and these were called Imalacualhuan, which means Prisoners of His Food. The year on which these died was a year of jubilee and indulgence.

At sunset, when everyone was weary of playing music, singing, eating, and drinking, the young women returned to their abode, bringing with them large clay plates similar to platters. These were filled with *tzoalli*, dough mixed with honey, covered with cloths decorated with skulls and crossbones. This repast was carried to the idol. Preceded by their leader, the girls ascended the steps to the small open space in front of the door of the shrine, where they left the food; then they descended again. After [the girls] had descended, the youths, in good order, moved rapidly toward the steps, and, having cast their staffs into the air, they rushed up the stairway of the temple. [They were] persistent, pushing one another in their effort to be the first in reaching the top, since the breads were given out by the dignitaries of the temple first to the first, then to the second, then to the third, and finally to the fourth. From the fifth on, no one was served until all were present. The honeyed tamales were snatched up eagerly and were carried away as relics. The four youths who arrived first were received by the dignitaries and elders of the temple and were shown into the holy place with great honors. They were bathed, given fine ornaments, and from this day on were respected and honored as men of renown.

When these activities ended, in the midst of great rejoicing and merrymaking, all the maidens who had served the idol and the youths of whom I have spoken were given liberty to go on their way, and they departed in order. As the girls left the place, all the boys from the different schools awaited them at the doorway of the courtyard, holding balls of sedge grass in their hands. The boys threw the balls at them and laughed at them, insinuating that since they had left the service of the gods they were free to do with their bodies as they wished.

Thus ended the solemn Feast of Tezcatlipoca and Toxcatl. We have described numerous ceremonies, more than those performed for Huitzilopochtli, with whom we dealt in [Chapter II]. And, since this chapter is already lengthy, we shall delay the description of the temple in which the deity was kept and of a second fashion in which he was represented and portrayed. We shall also deal with the priests who served him and the rites which were performed in his honor.

CHAPTER V

¶Which treats of the Temple of Tezcatlipoca, of the priestly hierarchies, and of the ceremonies.

Mexico and Tetzcoco were the two most magnificent cities in the land, where existed and flourished political organization, good order, and harmony, both in matters of government and in the fulfillment of the rites and ceremonies of the gods, all performed in the most orthodox fashion. The god Tezcatlipoca was represented or painted in two ways. One has been described in the last chapter. The other, which I shall now describe, can be seen in the drawing on this page [Plate 9]. It must be noted that in Mexico and in Tetzcoco, cities which (as I have said) were imitated in their customs, rites, laws, and ordinances by all the other towns and cities, the idol was kept in a temple, not in the fashion we have described, standing and dressed with numerous insignia, but seated upon a wooden bench of the native type. He was clad in a red mantle decorated with skulls and crossbones. In his left hand he carried a white shield with five balls of cotton set in the form of a cross, which are the raiment of the sky. In his right hand he held a spear, attached by a leather thong, in a threatening attitude. His arm was extended in such a way that he seemed ready to throw his atlatl.[1] Four arrows emerged from the shield. Tezcatlipoca sat there with his haughty countenance, his body all painted black, his head feathered with quail plumes. He was held to be the god who sent drought, famine, barrenness in the seasons, and plagues. And thus in this second effigy he was shown as dour and austere.

All the women whose children were ill took them to this temple to offer them to the deity, presenting them to the priests. The latter took the infants, dressed them in the garb and insignia of the idol, smearing them with the divine pitch and feathering their heads with the plumes of quail or turkey. This custom is similar to the Christian one in which children are offered to the saints of the order and are dressed in Dominican, Franciscan, or Augustinian habits. Let him who is jealous of the honor of our God beware. Every time he sees the native children with feathered heads, let him realize that these young people have been offered to the idol and are fulfilling the vow which their mother made in having them painted black and covered with plumes. Any servant of God should remove the feathers, punish him, and in this way gain his eternal reward. The soot used for tarring (and even in our times I have seen infants painted black in this fashion) was the same as that which covered the god and with which the priests and ministers besmeared themselves when they went to the woods to offer sacrifice. In this way they felt safe; they walked fearlessly, especially since these sacrifices were usually performed at night.

In Mexico this temple stood in the place where the Archbishop's palace is located today. He who has entered the latter must have noted that the entire building stands upon a terreplein without lower rooms, the entire ground floor being filled in.[2] There sat the god in his temple, which was no less ornamented, towering, and

---

[1] A short wooden spear thrower, used from prehistoric times, the Mexican weapon par excellence for both war and hunting. Even today it is employed in duck hunting on Lake Pátzcuaro, Michoacan.

[2] Durán is here referring not to the Great Temple but to a smaller temple dedicated to Tezcatlipoca which stood near the present-day corner of Moneda and Licenciado Verdad streets, opposite the Museo de las Culturas. The Archbishop's Palace would thus be the approximate site of the ancient temple.

castellated than that of Huitzilopochtli. It had been constructed with such a profusion of figures, sculpture, and work in stucco that it gave pleasure to gaze upon it from any point of view. Within its walled enclosure were many chambers, some occupied by the dignitaries of the temple, since there existed a hierarchy. These places can be compared to cathedrals, especially the temples of the greatest gods. There were others which were more like our parish churches, as we shall describe later. There were also apartments for young men who were in seclusion and who were old enough to serve in the rites and ceremonies of the priestly dignitaries. They lived in seclusion, poverty, and obedience and practiced the same mortifications as the elderly men. There were also communal dwellings for cloistered young women, nuns whose lives and garb we dealt with in the last chapter. I have spoken of how they served the god on his feast and of the way in which they dressed themselves, as the reader will see in a drawing on this page [Plate 10].

Before we continue describing the other idols in detail, I wish to speak of the priests of this temple, of their ceremonies and costume, and of their lives and habits, together with those of the other attendants. I had originally meant to write a separate chapter about this, describing the great and severe penance they endured, the austerity they suffered, and the tenacity with which they persevered in their painful and bloody practices. The priests and dignitaries of this temple were not appointed like the servants of Huitzilopochtli, each of whom was sent from a special ward. In the temple we now describe, things were not thus. The attendants had been offered from childhood to the temple by their parents, just as today people send children to the churches as altar boys or choirboys. There they are taught to sing, pray, and study and to become inclined to the priesthood. They are ordained and eventually rise to the hierarchy, just as I have seen many virtuous sons of common men rise. I have seen them wearing their long red cassocks and officiating, with the boys bearing candles, one carrying the staff. In this manner the parents placed their children in the temples in pagan times, offering the infants to the gods so that they might be taken care of and protected. The mothers and fathers did so when their children fell ill or were in danger. No people on earth have loved their children as the people of this nation do.

Consequently, they were offered to the gods in the temples to be educated and to learn the divine services [and] good breeding, together with ceremonial and ritual pertaining to the deities. A special home not unlike a boarding school was dedicated to these boys, and the great number of youths interned there were guided by teachers and masters who taught and formed them in good, praiseworthy exercises and customs. They were taught to be courteous, to show reverence for their elders, to serve, to obey; they were instructed in the manner of attending the lords, to be at ease among them and charming in their presence. The boys were taught to sing, to dance, and a thousand other refinements. They were also instructed in the arts of war: how to shoot an arrow skillfully, how to cast a spear or a dart from its leather thong, how to bear a shield, how to hold a sword. They were not permitted to sleep comfortably and also ate poorly so that from their childhood on they would be prepared for a harsh life, removed from all luxury.

In this house different social classes were represented. Some were the sons of noblemen; others came from the lowest rank. Though all lived within the same enclosure, the sons of monarchs and great men were always more highly respected and carefully attended, since food was brought to them from their homes, especially to the progeny of Moteczoma and the other braves and lords who had charged the elders to care for their sons. It was preached to them, they were admonished, to live chastely, to fast; food and drink were to be taken temperately; they were to eat calmly, with measure and without haste. The boys were tested in certain tasks and rough enterprises to determine which were learning to be strong. This house was known as the Telpochcalli, which means the House of the Youths or the House of the Boys.

After they had been taught and disciplined there in the ways I have mentioned, their teachers tried to discover their inclinations and decide what they would be best fitted for. If the boy seemed filled with courage and desire to go to war, as soon as he was old enough, as soon as there was occasion, he was sent to carry food and other supplies to the warriors so that he might see action and hardship. Thus, it was considered, he would lose his fear. Often the boy was given a great load to carry; and if he showed bravery on the battlefield, he was soon admitted to the company of the warriors. Consequently, he often went to the field with his load and returned a captain, bearing the insignia of a valorous man. Some, overdesirous of glory, were captured by the enemy or were slain on the field; often they preferred to be torn to pieces rather than be captured.[3] In general the youths most inclined to this sort of life were children of valiant men, of lords, of stout warriors, of chieftains. This is the rule in all the nations of the world: the highborn, always eager to gain honor for his person, defends his manner of life, his king, his native country and hopes to cover himself and his descendants with glory.

Other youths were more bent, more inclined, to religious matters and to cloistered life. When their inclination was noticed, they were immediately set aside and brought to the chambers and sleeping quarters of the temple and were decked with the insignia of the priesthood, as in our own Holy Church. When our boys show a vocation for the ecclesiastical life, they are given a tunic and a cap, the insignia and garb of the priesthood. Later they will be tonsured and ordained in the first minor order. Thus these natives took the youths from the schools and centers where they had learned the ceremonial and the cult of the gods and sent them to a house of higher learning. This institution was known as the Tlamacazcacalli, which is made up of *tlamacaz*, which means "perfect man," and *calli*, "house." Therefore, it was called the House of Young Men Who Have Reached the Perfection of Their Youth. The natives classified their ages with four terms: the first was Piltzintli, which means Childhood; the second was Tlamacazqui, which means Puberty; the third was Tlapaliuhqui, which means Mature and Perfected Age; and [the fourth was] Huehuetqui, which means

---

[3] As Durán makes clear, the Aztec lived for his society, and individual wishes and one's personal life depended totally upon the collective attitudes of the community. One can almost imagine the Aztec matron speaking the words of the Spartan mother: "Return with your shield or on it!"

Old Age.[4] Old age was highly regarded and revered by these nations as it is today among the native lords; old people are much esteemed, and so are their opinions and counsel, without which no steps are taken.

These youths were then taken to the higher institution, and in this house and its halls they found new teachers and authorities, who watched over them, advised them, and instructed them in the things they lacked. From the day they entered this second school, the young men allowed their hair to grow, like the long-haired Nazarenes. Second, they smeared themselves from head to foot with a black soot, hair and all. With the large amount of moist soot that covered them, presently vegetable growth appeared on their heads. Their braids grew to such an extent that they looked like a tightly curled horse's mane, and after a long time their hair reached the knee. The weight they bore on their head was so great that it was a hardship to carry it. This hair was never shorn or cut throughout their lives unless they retired in old age and were given an honored charge in government matters. This [charge] was called *tlazoyotl* and was similar to the posts given to the grandees in the court of His Majesty.

Some wore braids, while others braided their hair with white cotton ribbons no more than six fingers wide. These sooty and braided hairdresses were called *papa*. Even today I have seen boys with their hair long and sooty with pitch smeared on it by their mothers, perhaps imitating the ancestors. Because of the soot their hair is so blackened (and so tangled with this bitumen) that unless the hair is cut there is no other way of disentangling it. The soot ordinarily used came from the smoke of resinous wood. Resinous woods and their smoke were highly revered in ancient times and were an important offering to the gods. The priests invariably went about painted from head to foot with this soot, to the extent that they looked like the blackest of Negroes. The pitch for daily use was made from torch pine. At other times, when the people went

4 Age grading was an important element of the pattern of ancient Mesoamerican social life. Weitlaner and Castro (160–65) have pioneered in the study of age grading, at Tlacoatzintepec and Mayultianguis.

to perform sacrifices—especially to burn incense in dark and fearsome caves where the idols were kept, where special ceremonies were conducted—in order to lose all fear and to quicken their courage they painted themselves with a different pitch. This was called Teotlacualli, which means Food of God. This divine food varied depending upon the god who ate it. It was always made of poisonous beasts, such as spiders, scorpions, centipedes, lizards, vipers, and others. These animals were caught by the boys in the schools, who kept them in large numbers so as to have them on hand when the priests requested them, just as the pages in a palace keep toothpicks ready for their masters' table. Therefore, in their spare time the youths went about hunting these deadly beasts; and if one of the boys happened to be on an errand but came upon one of them, he trapped it as if his life depended upon it. Because of this the Indians are not afraid of touching these animals with their hands, as if they were not dangerous and loathsome.

This was the divine food with which the priests, ministers of the temples, and especially those with whom we are dealing, smeared themselves in ancient times. They took all these poisonous animals and burned them in the divine brazier which stood in the temple. After these had been burned, the ashes were placed within certain mortars, together with a great deal of tobacco; this herb is used by the Indians to relieve the body so as to calm the pains of toil. In this it is similar to Spanish henbane, which, when mixed with lime, loses its poisonous qualities, though it still causes faintness and is harmful to the stomach. This herb, then, was placed in the mortars together with scorpions, live spiders, and centipedes, and there they were ground, producing a diabolical, stinking, deadly ointment. After these had been crushed, a ground seed called *ololiuhqui*[5] was added, which the natives apply to their bodies and

[5] The seed of a type of morning-glory. "It has the heart-shaped, pointed leaves of most morning-glories, but the whitish, funnel-shaped flowers are hardly more than an inch long. These are followed by a small, fleshy fruit, in itself quite useless, but containing a single, lentil-like seed. This, and sometimes the plant itself, have been known as *ololiuhqui* since the Conquest, and long before. The Aztecs may have used the name for other plants, but commonly they applied it to the seeds of *Rivea corymbosa*" (Taylor, 128–29). Molina (1944) listed a noun, *ololiuhcayotl*, which he

drink to see visions. It is a drink which has inebriating effects. To all of this were added hairy black worms, their hair filled with venom, injuring those who touch them. Everything was mixed with soot and was poured into bowls and gourds. Then it was placed before the god as divine food. How can one doubt that the men smeared with this pitch became wizards or demons, capable of seeing and speaking to the devil himself, since the ointment had been prepared for this purpose? One is reminded of the ointment used by witches! May our Lord please that in this my writing I not cause harm to any honest matron who wishes to experiment with these things, as in *The Golden Ass*, where someone attempts to become a bird but, mistaking one jar for another, instead becomes an ass, according to the fable.[6] When the priests had been painted with this bitumen, they lost all fear. They slew men in sacrifice with the greatest of daring; still smeared, they went forth at night, alone, to the woods, to the dark caves, to somber and fearful cliffs, totally unafraid of injury or harm. But since they carried the divine food on their bodies, they sneered at the wild beasts. Well they knew that lions, tigers, and other deadly animals of the woods would flee because of that Pitch of God—or, let us be clear, of the devil. And although this black pigment did not frighten [the animals], they would have fled on seeing men turned into the image of the devil himself![7]

---

defined as "roundness such as that of a ball or of some other spherical object." In Mexican markets today *ololiuhqui* is called *Dondiego de día, Dompedro, maravilla, manto de Maria,* or *semilla de la Virgen.* The names are examples of syncretism carried even to narcotics: that which served for pre-Conquest rites now carries Christian names, even the names of saints and the Virgin.

According to some sources *ololiuhqui* was a "hellish, pagan thing" (Ruiz de Alarcón, 48–49). The plant and its seed were used both as an ointment and as a drink. The beverage was intoxicating, and men under its influence lost their senses and believed that they had become ferocious animals.

[6] A rare instance in which Durán cites a pagan Roman writer, in this case Lucius Apuleius, of the second century A.D., author of the *Metamorphoses,* or *The Golden Ass,* a witty satire which pokes fun at priests, wizards, and quacks. Durán is warning women against the potions, philters, cures, and beauty secrets of the native witch doctors who, though far superior as "beauticians" to their Spanish counterparts, are part of the magical world he so detests.

[7] The "divine pitch," frequently mentioned by Durán, was mixed with other

This pitch also served a medicinal purpose: it was used to cure the sick and little children. Therefore, it was called the Divine Medicine, and people came from all parts to pay a visit to the dignitaries of the temple so as to be rubbed with the Divine Medicine. The pitch was applied to the ailing part of the body where pain was felt, and the result was a remarkable relief. The cause of this cure (according to my own opinion, and I have persuaded many of the natives of this) was their extraordinary faith and trust. The Indians use the ointment to cure their ailments, since its properties are like those of *picietl* [tobacco] and *ololiuhqui*, which calm and soothe. Once it is applied as a plaster, it deadens pain; this it does by itself. But its effect is stronger when it is mixed with so many kinds of poisons. It has been proved that when it is applied to any aching place it will diminish the pain and give relief. Thus these priests cured, with the pitch or ointment, and [when they had]

ingredients, some potent, others with merely psychological effect. One is reminded of the witches' brew in *Macbeth*:

> Fillet of a fenny snake,
> In the cauldron boil and bake;
> Eye of newt and toe of frog,
> Wool of bat, and tongue of dog,
> Adder's fork, and blind-worm's sting,
> Lizard leg, and howlet's wing,
> For a charm of powerful trouble,
> Like a hell-broth boil and bubble.
>
> [4.1.12–20]

In his *History,* Durán wrote that the sixty sorcerers sent by Moteczoma I around the middle of the fifteenth century to seek the Aztec homeland "smeared themselves with the particular ointments which wizards still use nowadays" (Durán, 1964, 134).

Such venomous brews were prepared almost to modern times. One example was the virulent arrow poison prepared by the Seris of northwestern Mexico. Certain deadly roots and weeds, gathered on Tiburón Island were ground and mixed together. A rattlesnake was teased until it was infuriated, and was then offered a piece of meat, which it bit, injecting its deadly venom. To the meat were added the ground mixture and parts of other vipers, spiders, and scorpions. The mixture was placed over a slow fire and cooked in an airtight container for many hours. It was said that when the pot was opened the fumes were mortal. It was the custom for one man to test the poison at the expense of his own life. Smearing an arrow with the still-hot mixture, he scratched his arm with it. If the flesh turned white, it was certain that he would die within two days and that the poison would be effective against the enemy. Thus reassured, each warrior carried home a small portion of the brew in which to dip his arrows. McGee, 78.

anointed the body with this painkiller, the strong effects of the tobacco and the *ololiuhqui* seemed a sudden and miraculous thing to them. So people went to these priests as if they had been holy men, but the latter deceived and tricked the ignorant and persuaded them of any number of omens and superstitions, just as I believe they do today. The sorcerers urge the ignorant to have their medicines prepared for them and to perform satanical rites. The sorcerers persuade the people with such ease that they find it unnecessary to use menaces or torture or threaten them with the wheel of blades of Saint Catherine or the gridiron of Saint Lawrence. All they need to do is to ask the old people: "Do you want to live forever? Do you want to save the life of your son? Do the things that the ancient idol worshippers did!" The person addressed, without hesitation, in order to save the life of the son or the husband, turns to the ancient rites and superstitions: to the offerings of incense, rubber, *tzoalli*, and tortillas; to the superstition of the pitch and the feathers; to the shaving of the head; to the tying of ash papers to the neck; to the moving to and fro over the head of an incense burner filled with embers and incense; to the tying of colored threads, little snake bones, beads, and rings to the throat; to ritual bathing at set hours; to the night watch in front of a fire brazier; to abstention from all breads except those which have been offered to the gods. He also resorts to those who fan in the bathhouses; to those who suck out illnesses; to those who rub the bodies of men. All these things have been found to persist commonly without our knowing or understanding it, and this occurs sixty years after the end of paganism! The worst part is that, since they believed so strongly in omens (and they were intense believers in these things), they favored fortunetelling with grains of corn or by casting lots with pieces of thread. They turned to those who divined fates by looking into tubs of water. Let us hope that God has gradually decreased their number. I doubt that any of the latter exist—that any have survived till our times.

Though we have been dealing with these priests, it now behooves us to describe the cult and service performed before the god each day, together with the terrible penances that were carried out. The reader will find it convenient to see the painted form of the god. And once he has seen the picture, he will find it easier to understand what we are about to describe. These things were as the reader sees them on this page [Plate 11].

This illustration indicates that the occupation of these ministers is that of incensing the idol four times, day and night, with the incense burner in their hands, as we have seen. These are the four hours: the first at dawn, the second at noon, the third at dusk, and the fourth at midnight, when we rise to say matins. At this hour all the dignitaries and hierarchs of the temple rose, and, instead of ringing bells, the men called Tlamacazque took large conch shells; others took small flutes and produced an eerie, diabolical sound which lasted a long time. Afterward the man who was in charge for the week came forth. He was dressed in a long robe similar to a tunic [which reached] down to his knees. In one hand he carried a brazier or incense burner filled with embers from the divine fire of the god; in the other, a bag filled with incense. He then cast incense into the burner, went in to see the idol, and offered incense as priests now incense God's altar, lifting their hands and then lowering them. [The Tlamacazque] then put down the incense burner—which was called *tlemaitl*—and with a piece of cloth he dusted the altar and the cloths adorning the chamber. When the room was filled with the smoke of incense, the minister departed for his cell.

All these things were also performed at dawn, to the sound of the same conch shells, later, at noon, and then at sundown every day, not one being forgotten. Once the midnight ceremony had ended, everyone withdrew to an ample chamber which contained many seats made of wood and grass.[8] They seated themselves, each

---

[8] Durán's readers should bear in mind not only the stone and clay masterpieces of the Mexica people but also the other festive though perishable masterpieces which completely changed the faces of altars, interiors, staircases, and courtyards of the buildings. Several times a year the buildings were brought to life, enclosed with intricate wooden frameworks which were covered with brilliant dahlias, water lilies, *cempoalxochitl*, blue morning-glories, cotton flowers, purple cosmos, red poinsettias, luxuriant orchids, sunflowers, *flor de manita* ("hand-shaped flowers"), and tiger lilies—filling the temple with overpowering perfume. More humble blossoms were also interwoven: those of the bean plant, the pumpkin, the squash, the amaranth, the

one taking a maguey thorn to pierce the calves near the shinbone. They squeezed out the blood and wiped it on their temples. After they had smeared their temples, all the thorns used for piercing and for self-sacrifice were smeared with the remaining blood. Then the thorns were stuck into some large balls of straw which were placed between the merlons of the courtyard wall. These balls were always there for that purpose, decorated with branches.[9] The thorns were left there so that everyone could see the penance and suffering which [the ministers] had inflicted upon themselves, being men who endured pain for the people. In certain chambers of the temple a large number of these thorns were stored; the used thorns were removed every day, were put away, and new ones set into the straw balls, since no thorn could be used twice. On their arrival the Franciscan friars burned many of these. The Spaniards found the thorns so carefully kept and revered that they were amazed. They were preserved as a memorial to the vast amount of blood that had been shed.

When the penitential act was over, all the ministers left the temple and went to a pond near where Santa Veracruz Church now stands.[10] This pond was called Acapan, which means Bloody Water, and there they washed off the blood which had been smeared upon their temples. They washed like men still filthy with the sins committed that day. After their ablutions they returned to the temple sanctuary. Again they smeared themselves with soot. Then the

---

thistle, and the red colorin. Even the desert contributed its waxy maguey flowers, the buds from its prickly pears, and the pitahaya. Interwoven with this splendor nature had provided the Aztec artist were many creations of his own hand: flowers of wood, metal, feather, paper, grasses, reeds, rushes, seeds, and even the most apparently insignificant products of vegetable life.

[9] Thousands of maguey thorns of the century plant as described here have been discovered in recent excavations at Tlatelolco. Round bundles of thorns were found in offerings, lying upon the remains of cloth (Eduardo Contreras, personal communication, 1967).

[10] Though this pond has long since disappeared, the Church of La Santa Veracruz (founded by Cortés around 1526 in memory of his arrival in Veracruz on Good Friday, 1519) still stands behind Alameda Park in Mexico City. Today a parish church, at one time it was the chapel of a brotherhood of Mexicans who provided spiritual comfort and Christian burial for condemned criminals.

chief priests ordered the servants of the sanctuary to sweep the courtyard and the stairs, decorate it with branches, and bring firewood—for this was a ceremony in which no wood could be burned but that brought by these men. It could not be brought by others, since it was destined for the Divine Hearth, as this was called. Fire was never lacking in this brazier. It was never put out, just as today the lamp must always burn before the Holy Sacrament. These and no others were permitted to adorn the temples and decorate them with branches. They had their captains and chieftains, who are known as *telpochtlatoque*. This office has persisted to the present day, since youths decorate churches with foliage and adorn them with bouquets, flowers, and grass. These things are now permitted since it is not a superstition but simply an ancient custom.

These priests performed other fierce penances: they fasted ten, five, or seven days continuously before the main feasts, just as we do before the Ember days. They observed chastity and cut their virile members in the middle to become impotent so as not to offend their gods. They drank no wine. They slept little because most of their activities took place at night: they kept the fire going; they went to the hills to offer sacrifice on behalf of those who requested it. It was very common [for people] to resort to the [priests] so that they would offer sacrifice in the woods, bearing gifts of incense, food, wine, rubber, little bowls, and baskets. This is like the present-day custom of bringing alms so that a mass may be said for them, or, as under the Old Law, the sin offering of calves, lambs, and goats to the priests. In sum, they underwent the most terrible penance in order to be considered saints, fasters, and penitents, martyrs to a diabolical deity. He who could bear the most suffering did it in order to be highly regarded. Consequently they were called *tlamaceuhque* and *mozauhque*, which mean "those who do penance" and "they who fast." They received great satisfaction and elation from these activities.

It was also their duty to bury the dead and perform funeral rites. Some people were buried in the fields; others, in the courtyards of their own homes; others were taken to shrines in the wood;

others were cremated and their ashes buried in the temples. No one was interred without being dressed in his mantles, loincloths, and fine stones. In sum, none of his possessions were left behind; and if he was cremated, the jar which received his ashes was filled with his jewelry and stones, no matter how costly. Dirges similar to our responses were chanted, and [the dead] were mourned, great ceremonies taking place in their honor. At these funerals [people] ate and drank; and if [the deceased] had been a person of quality, lengths of cloth were presented to those who had attended the funeral. [The dead man] was laid out in a room for four days until [mourners] arrived from the places where he had friends. Gifts were brought to the dead man; and if the deceased was a king or chieftain of a town, slaves were killed in his honor to serve him in the afterlife. His priest or chaplain was slain (all the lords had a chaplain in their homes who administered the rites). He was killed so that he might perform the ceremonies in the afterlife. They slew the chief steward who had served him, the cup bearer, the male and female humpbacks, and the dwarfs who had been in his service. It was one of the glories of the noblemen to be attended by humpbacks and the ladies to be served by humpbacked women. They killed the grinders of corn so that these women might grind and prepare tortillas in the other world. The deceased was not to suffer poverty; therefore, he was buried with immense riches: gold, silver, jewels, precious stones, fine mantles, earplugs, bracelets, and feathers. If he was cremated, together with his body were burned those who had been slain to serve him [in the afterlife]. The ashes [of the victims] were mixed together and thus stirred [and] were buried with great solemnity. The funeral rites lasted for ten days filled with sorrowful, tearful chants. I have tried earnestly to find out their content, but I have been unable to discover the nature of these chants. Nor have I found a native willing to recite them, since all answer that they have been forgotten. May it please our God that this be true, that [these songs] have really fallen into oblivion. Nevertheless, I fear this is not always true, since they still hold their feasts for the dead: one for children and the other for adults. I am certain that they mix some [of the ancient practices] with our

Day of the Faithful Departed, just as they mix certain elements of the Christian feasts when they sing responses for the dead. They lament their ancient lords and gods, and, to keep us in ignorance, they claim they have forgotten these things. The priests granted their services to those who requested these things, performing so many special ceremonies that I would be forced to write a separate chapter [to describe them]. It is sufficient, however, that I describe a few of them here to give warning of what I wish to express. Just a few days before this was written, I discovered that, after [I had] married several young couples with all the ritual and ceremony of the Sacrament, they were taken straight from the church to the house of the old men and women. There they were married again with all the ancient ceremonies and rites I shall now describe.

First the priest took the bride and groom by the hand and asked them if they wished to be married. Once he heard their answer, the young man's mantle was tied to hers, making a knot. Thus bound, they were led to her house, where a fire was burning in the hearth, and she was then made to walk around the hearth seven times. After these seven turns [the young couple] was made to sit upon a new mat which lay near the hearth. They were left there alone to consummate the marriage. A new mat was placed there, never used before, in honor of his having bedded a virgin, and on it were shown the signs of her maidenhood. All of this was taken into account and consideration, and if [the girl] showed no signs of her virginity, all the baskets used for food in the banquet were perforated in order to proclaim the immorality of the girl and her family.[11] The plates and bowls were perforated to show the guests that she had not been a maiden on reaching the bridal bed, a thing lamented and wept over by the parents. Nevertheless, if she was

[11] The exhibition of the "hymenal sheet" was a very common custom in Europe in Durán's time. It is possible that the hymenal mat described by Durán is another aspect of his diffusionist tendencies. Covarrubias refers to the modern-day survival of this custom among the Zapotecs on the Isthmus of Tehuantepec: "The marriage consummated, the bridegroom emerges from the room to inform his mother that the girl was a virgin and that all is well. The news is received with general enthusiasm and fireworks, and the old women, already drunk, give loud hurrahs for the groom and his mother. The groom has brought out a blood-stained handkerchief of white silk as evidence of the girl's virginity" (Covarrubias, 352).

truly a virgin, offerings were made to the gods and banquets were held, one in her home and another in his. Then she was taken to her house.

A [written] account was made of his properties: jewelry, household goods, lands, and houses, and another account was made of her belongings. These documents were kept by the parents of the newlyweds and by the chieftains of the wards, in case of divorce. The latter was common among the natives; when [the mates] were incompatible, they asked for a divorce. A division of their wealth was made in accordance to what each had contributed. And each was given his freedom. He was given the male children, and she the girls, together with all the womanly things of the house. She was given license to marry again, and so was he. He was admonished never to return to his wife, under pain of death! These things were observed rigorously.[12]

The priests also performed another rite connected with newborn babes, whose ears and genital organs were slashed, in the manner of circumcision. Above all, [this was done] to the sons of the lord and rulers. If the newborn was a male child, the priests themselves washed him; and when he was bathed, they placed a tiny sword in his right hand and a small shield in the other. The child went through this rite four days in a row while the parents offered oblations for his sake. If it was a girl, after bathing her four times, they placed in her hands miniature implements for spinning and weaving, together with woven cloths. Other children received quivers of arrows around their necks and bows in their hands. Children of the common people received the symbol [of their future profession] according to what had been prognosticated by the sign under which they were born. If [the child's] signs indicated that he was to be a painter, a brush was placed in his hand; if

[12] In this passage Durán enlightens us further regarding the ancient written documents of Mesoamerica. In addition to almanacs, fortunetelling books, genealogies, tribute lists, and so on, records were kept of the personal property of brides and grooms, including lands and household goods. Copies were made and preserved by the families of the newlyweds, and one copy was kept in the registry office of the ward. Unfortunately, no such documents dealing with property rights of man and wife have been preserved.

a carpenter, he was given an adz; and the others [were treated] in a similar fashion.

We have already dealt with the activities and ceremonies of the ancient priests and have seen their superstitious ways. Now I wish the reader to know, to understand, the intention with which I have written these things. It has not been my purpose to tell fables and ancient customs but to warn with Christian zeal the ministers of God who with such fervor practice the ministry which God gave them and for which they were chosen [to fulfill] their blessed works. Let them search out, let them uproot the tares which grow among the wheat. Let them be ripped out so that they not grow side by side with the divine law and doctrine. Let [our ministers] in their laxity and negligence, in their idleness and recreation, not permit the Indians to practice even small things, such as the shearing of children's heads, the feathering with plumes of wild fowl, nor the smearing of rubber upon their heads or on their foreheads, nor the smearing with pitch, nor the anointing with divine bitumen. [The children] grow long braids until they look like demons. Let not [our ministers] tolerate a new superstition invented among them: that of allowing children to grow crowns of hair on their heads. For this new [practice] new doctors and masters in the art of tonsuring have arisen, not only for children but for adults.

As a proof of my veracity I wish to tell something which happened to me in a certain village. I was called to hear the confession of a sick person, and there I found a woman of some eighty years with a great piece of cloth on her head. As soon as I saw her, (experience had opened my eyes), I immediately removed this cloth, and when I did so, I saw that she was tonsured with a friar's crown. It was so white and venerable that had she not been so ill she deserved to be appointed to the high dignity of standing with a miter at the door of the church. When I reported to some friars that I had ordered [the crown] removed, they answered that these things were done only as a devotion to the monks. I have tried to believe their explanation, given in such holy simplicity, and I must persuade myself that it is [the result of] extreme ignorance on their part and lack of understanding of the language of the Indians.

[The latter] are moved not by any ardent zeal but by their ancient rites and superstitions. If this is not true, let them ask that old woman just how strong her devotion was toward the monks, friars, and priests when she allowed that crown to be fashioned; then the evidence will be clear when we observe that this custom has spread throughout the land and has been permitted in the woods, in the rocky country, and in the most remote villages. [There one sees] the boys tonsured, and, if we are to believe their great love for the monks, they run and flee from them, scarcely knowing where to hide; though we have been here fifty-five years, [the Indians] flee from us as they did on the first day.

In ending this chapter, I wish to say something about what the priests did after having sacrificed the person disguised as a counterpart of the god Tezcatlipoca. It should be noted, as we have related in the last chapter, that on the feast of this god a slave was offered up. Once he had been sacrificed, another slave was immolated on the same day, [one] who had consecrated himself or made a vow to that end. He was delivered to the priests so that the likeness of the god might not be wanting. It was a ceremony involving the renewal of the live god, just as the Holy Sacrament is renewed in the churches. After the man was bathed and washed carefully, he was dressed in the complete attire and insignia of the deity, as shown in our illustration [Plate 9]. He was given the name of the god Tezcatlipoca, and all year he went about honored and revered as the god himself. Twelve guards constantly accompanied him to prevent him from fleeing. He was allowed to walk where he pleased, but the guards were always alert, their eyes upon him. If [the man managed] to flee, the most negligent guard took his place, representing the deity until his own death. The man to be sacrificed dwelt in the most sacred chamber of the temple; there he ate and drank; there the lords and the principal men came to revere and serve him. There he was brought victuals like those [eaten by] the great ones; and when he walked about the city, he was accompanied by lords and dignitaries. [The victim] carried a flute in his hand and occasionally played it so that it might be known that he was passing. Women with children in their arms came out, placing the little ones before him, greeting him like a deity, and this was done by most of the people. At night he was placed in a cage made of heavy wooden boards to prevent his escape. When the day of the feast arrived, he was sacrificed at noon as described, and every four years many others [were sacrificed and went] his way.

The ceremony of this god lasted for periods of twenty days, [similar to our] octaves. Thus ended the feast of this idol and devil, and so does our chapter, which, because of its numerous rites, has forced us to be unduly prolix.

CHAPTER VI

¶Which treats of the god known as Quetzalcoatl, deity of the Cholultecs, highly venerated and held in awe by them. [He was the] father of the Toltecs and of the Spaniards, inasmuch as he predicted the coming of the latter.[1]

IN pagan times each of the cities, towns, and villages of New Spain had its own god [worshiped by] the natives. And though [the gods] were revered by all, adored, and their feasts celebrated, [each town] had a special one who served as patron of the place, honored with greater ceremonies and sacrifices. The same situation exists today, for, though the people solemnize the feasts of all the saints, the feast of the town and its patron is carried out with the utmost solemnity. So in ancient times on the feasts of the idols each village had its own idol as patron. On his day extremely elaborate festivities and expenditures were common.

Thus the idol we deal with in this chapter was the god and patron of the Cholultecs, highly exalted and celebrated to the

[1] "Quetzalcoatl, . . . father of the Toltecs and of the Spaniards"! With what innocence Durán presents in a brief phrase this recurring theme in the development of Mexico, coloring her racial, economic, social, military, and political history during the last thousand years. Quetzalcoatl, high priest and king of paradisiacal Tula in the tenth century A.D., was the spiritual progenitor of Cortés and of the white man in general. In the Tula of Quetzalcoatl, pumpkins were large, ears of corn were wonderfully long, cotton grew in colors, birds of precious feathers sang marvelously—in that Aztec Garden of Eden there was no poverty, sorrow, or labor. To the Indians of the

extent that on the day of his celebration, since the Cholultecs were merchants and wealthy people, they celebrated a superb, a costly feast for the god called Quetzalcoatl, the deity of the merchants. They spent all they had earned during the year to surpass the other cities and to show and make evident the grandeur and opulence of Cholula.

Generosity and liberality are natural to the inhabitants of this land, to the extent that gold, silver, and precious stones mean nothing to them. When they are desirous of ostentation (not only those who are well off but even the most wretched Indians), they find generosity and liberality very natural, generosity of spirit to be lavish with one's own possessions and be proud, showing neither timidity nor weakness—as naturally as the spring flows and the earth gives her fruits.

Today the natives of Cholula continue their trade and commerce with different merchandise, traveling through the most remote and distant parts of the land, such as Cuauhtemallan and Xoconochco, all along those coasts and mines, with their loads of peddlers' trinkets, just as they did in ancient times. Let us pray to God that they no longer do these things with faith in the old god, formerly trusted as patron of the merchants.

New World, Cortés was Quetzalcoatl himself, who, after an exile of over four hundred years, returned to the shores of his native land in 1519. Thus the Lord Cortés-Quetzalcoatl, the Great White Man, the Messiah, the Redeemer, had at last come back to restore Mexico to its primeval wealth and bliss.

But the Lord Cortés-Quetzalcoatl did not restore the misty, longed-for dream-world of a past utopia. He brought new patterns not at all Toltec, which supplanted the native society. That Cortés was not Quetzalcoatl must have become apparent even to the least perceptive natives of Durán's time. By the end of the eighteenth century, long before independence, "Quetzalcoatlism," the hope for a foreign redeemer, had weakened to the point of all but total collapse. The blond god had been forgotten in the rise of a nativism, engendered by belief in the dark-skinned Virgin of Guadalupe; the writings of "Indian lovers" such as the Jesuit Clavijero, with his glorification of the Aztec past; and a general disdain of the constant influx of Spanish fortune seekers who bore little resemblance to the loving Quetzalcoatl.

Those who still felt strong attachment to the foreigner's ways (Spanish or not) began to be labeled Malinchistas, or followers of La Malinche, the woman who abandoned her people to follow Cortés. Even today Mexicans who overesteem "foreign" characteristics—including fair skin and hair—are known as Malinchistas. Maximilian, emperor of Mexico from 1864 to 1867, was the last "Quetzalcoatl."

This god Quetzalcoatl was adored in all the villages of the land, especially in Cholula, where he stood in a lofty and prominent temple, in whose courtyard the Marqués del Valle, Don Hernando Cortés, ordered a massacre of five hundred natives. He had asked them to bring food, and in its place they had brought firewood. This went on for three days, and on the third day all were slaughtered. After this [the Indians] brought food not only to the human beings but to the horses, so that when they brought a turkey for a man they brought another for his horse and did so with the other foods. If the people [of Cholula] had, from the beginning, behaved as [the people] of the other towns, that cruel massacre would not have taken place.

This idol stood in a wide, long chamber placed on an elaborately decorated altar, all its ornaments [being] of gold, silver, jewels, feathers, finely worked and splendid cloth.

The image was of wood and was shaped in the form we have seen in the illustration [Plate 12]. That is, his body was that of a man, and his countenance that of a red-beaked bird. From the beak emerged a crest covered with warts like that of a Peruvian mallard. Within the same beak were rows of teeth and a protruding tongue. From the beak to the middle of the face he was painted yellow, and next to the eye was a black stripe which passed below the beak.

The idol was adorned in this manner: it was crowned with a pointed paper miter painted in black, white, and yellow. From behind this miter long painted strips with tufts at their ends hung down his back. On his ears he wore golden ear-shaped plugs. Around his neck hung a large golden jewel shaped like a butterfly wing attached to a red leather band.[2] He wore an elaborate feather mantle done in black, red, and white, designed like the jewel—a butterfly wing. His splendid breechcloth was of the same hues and pattern, and it ended below his knees. On his legs he wore golden anklets, and [he] was shod with sandals. In his right hand he held

---

[2] This jewel was famed as the *ehecacozcatl* (a cross section of a sea snail with a spiral shell), symbolic of the god Quetzalcoatl. This conch shell was a musical instrument which emitted sounds imitating the wind; hence its name, *ehecacozcatl*, "wind necklace."

an ax made in the shape of a sickle. This was of wood and was colored black, white, and red, and next to the hilt it was decorated with a fringe of white-and-black skin. In his left hand he carried a shield of white-and-black marine bird feathers—from herons and cormorants—with a great number of thick tufts of the same feathers. What I have described was the daily garb of the idol. Some have told me that at times it was changed. In order to avoid prolixity, I have not bothered to set this down, since everything can be summed up in the changing of one mantle for another—changing today's miter for another—but the usual style was the one I have described.[3]

The natives celebrated the feast of this god on February 3, one day after Candlemas, according to our missal. This festivity was solemnized in the following manner: forty days before this feast the merchants bought a man who was flawless of hands and feet, without stain or blemish, nor one-eyed, nor with a cloud in his eye, nor lame, nor lacking one hand, nor crippled, nor with bleary eyes, nor drooling, nor lacking teeth. He was to have no blemish—none whatsoever—the sutures of his skull closed, nor signs of a cleft chin, nor pustules, nor scrofula—he was to be free of all imperfections!

This slave was bought so that, arrayed as a god, he might represent him during those forty days. Before he donned his costume, he was purified by being washed twice in the "divine water." After he had been washed and purified, he was dressed like the idol, exactly as has been described. He was then garbed with the conical hat, the bird's beak, the mantle, the jewelry, the golden anklets and earrings, the breechcloth, the shield. This living man was bought to represent the god for forty days, and he was served and revered as such. He was accompanied by his guards and many other persons

[3] The custom of changing the garb of religious images in accordance with the ceremonial occasion is one of the many cases of religious parallelism stressed by Durán and is, of course, either a conscious or a subconscious effort to influence the reader in favor of his diffusionist theories. Mediterranean Christians had long been accustomed to change the dress of images of the Virgin Mary during the year—black for mourning, white for rejoicing, and so on—as is evident in the closets of many shrines, such as those of Macarena in Seville, Loretto in Italy, and Cholula in Mexico, where the wardrobes of the Virgin are stored.

who attended him during those days. At night he was shut up in a cage to prevent his escaping—as was the impersonator of Tezcatlipoca. In the morning he was brought out of the cage and placed in a prominent place. He was served very good food, and, after he had breakfasted, flowers were placed in his hands and flowery garlands about his neck. Then they went with him about the city as he sang and danced in order to be recognized as the impersonator of the god. These things [were] substituted [for] the flute which the other [Tezcatlipoca] played for the same reason—that of being recognized. When the women and children heard his song, they came out of the houses to greet him and offer him many things as though he were divine.

Nine days before the feast two venerable elders, hierarchs of the temple, came before him. Humbling themselves in his presence, they whispered in a low, meek, deferential, and respectful voice:

"O Lord, let your worship know that nine days from now your task of singing and dancing will end. Know that you are to die!"

And he was expected to answer, "So be it!"

This ceremony was called *neyolmaxiltiliztli*, which means "realization" or "fulfillment." Once he had been advised, they kept their eyes on him; and if they saw that he became melancholy, that he stopped dancing joyously, with the happiness he had shown, and with the gaiety they desired, they prepared a heathen, a loathsome spell for him: they went immediately to procure sacrificial knives, washed off the human blood adhering to them (the result of past sacrifices), and with that filthy water prepared a gourd of chocolate, giving it to him to drink. It is said that the draught had this effect upon him: he became almost unconscious and forgot what he had been told. Then he returned to his usual cheerfulness and dance, having forgotten the warning he had been given. It is believed that he offered himself for death with great joy and gladness, bewitched by the beverage. This drink was called *itzpacalatl*, which means "water from the washing of the obsidian blades." They gave him this beverage because if the man became sorrowful owing to the warning it was held as an evil omen or sign pronosticating some future disaster. When the feast day arrived (which as I have said was on the third of February), after having honored [the youth] with incense and music, he was taken away and sacrificed at midnight in the manner I have described.

At that same time, having offered his heart to the moon[4] and having thrown it to the god in whose presence he had been slain, they let the dead body roll down the steps. There those who had sacrificed him (the merchants, as I have stated, whose feast it was) picked him up and carried him to the home of the chieftain. There he was cooked, and different dishes were made [of his flesh] so that by dawn this food would be ready for the meal and banquet.

First, the god was greeted with a little dance performed at dawn, while the representative of the god was being cooked. Today, on the principal feasts, this little dance is performed in the morning next to a bonfire. This solemn banquet of the slave was attended by all the merchants, who dealt in all kinds of wares, especially in buying and selling slaves. Each year they offered up this slave as a likeness of their deity. He was bought by all of them at the market of Azcapotzalco or in that of Itzocan, which was the market place specializing in slaves; this type of slave could be sold nowhere else. The ceremony of washing and purifying them was carried out by the priests after they had been purchased and they were cleansed of the stain of captivity.

This god was one of the main deities of the natives, and thus the temple in which he stood was of supreme importance, especially the one in Cholula. In the City of Mexico, since [Quetzalcoatl] was not the patron of the city, [the people] did not pay so much heed to his glorification as in Cholula. [This temple in Mexico] had only sixty steps to be climbed and its form was thus. Above the steps lay a stuccoed courtyard of medium width, where stood a round hall. Though this was large, it was made in the form of an oven, and the entrance was wide and low, like the mouth of an oven. In order to enter, it was necessary to stoop low. The round vault of the straw roof was called *xacalli*.

---

[4] A human sacrifice to the moon was unusual among the Aztecs of Mexico. Sahagún, however, states that the neighboring Indians of Xaltocan (probably the Otomis) adored the moon as a principal deity (Sahagún, 1950, VII:9).

This temple had its chambers like all the rest, with its cloisters for the many [attendants] who served this god and learned the ceremonies of this cult. Later they were to follow, to succeed, the priests [of the temple]. There was only one resident priest here, and he was responsible for the education and instruction of the youths, performing all the rites of the god. His obligations lasted one week; since three or four ministers or abbots attended that temple, each served one week without leaving the place during all this time. His daily task was to beat a great drum (the like of which existed only in this temple) at sunset, sending his message, just as today we are accustomed to ringing the Ave Maria. This drum was so big that its hoarse sound was heard throughout the city. Having heard it, the city was plunged into such silence that one would have thought it uninhabited. The markets were dismantled; the people went home. Everything remained in such quiet and peace that it was a wondrous thing. This signal for withdrawal was like the ringing of the curfew bell in cities so that the people will retire. Thus, when the Indians heard the sound of the drum, they said, "Let us retire, for Yecatl has sounded!" This was the god's second name. At dawn when the sun was rising, the priest again sounded his drum, at the hour when bells ring at daybreak today. With this sound he announced the birth of the day, and thus travelers and strangers prepared for their journey according to that signal, as if they had been prohibited from leaving the city until then. Likewise, the farmers, traders, and merchants made themselves ready—with that sign—some going to the market places, others to their fields. Women also rose to sweep their homes. The latter was based upon some pagan belief, and even today there exists the idolatrous custom of rising at dawn to sweep one's property and occasionally that of someone else.

This temple contained a fair-sized courtyard, where, on the day of the feast, were performed splendid dances, merry celebrations, and amusing farces. For these things a small stage or platform stood in the middle of the courtyard.[5] It was about thirty feet

---

[5] Durán's description of these rudimentary theatricals, together with platforms almost invariably found in large courtyards, such as those of Tlatelolco and, hundreds

square, neatly stuccoed, and was adorned with branches and beautifully decorated for the feast. It was hemmed in by arches made of all kinds of flowers and rich featherwork which were hung at certain intervals. There were different birds, rabbits, and other festive things highly pleasing to the eye. After dining, the merchants and lords danced around that theater with all their finery and splendid dress. The dance then ceased, and the players appeared. The first who came out [played] a farce of a man swollen with tumors, feigning to be sorely afflicted by them, moaning over the pains he felt, mixing with [these complaints] many joking words and sayings, all of which caused laughter among the people. When this farce had ended, another began: two blind men and two bleary-eyed individuals appeared. These four acted out a funny quarrel filled with clever sayings, the bleary-eyed men and the blind mocking one another.

When this farce had ended, another man appeared, representing a person with a cold, coughing constantly, feigning a chill, making wild and funny gestures. Then the actors were a large fly and a beetle; they came out imitating these creatures in lifelike fashion. One of them buzzed like a fly when it comes near meat, while the other watched him and said a thousand funny sayings. Then this other, disguised as a beetle, poked about the rubbish. All these native farces were highly amusing and pleasant, but were not acted out without pagan meaning, for they stemmed from the fact that the god Quetzalcoatl was held to be the advocate for tumors, eye disease, colds, and coughing. Thus in these same farces they included words of pleading directed to this deity. They begged for help, and so it was that all those suffering from these ills and diseases came with their offerings and prayers to this idol and his temple.

of years earlier, in the Ciudadela at Teotihuacan, should be clues to archaeologists regarding their function. Aside from Durán's description, only a few lines of the comedians' dialogue have survived in one or two ancient Nahuatl manuscripts copied by the Spanish missionaries: ". . . I am the jester. . . . I am a precious bird; I have come flying from the place of anguish. . . . I am the red-throated thrush. I have come flying. I have turned into a flower." "I am the rabbit who sacrificed himself. Behold me; I am now speaking seriously. Hold on to your ribs." "I am the trickster; I am he who goes about jeering" (Garibay, 1952, 142–67).

On this day in the temple the gift which the common people offered to this false god consisted of breads and fowl, some of the latter alive, others cooked. Those already cooked were [presented] in this manner: in woven containers of dry cornstalks, all interlaced. This did not lack its symbolism, since it indicated the dryness of the season. On top of those small containers, or plates, they placed tamales as large as fat melons. These tamales are the native bread. Upon the tamales were placed large pieces of cooked hen or male turkeys. An enormous offering of these things was made before the altar of the idol. Others presented the usual gifts, that is, incense, rubber, feathers, pine torches, quail, paper, unleavened bread, small tortillas in the shape of feet and hands. Each one of these things had its special aim and purpose.

All the nations of this land ate azymous, or, as we say, "unleavened," bread on this day. The Huaxtecs were an exception, since they were considered [by the Mexicas] idolatrous heathens, not keeping the law, like the Canaanites in relation to the Jews. In order to understand this custom and the difference between leavened and unleavened bread, it must be explained that these people cooked their maize with lime and ashes to flavor, soften, and season the bread. The lime was used for corn, as our wheat contains leavening to soften it. On this day all the bread was prepared without cooking it in lime, but only in water. This was the custom: When the corn had been [brought to a boil] in plain water, it was ground. Once ground, the dough was dissolved in water until it became like paste; then it was strained through thin cloths. The paste was wrapped in cornhusks and cooked in pots, thickening in the husks with the heat. [On this feast] this bread was eaten and no other. In the native language this bread is called *atamalli*, which means "plain-water bread," which actually means "unleavened bread, kneaded with water, lacking salt or leavening."[6]

[6] The modern Mexican tortilla, or maize bread, is made in the following manner. Grains of corn are soaked in water with chunks of lime and ashes. When softened, the mixture is heated almost to the boiling point; if it is cooked too long, it becomes mushy and inedible. The mixture is then ground to form the dough from which thin cakes are patted out. The cakes are then baked on an ungreased griddle. Although lime was omitted from the tortillas on the ritual occasion Durán describes,

COLOR PLATES

Topiltzin-Quetzalcoatl

(See Plate 1)

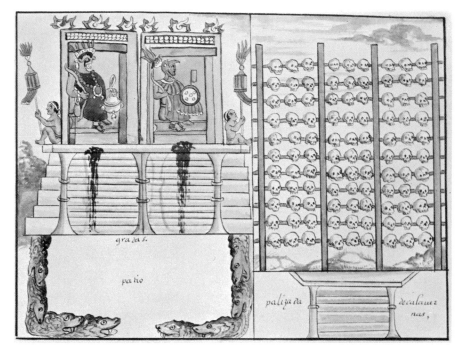

The Great Temple of Tenochtitlan and skull rack

(See Plate 4)

A fire sacrifice to Cihuacoatl

(See Plate 21)

Xochiquetzal, Goddess of Flowers and Love

(See Plate 25)

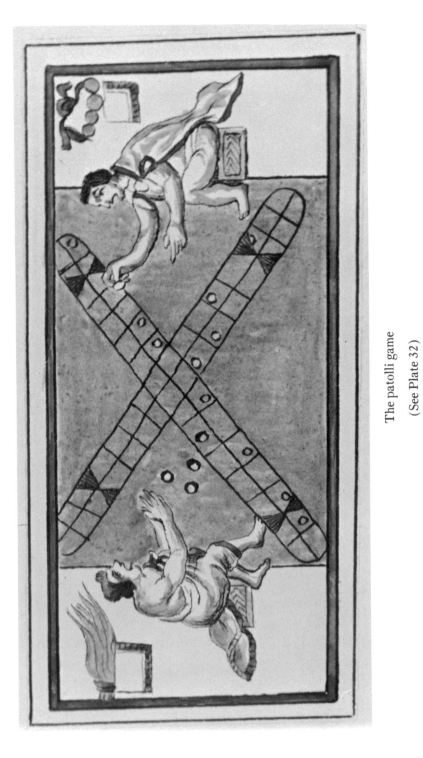

The patolli game
(See Plate 32)

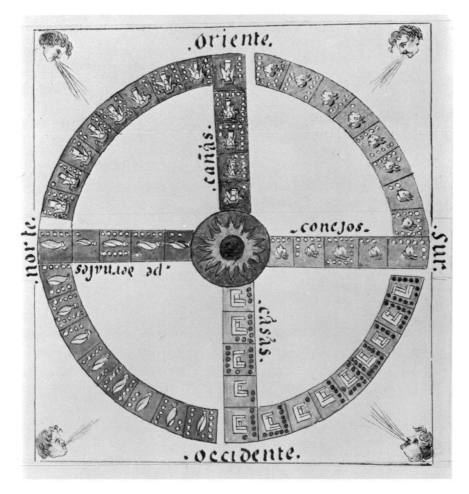

The Aztec cycle of fifty-two years
(See Plate 35)

The first month of the Aztec year
(See Plate 38)

It now remains to explain why this feast belonged more to the merchants than to others. For this reason I wished to prepare a special chapter; but since I realized that it was connected with the theme we are discussing in relation to this idol, it did not seem amiss to include it in this place.

In this land in pagan times the ancient kings and princes took very special care and caution in rewarding and honoring the upright, the virtuous, and the brave so that the rest might find heart to imitate their strength, when they saw the reward given [for this virtue] by kings and lords to those who practiced it. Thus many strove, in every possible way, to lift their names on high, to obtain glory, to procure greater honors, to found lineages and titles, and [to gain] good fame for their persons. There were three established and honored ways in all the nations [for obtaining these rewards]. The first and principal path which the kings designated was soldiery —to make oneself known in war through valiant feats, to be outstanding in killing, taking prisoners, to destroy armies and squadrons, to have directed these things. These [warriors] were given great honors, rewards, weapons, and insignia which were proof of their splendid deeds and valor. These [men] were given a new name, *tequiuaque* which is the equivalent of saying "man who makes good use of the soldier's calling." This term is made up of *tequitl*, which means "work," and the syllable *uaque*, which refers to a person who has performed his work well. In our own language we could give him the title captain.

The second way in which men rose was through religion, entering the priesthood. After having served in the temples in a virtuous, penitential, and cloistered way of life, in their old age they were sent out to high and honorable posts (which exist to this day) in the different nations. They were given high-sounding names and titles, which in our language today, to judge by the respect and reverence they enjoyed and still do, can be considered to have been the equivalent of counts, dukes, or marquises; bishops or archbishops; and so forth. They were present when the government

it never was actually a leavening agent. Durán, in his eagerness to compare New and Old World customs, equates lime with yeast.

councils were held, their opinions and advice were listened to, and they were part of the ruling boards and juntas. Without their council and opinion kings did not dare act, very much like the councils that His Majesty holds in order to clear his royal conscience. Thus, in the same manner, the positions were held by these dignitaries after long penance, toil, and exemplary life. When they were given these exalted posts and distinctions, many rites were performed. Their long hair was cut; the soot which had at all times covered their faces was washed off. We might almost call it a "doctorate," since through those ceremonies they gained great privileges and the position of knights, and a sumptuous banquet and fiesta was held. Today these things are carried out in the old manner. I can affirm this, for I have been an eyewitness at more than four of these "graduations." For those who know, who understand, the language of the people, I want to set down here the titles, which are *tlaca-tecuhtli, mexicaltecuhtli, tlacochcalcatl-tecuhtli, tecpannecatl, miz-toncatltecuhtli, amiztlato*, and so forth.

The third and least glorious manner of [rising in the world] was that of becoming a merchant or trader, that of buying and selling, going forth to all the markets of the land, bartering cloth for jewels, jewels for feathers, feathers for stones, and stones for slaves, always dealing in things of importance, of renown, and of high value. These [men] strengthened their social position with their wealth. We have seen many men of low birth and worse blood rise to a state which has permitted them to marry daughters of dukes, counts, and marquises and to form magnificent and rich family estates, mixing their humble blood with that of the highest of Spain. The same was true of these Indian merchants. They acquired wealth and obtained slaves to sacrifice to this their god [Quetzalcoatl]. And so they were considered among the magnates of the land, just as the valorous soldier brought sacrificial captives from war, gaining fame as a brave. He received people and prepared a banquet with the flesh of the man he had brought back as an offering to this god, all the lords and chieftains granting him in return insignia and high privileges—the same was true of the merchants. They offered one or two sacrificial slaves with the usual ceremonies of eating and dancing, presenting gifts of mantles, breechcloths, and sandals to all the lords, preparing different dishes for all the guests. [These merchants] were given the title of noblemen and were honored with the same pomp as the warriors. [Each one] was given an appropriate name, different from the rest, which indicated the way in which he had gained his honors. They were called *tla altique*, which means "purifiers of sacrificial victims." Thus at the beginning of this chapter we spoke of how the merchants celebrated this feast, offering up slaves for sacrifice, purifying them in the manner described.

The merchants celebrated the feast in honor of their god because their divine patron had been the most excellent, the richest merchant in his time, and possibly the one who gave them the patterns and rules of their trade.

With these things I shall terminate this chapter. I wish to give warning that even today there is a diabolical custom among the natives, especially in Cholula, where the god [Quetzalcoatl] was worshiped; peddlers will traffic for ten, twelve, and even twenty years, earning and saving up to two or three hundred pesos. And after all their toil, wretched eating and sleeping—without aim or reason—they offer a most lavish banquet. There they spend all their savings. What I most regret is that they follow the ancient custom of holding that memorial feast in order to celebrate their [ancient] titles and set themselves on high. This would not be wrong except that for their celebration they await the day on which the god [Quetzalcoatl] was honored.

May the Lord our God, in His infinite kindness and mercy, erase these things! May He remove the memory of Amalech from their minds and bring them to His fold! Amen.

CHAPTER VII

¶Which treats of the idol Camaxtli, god of the people of Huexotzinco and of Tlaxcala.

WE have dealt with the festivities of the most important gods of the land, and it now behooves us to speak of another divinity, no less attended and revered, with as many and as curious rites and ceremonies as the indigenous peoples could provide. This account will be pleasant and gratifying, and I set down the details carefully, as my history demands, since it contains nothing that we cannot profit by or that cannot give us useful information. I shall try to be as brief as possible (in order to avoid wordiness), though I have been accused of being too succinct and concise. I have been told that since I was writing such a novel and interesting account I should not abridge as I have done. By following this convenient and less tiresome path, I cannot help but tell all that should be described in this account. Thus, since I am dealing with the idol called Camaxtli, deity of the province of Huexotzinco, I cannot refrain from letting my pen flow, because of the great rites and festivals performed in that city and in others.

Since we have already dealt with Quetzalcoatl, god of the people of Cholula, let us now speak of [the deity] of Huexotzinco.

The latter was looked upon with as much reverence and veneration as that shown by the Mexicas [in their adoration of] Huitzilopochtli. The idol [of the people of Huexotzinco] was the god of the chase. He was known as Camaxtli or Yemaxtli. His feast was celebrated by hunters and performed with great rejoicing and ceremony, since there were forests and game [in abundance]. So it was that the Huexotzincas, people who were proud of their love of forests and of the chase, adopted this god as their advocate, and they honored, revered, and served him as much as can be imagined. Would that His Divine Majesty permit all this care, fear, and reverence be turned and applied to His Divine Service since He is the True God, our Lord.

[Camaxtli] was called the Lord of the Chase because he was the inventor of ways and manners of hunting and because he was skillful and cunning in this art. He was also the first sovereign of the Chichimec hunters. Thus no image of him stood in Mexico or in Tetzcoco, nor was a festival held in his honor [in those cities]. This was in part because he was a new [god] and in part because the Mexicas and the Tetzcocans waged a perpetual war against Huexotzinco. [The Huexotzincas] had never been willing to surrender [the image], nor had the others been able to take it by force. Thus, four or six years before the arrival of the Spaniards in this land, King Moteczoma attempted to steal the idol from the Huexotzincas and bring it to his own city. To do so he resorted to much trickery, feigning, and deceit. But the Huexotzincas suspected Moteczoma's treason and trickery to steal their god. It was said that the idol himself warned them, while the Mexicas were lodged in the royal chambers of the city, planning to prepare a trap or snare to attack the temple and carry off the idol by force. Nevertheless, the Huexotzincas surrounded those chambers and fell upon them with murderous intentions. But the Mexicas realized the terrible thing about to befall them—that they could not escape without being captured or killed. They climbed up through the hearths and chimneys[1] of the rooms up to the roofs of the houses.

[1] Archaeologists have found no remains of true chimneys in pre-Conquest Mexico. Durán is undoubtedly referring to the escape holes in the thatched roofs of the windowless Aztec houses.

The Huexotzincas entered, [but the enemy] was not to be found. When the Mexicas saw that all the [Huexotzincas] were inside, they leaped down to the street and fled. When the people of the city realized this, they attempted to follow them, but night[fall] stopped the pursuers. Those of Huexotzinco had the consolation [that the Mexicas] had fled without taking what they had come seeking.

The feast of this god was celebrated in two places. The first and most important took place in Huexotzinco and Tlaxcala; the other, in Coatepec, a town which borders on Huexotzinco. In very ancient times the people of Coatepec were subject to but friendly toward [Huexotzinco]; therefore, this idol was lent to them, since they were also Chichimec hunters. "Why then," someone might ask, "did the Mexicas and Tetzcocans not go to that village, since it was in their own territory?" My answer is that the rulers [of these two cities] did not seek relics but the image itself. In Coatepec only relics were given by the Huexotzincas, who kept [in their city the god itself], so desired and coveted [by the people of Mexico and Tetzcoco]. If the arrival of the Spaniards had not blocked Motec-zoma's plans, he would have captured [the idol] in spite of the Huexotzincas, and he would have conquered them also.

This feast fell on the fifteenth of November. It was the greatest of all, and was received with all the applause in the world, with a maximum of merrymaking. [It was the feast] in which the largest number of people died in sacrifice. This occasion [was commemorated] every eighty days, and a small festival was held. Therefore, if the principal feast contained twenty-five "layers" (as they say), the one which took place every eighty days had only four [layers]. I mean that if on the main feast they slew only thirty or forty men, in the sacrifice of the commemoration, only one or two were killed.[2]

2 Durán's reference to *capas*, or "layers," in his description of ceremonial days is reminiscent of the curious varieties of numerical Nahuatl terms described by Molina (118–20) and by others acquainted with the intricacies of the Nahuatl language. The words for one, two, three, or four—any number at all—varied, depending on the aspect or qualities of an object as it was perceived by the Nahuatl-speaking people. Thus, to count "animate" objects such as eggs, squash, pumpkins, prickly pears, and beans, distinctive numerical suffixes were employed. A different type of

The image of this idol was of wood. It was made in the form of a man with very long hair, his forehead and eyes black. On his head he wore a crown of plumes, and his nose was pierced with a beryl stone. On his arms he wore silver bracelets, in the fashion of knotted cords, with arrows set into them, three on each arm. From his armpits hung rabbitskins similar to the stole of a priest. In his right hand he carried a net basket which contained the food he carried to the woods when he went hunting. In his left he bore his bow and arrow. His breechcloth was highly adorned, and he wore shoes on his feet. His entire body was striped from top to bottom with white stripes [Plate 13].

The temple of this god was most beautiful, a hundred steps high, so crowded with people and so well carved that it surpassed that of the City of Mexico in beauty, in good taste, and in magnificence. At the top of the steps stood a beauteous round chamber with a thatched roof, so finely and carefully worked that nothing better could be made in straw. This roof ended in a long peak, at the top of which stood a clay monkey done in a realistic manner. Inside, [the chamber] was decorated with splendid cloth, feathers, jewels, and other ornaments, the best these rustic people could produce. At the foot of the idol (which stood upon an altar) there lay a small round coffer like a case. The [coffer] was a little less than a yard high and was covered with a lid. It contained some fire sticks which this god had originally used with a little ember to strike fire. In that case were also the feathers of different birds—blue, green, red, and yellow—all from rare birds. This box or case was held in as great respect and deference as the idol itself. It was carefully concealed, covered with cloth, very much like the Ark of the Covenant, in which were deposited the Tables of the Law and the staff of

word was used for numbers of objects that stood in line. "Things folded one upon another" had yet another numeral terminology. "Long" objects also had their own distinctive numbers. "Animated," "round," "folded," and "long" things differed considerably from our visual concept of material objects. The *capas*, or "layers," probably belonged to the category of the heavens described by Molina, who saw such things as plates, bowls, or "heavens" piled one upon another. It is not surprising, therefore, that Durán, who was thoroughly familiar with the Nahuatl way of counting, wrote of feasts in "layers." No thoroughgoing study has yet been made of the Aztec method of enumeration based on form, position, time, and space.

Aaron, together with the vessel of manna. Thus was this small coffer preserved in the temple with those feathers and fire sticks, which we call tinder, and a flint, and among them some old broken arrows which must have belonged to the god, together with a small bow. It seems that these insignia guided the Chichimecs and brought them to the places where they now dwell. Those instruments taught them how to survive in the wilderness when [the god] brought them, guided them, into this land. And in thanksgiving they guarded and revered those insignia as relics of a divine, celestial thing. Thus, in the town of Coatepec, this god [Camaxtli] was not represented in wood nor in stone nor as a man, as in the cities of Huexotzinco and Tlaxcala. The people of [Coatepec] adored and revered only the little coffer which, carefully covered and adorned, stood upon an altar. Within it were kept some of the feathers, the tinder, the flint knife, the arrows, and a small bow which their friends from Huexotzinco had given them.[3] As I have said, the people of Mexico were not interested in obtaining relics: they wanted the very idol itself.[4]

Eighty days before the arrival of the feast an ancient priest from the temple was appointed for a number of days. He himself had volunteered [for this office], and from that day on he began to fast on bread and water. He fasted eighty days, consuming nothing but bread and water, and that only once a day. When the eighty

[3] Coatepec, on the western slopes of Mount Tlaloc, though barely twenty miles from the Aztec center at Mexico-Tenochtitlan, is here presented as an ally of Huexotzinco and Tlaxcala against the Aztecs. It seems strange that the Aztecs, who had established outposts beyond the present-day border of Guatemala, had enemies within their own valley. Yet it must be remembered that the people of Tlatelolco, barely a mile from the Great Temple of Huitzilopochtli, were still resentful of their defeat in 1473 and were potential foes. The lake towns of the southern part of the Valley of Mexico—Xochimilco, Mixquic, Chalco, Cuitlahuac—were not to be trusted either, as was to be seen later during the siege of Mexico by the Spaniards. On the west the Tarascans of Michoacan had defeated the Mexicas in battle. Perhaps the worst threat lay on the east, in the Puebla-Tlaxcala region—in Huexotzinco, Cholula, Tlaxcala, and a dozen other small kingdoms which were rich and independent and fierce enemies of the Mexico of the Aztecs. Tens of thousands of their warriors would become allies of the Spaniards in 1519, a dynamic and decisive force in the Conquest.

[4] Like the Romans in their last days, the Aztecs of Mexico undoubtedly had rashly overextended their empire and were finding it difficult to control it.

days had ended, he was so thin, weak, and emaciated that he could barely stand or speak. The long fast having ended on the eve of the festival, this man was painted from head to foot with the same white stripes which adorned the idol. He was dressed in the same way and fashion as the god, which we have already described: a headdress of plumes, bracelets, and a stole made of rabbitskins. He was given his bow and arrows [for one hand], and in the other [he held] a basket with his food. He was dressed in a splendid breechcloth, and on his ankles he wore short golden anklets. Thus dressed and adorned, after having fasted those eighty days in order to be honored on the feast day and to be adored as an idol and god, this elderly minister was called forth from his chambers. Very early, before sunrise, all the dignitaries of the temple, together with the ministers, the youths, and the boys of the schools and of the monasteries, went up with him to the summit of the pyramid, accompanied by the din of shell trumpets and drums. When he arrived, all the young men and boys I have mentioned, dressed and adorned as hunters, each with bow and arrows in his hands, formed a squadron. Amid tremendous shouts and screams they [feigned] attack against the emaciated elder who represented the god, shooting many arrows innocently into the air so as not to offend the god. When the rites and shouting had ended, all the priests took hold of the lean old man and helped him [down the steps] with marked reverence.

From there they made their way to the woods, all walking in order as in a procession. Eighty days before this feast a public edict had been issued which prohibited anyone from entering this forest [to cut] firewood or lumber or branches or any other thing, and guards had been placed there. Anyone caught doing these things lost his ax and his tumpline. He was also deprived of his mantle and his other possessions. All these things were done so that the game would not be scared or frightened away. Besides being the feast of the god Camaxtli, it was also a day of great solemnity in the calendar, and was called Quecholli, which may be translated as Festival of the Hunt.

This feast was celebrated in all the land, and in Huexotzinco the two feasts were celebrated together: one for the god Camaxtli, and the other for the solemn day of Quecholli. [Later] we shall deal with the latter day in more detail.

But let us return to the purpose of our story. The lords, hunters, and leaders of the hunt arrived in the woods (all of them had been given such titles as Amiztequihuaque and Amiztlatoque, which mean Captains or Lords of the Hunters and of their Leaders. They had fasted for five days before this feast, praying for good fortune and abundance of game.

When dawn came, before the men from the city arrived, all these noblemen and hunters arrayed themselves in the following way. First, they painted a black circle around their mouths, and they did the same to their eyes; they feathered their heads and ears with red plumes; they encircled their heads with bands of red leather; and in the knot or bow made by the leather at the nape of the neck was tied a bunch of feathers from the eagle and other [birds], which hung down their backs. They smeared their bodies with stripes of white paint. All of them were nude except for their beautifully adorned breechcloths.

When the man representing Quecholli appeared, the men came out to meet him in good order. Having received him, they led him to the place where the hunt was to be. An idol, together with a bower, had already been set up on this site, the summit of the hill. [This bower] was finely constructed of flowers, feathers, and cloth, and bore the name Mixcoateocalli, which means Sacred Place of Mixcoatl. Mixcoatl means Cloud Serpent.

When [the men] arrived, they surrounded the woods in wing formation, leaving the hill with the shrine, or bower, in the center. This accomplished, a warning was given and was heard by the leaders and the captains of the chase. They set out for the hill with such cries and shrieks that it seemed that the mountain might collapse. [The men] went in such good order, so close to one another, that a mouse would have found it impossible to escape. And in this disciplined form they finally arrived at the shrine on the crest of the hill. Before them fled all the game and creatures of the woods, which, seeing themselves surrounded, struggled to escape. The killing, the shooting with arrows, took place now, together with the catching of deer, hares, rabbits, pumas, mountain lions, and other beasts, squirrels, weasel, and snakes. They captured alive all the game they could. Great honors were awarded to those who caught or killed the largest number of animals. They were granted new and fine gifts of mantles, splendid loincloths, featherwork, and other things.

After the hunt the game was placed before the idol, where it was sacrificed and slain as if it had been human. The oblation terminated, all descended to the plain, where they split into two paths. There they spread a great deal of grass (the place was called Zacapan, which means On the Grass), and all sat down. Then they took the tinder, flint, and other instruments for kindling fire from the case, and the priests lighted a new fire, blessing it with certain ceremonies. They built great bonfires to roast all the game, and this was eaten with much reverence and pleasure, together with *tzoalli* bread, which—as I have remarked—is a bread made of amaranth seeds, much like our own rye bread. On this day they all remained in the woods until the following morning. But at dawn they returned to the hunt, and if [animals] were taken, they repeated the actions of the previous day. After having eaten, they returned in the same good order with which they had come, carrying with them the image of the god with much reverence. Having arrived, they carried [the god] to the summit of the temple. Thus the feast was suspended for ten days until the octave of Quecholli had passed. Thus was named the feast and the day of which we have spoken: *tlaco Quecholli*, which means "halfway through Quecholli." Thus during those ten days there was great rejoicing, dancing, banqueting, and feasting until the tenth day came; then the feast had ended, terminated.

When the tenth day arrived—this being like the octave of the feast—early in the morning the dignitaries and priests of the temple took charge of a man and a woman. The woman was given the name Yoztlamiyahual, and the man was called Mixcoatontli, and both were dressed in the raiment of the gods they represented. She was [clad] just like the goddess of that name, and he was [dressed] precisely like the god he represented, who was Mixcoatl. These [two] were taken out in public, and the people paid homage to them. Once their public appearance ended, many youths disguised in the same manner as the man offered themselves up as vassals and servants of the [god] Mixcoatontli. They were called Mimixcoa, which is a generic term; this transmitted some of the divine essence to these men. And so [the god] received them and gathered them unto him.

Then they took the woman and knocked her head four times against a large rock which stood in the temple. This rock was known as *teocomitl*, which means "divine pot." Half-conscious, before she had died of the blows, her throat was slit as one cuts the throat of a lamb. And her blood flowed upon that rock. Once she was dead, she was decapitated, and the head was carried to Mixcoatontli, who took it by the hair and then went to stand in the midst of his attendants. In good order the people made a procession around the courtyard four times. And he who was representing the god Mixcoatontli in the midst of his servants, with the head in his hands, kept turning to one and another, talking to them and preaching divine things and the cult of the gods. When the procession had finished its four turns, they directed themselves to the one who had represented the god Mixcoatontli, and sacrificed him in the usual way. He was cast down the steps, and thus ended the feast and the day of the octave, [dedicated] to both the idol Camaxtli and the feast of Quecholli.

Many priests and groups of young men served this temple and this god. Just as we have told in previous chapters, they learned a good way of life. Most of them emerged as great hunters, since the main activity there was to learn hunting. Two opposite ways of life existed in this monastery: one the way of chastity; and the other, of incontinence. We should explain that he who was to remain there in the service of the god (whether in the priesthood or in some other ministry) was prohibited from knowing women, nor was he to feel lust, nor curiosity on looking [at women], whether in acts or words, under pain of death. The other extreme was that some were permitted normal sexual relations, and a great deal of freedom was given to those who wished [to take advantage of this privilege]. Thus one undesirous of remaining as a minister of the temple was allowed to live with a young woman, with whom he could live in free concubinage as long as he wished. She was given to him on trial; if she bore children and he desired to marry her later, he could do so. If not, he was allowed to abandon her and marry someone else. Thus those who proved themselves in giving life to children (both men and women) were highly honored, their fecundity and fertility praised.

Every eight years this temple was renewed, rebuilt, and at the renovation a man was sacrificed. Many other ceremonies [took place], similar to the dedication of a church or the consecration of a place of worship. This type of blessing is still common, since today it is practiced in newly finished houses before the owners have taken possession. [The Indians] perform the same ritual used in ancient times for the renovation or construction of houses or temples. As witnesses of this, I wish to call on the ministers who understand [the Indians] and who have penetrated their consciences, [though I cannot call upon those] who do not understand, penetrate, or know what the native says, nor what he tries to say. This ceremony is very common: [When the natives] go to live in a new house, no one will enter without first performing the *calmamalihua*, as this rite is called by them. On this occasion they eat, drink, dance, and pour pulque in all the corners, and the host himself takes a newly lighted firebrand and points it in one direction and in another, thus taking possession of the home he built. As I have stated, this [custom] continues in use today, and I have seen it [practiced] everywhere.[5]

[5] There has been much speculation about the periodic covering up and rebuilding of temples in Mesoamerica, a custom in which a layer of earth and stone was placed over the nucleus of the previous temple, until finally a pyramid resulted, formed of a series of superimposed stuccoed layers, each enveloping the previous structure. It has been calculated that such renovations took place every fifty-two years, or each lunar year. Here Durán states that the pyramids were rebuilt every eight years. Mesoamerican archaeologists have not as yet determined the pattern of this ancient system. Superimposed pyramids, such as those at Tenayuca, Cholula, Calixtlahuaca, and Teopanzolco, may still hold surprises for the archaeologist, to which Durán's brief words may provide a clue.

I consider [these practices] and the tolerating of them harmful; thus I fulfill my obligation in denouncing them. Let him who feels this responsibility find a remedy for these things! Let him not burden his conscience by feigning ignorance and consenting to these and other superstitions! Let him not consider them things of little concern! If he does not fight against them, reprehend them, showing wrath and grief over them, the natives become accustomed [to our lenience] and do things of more weight and gravity. They are still idolators, in spite of many years of [Christian] teaching, and are more superstitious than they were under the [old] law, all owing to the negligence and carelessness of those who are in charge of them. "And if you don't believe that the pot was broken, behold the pieces on the floor." And I am referring to what we see, find, and discover every minute of the day, not only in villages far removed from the City of Mexico, where there would be some excuse [for idolatry] through lack of catechism. I am referring to [places] very close to Mexico, and even to the city itself. There are as many evils, superstitions, and idolatrous natives as [there were] under the old law; there are [as many] witch doctors, fortunetellers, fakirs, and old men who preach their cursed religion, preventing it from falling into oblivion. They teach it to youths and to children, making up and inventing superstitions in things which in themselves are not evil. They have introduced magic beliefs even in the perforating and the placing of earrings in the ears of women and girls. Let the truth be told. One day I entered a home to visit and console some ailing people during the great plague which raged in this year. I found a sick old man seated, wearing some earrings which he had donned on the orders of a deceitful doctor, who had made him believe that if [he placed them in his ears] he would not die. And therefore you will see these [earrings] worn by old women who have almost turned into dust, who believe with a faith as strong as ours in the Most Holy Trinity that their life will be prolonged by wearing them. To remove this ironical deception it would be necessary to receive the special grace of the Holy Spirit.

We have also allowed [the following situation to exist]. When someone asks for the hand of a daughter, he must first carry food and presents [to her family]. And if he does not offer these first, following the ancient custom (though the girl is willing and even obstinate), we shall observe that her parents and kinsmen are against it and will refuse to give her up. And if her father is a chieftain and he is reprehended [for his refusal, he says:] "He did not ask for her hand in the proper way. He brought nothing." Some will say that these things are of no importance. But I say that it is a subtle form of idolatry, besides being an ancient custom. All the heathen customs [of the natives] were based on eating and drinking—worse than the Epicureans.[6] They find their happiness in these things. He who has known and become acquainted with [the Indians'] low way of life must have seen and become familiar with [such practices]. When the natives go to visit someone—whether he is ill or in good health—if they are not fed and given to drink, they will not return, even though he is their own brother or close kinsman—even though he dies. The same thing occurs at the wakes, which I have described. On that day a banquet is offered to the entire ward, to the chanters and acolytes, since everyone (with the corpse still present) eats the host out of house and home. The funeral rites are performed right there. The house is stripped, the soul goes to the underworld, and the wife and children become destitute. And nothing should be lacking for this occasion, since it is an ancient custom, an idolatrous custom to which little heed has been paid in the past and in the present. Thus no one can extirpate these things, nor is there a remedy for them. The error was in not seeing [such customs] and prohibiting them from the very beginning so that [superstitious] practices would not take root to the extent that only God could now tear them out. And had the Spaniards in their cruel, atrocious massacres of men, women, and children slain the old men and women so that those of the new generation would not preserve knowledge of the ancient [religion] —had this [killing] been done with godly zeal, [it would be a] more pardonable sin before His Divine Majesty than in having murdered, impaled, cast them to the hounds, and hanged them in

[6] Undoubtedly Durán is referring to ceremonial occasions rather than to the daily life of the Mesoamerican Indian, whose fare was and is exceptionally frugal.

order to steal their gold, silver, and jewels. Because of their misdeeds they may have gone to Hell; but had they mixed godly zeal [with their acts], they could have been saved and, repentant of their sins, attained Heaven.

The priests of the god we have been describing taught the common people to conjure the chase by magical incantations. These spells and sorcery were used by the hunters to prevent the game from fleeing, scattering, escaping from the snares and nets. Before leaving the house, [the hunters] were also instructed to offer sacrifices and prayers to the fire and to the threshold of the house; and when they had reached the hills, [these hunters] were to greet the hills and make sacrifices and oaths. They were ordered to salute the cliffs, the ravines, the wild grass, the thickets, the trees, and the snakes. Finally, they were to make a general invocation to all the things of the woods, together with a promise of offering sacrifice to the fire by roasting the fat of the game which was captured.

These incantations have been written down, and I have had them in my hands, and I could set them down here if they were important. Aside from their not being necessary, however, once they have been translated into our Spanish language, they become nonsensical, since they are only an invocation to hills, waters, trees, clouds, and the sun, moon, and stars. Together with these, [they invoked] all the gods they adored and all the animals of the woods.

These things have not been forgotten; I can affirm that today they are still in use, together with a thousand other incantations with which they conjure clouds, water, mountains, hail, and stones. All these things are founded on idolatry and the ancient rites. Would that our True and Immense God were pleased that [the Indians] had forgotten [them], so that this book not be a reminder [to the natives], like those [works] that some are compiling, to the detriment of the good which an understanding of the facts in this book would bring about. I believe that, incited by the cursed devil (since the good that I seek has not been realized), these wretched Indians remain confused and are neither fish nor fowl in matters of the Faith. On one hand they believe in God, and on the other they worship idols. They practice their ancient superstitions and rites and mix one with the other, and all of this is the fault of the ministers who are with them and do not understand them.

But I find consolation: God is with me, and the rationalizations [of the Christian ministers] are so feeble that [in the end] we shall prevail against these Philistines!

CHAPTER VIII

¶Which deals with the idol named Tlaloc, God of Rain, Thunder, and Lightning, who was revered by all the people of the land. The name means Path Under the Earth or Long Cave.

WHEN we spoke of the god named Huitzilopochtli, in whose honor the Mexicas celebrated a most solemn feast, I wrote that next to the chamber where he stood, within the same temple, was a companion of his, [Tlaloc], who was no less honored or revered than [Huitzilopochtli]. [Tlaloc] was also held to be a god like the others, and he was honored with as many sacrifices and ceremonies as any. He was worshiped as God of Rain and of Lightning, Thunder, and Thunderbolts and of all kinds of storms. His story will please my listeners because it contains remarkable things and will also make them give thanks to our God for having cleansed these wretched people from their great errors and blindness, for they were sunk in the most intolerable deceits and depravity.

First of all, it must be noted that the idol is known as Tlaloc and was venerated and feared throughout the entire land. The whole country was dedicated to his service—lords, kings, noblemen, and the common people. His permanent home was in the same temple of the great Huitzilopochtli, next to him, where a special chamber had been erected. It was beautifully adorned with the usual decoration of cloth, feathers, jewelry, and stones—all of the finest quality. His statue was carved of stone, representing a frightful monster. Its horrendous face was like that of a serpent with huge fangs; it was bright and red like a flaming fire. This was a symbol of the brilliance of the lightning and rays cast from the heavens when he sent tempests and thunderbolts; to express the same thing, he was clad totally in red. His head was crowned with a great panache of green feathers, shining, beautiful, rich. From his neck hung a string of green beads called *chalchihuitl* [jade] in the form of a necklace and hanging from it a round emerald set in gold. In his ears were [earplugs] made of the stone we call jade, from which hung hoops of silver. On his wrists were bracelets of precious stones, and he wore [similar jewelry] on his ankles.

Thus no other idol was more adorned or enriched with stones and splendid jewels than this, since all the foremost warriors and noblemen came to him with their gifts of magnificent stones and jewels. These were offered because it was believed that anyone who had been struck by lightning and killed had been injured by a stone. Thus most of the offerings placed before this idol were stones and fine jewels. In his right hand [Tlaloc] carried a purple wooden thunderbolt, curved like the lightning which falls from the clouds, wriggling like a snake toward the earth. In his left hand he held a leather bag which was always kept filled with copal, an incense which we call myrrh. This idol sat on a splendid dais covered with green cloth and decorated with handsome designs. His body was that of a man, even though his face (as I have said) was that of a fierce and terrifying monster.

This same name of the god [Tlaloc] was given to a lofty mountain which is bounded by Coatlichan and Coatepec on one side and by Huexotzinco on the other. Today this mountain is called Tlalocan, and it would be difficult to say which received its name from which—the god from the mountain [or the mountain] from the god. Perhaps it is more believable that the mountain took its name from the god because on that whole sierra the clouds become cold, and storms of thunder, lightning, thunderbolts, and hail are formed. Therefore it was named Tlalocan, which means Place of Tlaloc.

On the summit of the mountain stood a great square courtyard surrounded by a finely built wall about eight feet high, crowned with a series of merlons and plastered with stucco. It could be seen from a distance of many leagues. On one side of this courtyard was a wooden chamber neither large nor small, with a flat roof. It was stuccoed both within and without and possessed a beautifully worked and handsome [castellated] crown. In the middle of this room, upon a small platform, stood the stone idol Tlaloc, in the same manner in which Huitzilopochtli was kept in the temple [of Mexico]. Around [Tlaloc] were a number of small idols, but he stood in the center as their supreme lord. These little idols represented the other hills and cliffs which surrounded this great mountain. Each one of them was named according to the hill he stood for. These names still exist, for there is no hill lacking its proper designation. Thus the small idols which stood around the great god Tlaloc had their own names, just like the hills which encircle the great mountain.

The feast of this god fell on the twenty-ninth of April, and it was celebrated in such a solemn way that men came from all parts of the land to commemorate it, to the point that no king or lord great or small failed to bring his offerings. This god was honored on one of the principal feasts of the calendar. It was called Huey Tozoztli [Great Vigil], which indicated that the feast was most solemn and elaborate, with double ceremonies and rites inasmuch as it coincided with one of the celebrations held every twenty days. These were like Sundays on which people abstained from manual and servile labor; these people, therefore, observed our same precept of "keeping the holy days." The purpose of this feast was that of asking for a good year, since all the maize which had been sown had now sprouted.

As I have mentioned, the mighty King Moteczoma, together with all the great men of Mexico—knights, lords, and nobles— came to the celebration on the great mountain. Nezahualpiltzintli, king of Acolhuacan, [arrived] with all the nobility of his land and kingdom. At the same time came the rulers of Xochimilco and of Tlacopan with their leading chieftains. So everyone came to the Mountain of Tlalocan: the entire nobility of the land, princes and kings, and great lords, both from this side of the snowy mountain [Iztaccihuatl] and from the other, Tlaxcala and Huexotzinco. For these lords large, fine shelters of boughs were made, according to their rank, for these were mighty kings and lords, greatly feared and venerated. For each sovereign and his followers were built, on different parts of the mountain, houses of straw with their rooms and apartments, as if they had been meant to be permanent. All of them were constructed around the great courtyard which, as I have mentioned, was at the summit.

Just after dawn these kings and lords with their followers left [their shelters]. They took a child of six or seven years and placed him within an enclosed litter so that he would not be seen. This was placed on the shoulders of the leaders. All in order, they went in the form of a procession to the courtyard, which was called Tetzacualco. When they arrived before the image of the god Tlaloc, the men slew the child within the litter, hidden [from those present]. He was slain by this god's own priests, to the sound of many trumpets, conch shells, and flutes. The child dead, King Moteczoma, together with all his great men and chieftains, approached [the idol] and presented finery and a rich garment for the god. They entered the place where the image stood, and [Moteczoma] with his own hands placed a headdress of fine feathers on its head. He then covered it with the most costly, splendid mantle to be had, exquisitely worked in feathers and done in designs of snakes. [The idol] was also girded with a great and ample breechcloth, as splendid as the mantle. They threw about its neck valuable stones and golden jewels. Rich earrings of gold and stones were placed upon him, and on his ankles also. [The king] adorned all the smaller idols who stood next [to Tlaloc] in a similar fashion. After Moteczoma had dressed the idol and had offered it many splendid things, Nezahualpilli, king of Tetzcoco, entered. He was also surrounded and accompanied by great men and lords, and he carried a similar garment [for the idol]; and if it was superior [to that offered by Moteczoma], so much the better. He dressed it and the smaller images with much splendor, except that he did not place the headdress upon the head but hung it from the neck and down its back. Then he departed. The king of Tlacopan then came in with another garment and offering. Finally the [sovereign of] Xochimilco, accompanied by all the rest, entered with more fine adornments: textiles, bracelets, necklaces, wristbands, and earplugs, just as the others had done. The headdress was placed at the feet [of the idol]. Thus everyone came in to make his offerings: one of them a mantle, another a jewel, another a precious stone or feathers, exactly as [people] enter [the church] on Good Friday for the Adoration of the Cross. After the offerings had been made, all went outside, leaving the chamber so rich in gold, jewels, stones, cloths, and feathers that [this wealth] might have enriched many paupers.

The idol and the smaller images had now been dressed in the manner described. Then was brought forth the sumptuous food which had been prepared for each king [to offer the god]: turkeys and their hens and game with a number of different kinds of bread. Moteczoma himself, acting as steward, entered the chamber where the idol stood, and his great men aided him in the serving of the food. The rest of the chamber was filled to bursting with stews of fowl and game, many small baskets of various breads, and gourds of chocolate. Everything was beautifully prepared and cooked, and there was such abundance in the room that some of it had to be left outside. At that time the king of Tetzcoco entered with his viands, which were no less rich and superb. And he fed the god in the same way as Moteczoma, he himself as steward. Then came [the ruler] of Tlacopan, who did likewise. And afer him that of Xochimilco. They offered so much food that those who tell this story (they are men who actually saw these things) affirm that the food was so plentiful—stews, breads, and chocolate in the native style—that most of the courtyard was crowded, and it was a sight to see. It was especially notable that all the pottery was new, and so were the baskets and the vessels—never used before. When the food had been put in its place, the priests who had slit the throat of the child came in with his blood in a small basin. The high priest wet the hyssop which he held in his hand in that innocent blood and sprinkled the idol [and] all the offerings and food. And if any blood was left, he went to the idol Tlaloc and bathed its face and body with it, together with all the companion idols, and the floor. And it is said that if the blood of that child was not sufficient one or two other children were killed to complete the ceremony and compensate for what had been lacking.

When all these rites had terminated, everyone descended to the living quarters to dine, since they could not eat in that place because of their pagan superstition. Meanwhile, in the neighboring towns down below an abundant and sumptuous repast, for kings, princes, and great lords, had been prepared. So it was that each returned to his city.

When one of the sovereigns found himself unable to go in person (because of some urgent matter), he sent his envoy or delegate with all the pomp and offerings described, so that these might be offered in his name and all the ceremonies of which we have spoken might be performed.

When all these things had been done, a company of one hundred soldiers was formed—the most courageous and valorous to be found, [led by] a commander. They were left to guard the rich offerings and abundant victuals which had been presented. This was done to prevent the foe (from Huexotzinco and Tlaxcala) from robbing and sacking. If by chance [the Mexicas] were neglectful of placing that guard or the sentinels of their watch, the enemy came at night and, having stripped the idol, stole all the wealth that had been offered. Should this happen, the Mexicas and all the other provinces of the Mexica country were greatly offended and outraged. Thus the soldier who was careless paid for his neglect with his own life. Nevertheless, since the cunning and the trickery of the Mexicas were always great, it is said that more often than not, while pretending to be asleep, they allowed the enemies to enter with the riches as bait, and after they had been thus baited and were at the mercy [of the Mexicas], the latter appeared suddenly in an assault which left no man alive. This guard lasted until all the food, baskets, and gourds rotted and the feathers disintegrated from the moisture. Everything else was buried there, and the chamber was walled in until the next year, for in that place there were no priests or ministers in attendance, only the guard we have mentioned, which was changed every six days. [To maintain this guard], certain nearby towns had been chosen to provide soldiers to keep watch as long as there was any fear that the foe might sack the idol and the offerings. After the oblations on the mountain [of Tlaloc] and everything I have described had ended, the lords hastened to descend to the celebration and sanctification of the waters, which were performed on that same day in the lake, streams, springs, and cultivated fields. Here sacrifices and oblations were offered, and these I shall describe in a detailed manner when we deal with the festive day Huey Tozoztli, since all these things pertain to that place.

At dawn the lords celebrated the Feast of Tlaloc on the mountain (this Mountain of Tlalocan) with the solemnity and lavishness I have mentioned, in great haste, since they wished to be present at the sacrifice of the waters. [While these rites were being performed], those who had remained in the city [of Mexico], where the image of the god, sumptuously and richly adorned, was kept in the temple of Huitzilopochtli, prepared for the same feast of the waters. This was especially true of the priests and dignitaries of the temples and of all the youths and boys who lived in seclusion and in the schools. [All of them] donned new ornaments and performed many different dances, farces, and games. They wore various disguises as if it were their principal feast day, very much the way [our] students celebrate the Feast of Saint Nicholas. All these games and festivities were carried out in an [artificial] forest set up in the courtyard of the temple in front of the image of the god Tlaloc. In the middle of this forest was placed a very large tree. It was the tallest that could be found in the woods, and it was called Tota, which means Our Father. This indicated that the idol was the god of the woods, forests, and waters. When the news arrived [that the lords who had been on Mount Tlaloc] were descending from the mountains and drawing close to the waters to embark in the canoes which awaited them, this solemnity and feast ended in the lagoon. These [canoes] were as numerous as the lords, chieftains, and men who had made the journey, and they covered the shores of the lake. All were richly adorned and covered with awnings, especially those of the sovereigns, each one possessing his own boat with a great number of rowers who propelled it swiftly. But before we continue in regard to this second feast which came out of the city, I wish to speak of the [artificial] forest and of the tree called Tota, which can be seen in the illustration [Plate 14].

It is to be noticed that this image was honored in name of the Father, which is translated as Tota; thus we know that [the people] revered the Father, the Son, and the Holy Ghost, and called them Tota, Topiltzin, and Yolometl. These words mean Our Father, Our Son, and the Heart of Both, honoring each one separately and all three as a unit. Here we see evidence that these people knew something about the Trinity.

In order to fulfill our purpose and avoid incompleteness in our account, it is to be noted that before the actual day of the feast of this god a small forest was set up in the courtyard of the temple in front of the shrine of the idol Tlaloc. There were placed many bushes, little hills, branches, and rocks, all of which seemed the work of nature, yet [were] not arranged in imitation of nature. In the midst of this forest was set a tall tree of luxuriant foliage, and around it were four smaller ones. This tree was obtained in the manner which I shall describe. All of them—the ministers, youths of the temples and monasteries, schools, colleges, boarding schools (not excepting young or old, youth or elder)—went to the Hill of Colhuacan.[1] And on the entire [hill] they sought out the tallest, the

[1] The Hill of Colhuacan, today known as Cerro de la Estrella (Hill of the Star), is near the towns of San Francisco Culhuacan and Iztapalapa, both on the periphery of Mexico City. In ancient times this small volcanic prominence was known as Huixachtepetl or Mixcoatepetl, on which stood a temple dedicated to Mixcoatl, father of Ce Acatl Topiltzin-Quetzalcoatl. The ruins of the small temple may still be seen. According to some scholars, such as Wigberto Jiménez Moreno, Mixcoatl was assassinated by an usurper named Ihuitimal. When Topiltzin reached manhood, he killed his father's murderer, sought out his father's bones, and buried them on the Cerro de la Estrella. At the end of each fifty-two-year cycle, fearing that the world might end, the Aztecs held a dramatic ceremony on the summit of the mountain. Dreading that

fullest, the most beautiful tree that could be found, the straightest and the thickest. As soon as the desired tree had been found, all its branches were tied with ropes and were bound to the trunk. They were tied carefully so that not a branch or a leaf would touch the ground while [the tree] was carried in. Once it had been tied, the woodsmen came to cut the tree, which had already been bound with other ropes so that when it fell it would not touch the ground. On the contrary, while it tottered it was supported by the ropes and by forked poles so that it was lowered into the hands [of the men]. After the full [weight of the tree] had been received without its touching the ground, it was carried out of the woods. At certain intervals, when [those who carried it grew tired], they released it, and it was taken by others who did not allow it to rest on the ground. One relieved another, and so many men took part that their toil was not wearisome. On the contrary, they returned bringing [the tree] with great merrymaking, with songs and dancing, with a joyous clamor, and thus it was brought into Mexico with the same excitement that is usual [even today]. It was brought to the temple we have mentioned, where, in the midst of the [artificial] forest, a deep hole had been dug.

Having arrived, [the men] planted it so straight and fine that it seemed to have been born there. Then the ropes which had bound it were untied from the branches, and the latter opened up and became full again, as they had been in the woods. This tree was called Tota, which means Our Father, because around it were placed four smaller [trees], [the main one] seeming to be the father of the others. Once the great tree and the four small ones had been set up in the form of a square with Tota in the center, from each of the small trees emerged a twisted straw rope, attached to the large one in the center. From the four small trees, therefore,

---

the sun might not appear the next day, the priests held vigil throughout the night on top of the hill, while all the fires of the Valley of Mexico were extinguished. On the appearance of Tlahuizcalpantecuhtli-Quetzalcoatl, the Lord of Dawn, the Morning Star, a new fire was lit on the chest of a sacrificial victim at the summit of the Cerro de la Estrella. The people rejoiced, knowing that the world had been granted another fifty-two years of life.

emerged four ropes, and all four were tied to the central tree, called Tota.[2] These ropes, which stretched across the space between the large tree and the little ones, were decorated with tassels hung at intervals, made of the same grasses or straw. It is said that these rough cords represented the penance and harshness of the life led by those who served the gods. So it is said that Nezahualcoyotl and his son Nezahualpilli took their name from these ropes, because Nezahualpilli means Penitent Lord or Fasting Lord. And I affirm that he took the name from these ropes because they were called *nezahualmecatl*, which means "cords of penance." In our terms it means almost the same as a penitential chain, because in truth the penitents in ancient times used those rough cords on their bodies to chastise the flesh.

When that great pole or tree had been set in place, together with the smaller ones and the penitential ropes, the high priests and

[2] Many ancient customs described by Durán survive in modern times. In the highlands of Puebla and in Veracruz the main pole in the *palo volador* (flying-pole dance) is still held in reverence. The celebration has been described as follows: "After finding the tree, the groups dance around it and beg its pardon for cutting it down. Then before cutting the branches off, the men give it a drink of *tepache* (a fermented pineapple beverage) and spill a little on the ground after the first twenty blows to make it forget its pain. And some of them sing, play, and dance until it falls. The cutting off of the branches, the felling and transportation of the trunk are done with the greatest care so that there will be no scars on the tree when it is put up. Whenever it is necessary to stop to rest on the way in, the men sprinkle the trunk with brandy in the middle and at the ends.

"A messenger informs the people at home when the party is to arrive, and many men go outside of the town, to meet them at a place called La Garita. When they reach the plaza, more people are there to welcome them. Church bells ring, rockets burst, and the band plays. Then all are given a festal meal at the home of the moyordomo, but before going there, the flyers go to church to pray. Afterwards the tree is also fed, for the hole in which it is to stand is blessed with holy water and in it is placed an offering of food, drinks, and smokes so that it may be content and not claim the life of a flyer" (Toor, 321).

On August 14, 1966, *Excelsior*, a Mexico City newspaper, reported the death of two dancers and the serious injuries of two others when the four performers fell from a pole during a visit to a state fair at Saltillo, Coahuila. The head of the group claimed that the accident was due to the lack of the accustomed religious ceremony honoring the pole before the dance: ". . . the base of the tree should be sprinkled with the blood of a hen and a liter of mezcal liquor, but they could not get a hen and poured only the mezcal into the hole. . . . The leader insists that the accident was due to this."

dignitaries, dressed up in their pontifical robes (as these are called), carried forth a little girl seven or eight years old in a covered litter, so completely shrouded that she was invisible to all eyes, in the same way that the lords had carried the boy we mentioned to the hill. In the same manner the priests carried this girl on their shoulders enclosed within the covered litter. She was dressed in blue, representing the great lake and other springs and creeks. On her head she wore a garland of red leather, and on top was a bow-knot with a blue tuft of feathers. The little girl was carried within the covered litter into the forest and was set down. Then a drum was brought forth, and everyone was seated, without dancing; then they sang various chants before the girl. This chanting lasted until news arrived that the lords had completed their offerings and sacrifices on the mountain and were now ready to board their canoes. Having received this news, [the people] took the child in her litter and sent her off in a canoe. At the same time the great tree was removed, its branches were bound again, [and] it was placed on a raft in the water. The music and singing did not cease, and innumerable canoes [filled with] women, men, and children [who desired to] see the feast went along with her to the middle of the lake, swiftly. Then they arrived at the place called Pantitlan, where the lake had its drain. (Occasionally a tremendous whirlpool appears when the water is sucked down.) In this way many canoes are in peril because of carelessness and lack of knowledge as they pass on the surface.

When the great lords on one hand and those of the city on the other had arrived at that place, the great tree called Tota was taken and was thrust into the mud next to the spring or drain. Its branches were untied, and it filled out again. Then [the people] took the child within the litter and slit her throat with a small spear (used for killing ducks), and her blood was allowed to flow into the water. Once [the blood] had flowed, she was cast into the waters, right into the whirlpool. It is said that the latter swallowed her so that she was never seen again. After the little girl had been cast in, the sovereigns came to make offerings, one after the other, and so did the lords. They offered as many rich things (such as jewels, stones, necklaces, and bracelets) as had been given on the mountain. These were thrown into the lake in the same place where the girl had been cast. Here each year such quantities of gold, stones, and jewels were cast that it was a marvelous thing to see.

Today some people think that the great treasure of Moteczoma was thrown by the Indians into that spring. [The treasure] disappeared when this land was conquered, during the feast which took place while Don Hernando Cortés was reorganizing [his forces] in Tlaxcala. The spring has been stopped up with mud and bog, for it was not cleaned as it had been when sacrifice was offered there.

[The sacrifice] and offerings terminated, together with the other ceremonies, [such as that of] setting up the tree Tota, the music ended, and so did the singing and all the other festivities. In grave silence all returned to the city. In this way the feast ended. But the ceremonies did not, since the peasants and the common men continued them in their tilling and sowing in the fields, in the rivers, springs, and streams. And since it is very important [to consider this point], I will leave [my warning] for its proper place. It is a most important warning, which must be given so that the ministers and confessors will be on their guard and keep clear consciences. [These ceremonies] are performed today, and I have found them very common, especially in the towns near mountains.

The tree of which I spoke was left fixed there until it rotted and fell. And since each year they set up a new tree, it is said that there were so many dried ones next to the spring that finally they had to place them farther away owing to lack of space. This is true because I remember that, on crossing the lake by canoe many times, I saw the great hoary tree trunks rising out of the water. And since I have always been curious and fond of asking questions, I wished to discover [what these trees were]. I was told that they were trees which had been there in olden times, and inasmuch as I was unaware of their true origin, I believed them to have been trees which had grown there, until I came to discover their true significance. I believe that today there are still remains of them; the natives say that if that spring could be dredged and cleaned one would find many precious things, such as gold, silver, jewels, stones, and notable signs and vestiges of ancient sacrifice.

I do not wish to create confusion because of the many versions I was told of this account. Some say that it was a drain. Others disagree, [saying] that it was a spring and that during the rainy season a great quantity of water burst forth, filling the entire City of Mexico and its canals with water, almost flooding all the towns which stood on the beaches and shores [of the lake], and occasionally the water rose as far as their homes. This is affirmed by those from Chimalhuacan-Atenco and from Chicoloapan and by those from all the small towns on the slopes of the mountains next to the lake as far as Tetzcoco. Today they wonder how each year there can be less [water and not more]. If it were not for the rivers and great springs that flow into [the lake] and feed it, it is believed that it would have dried up.[3] Those who claim that this depression in the water was a spring base their reasoning upon these things. [They say that] it dries up because it is not dredged; therefore, the main spring has become blocked and is drying up. [They say] that if it were cleaned out again the city would be in great danger, for the canals which existed in Mexico in pagan times (and they were many) are stopped up, and the water would find no place to flow, and therefore a flood would take place.

Those who have an opposite opinion (that it was a suction drain) say that the springs of the Marquesado proceed from here and that experiments have shown this clearly. Furthermore, another reason is given—that which miners claim—that it burst forth under the earth and goes to the City of Mexico. Thus the water is found so close to the surface where everyone digs, and the swallowing up of the little girl shows that it was a suction drain.

[3] Durán's speculations about the rise and fall of the waters of the Basin of Mexico remain unproved. The enigma of the workings of the volcanic clefts under the soil of Mexico City and of the movements of the subterranean waters have never been satisfactorily mapped. An example is the lake village of Mixquic, near Xochimilco. In 1955 its canals and ponds almost completely dried up. The villagers, distraught at the sight of parched cornfields and vegetable plots, prayed for the water to return. On May 3, the Feast of the Holy Cross, a sizable spout of water erupted near the village and has since continued to grow. On May 3 of each year visitors to Mixquic can observe the thanksgiving ceremonies of the villagers.

This reason, however, is not satisfactory, because, when the water seized the child, there might have been trickery and falseness among the priests who were the deceivers. Their only concern was to make the common people believe that the idols performed miracles and wonders so that they would be held in greater fear and reverence. Because these people are more moved by what they see than by what they hear, great devotees of doubting Thomas and of seeing and believing, like their forebears the Jews, who beseeched Christ for signs in the heavens. Therefore, [the natives] saw that the sacrificed child (offered to the god Tlaloc and in the name of the lake), once thrown into the water, was swallowed, never to appear again as is customary with bloated corpses. They did not realize that those cursed ministers of the devil must have attached stones to them so that they would go to the bottom. They believed so strongly that the God of the Water ate her and carried her with him that even today it has been difficult for me to persuade them to the contrary, since they say that as soon as the little girl was cast into the water it made a mighty sound. And when it swallowed her, the water produced, together with this sound, a great whirlpool. Since this is not a matter of Faith, it is easy to believe that each one [of the Indians] in his own way believes that his good judgment carries weight and the appearance of the truth. I will say that those who navigate this lake today flee from that place and do not dare to pass it. They remember the many disasters which occurred to those who crossed this place and the calamities which happen when someone drowns here; therefore, it is necessary to pass [the lake] at night through fear of the tempests and the winds which rise upon it during the day.

There is a remarkable thing about this lake. Many times it becomes angry and turbulent in that place, even though there is no wind. There the water boils and froths; according to my conjectures regarding its cause, it seems to be that spring or vent in the lake. [This whole opening] is stopped up with mud, and the water and air are held back so that they cannot emerge and follow their course, as they would wish. These two elements react violently and must be the cause of that strange movement and great winds in the lake. As an eyewitness I swear that I shall tell the truth about what happened to me and another friar in the midst [of the lake]. One morning we were navigating peacefully and quietly, when suddenly, without any air or wind from any direction, there arose a hurricane and a movement so strange that we thought we would drown. When I asked the rowers who carried us (who were no less frightened, terrified, than we) the reason for that unexpected tempest or hurricane without wind or warning of it, they answered that it was the air below which sought an exit. [They added that] this happened quite often. I understand it to be as I have described: that the air in the pores of the earth in that region causes this movement, which escapes through the water; it is not much, but it creates earthquakes and shakes the world.

In order to understand the humbug, the fable, regarding the origin of Our Mother, the Lake,[4] I wish to repeat what was told to me in all seriousness by certain solemn old men. When I asked them what they knew about the origin of the lake or their thoughts on the subject, they answered the following: "It comes from the sea." I asked them the reasons and circumstances that made them think thus, and they said to me:

> The kings of ancient times, desirous of knowing the origins of this lake, endeavored in the most serious manner to discover and clarify this [point], especially as they saw [the lake] ebb and flow; sometimes it was one color, sometimes another. They sent men to many regions [to investigate the origins of the lake]. It is said that near the coast they saw a river that came out of the sea, which soon sank [into the ground], as it does today. In order to discover where this river would reappear, they cast into the hole a heavy, smooth, round gourd, all filled with cotton and tightly closed to keep out the water. Once they had tossed it in, they sent the news to Mexico so that [everyone] would watch to see if the gourd appeared somewhere on

4 Our Mother, the Lake is surely a translation of the Nahuatl Tonanhueyatl, referring to the mother goddess. The lake, giving moisture to the cornfields and teeming with edible things such as algae, mosquito eggs, water plants, shrimp, fish of a dozen varieties, frogs, ducks, and other birds, such as wading birds, was really the mother of ancient Mexico-Tenochtitlan. The Aztecs saw her as Our Lady Tonan, who suckled her favorite children with her lake milk.

the lake or in some river or spring. Many observers and searchers were placed around the lake and after some days they found the gourd floating on top of the water in the great lake.

This is possible and may well be believed, since the water speaks for itself, its origins, and vegetation. For one thing, it is salty, thick, and dirty; at times it is clear, at others it is turbid. Sometimes it is blue, sometimes green, at other times very black. It is water where fish do not breed, and all [fish] from fresh waters or springs that enter it immediately die and are cast to the shore. [The lake] brings little health to Mexico with its bad vapors and stench, especially in the dry season.

I have brought up all of this in order to explain the sacrifice performed to the lake on the day of [the festival] of Tlaloc. This day, as we have seen, was most solemn, festive, and—if we well consider the care and attentiveness with which these people solemnized it—the toil of going to and coming from the mountain, of going to and coming from the lake, the offering of so many precious and fine things, the sacrifice of one's own sons and daughters, the service to the devil day and night on hills and cliffs without failing to carry out the rites of any year—it is grievously disturbing to us to behold the laxity and lukewarmness, the cracks and failings with which we serve our True God. Yet we still permit Him to be served more in the worldly sense than in the spiritual one. We calm our consciences with the appearance of "Christians" which the Indians feign for us. We make no effort to uproot tares which are mixed with the wheat. Truly, it perplexes us and causes great shame to know that, though the devil was served with such painstaking care night and day, we now allow the great bounty of our True God and Lord to be received with such laxity and negligence. He is revered, believed in, and worshiped without diligence, care, and life (for we have the obligation to give this for His love) so that His name is hallowed and so that His holy law and faith is kept. We try to extirpate the deceitful, lying faith and error of these wretched people in which they still deposit and place their trust. This faith is a lie and deceitful falseness! And [yet] what we teach them is the eternal and highest truth and blessedness!

In regard to all of this, those who deal [with the natives] and have intercourse with them should know the language well and understand them if they have any pretense of obtaining fruit. [On this understanding depends] the salvation and life of the soul, or the damnation of one and the other. And [the ministers] should not conform by saying that they know a little bit of the tongue in order to hear confession and that is enough, for this is an intolerable error; for the Sacrament it is necessary to have more knowledge and understanding of [the language] than for any other [rite], in order to examine the tangled consciences of penitents who have been hiding idolatry for many years.

Let it not be that the prelates fall into such a great error as to say that the minister knows enough of the language to confess a sick man and so give him the Sacrament.

I repeat: it is a great error, because of the small intelligence of the Indians, because it is necessary to speak to the sick man on his deathbed in his own language, to have good persuasion, and to explain that the Sacrament he receives contains, as a mediator, the Passion of Christ and His Precious Blood. [It should be explained to him] that he will receive remission and pardon for all his sins, and he must be filled with the fear that if he does not reveal his sins he will go to Hell. Sometimes the sick person, filled with dread and fully persuaded, will make known that which he has hidden for forty or fifty years; this has happened and it continues to happen constantly.

Let those who are in charge of this most important endeavor take care, for the love of Christ crucified! It is not enough that they are mediocre translators. [Their obligation is] to preach, to explain the mysteries of the Faith, and to teach them the truth; but they will preach only errors and lies [if they do not have a true understanding of the language]. All of this [ignorance] is harmful and bad for the consciences of those who order these things to be done without great certainty. I wonder at some persons who are so sure of themselves that they take charge of these things. They eat, they drink, they sleep unheedingly as if they had no obligation to give God an accounting for those who, because of their own faults, go to Hell. They are satisfied with two useful words. They are *tleitoca* ["What do you call this?"] and *igualaz* ["It's coming."]. These are the first words learned by the conquerors when they came to this land, together with others so crude and rough that the Indians not only laugh at them, mock them, and scorn them but [hardly] understand them or know their meaning.

CHAPTER IX

¶Which treats of the great feast called Tlacaxipehual-iztli, which means Skinning of Men, on which day was honored an idol known as Totec, Xipe, and Tlatlauhquit-ezcatl. Under these three names he was adored as a Trinity. He was also known as Tota, Topiltzin, and Yolometl, which mean Father, Son, and the Heart of Both, honored at this feast.[1]

ON March 20, one day after the date on which our Holy Church keeps the feast of the glorious Saint Joseph, the Indians of this land performed a most solemn, festive, bloody ceremony, which cost so many human lives that no other rivaled it. It was called Tlacaxipe-hualiztli, which means Skinning of Men, and was the first feast of the year within the number of their calendar, celebrated every twenty days. Besides being one of the feasts within this number, during its course was honored an idol which, though one, was adored under three names. In spite of these three names it was adored as one, very much as we believe in the Most Holy Trinity, who is three distinct persons and One True God. So it was that these

---

[1] Totec means Our Lord; Xipe means the Flayed One, and Tlatlauhquitezcatl signifies Red Mirror. The three names describe some of the attributes of Tezcatlipoca, the Smoking Mirror, the god who delighted in playing pranks on mankind. Tota means Our Father; Topiltzin is Our Lord, Our Prince, or Our Child. Yolometl is derived from the word *yolotl*, "heart." In his endeavors to relate the religion of the Aztecs to Christianity, Durán overemphasized the superficial similarities between the Trinity and three of the attributes of the Aztec divinity in whose name this feast was held.

blind people believed that this idol was one being under the names of Totec-Xipe-Tlatlauhquitezcatl. It will be necessary to explain these names in order to understand their meaning. All the ceremonies and solemnities were prepared in honor of these three names and of each one in particular.

The first name is Totec. At the beginning its meaning seemed obscure to me, and I was filled with doubts. After asking questions again and again, I finally discovered that it means Awesome and Terrible Lord Who Fills One with Dread.

The second is Xipe, which means Man Who Has Been Flayed and Ill-treated.[2]

[2] Xipe, the Flayed One, is one of the most ancient gods of Mexico, rivaled in antiquity only by Tonantzin, Earth Mother; Tlaloc, God of Water; Huehueteotl, Old God of Fire; and Quetzalcoatl, Feathered Serpent. Archaeologists have discovered clay figurines of Xipe in Teotihuacan II culture, dating to about A.D. 100. An astonishing number of small clay statuettes representing Xipe are found today by Mexican peasants in the area once dominated by the Aztecs. Probably Xipe's only rival in number of figurines is Tonantzin.

Some of the scholars who have studied this divinity and his strange ceremonial have concluded that the cult was essentially an agricultural rite in which the skin of the victim represented the husk of an ear of corn about to ripen. Xipe was also God of Spring; a famous sculpture in the National Museum of Anthropology of Mexico shows him clad in a human skin covered with flowers. Like the classical Prosperpine who appeared in the springtime, Xipe clad the earth with new vegetation.

The theme of Xipe is expressed in a masterly way in the following Aztec poem, recorded in Nahuatl in the European alphabet shortly after the Conquest:

OUR LORD THE FLAYED, THE DRINKER BY NIGHT: HIS SONG

> Thou, Night-drinker,
> Why must we beseech thee?
> Put on they disguise:
> They golden garment, put it on!
>
> My God, thy jade water descended.
> The cypress is become a quetzal-bird:
> The fire-snake is become a quetzal-snake
> And has left me.
>
> It may be, it may be, that I go to destruction;
> I the tender maize plant,
> My heart is jade
> But I shall yet see gold there.
> I shall rejoice if it ripen early.
> "The war-chief is born."

(continued)

The third name, Tlatlauhquitezcatl, signifies Mirror of Fiery Brightness. He was not a local god commemorated here or there; his feast was observed in the entire land. Every one did honor to him because he was a universal god, and thus a special temple was dedicated to him with all the honor and magnificence befitting such a deity.

On his feast more men were slain than on any other because it was the most popular of all the solemnities. Even in the most wretched villages and in the wards of the towns men were sacrificed, to the point that the more I write and ask the more I am astonished to learn of so many rational human beings who died throughout the entire land each year, sacrificed to the devil. We may affirm that more were killed this way on those days than [there were] those who died a natural death. In order to prove my point, I wish the reader who wants to make comparisons to study this, and he will see that I am right. Let him observe that only on this day Tlacaxipehualiztli (for that is the name of the feast we describe here) in Mexico City alone at least sixty persons were slain. And if he travels through all the provinces, cities, and kingdoms, he will learn that on this single day a thousand or more men were sacrificed. All these numbers do not include the other feasts, none of which took place without the killing of men and women.

The image or figure of this idol was of stone, about as tall as a man. His mouth was open like a man speaking. He was dressed in the skin of a sacrificed man, and on his wrists hung the hands of the skin. In his right hand he carried a staff, at the end of which were attached some rattles. In his left hand he carried a shield decorated with yellow and red feathers, and from the handle emerged a small red banner with feathers at the end. Upon his head was a red headdress with a ribbon, also red. This was tied in an elaborate bow on

---

My God, let there be abundance of maize-plants
In a few places at least.
Thy worshipper turns his gaze to thy mountain,
Toward thee.
I shall rejoice if it ripen early.
"The war-chief is born."

(Barlow, 1963, 186)

his forehead, and in the middle of this bow was a golden jewel. On his back hung another headdress with three small banners protruding, from which were suspended three red bands in honor of the three names of this deity. He also wore an elaborate, splendid breechcloth, which seemed to be part of the human skin in which he was attired. This was the dress he always wore; it was never changed or altered [Plate 15].

Forty days before the feast the people dressed a man as a representation of the idol with his same adornments, so that this live Indian slave should be an image of the idol. Once he had been purified, they honored and glorified him during the forty days, exhibiting him in public as if he had been the god himself. The same was done in each ward, and these wards were like our parishes. Thus they had the name and avocation of the idol who made his home there; this was the church of the ward. In each ward and on each feast they also dressed a slave in the same manner; he was attired in the main temple so that he represented the deity. This was not done on all the feasts of the year. Thus, if twenty wards existed, twenty men went about impersonating this god of the entire land. Each ward honored and revered this man who personified the deity, just as in the main temple. I understand that on this feast all the gods were honored as one. In order to demonstrate this, I will state that when the dawn of the feast day arrived, the man who for forty days was the live representation of the god was brought out. After him came the impersonator of the sun, then one disguised as Huitzilopochtli, then Quetzalcoatl, then Macuilxochitl, then Chililico, then Tlacahuepan, then Ixtliltzin, then Mayahuel.[3] All of these

---

[3] It is probable that the costume of the man representing Quetzalcoatl was that of the god in his attribute as Ehecatl, God of Wind, including the famous conical hat and duck beak.

Macuilxochitl bore the calendrical name Five Flower. He was also known as Xochipilli, Flowery Prince, and his worship was intimately connected with that of Xipe. This Dionysus-like deity was thought to bring venereal disease to mankind. He was also the patron of gamblers.

According to Sahagún, Chililico was one of the shrines of the nobility in the Great Temple of Mexico.

Tlacahuepan was a divine and semilegendary personage associated with the war god Huitzilopochtli. Sahagún described Tlacahuepan as one of the wicked men

were the most important deities of the main wards. One after another they were slain, their hearts being torn out in the usual way; these were then raised with uplifted hand toward the east. Then they were cast into a place called Zacapan, which means On the Straw, where the sacrificer of the gods stood. While he stood there next to the hearts, the people made offerings. They gave bunches of ears of corn, such as those the Indians still hang from the beams of the ceiling, just as Spaniards hang bunches of grapes. Before I forget, I wish to state that these suspended ears of corn are a superstition, a remnant of the ancient idolatry and offerings. They were offered there and had to be placed upon green leaves from the sapota tree. In all of this there was much mystery and superstition. After the god impersonators had been sacrificed, all of them were skinned very rapidly in the way I have described. When the heart had been removed and offered to the east, the skinners (whose task it was) cast the dead body down and split it from the nape of the neck to the heel, skinning it as a lamb. The skin came off complete. After the skinning had taken place, the flesh was given to the man who had owned the slave. Other men donned the skins immediately and then took the names of the gods who had been impersonated. Over the skins they wore the garments and insignia of the same divinities, each man bearing the name of the god and considering himself divine. So it was that one faced the east, another the west, another the north, and still a fourth the south; and each one walked in that direction toward the people. Each of these had tied to him certain men as if they were his prisoners, thus showing his might. This ceremony was called Neteotoquiliztli, which means Impersonation of a God.[4]

---

who caused the destruction of the glorious Tula, or Tollan, capital city of the Toltecs. Tlacahuepan was a name commonly given to Aztec noblemen. One heroic son of the Emperor Axayacatl (who ruled from 1469 to 1481) was called Tlacahuepan, and as late as 1566 a Pedro Tlacahuepantzi, Lord of Tula, requested certain favors of King Philip II of Spain.

Ixtliltzin, also known as Ixtlilton, the Little Black-Faced One, was one of the four hundred divinities of wine and drunkenness.

Mayahuel was the goddess of the century plant, or maguey cactus, from which the natives extracted the juice now known as *aguamiel* and made pulque, the native wine of ancient and modern Mexico.

176

This rite, which showed that all constituted one power and one unity, then ended, and the gods came together. The right foot of one was tied to the left foot of the man next to him, the legs bound up to the knee. Tied in this manner, they spent the rest of the day supporting each other. In this way, as I have explained, they demonstrated their equality, conformity, their power and unity. Still tied, they were taken to a place of sacrifice, which was called *cuauhxicalli*, a smooth and plastered courtyard measuring about seven yards around. In this enclosure stood two stones; one was called *temalacatl*, which means "stone wheel"; and the other *cuauhxicalli*, which means wooden tub or eagle vessel. These two round stones were fixed within that courtyard one next to the other.[5]

Then appeared four men wearing armor, two wearing tiger [jaguar] devices and the others wearing eagle devices, the four carrying their shields and swords in their hands. Those who bore the device of the jaguar were known as the Great Jaguar and the Little Jaguar. In the same way those who were clad with the device of the eagle were called Great Eagle and the Little Eagle. These four surrounded the men dressed as gods. Then all the dignitaries of the temples appeared in order. They had brought a drum with them and commenced the chant of the feast and of the idol, whereupon an ancient man dressed in the skin of a mountain lion made his appearance. Four men came with him—one dressed in white, another in green, another in yellow, and yet another in red; these were known as the Four Dawns. With them came the gods Ixcozauhqui and Titlacahuan.[6] The old man put them in a certain place, and, having set them there, he brought forth one of the prisoners

[4] Neteotoquiliztli appears in Molina's Nahuatl dictionary as *neteomachtlaniliztli*, "the desire to be regarded as a god."

[5] The cuauhxicalli was generally a tub in which human hearts were placed after sacrifice.

The *temalacatl* was a stone wheel upon which gladiatorial sacrifice took place. Probably the most famous such wheel is that of the Aztec Emperor Tizoc (who ruled from 1481 to 1486), now in the National Museum of Anthropology of Mexico. Carved in relief, it shows the ruler's conquests in various provinces.

[6] According to Sahagún, Ixcozauhqui was one of the attributes of Xiuhtecuhtli, the Fire God. Titlacahuan was one of the numerous attributes of Tezcatlipoca, He Whose Slaves We Are.

to be sacrificed, making him ascend the *temalacatl* stone. This stone had a hole carved in its center, and from this emerged a rope four yards long, the rope called *centzonmecatl*.[7] The prisoner was tied by one foot with this rope and was given a shield and a feathered sword in his hand.[8] The victim carried a vessel of Teooctli, Divine Wine, which he was forced to drink.[9] At the feet of the naked[10] captive the elder set four wooden balls with which he was to defend himself. The old man, known as the Old Mountain Lion, withdrew. Then, to the throbbing of the drum and in the midst of the chanting, the man called Great Jaguar came out, dancing with his shield and sword, as he approached the bound prisoner. The latter picked up the wooden balls and hurled them down. But the Great Jaguar, being skillful, intercepted the blows with his shield. When the balls

[7] Literally, "four hundred strands," so called because the rope was elaborately woven. It has not been established to which part of the stone the rope was attached.

[8] By "sword" Durán is referring to the macana, a long stick edged with razor-sharp blades made of obsidian.

[9] Teooctli, the Divine Wine, Authentic Wine, Real Wine, or Wine of the Gods, is mentioned more than once in Durán's works, but exclusively in connection with men who were about to endure a terrible fate, such as the Tlacaxipehualiztli, the Skinning of Men, and other sacrificial ceremonies. This wine, made primarily of fermented juice of the maguey, gave valor to those who were about to die. It is difficult today to determine the other ingredients of the drink. Numerous drugs were common to ancient Mexico. Some of them, such as peyotl, or peyote (a mescal button which when chewed produces visions), *teonanacatl* (the "divine mushroom," which is eaten in pairs and produces ecstasy and wild dreams), and other plants may have been used in preparing the Divine Wine. The most likely ingredient was peyotl, which for centuries has been used to dull the senses and give courage and hardiness. Today the bulb is well known to the Huichols of Nayarit, the Tarahumaras of Chihuahua, and certain tribes in the southwestern United States. The Huichols carry out an arduous forty-day pilgrimage to the deserts of San Luis Potosi to pick this wild cactus. The bulbs are chewed on the way back to help the men withstand fatigue, hunger, and thirst on the journey, and the witch doctor and many of his followers are almost insensible by the time they have returned to their village. The drug is also used on long religious pilgrimages. Those who have used peyote report amazing visual sensations, such as cubic patterns, spirals, and remarkable color visions. Aldous Huxley has recorded his sensations to the drug in *Doors of Perception*.

To judge from prohibitive decrees issued by the Spanish viceroys during the colonial period, several such stimulants were added to pulque.

Pre-Hispanic drugs are still used in Mexico, among them peyote and *teonanacatl* (*Amanita muscaria*).

[10] By "naked," Durán usually means clad only in a loincloth.

were gone, the wretched prisoner took hold of his shield and wielded his sword, defending himself from the Great Jaguar, who sought to wound him. However, since one was armed and the other naked, since one carried a sword inlaid with blades while the other had only a feathered stick, after a few turns around [the stone] the captive was wounded on his leg, thigh, arms, or head. And so, once he had been smitten, to the sounding of the trumpets, shells and flutes, the prisoner fell.

After he had fallen, the sacrificers came to untie him and carried him to the other stone, which, as we have said, was called *cuauhxicalli*. There they opened his breast, took out his heart, and offered it to the Sun, hand on high. Twenty or thirty prisoners were sacrificed in the manner I have narrated. Old Mountain Lion brought them forth one by one and bound them for the contest, and the four Jaguars and Eagles were always present so that when one was weary another could take his place. If one became tired and the prisoners were many, the men called the Four Dawns would come to their aid. These were to fight with the left hand. Since this was their occupation, they were as skillful in fencing and wounding with their left hands as with their right. The captive who was being attacked was permitted to wound and to kill in defense of his life against his aggressors. And in truth, some of the prisoners were so spirited and dexterous that occasionally they would kill the Great or the Little Jaguar, or the Great or the Little Eagle. With the balls they cast or with the shield or the wooden sword which they held in their hands, they defended themselves bravely. Some managed to escape from the rope with which they were bound, and once free they attacked the adversary, and both would be slain. This occurred when the prisoner was a great man who had been a captain in the war in which he had been captured. Yet others were so fainthearted, so cowardly, that as soon as they were bound they lost all spirit, crouched, and allowed themselves to be wounded.

This combat lasted until all the captives had been sacrificed. Every one of them was forced to go through this rite, which was called Tlahuahuanaliztli. This means Marking or Scratching with the Sword. In our own language it could be called *toque* [*touché*], as in fencing with harmless swords. Thus he who fought the prisoner, when he had drawn blood from the foot, hand, head, or some other part of the body, withdrew. Then the musical instruments sounded, and the wounded man was sacrificed. In this way those who were tied, with spirit and adroitness, took care not to be wounded quickly, in order to prolong their lives. In the end, however, they were slain. This combat and sacrificial rite lasted all day, and forty, fifty, or more men would die in this manner. This does not include those who were killed in the wards, all of whom had represented the god. All these things cause compassion, pity, and great sorrow!

The entire city was present at this spectacle, which was celebrated at the temple of the god where that sacrifice was offered. It was a special temple, an elaborate one, for its height as well as for the varied kinds of sacrificial stones. The shrine or hall where this idol was kept was small but richly decorated. In front of this room was a stuccoed courtyard some seven or eight yards square. There stood the two fixed stones; to ascend to them there were four small stairways consisting of four steps each. On one was painted the image of the Sun and on the others the count of the years, months, and days. Many rooms surrounded this courtyard. In these were kept the skins of those who had been flayed during the forty days. At the end of this time they were buried in a vault or cellar which was at the foot of the stairs. One of the stones which I have mentioned stood where sacrifices were begun, and the other where the sacrifice ended. Many of us today have some knowledge regarding them, and one of the stones was in the main square of the city for a long time. It stood next to the canal where today an open-air market is held in front of the Royal Mansion.[11]

Here a large number of Negroes formerly gathered continually to sport and to commit atrocities, sometimes killing one another.

---

[11] The Royal Mansion, or Royal Palace, was originally the residence of Moteczoma II. The land occupied by this complex of buildings, situated in the heart of Mexico City, was granted to Cortés by the king of Spain in 1529. The heirs of the conqueror sold the property to the Spanish government in 1562, and it was there that the Viceregal Palace was constructed. Today this enormous building is the National Palace of the Federal Government of Mexico.

That is why the Most Illustrious and Reverend Lord Fray Alonso de Montúfar, of holy and laudable memory, Most Worthy Archbishop of Mexico of the Dominican Order, had it buried, in view of the crimes and homicides committed there.[12]

The second stone was the one that has been unearthed for the second time at the site where the Cathedral of Mexico City is being constructed. This stone now stands at the western doorway of the church. The ancients called this the "basin," because it had a concavity in the center and a channel through which ran the blood of the victims, which were more numerous than the hairs on my head. I would like to see this stone removed from the doorway of the church.[13] And once the old cathedral is torn down and the new one is erected, we should also remove the stone serpents which serve as the bases of the columns. These used to stand near the courtyard of Huitzilopochtli.[14]

In front of the Royal Palace was the huge main square of the city, the Zocalo, which then served as a market place. Immediately south of the palace lay another market place, where the Aztecs held one of their most important ceremonies, the flying-pole dance.

[12] The Negroes mentioned by Durán were African slaves, who apparently fought like gladiators upon this stone after the Aztecs themselves had ceased doing so. Possibly the slaves' Spanish masters were also present, enjoying the bloody spectacle and betting on the participants.

[13] It is likely that this stone is the Stone of Tizoc, now in the National Museum of Anthropology of Mexico.

[14] The columns of the primitive Cathedral of Mexico City, carved from pre-Hispanic sculptures, still stand at the southwestern corner of the atrium of the present-day church. In 1964 the Municipal Government built a low stone platform for these relics of ancient times, which today surround a bronze bust of Cuauhtemoc. On entering the crypt where the archbishops are buried, the visitor to the Cathedral of Mexico finds the sarcophagus of Juan de Zumárraga, first bishop of Mexico (1527–48), inlaid with a large Aztec death's-head carved in stone. In a sense this great crypt, conceived by Luis Maria Martínez, archbishop of Mexico from 1936 to 1958, and situated under the Royal Altar of the cathedral, unifies the Aztec and Roman Catholic worlds of Mexico.

When Durán wrote these observations, it had been decided to replace the original cathedral, erected shortly after the Conquest, with a new and much larger one. Though Philip II ordered the construction of the new building in 1573, it was not until 1626 that the original cathedral was torn down, long after Durán's death. Thus Durán can only have known by hearsay of the pagan motifs hidden inside the columns. Fortunately, his hopes for the total destruction of pre-Hispanic sculptures were not destined to be fulfilled.

I happen to know of old men and women who have gone there to weep over these relics because of the destruction of their temple. I trust that in His goodness our God has not permitted those Indians to go there to adore the stones and not God.[15]

In honor of this feast a ritual food was eaten. This consisted of tortillas and tamales, both made of corn dough mixed with honey and beans. It was forbidden to eat any other bread, since it was considered a sacrilege and against the Divine Commandments.

After the rites I described previously, all those who had represented the gods dressed in human skins departed, after the priests had removed these skins, washed them with their own hands, and hung them with great reverence upon rods. Very early the next day men would go to ask the owner of the slaves who had been skinned if they could borrow the skins in order to go begging. The owner then ordered that they be lent to the beggers. Poor people would do this in all the wards: borrow the skins, put them on, and over these wear the garments of the god Xipe. They then went about the city and in each of the wards solicited alms from door to door. [The numbers of] these mendicants were twenty or twenty-five, depending upon the number of wards. They were not supposed to meet each other anywhere, in a home, on the street, or at crossroads, because if they encountered one another they were supposed to attack, assault, one another, fight until the skin and clothing had been torn. This was a statute, an ordinance of the temples. So the men avoided encountering one another, and because of this were accompanied by little boys who followed them. Others spied for them and carried the gifts which they had gathered. Regarding these gifts there was a superstition: no one could refuse the beggars —everyone was obliged to give something, be it little or much. The gifts usually consisted of numerous ears of corn, squash, beans, and many seeds, according to the wealth of each person. Some would also offer bread, meat, pumpkin cooked in honey. Others

[15] This pathetic Indian pilgrimage to the ruins of the Aztec holy city is reminiscent of the Jews' pilgrimages to the Wailing Wall of Jerusalem. Perhaps Durán, preoccupied with his theories about the Jewish origins of the Indians, associated the two rites.

gave bread that had been left over from the previous day. Still others, such as the lords and nobles, gave more costly things: mantles, loincloths, sandals, featherwork, and jewelry. All of this was gathered in the temple. When the twenty days dedicated to begging ended, the mendicants divided the alms with the owner of the slave whose skin they had borrowed. In this way many indigents helped themselves in their poverty. Every night each beggar had to return his skin to the temple, where it was kept in a special room. And every morning each one went to pick it up.[16]

As the beggars passed along the streets, women bearing children in their arms approached them, asking for their blessing, just as the people today request the blessing of the monks. The Xipes took the children in their arms and muttered certain words over them. They went about the courtyard of the house four times and then gave the child back to the mother, who offered alms to the beggar. Once the twenty days in honor of the god—similar to one of our octaves—passed, the almsgiving ceased. A ceremony was celebrated on this day; the skins were buried, stripped from those who had worn them. The people placed a drum in the middle of the market place, and all the old soldiers and their captains who had captured the victims in war were present. Each was adorned with new insignia, and they carried prizes given them by the king. Each was attired in his net mantle. The warriors danced around the skin-clad beggars. During that feast, which lasted twenty days, one or two skins were removed each day. The men ate and drank during this festivity, and their hearts were gladdened. When the time had come to remove the skins, they stank, were black, abominable, nauseating, and ghastly to behold.

After these forty solemn and festive days had passed, the skins were taken to the very temple of the god Xipe. There they were buried at the foot of the steps in an underground place, or vault, which had a movable stone doorway. With much chanting and cere-

[16] The pattern of institutionalized begging from house to house is universal and has many modern parallels in Mexico—and in the United States on Halloween, when children dressed in costume go from door to door begging. The house owner, like the Aztec citizen of antiquity, feels obliged to give "little or much" food.

mony the skins, considered sacred, were then buried. Everyone in the land attended this burial, each man in his own temple; and when the ceremony had ended, a great sermon was pronounced by one of the dignitaries. This speech was filled with rhetoric and metaphors, delivered in the most elegant language. In this sermon the orator referred to our human misery, our low state, and to how much we owe to Him who created us. He advised everyone to live a quiet, peaceful life. He extolled fear, reverence, modesty, breeding, prudence, civility, submission and obedience, charity toward poor and wandering strangers. The preacher also condemned theft, fornication, adultery, the coveting of another's goods. At the end he extolled many virtues and condemned all evil, just as a Catholic preacher would moralize or preach, with all the fervor in the world. He warned the man who had sinned that he would leave a wicked, evil name in the world and that he would descend to Hell as a perverse man and would be held there as such. He also admonished the good people, encouraged them, and promised them that, if they continued in their good, quiet and pacific lives, the Lord of the Heavens would love them, and they would receive their reward. Each one would depart from this life and go to the other with a good name, and would be honored in the afterlife.[17]

Everything I have described here shows that these people knew something of the Divine Law, the Holy Gospel, and of the Beatitudes, since rewards were promised for a good life and punishment for a wicked one. I interrogated the Indians regarding their ancient preachers, and I myself have written down their sermons, with the same rhetoric and style and metaphors. In reality they were Catholic. When I realized the knowledge the Indians had regarding the Beatitudes, of Eternal Rest and the holy life that must be lived on earth in order to obtain these things, I was amazed. However, all of this was mixed with their idolatry, bloody and abominable, and it tarnished the good. I simply mention these things because I

17 The rewards and punishments in the afterlife described by the temple dignitary may have been distorted by the Christian training of Durán's post-Conquest informants and by Durán's endeavors to connect the Indian religion with Judaism and Christianity. In general, Aztec sources give the impression that the Indian's fate in the hells and heavens of his religion was not the consequence of his conduct on earth.

believe there actually was an evangelist in this land who left the natives this information. I pray therefore to our Lord God, blessed and praised forever, who deigned to save these wretches from their enormous errors and blind servitude. I invoke Him who eliminated these loathsome sacrifices of blood and human hearts offered to the devil. Some of the natives have recognized the benefit which has come to them with the kind Law of God, and these offer praise to the giver of these good things. Let Him be praised forever!

Another feast honoring the sun was celebrated with no less ceremonial or heathen rites than those we have described, and I believe it will give [the reader] as much pleasure as the others. [The feast] will deal with so many rites that I shall be forced [to discuss] it as lengthily as the other chapters. I shall describe numerous ceremonies and sacrifices, together with the splendor of this feast, for it was patronized by illustrious men who belonged to an order of knights who had vowed to end their days in the military career. These were of such gallant, courageous hearts that they were committed to a promise. If, on the battlefield, ten or twelve men fell upon them, they were never to turn their faces or their backs, nor to move their feet [as if in retreat]. It seems to me that if these knights had formed part of the German army the latter would have learned the custom of fighting while remaining motionless; [this position] is described in many historical accounts. This vow, this discipline, was kept and fulfilled so bravely and calmly that [the knights] never budged an inch, willing rather to be torn to pieces on the spot. And because of their dauntless hearts and their bravery they were so highly regarded and loved by their king and lords that those who performed the greatest deeds in war were given honors, large rewards, and titles. Since this festivity belonged to the [Knights of the Sun], it is well that the next chapter conform to the worth that such [great warriors] deserve. In this chapter I shall describe [these things] with the brevity and method that my work requires, and I beg to be pardoned if I dwell too long on the subject.

CHAPTER X

¶Which treats of the feast in honor of the Sun, known as Nauholin.

IN this land there was an order of knights who were dedicated to war. They made a vow and promise to die in the defense of their country and not to flee in the face of ten or twelve [foes] who might attack them. The Sun was their god and leader. They held him to be their patron, as the Spaniards [are led by] St. James.[1] All those who made vows and entered this institution were illustrious and brave men, all sons of knights and lords, the common man being excluded, no matter how brave.

And thus the feast of knights and noblemen was held in honor of their god the Sun, and was called Nauholin, which means Four Motion. With this name it was solemnized according to the high position of the persons whose feast it was. The feast was celebrated twice a year: the first time on March 17 and the other on the second

[1] Durán could give no more effective example than this one in which he compares Nauholin with Saint James, the militant patron saint of Spain. The Aztec armies heard "Santiago y a ellos!" ("Saint James and at them!") thousands of times during the death throes of their nation. According to legend, Saint James won battles for the Spaniards more than once: at Queretaro, and in an earlier fray mentioned in a celebrated passage by Bernal Díaz del Castillo (1939, I:137).

day of December—that is, on the two occasions on which the number Four Motion or Movement fell in the year. To better understand this, it is necessary to know that the native week covered a thirteen-day period and that after the thirteen days had terminated the count from one to thirteen began again. The months contained only twenty days, and for each of these twenty a sign was designated. These signs were twenty, each having its own, just as we say Monday, Tuesday, and so forth. This way the days of the month were indicated, and among them was the sign *ollin*, in the form of a butterfly. When this sign (counting, as they did, the weeks by thirteen) fell on the number four (which occurred only twice a year), the feast called Four Motion was celebrated splendidly, as we shall see.

This military order possessed its own temple and house, finely decorated, containing many halls and chambers. There [the warriors] retired and served the image of the Sun, and although all were married and had their own homes and things to do, they also had within the halls and apartments of that temple prelates and hierarchs to be obeyed, and were governed by their orders. Great numbers of youths were here—boys, sons of the nobility, who had made vows to become members of that knightly order. They were educated there and were taught all forms of warfare with every type of native weapon. This order can be compared to our knights commanders of Spain, some belonging to Saint John, others to [the Order of] Calatrava, others to Saint James. In order to be distinguished from the others, each had his own badge, according to the rank he held within his military order. We could call them the Knights Commanders of the Sun, whose symbol they wore in battle.

This Temple of the Sun stood on exactly the same place now occupied by the [old] Cathedral of Mexico and because of its nature was called Cuacuauhtinchan, which means the House of the Eagles. These titles, Eagles or Jaguars, were used as metaphors to exalt and honor men of great deeds. Thus that temple called the House of the Eagles could just as well have been the House of the Braves, inasmuch as—through a metaphor—their courage was compared to that of the eagle or of the jaguar. Among the birds the eagle is the most valiant, and among the animals the jaguar is the bravest and the most ferocious.

In the upper part of this temple there was a room of medium size next to the courtyard we described in the last chapter; it was about forty by fifty feet and was handsomely stuccoed. On one side of this courtyard stood the hall I have mentioned, and above an altar there hung on the wall a painting done with brush on cloth: the image of the Sun. This figure was in the form of a butterfly with wings and around it a golden circle emitting radiant beams and glowing lines; and the whole chamber was decorated with splendor and magnificence. Approximately forty steps led up to this room.

All the rites performed in the other temples also took place here: the incensing of the image four times day and night [and] the vowing and fulfilling of all the rites of offering and sacrifice done for the other gods. [Special] priests and dignitaries existed for these things with all the usual rights and privileges. They solemnized the festivity in the following manner.

First, on this feast all the people of the city had to fast so strictly and rigorously that not even children or the ailing were allowed to break the fast until the sun had indicated high noon. At this moment the priests and ministers of that temple took up their conch shells and trumpets and summoned the people to the temple. When they had heard this, [the people] came with the greatest haste and respect, as today they come to mass on Sundays. When they had gathered to the sound of the conch shells and trumpets, a captive taken in war [was brought forth], accompanied and surrounded by some of the principal men. His legs were smeared with white stripes; half of his face was [painted] red; white feathers were [placed] on his head. In his hand he carried an elaborate staff with leather bows and ties and white feathers attached to it. In his other hand he bore a shield with five cotton tufts on it. On his back was a small box which contained eagle feathers, red ocher, and pieces of lime plaster, pine incense, and papers striped with rubber. With all these childlike objects they formed a bundle [Plate 16]. The man carried it out on his back, and it was placed it at the foot of the temple steps; and there in a loud voice, so that the whole crowd would hear, [the priests] addressed him:

O Lord,
We beg you to go before our god
In our behalf.
Greet him in our behalf!
Tell him that his children,
The knights and chieftains
Who have remained here [on this earth]
Beg him to remember them.
Let him protect them where he may be!
Let him receive this humble present which we send him.
Give him this staff
So that he use it while walking.
This shield
So that he use it to defend himself.
[Give him these things]
Together with everything you carry in the bundle!

When the man had heard the message he was to deliver, he said, "So be it." They let go of him, and he began his ascent up the steps of the temple, little by little, pausing at each step. He lingered for a while, and, after going up to the next step, he tarried again. He did this according to instructions he had received regarding the time he was to spend on each step. He was also supposed to illustrate the movement of the sun by going up little by little, imitating [the sun's] course here upon the earth. Thus it took him a long time to ascend the steps.

After he had reached the top, [the man] walked to the stone which we call the Cuauhxicalli. He stood upon it. (As we have said, its center was carved with the symbols of the Sun.) Standing there, turning to the image of the sun which hung above the altar in that chamber, he cried out in a loud voice. Now and then turning to the True Sun, he spoke his message.[2]

[2] The message of the sacrificial victim, based on the priests' instructions to him, might be reconstructed as follows:
"O, our God,
Here I am before you.

189

Once he had spoken, four sacrificial ministers ascended the four staircases to the stone (which I have described). They took his staff away from him, his shield, the bundle he carried; they took him by his hands and feet. Then the main sacrificer came up, knife in hand, and slit his throat, commanding him to go up with his message to the True Sun, to the other world. His blood spilled upon that font along its groove. It flowed there, in front of the chamber of the Sun, before the sun painted above the stone which became bloated with that blood.[3] When all the blood had run out, they opened his chest and took out the heart, and holding it up, they presented it to the Sun until its steam had cooled. Thus ended the life of the wretched Messenger of the Sun. And he journeyed with his message to Hell itself, where he bore witness to the terrible blindness of these people.

So this man was offered up. His sacrifice was attended by all the people, who fasted. The hour had been calculated so artfully that by the time the man had finished his ascent to the place of sacrifice it was high noon.

I entreat you in their behalf,
I greet you!
Your children, the knights, and the chieftains
Who are still on this earth—
Remember them!
Protect them from where you are!
Receive, O Sun, this humble present
Which they send you.
Take this staff
For your walking.
Take this shield
To defend yourself.
Take these things,
Together with everything this bundle contains
For they are yours."

[3] The "groove" in the Stone of Tizoc mentioned in this passage did not exist in the pre-Hispanic period. It is likely that in early post-Conquest times the stone was intended to be cut up and used as building material for the primitive cathedral but was too hard and therefore discarded. Fray Diego undoubtedly saw this stone many times while it stood next to the old cathedral and concluded that the groove had served as an outlet for the blood of sacrificial victims.

As soon as his throat had been slit and the rites had been completed, the conch shells and trumpets were blown by the priests of the temple. By this they indicated that everyone could eat and that the interdict and ban of fasting was lifted. Otherwise, the penalty would have been to suffer the wrath of the Sun and dreadful omens and signs of evil for anyone who broke [the rules]; therefore, no one dared break them. When the summons had been heard, everyone went to dine. Some went home, and others who had come from afar, who had brought their food, ate there. While the people ate, the priests were not idle: they took the gift brought by the man who had gone up [the steps]. With his staff and shield this was hung next to the image of the Sun, as trophies. Then they took the sacrificed slave and returned him to his master, and with this flesh the feast was solemnized. The flesh of all those who died in sacrifice was held truly to be consecrated and blessed. It was eaten with reverence, ritual, and fastidiousness—as if it were something from heaven. Commoners never ate it; [it was reserved] for illustrious and noble people.

The common people having dined, summons again were given with the instruments (which are the equivalent of our bells), and everyone went again to the temple to take part in the conclusion of the ceremony. When the temple was full, the noble youths appeared with small blades in one hand and in the other a bunch of thin, smooth wicker reeds, and sat down in rows. On their own persons they practiced a strange sacrifice. With those blades they wounded the fleshy parts of their left arms between the skin and the flesh in such a way that a finger's width would allow the passing of the blade from one part to the other, and through those self-inflicted wounds reeds were passed. One by one they were put in and pulled out on the other side. Covered with blood, [the reed] was cast in front of the image of the sun, and he who extracted the most reeds was considered to be the bravest, the most penitent, the one who was to obtain the greatest glory. This sacrifice was done not only on the feast day. After they had done their penance, [the warriors] went to bathe, the drums were brought out, and a great feast was held, attended only by lords and chieftains. No one else could take part. At this dance these noblemen displayed many finely worked jewels, feathers, and necklaces, all very splendid and magnificent, especially the knights of this order who had brought out the insignia and weapons of their patron the Sun on their shields and featherwork.

In this temple on this day everyone who could presented splendid offerings of all kinds of things. Each one gave generously of what he had, according to his means. They followed this custom of offerings dating from ancient times. In olden times the presenting of offerings was a great pleasure because it filled [the people] with vainglory, just as today they become puffed up [for the same reason]. I hold it certain that few or none make an offering in which the object is offered up exclusively to God. May the Lord grant that I be mistaken, and if my judgment is rash, may He pardon me, because the fact is that they keep back the offering until someone is looking. Often they have [the gift] put away; then suddenly they arrive to place the offering on the altar itself, not at one side (placing the gift in the middle of the altar to attract the attention of the priest, though they could have placed it on the bottom step). Surely all this seems like vainglory to me.

It is also said that when gifts were presented on this day [the people] raised their eyes to the sun, and they invoked the Lord of Created Things with ardent desire and feeling. And I believe that it was an invocation of the Sun, whom they considered to be the Creator and Cause of all things.[4]

Here ends the Feast of the Sun and its knights, whose deeds did not seem too much outside my subject. I felt it convenient to

[4] Syncretism of the old and the new is shown by identification of the Sun with the Christian God in modern Indian Mexico:

Here in Tetelcingo when the Sun rises the old men and women elevate their hands in the direction in which the Sun is dawning and they cry out, "God is now appearing to us! Here he comes to give us light. Aaaaay, Dios . . . !"

At noon they say, "Aaaaay, Dios . . . ! O Lord our God! You are passing over us again! Again you are going to disappear from us."

And when the Sun has set, again the old men and the old women cry out, "Aaaaay, Dios, O Lord our God, you have abandoned us now! You have given us light. Now you have brought darkness to us. Now, watch over us during this night. Watch over us, merciful God." [Icaza, 227]

describe them in the last chapter in order to avoid prolixity in the feast and ceremonies. [I have spoken] briefly, passing over fine points but not essential ones, and all has been told as best as I could extract it from the native language.

CHAPTER XI

¶Which treats of the feats of the Knights of the Sun and how the highest authorities honored them and other braves.

I T has always been a celebrated and common thing among all nations (not only among the polished and civilized but even among the most barbarous) for kings and great lords to honor and favor their personal assistants in their own kingdoms according to the great deeds and merits of their persons. Some rise in dignity through the literary arts, others to privileges and estates through arms. Thus kings, in rewarding the chief men, exalt their own realms, states, and personal authority, for, while the king makes his grandees, the grandees make the king. Through the great rewards they are given (assuming that such honors have been merited by these men or by their ancestors), they receive glory for their deeds and strength. Consequently, as loyal and grateful [subjects], they support their legitimate masters, the monarchs, defending and aiding them with their persons and estates to the point of death itself.

I have brought up these things because I shall now tell of the great care and solicitude which—since the beginning—the monarchs of this land have taken to reward, to remunerate, with notable privileges and ranks, gifts and generous offerings, as well as great prerogatives, liberties, and exemptions, [all given] to their subjects, vassals, and personal assistants of their realms. [These men] were given great honors, good and generous grants, according to their needs and customs; and even though their way of life is lowly, the grants were not so despicable. [They received] hamlets, towns, villages, and material things, gold and silver, jewels and rich stones, precious, valuable featherwork and insignia, articles of dress [such as] fine mantles and breechcloths, all given in recompense for the valorous deeds they had accomplished. [These things were granted] not only to men of lineage but also to those of humble birth who were outstanding. For these were special rewards and privileges which distinguished them from those of noble birth. They were given special devices and weapons which indicated that they were the Gray Privy Knights and therefore could be told from the rest.[1]

Just as among these nations a difference existed between those who were aristocrats and those who were not, thus in the royal palaces and in the temples there were rooms and chambers which accommodated or received different qualities of persons so that the first would not mingle with the second, so that those of good blood would not be on the same level with the lower class. This is an admirable thing, a remarkable thing, and does not pertain to a people as brutish and barbarous as we would like to think these people were. In pagan times they possessed as much good order and government, harmony and concert, as any people in the world could have had, particularly regarding this custom of granting renown, special honors, distinction, and glory to knights. [One could identify] a knight [and distinguish] a gentlemen from a hidalgo, a hidalgo from a squire, a squire from a clerk, and [a clerk] from a plebeian of the lower class. Thus, in good and orderly re-publics and communities, great attention was paid to these things, unlike the disorder that prevails in our modern republics, where

---

[1] In other words, the Gray Privy Knights were commoners who had risen through their own efforts and obtained special privileges from the king. The term used by Durán for such men, Caballeros Pardos, was the title given in Spain to commoners who obtained special privileges from the king for similar feats.

one can barely tell who is the knight, who the muleteer, who the squire, who the sailor. Today it is clothes and fine embroidery that make all men esteemed alike, and this is the cause of our decadence. Therefore, in order to avoid this confusion and turmoil and so that each one would keep his place, the natives possessed important laws, decrees, and ordinances. To explain them I have decided to include them in this chapter as something belonging to the ancient past and to the Knights of the Sun, whose special privileges are worthy of note.[2]

The first and most remarkable thing to be noted is that the palaces of the kings and lords were always built next to the temple. Adjoining those temples or enclosed within them were palaces, great halls, and apartments for different kinds and qualities of persons. On entering the door, each one knew his place, according to his rank. The great men had their own palace, the knights theirs, the hidalgos their own, and the squires theirs also, so that the noblemen had no reason to go to [the house of] the knights, nor the knights to that of the squires, in the same way that the dean takes his place, the archdean his place, the precentor his place, and so forth. Their rules were so rigorous that under pain of death no common man dared pass the threshold of the royal houses and chambers. For the servants who brought water and firewood, therefore, there were secret doors, separated and very distant from the main one. In order to confirm what has been said it should be known that each apartment had a special name so that men of every rank recognized their own. Each was called by the corresponding rank; for instance, the one belonging to the princes and great lords was called Teccalli, which means Palace of the Princes. In order to explain this further it must be known that the term *tecutli* is a generic term for princes, counts, dukes, marquises, and men of rank and that the term *calli* means "house," from which came Tec Calli, which means Palace of the Princes and Great Lords. No one dared enter, much less sleep

[2] Durán's comparison of the chaotic social conditions in the Mexico of the 1580's (among both Indians and Spaniards) and the stability of the social world before the Conquest is unusual in that he seldom displays interest in social classes. He seems to sigh for a world which, though heathen, had based its disciplined social system upon lineages and individual merit.

in these apartments, except these great chieftains. Therefore, when one came to the court accompanied by his knights and nobles, all went with him as far as the door of the apartment, left him there, and then turned back. The same was done with all the lords who recognized that place as pertaining to them.

The second apartments were those known as the Pilcalli, which means House of the Nobles, because *pilli* means "noble," and [the term] was formed like the one above. All the nobles went directly there, recognizing it as the seat and place assigned to them. These were the courtly nobles, sons, brothers, or nephews of the great men who were permanently in the palace, together with all the other nobles of well-known families.

Then came the House of Eagles, which was called Quauhcalli, which [name] is made up of *quauhtli*, "eagle," and *calli*, "house." We dealt with this type of knight in the last chapter. As I stated, they were knights who were dedicated to soldiery. Flying like eagles in battle with invincible bravery and courage *par excellence*, they were called Eagles or Jaguars. They were the men whom the sovereigns most loved and esteemed, the men who obtained most privileges and prerogatives. To them the kings granted most generous favors, adorning them with brilliant, splendid weapons and insignia. No decision in war could be reached without them; not even the monarchs could contradict their ordinances and commands, and soon confirmed them. The Sun was their patron; they honored and served his temple with all the care and reverence in the world. That is why I call them the Knights of the Sun. I understand that in our language they would be called Knights Commanders, for, just as the King our Lord grants a gentleman a post with the habit of Saint James or of Saint John or of Calatrava, so the kings gave to these gentlemen insignia which served as titles, which distinguished them as grandees. In order to explain this further, it must be known that when one of these knights performed a great feat in war, capturing or slaying, he obtained these distinctions. As soon as [the warrior] returned to the court, the king was informed of the brave deed of the knight, who was brought before him. After manifesting his appreciation, [the king] dubbed him a knight and

197

gave him this honor. [This knight] was granted the name *tequihua* which was a general name applied to brave men. Aside from [receiving] this title, he was given the signs of a knight commander which I have described. The hair on the top of his head was parted in two, and a red cord wrapped around it; in this same cord was attached an ornament of green, blue, and red feathers. From this knot emerged a cord which hung down his back, at the end of which was suspended a red tassel. This meant that he had performed a great deed; and when he had performed two [feats], he was awarded two tassels, depending upon his acts. When this had been done, the king himself presented [the warrior] with a shield and a cuirass of fine featherwork. The shield bore insignia which served as his [coat of arms], and also a feathered native helmet which served as his personal device. He was then dressed in a rich mantle and breechcloth; he was given jewelry, necklaces, earplugs, and labrets [Plate 17]. He was exempted from all types of taxes, tributes, contributions, and such. He and his children were granted the privilege of wearing cotton and sandals, and he could keep all the women he could support. From that day on he could enter the palace; he could sit [with the rest] in the House of Eagles!

Everything we have stated regarding the Knights of the Sun, the prerogatives and favors with which they were honored, can be applied to the principal men who gained renown. Among them was another kind of knight even more highly respected because he excelled. After having passed through the stage of the *tequihuaque* and having performed more than twenty deeds and brave acts, he was given new names, new insignia and arms, new grants and titles. It should be known that the new name given was Cuachic. This term means Shorn Man, and thus for this new knightly order his entire head was shorn with a blade, though a lock of hair was left above the left ear. It was as thick as a thumb and was braided with a red ribbon. One half of his head was painted blue and the other half red or yellow. He was given a large and magnificent breechcloth and was covered with a net mantle, an open-weave net of maguey fiber. This provided no defense or protection for the body, since he went about as if naked. He was forced to wear this net mantle always in public, even if there was frost, rain, or hot sun, since it was the garb of his profession, just as I believe that knights commanders today are obliged to wear the habit pertaining to their title.

This order of knights always constituted the rear guard of the armies so that when their own men retreated, when they saw that they were in trouble, [the Cuachic] came out as a reinforcement with such daring and high spirits that they frightened away and routed armies, caught and killed large numbers of men. They fought face to face with numerous warriors, having been ordered not to flee before [fewer] than twenty attackers. Skillful and dexterous, they had lost their fear of battle to the extent that, once they had set one foot in a place, one hundred men were not capable of removing it. Occasionally two or three [Cuachic] were capable of destroying a whole army. They were highly esteemed by the kings, honored with great solicitude, daily granted large and plentiful favors. [The sovereigns] called them the light of their eyes!

A third order of knights was called the Gray Knights. These were born of the lower classes and of men of little fortune. Through their bold spirit, courage, and pluckiness they managed to be admitted into the numbers of the Eagles and thus be called conquerors, or *tequihua*. In manner different from those of high birth, they belonged to an order and were dubbed knights. This ceremony was performed for the common man who had risen and accomplished some distinguished feat in warfare [and] returned to the court from battle. He was brought into the presence of the great lord, who praised his deed and had the [warrior's] queue cut above the ears. [The lord] gave him a jacket covered with skin bearing the head of a jaguar or white strips of chamois, covering him down to the waist. A wide and magnificent breechcloth covered his thighs. He was given ear plugs and a labret [and] also a white shield bearing five tufts of feathers. He was granted the right to dress in cotton and wear sandals in the royal abode, to eat human flesh and drink wine (that is, in public, for in private all did). He could keep two or three concubines. He was freed from paying tribute and taxes and contributions. He was given lands and properties. [He was given] permission to dine as often as he wished within the royal houses, where he was given his ration. He was allowed to dance with the lords whenever dances and celebrations took place. In sum, these men began a new lineage, and their children enjoyed their privileges, calling themselves knights.

So I have seen among our Indians of today a few disputes, especially about lands or houses, [between those] who come to quarrel, who call each other "scum" and "lowborn," aware of the fact that their ancestors were humble people and who because of their individual deeds had become Gray Knights, all recognizing, all revealing each other's genealogy. This is still very common within our nation: he who had been a sandal maker had risen by his own merits to become a gentleman because he went on the campaign and conquest of the *bacallaos*.[3] Yet someone will always say to his children, "Look how he struts! His father pulled more leather with his teeth, and his hands are more stained with tanning liquid than with perfume!"

But let us return to our theme. Thus the common man was rewarded to distinguish him from the noble, and the difference was this: the noble knights were dressed from head to foot in quilted armor covered with feathers, while the common men were given no feathers but wore the skins of different animals over the quilted material. This was due to a law prohibiting the wearing of feather-work without the permission of the sovereign, for [the featherwork] was the Shadow of the Lords and Kings and was called by this name. This ruling, by the way, was enforced more strictly than our modern ones regarding the wearing of silk. In the ancient times, therefore, among the pagan natives no one wore cotton but [had to wear] maguey fiber, unless he was of the privileged class, which I have described; even less could he drink chocolate (which is a native drink) unless he was a lord or chieftain. Nor could the common people wear elegant skin sandals, but only [ones] of woven reeds, and these only on the highways, because no one went

[3] The Spanish text reads ". . . nunca falta quien diga a sus hijos: 'Beyslo qual ba, pues, su padre estiró más cueros con los dientes y tenía más teñidas las manos de zuma, que que no de algalia.' " Thus Durán indicates that a manual laborer could rise from a humble position to that of a knight, a change in status not uncommon in both ancient Mexico and sixteenth-century Spain.

about shod in the city except the chiefs and knights. When these [men] entered the temples and were in the presence of the monarch, they removed their sandals. They wore no hats or any other covering on their heads except their long hair clipped below their ears. Kings and great men, however, wore their hair down to the shoulder as a sign of authority, and the monarchs wore rich miters of gold and stones which served as crowns. These were worn when the lords appeared in public or when official visits were made.

I have already stated that there was another house where the *calpixque* gathered. These were like judges or heads of the wards in charge of the distribution of jobs and public works, such as building roads, cleaning the streets and canals, obtaining the necessary provisions for the community. These [*calpixque*] resided in these apartments, where usually they were to be found. They gathered to hear the decisions and commands of the royal council. To them were sent edicts, the laws, to be enforced. Thus, if in a council of war it was decided that a certain city or town was to be attacked, because of rebelliousness, on a given date, those of the council gave orders to notify the nearby villages so that they might obtain provisions and equipment for war, clean the roads and make them clear for the army, place sentinels so that the army would be received in the villages and that each one would be notified of the [soldiers' coming]. These orders came from the council and were carried to the chambers of the *calpixque*, who immediately sent them to the officials of a village, and from that village they were transmitted to another, and from another to another; such was the task of the men of the fourth group.

One could write a detailed history about these ancient ordinances, laws, and system describing the order and concert with which they governed themselves, the rigor with which [the laws] were executed, the ranks and honors with which the knights and braves were rewarded. It would be longer than [my description]. A summary in this chapter would be too lengthy because in the smallest details there were special provisions, customs, and such good order that even in the sweeping of the royal abode there were specific rulings and special authorities in charge. And so it was with everything else. The same order and good government is found among these people today to the extent that not a man is lost nor a thing mislaid.

May His Divine Majesty give me enough days to write a detailed treatise in which could be seen the order and good government of the [ancient] nations! And the just and righteous laws that existed among them! Some, however, were tyrannical, founded upon the unwholesome awe in which the vassals held their lords and the fear and submission in which they were kept. The lords were [often] most cruel, tyrannical, and merciless!

CHAPTER XII

¶Which treats of the Feast of Xocotl Huetzi, the particular divinity of the Tecpanecs, people of Coyoacan, held in great esteem by them.

Every time I stop to consider the childlike things on which these people based and founded their faith, I am filled with wonder at the ignorance which blinded them—a people who were not ignorant or brutish but skillful and wise in all worldly things, especially the elite. I say this because we are going to deal with a god so base that, though he received a joyous and solemn feast, he was only an idol in this feast, and yet he was practically the creator of it and its festivities. [He was the cause of great joy], as much to those who celebrated it as to all the people, since the idol served as a doll to those who performed the ceremonies and rites.

This idol was called Xocotl, and (to tell the truth) I do not know the Spanish word for its accurate meaning, unless it is the name of a bird it represented and whose figure was adored. This bird must have been called thus because on the day of the feast [the people] made a bird with the dough of amaranth seed which we have called *tzoalli*.

This dough was always used to make images of the gods—the "flesh" and "bones" of the deities, as I have stated. Afterward they ate the dough, calling it "the flesh of God." They formed the idol of the dough thus. Taking a large piece of dough, they placed it within a net. Then of the same dough they fabricated the head of a bird, gilding its beak, attaching fancy green feathers to make the wings and tail, setting it up so that it looked like a splendid bird indeed. The other four pieces of dough were fashioned into [special shapes], finely painted, to be placed at [the bird's] feet, serving him as a support in the form of branches and flowers. This bird-shaped idol upon its [flowery] branches was placed on top of a tall pole. It must have been at least one hundred ten to one hundred forty feet tall. This pole was brought from the woods and was placed at the entrance to the city twenty days before the feast, on the day called Micailhuitontli, which means the Feast of the Little Dead Ones.[1] On this day they cut the tree, brought it from the woods, and laid it down at the entrance of the city, where it was sanctified daily with special ceremonies while the bark was removed and the tree smoothed.

On the same day the merchants offered up five slaves, four males and one female. All were washed and purified according to the ways and customs of cleansing slaves who were to represent gods. When these slaves had been presented and dedicated, one was given the name Yacatecutli [He Who Goes First]; another, Chiconquiahuitl [Seven Rain]; another, Cuauhtlaxayauh [Eagle Face]; another, Coatlinahual [Weresnake]; and the woman was named Chachalmecacihuatl [Lady of the Chachalmec People(?)]. These were the names of the five deities adored, revered, and celebrated on this day by these people, together with Xocotl, [whom the slaves] represented. These five slaves impersonated them for twenty days, being honored as if they had been the gods themselves.

Ten days after the tree was brought in and the [slaves] (who had been offered by the merchants, chieftains, and lords ten days

[1] Though the Spanish text translates *Micailhuitontli* as the *Fiesta de los muertecillos*, a more literal translation would be Small Feast of the Dead. Later Durán calls the Huey Micailhuitl the Great Feast of the Dead, in reference to the large number of adult victims sacrificed. Micailhuitontli, in our opinion, translates best as Small Feast of the Dead, meaning a feast for children, and Huey Micailhuitl, Great Feast of the Dead, for adults.

before the feast) had been attired in the garb of the gods, those who were to be sacrificed by fire were consecrated. Before noon on the eve of the feast day the pole was brought into the city and erected in the courtyard of the Great Temple. At the top was placed the bird of amaranth dough, with the [branches] of the same dough at his feet, upon which it seemed to be sitting. When [the pole] had been set up, they went to the Divine Brazier (for so it was called) and lighted a fire, casting into it so much firewood that it made a splendid blaze. The bonfire prepared, it was left there until the next morning, [the people] not failing during the night to keep the fire going so that by morning there was an enormous mass of embers as the day of Xocotl dawned. This was also called the Great Feast of the Dead, or Huey Miccailhuitl, which was one of the many feasts of the calendar. It was called the Great Feast of the Dead because of the many slaves sacrificed then. This fiesta fell on the twenty-seventh of August.

After dawn all those who were to be sacrificed were dressed in the garb and habit of the main gods, and according to seniority they were placed in a row next to the great fire. While they stood in that place, a man appeared who bore the name the Fighter. One by one he bound their hands. Then came five other ministers and one called Tlehua. [This Possessor of the Fire] swept carefully around the glowing coals. When he had finished sweeping, they took the "gods" one by one, alive as they were, and cast them into the fire. Half-roasted, before they were dead, [these victims] were pulled out and sacrificed, their chests opened.

After each of these gods [had perished], four or five male slaves were sacrificed. And so the thing continued, [the people] sacrificing [slaves] and burning their gods. It was a loathsome and frightful thing!

Moreover, since the gods were many and those slain after each god were also numerous, the entire floor was covered with dead bodies. It was dreadful to behold! Therefore, this was called the Great Feast of the Dead.

All the people came to this great feast and solemnity, worshiping the image of dough which stood on top of the pole, raising their eyes toward it with great piety, just as the children of Israel adored the serpent in the wilderness. It is no wonder that this feast is called the Great Feast of the Dead, in remembrance of those who died in the wilderness, since the ceremony involving the pole with the idol on top represents it so vividly. When this act of worship ended (even though these people did not know how to kneel or place their hands as we do to worship, since their own way was squatting, crossing their hands upon their breasts, or prostrating themselves upon the ground), they came out with their offerings. These consisted of breads, native wine, pine torches which served as candles, copal, and so on.[2] Once these offerings had ended, at evening the youths and maidens came out of their cloisters in the Great Temple. [The young girls and boys] were well garbed and highly adorned. On their heads [the boys] wore feathers, as well as earplugs and imitation labrets,[3] all holding gay feathers in their hands [and wearing] golden bracelets. [The girls] came wearing brand-new garments, their faces made up and colored, their arms and feet covered with feathers. To the sound of a drum they danced all that evening around the courtyard. To this dance came all the high lords, splendidly arrayed, and these formed a circle with much pomp and majesty, keeping the youths and maidens in the center. Instead of flowers the young people carried in their hands small idols and branches made of the same dough as the idol. Each wore a net mantle. The net was white and black with white featherwork, and attached to the middle of their heads [were headdresses] of black feathers which matched their costumes.

2 The Great Feast of the Dead described by Durán has its counterpart in modern Indian Mexico. On November 2 altars, smoking with incense, are set up in the homes of the villagers. The altars are adorned with paper cut in designs and with marigolds. The table is laden with mole stew, liquor, ceremonial breads, candies, *calabaza en tacha* (pumpkin cooked with brown sugar), tamales, and cigarettes. It is thought that the essence of these offerings is consumed by the souls of the deceased, who deeply appreciate the gifts.

3 Since these youths had not yet captured an enemy in battle, their labrets were imitation ones. When a youth finally took a victim on the battlefield, a perforation was made under his lower lip in which he wore an elaborate lip plug as a sign of bravery.

The leader of the dance, who stood in front of the others, was dressed according to the native fashion. This god was disguised as a bird or as a bat, its wings and crest made of large and splendid feathers. From his wrists and ankles hung gold bells; in both his hands he carried native rattles. He made much noise and clamor with these [rattles] and with his own mouth. He went twisting along completely out of order and rhythm with the other dancers. From time to time he spoke loudly, using terms which few—perhaps none at all—understood. Thus this man went along merrily [Plate 18].

Let our priests and laymen take note of what they may have seen often in the native dances. How common it is to see one or two natives precede the circling dancers without following the rhythm of the rest; yet [this man] is their guide. He dances as he pleases; he is attired in a different disguise. Once in a while he becomes merry and makes the pleasant sounds which I have described.

How ignorant we are of their ancient rites, while how well informed [the natives] are! They show off the god they are adoring right in front of us in the ancient manner. They chant the songs which the elders bequeathed to them especially for that purpose. It behooves our priests to remember my warning so as to recognize things that are evil. My intention has been to warn—not to teach idolatry, old or new—as some ignorant critics have stated falsely, in order to hinder and obstruct the good that could come from this book, [which has been written] as advice to our priests to the honor of God and to the extirpation of the heathen, idolatrous customs still in existence. I should not wonder, however, that there are those who want to obscure what is good because there was One who wished to obscure the works of Him who was the Light of the World, claiming that they were the works of Beelzebub, prince of demons. Continuing with our warning, however, I state that one should not dissimulate or permit natives to go around representing the god or the rest singing their idolatrous chants and lamentations. They sing these things when there is no one around who understands, but, as soon as a person appears who might understand, they change their tune and sing the song made up for Saint Francis with a hallelujah at the end, all to cover up their unrighteousness—interchanging religious themes with pagan gods.

The dance ended one hour before sunset, and all the youths and maidens who had participated cast off the feathers and adornments in which they had danced and then came to the contest—to see who could climb the pole fastest, reach the idol, and cast it down. That is why I said that the very idol served as a toy and fun at the feast, as I shall explain. Those who were brought up in Spain will have seen how this game is conducted. According to the story (since I must confess that I have not seen this done), it is said that [in Spain sailors] place lengths of velvet on top of a smooth, greased mast of the ship. Those who are to run strip, stand in order, then assault the mast in a wild rush, those in advance tussling among themselves. (As Saint Paul says) all run, but only one manages to reach the top first and take the prize, being the lightest and most adroit.

Well, try to imagine the same thing: these [Mexica] youths forming, stripping, placing themselves in order, and climbing the pole. These were not worthless or lowly boys—all of them were sons of lords and chieftains, skillful, courageous, and nimble, [eager to] prove themselves in the game of Xocotl, to see whether the god granted them good fortune. As they stood in a row, the signal was given, and they dashed for the pole with spirit, fury, and speed, struggling to climb one after another, getting in each other's way, tussling so that some fell from the lower part, others from the top, still others halfway up. The most deft climbed as swiftly as they could so as not to be reached by those who followed. Thus the swiftest who reached the bird tore off its head, the second a wing, the third another wing, the fourth the tail. Once the fourth had finished, there was nothing left. There it finished, and these four descended rapidly with great joy and vainglory, as if they were brave men, the chosen ones of the god [Plate 19].

When [the victors] descended with their prize, the dignitaries and the elders from the sleeping quarters came up and took those four youths in their midst. They were conducted to the chambers, where their ears were bled with knives and a few drops of blood were drawn. They remained cloistered there four days, fasting the entire time. When this had ended, they went to bathe to be purified for the sacrilege committed of having taken possession of the idol—a Jewish rite.

When those youths had finished, axmen appeared and chopped the pole to the ground. Then such a multitude fell upon it that in less than an hour nothing was left, and he who did not carry away a small or large part of the pole, no matter how tiny the splinter, thought himself very unfortunate. Thus all struggling to carry something away—be it of the idol's dough or of the four [dough] balls [or branches]—considered themselves lucky and revered them as we revere the relics of Agnus Dei or the wood of Lignum Crucis.[4]

It must be explained that the fall of this Xocotl pole was called Xocotl Huetzi, which means Fall of Xocotl.[5] The four boys who had so nimbly climbed the pole were obliged to contribute the amaranth seed a year later for the body of the idol.

With this we are finished with the feast of Xocotl Huetzi, and thus ends our description of the festivities of the highest male deities, excepting those which appear in the calendar, celebrated every twenty days, as we shall see later. Though they were gods, they were also [calendrical] signs, and they ruled, governed, and measured time.

Leaving these things for their proper place, we shall now deal with the goddesses who were worshiped in this land.

[4] The Agnus Dei is a medallion of beeswax, from the Paschal candle, stamped with the image of a lamb. The Lignum Crucis is a relic of the true cross.

[5] A more literal translation would be Fall of the Fruits.

CHAPTER XIII

¶Which treats of the goddess Cihuacoatl [Snake Woman], also called Quilaztli, goddess and patroness of the Xochimilcas.

Just as this Mexican nation had male gods, it also worshiped female deities, honored in the most solemn and elaborate festivities.

[Perhaps] some of these goddesses originated through qualities or graces or took the name of the rugged mountain where each was worshiped or of some idol to whom sacrifice was offered or of some place where there was a dark cave for the offering of sacrifice or of a place which gave birth to furious showers and thunderstorms, places called by the names of gods and goddesses (as we have said of the god Tlaloc and of the Sierra Nevada, celebrated as the Iztaccihuatl, or White Woman, who will be described later).

But let us deal with each goddess in her place. The main goddess was called Cihuacoatl, deity of the people of Xochimilco; and though she was the special goddess of Xochimilco, she was revered and greatly exalted in Mexico, Tetzcoco, and all the land.

The goddess Cihuacoatl was made of stone. She had a huge, open mouth and ferocious teeth. The hair on her head was long and bulky, and she was clad in womanly garb—skirt, blouse, and mantle—all white [Plate 20]. This was the usual habit in which she was kept in her lofty and sumptuous temples, especially in that of Xochimilco, whose patroness she was. It was not quite as elaborate in Mexico or Tetzcoco. But even in these cities at the top of the steps [of the temple] stood a large chamber some sixty or seventy feet in length and thirty in width. This hall was elaborately decorated, and the goddess stood upon an altar no less ornate than the rest. This room was always pitch-black. It had no small openings, no windows, no main door save for a small one through which one could barely crawl. This door was always hidden by a sort of lid so that no one would see it and enter the chamber except for the priests who served the goddess. These were elders who performed the usual ceremonies. This room was called Tlillan, which means Blackness or the Place [of Blackness]. Next to the walls of this temple stood all the gods of the land, some large, some small. They were called Tecuacuiltin, which means Image of Stone or In the Round. All these idols were attired with paper scapulars striped with rubber (a gum we call *batel* [rubber], very common in the native offerings). These idols also wore paper headdresses or miters painted and striped with the same rubber.

The idols were taken out whenever it was necessary to perform a special feast for them or when their day arrived or when their help was needed. They were carried out in a procession to the woods, to the mountains, or to the caves from which they had taken their names. There, in that cave or in that forest, they were presented with the usual offerings and sacrifices, and the mountain was invoked for some special need—lack of water, a plague or famine, or a future war. When the ceremony had ended, [the image] was returned to the hall, to the place where it always stood.

The celebration of this goddess was held on the eighteenth of July according to our calendar, and according to theirs it was the festivity known as the Feast of Huey Tecuilhuitl, which was the eighth festivity of the calendar. Besides being the day of the commemoration of the goddess, it was a solemn day among the feasts of the calendar. It can be compared to the following: if a holy day falls on Sunday, besides being the day of some important saint, it is also the Lord's Day.

Huey Tecuilhuitl means the Great Feast of the Lords, and was celebrated by the lords in a lordly way. Twenty days before the date this was done: a female slave was bought, purified, and dressed in the same manner as the stone idol—all in white with her white mantle. Thus dressed, she represented the goddess and received the honors and courtly attentions [the goddess herself] would have received had she been alive. She was taken from one feast to another, from one banquet to the next; she was led to all the market places and was regaled with every known type of gaiety and merriment. She was always kept drunk, tipsy, inebriated, out of her wits. Some say that this was done with wine; others say that, besides drinking wine, she was bewitched in one manner or another. This was done so that she would always walk about gaily, forgetting that she was to be slain. At night she slept in a cage, for they feared she might try to escape. The woman was named Xilonen.

Thus it went, from the day of her purification to that of her death.

First of all, on the day of her feast, one hour before dawn, the four captives were slain, and their bodies were cast upon the ground close together. The woman was thrown upon them, and her throat was slit. Her blood was then gathered in a bowl, and her heart was torn out. The stone goddess was touched with it and sprinkled with blood. The entire chamber and the idols were also sprinkled, and the bodies were given back to their owners for the banquet. All this was done early, one hour before dawn. The bodies of these four men were called the Dais of the Captives of the Goddess. It should be remarked, however, that the goddess was offered the same fire sacrifice as that offered to Xocotl, according to what some tell me and according to a picture I saw, dedicated to this deity. I wish here to tell some particulars about this and relate the method and manner used in sacrificing—a frightful thing.

Four days before the principal feast day of this goddess a fire was prepared in a great hearth within a room in front of the goddess's chamber; for four days and nights they never ceased feeding oakwood to that brazier, or hearth. The brazier, which was in the floor of the chamber, was made of finely carved stone and was called

Teotlecuilli, which means Divine Brazier or Divine Hearth. This hearth was so stuffed with the live coals of oakwood that it burned like a furnace, furiously. On the same day, before the sacrifice of the woman who represented the goddess was performed, she was made to sit in the chamber in front of the fire and was greatly revered and honored. In her presence, in the place of the goddess, the sacrifice was offered [Plate 21]. The sacrifice was performed before this live woman and not before the stone one because the stone goddess was kept concealed within the dark chamber. No one was ever allowed to enter or leave that place unless he was [a person] of great importance and majesty. She was kept within that sacred place, and no priest, no other person, dared touch the statue. The same can be applied to the other gods. To prove this, I shall tell what a conqueror narrated to me. When the land had been conquered, the Marqués del Valle [Cortés] ordered the Indians to ascend and cast down the great Huitzilopochtli. And he [the informant] assured me that there had not been a native in the entire land who had been persuaded [to do so]—either by threats or [by] loving words. Having realized this, the marqués sent up Gil González de Benavides (father of Alonso de Ávila) to cast it down. He ascended [the pyramid], though harassed and obstructed by the Indians. He sent [the idol] rolling down, and this is narrated by the Indian elders as an extraordinary, remarkable, and daring feat—a human being touching the god Huitzilopochtli. I tell these things [to make clear] the reverence in which this goddess was held, though she was simply represented by the seated woman.

The four prisoners who were to serve her as a dais were then brought to the Divine Hearth, and each was sacrificed in the following way. The ministers of the temple took hold of him, two by the hands and two by the feet, and swung him four times. On the fourth [swing] they let him fall into the live coals, and before he was dead they pulled him out swiftly. Thus, half-roasted, he was placed upon a stone, his chest was opened in the manner I have described, his heart was extracted and cast down in front of him. The same was done to the second, the third, and the fourth. They were sacrificed and placed upon the floor as a seat. The divine woman was then slain and her blood gathered for the performance of the ceremony which has been described. At that time the fire was sprinkled with her blood. Fire was known by the name of the god Xiuhtecuhtli [and was] worshiped and given generous offerings under this name.

The fire sacrifice having ended, the man in charge of sweeping appeared and swept around the fire. After he had swept, all the priests of the wards came, each placing near the fire a folded mantle of his deity, a breechcloth, and a belt. On top of these [he placed] a small image. After having made these offerings, each sat down and stripped. Each took two incense torches, each about a yard long, in his hands and lighted them in the sacred fire. Squatting, they held the torches in their hands; the burning, melting resin ran down their arms, bodies, and legs, roasting them alive in their fiery penitence to the god Xiuhtecuhtli. On that day of sacrifice what was left of their torches was cast into the fire, and all that had dripped on their bodies, arms, and legs was torn off and cast into the fire, together with heavy loads of incense, which in the fire produced a tremendous cloud of smoke. While it was still smoldering, they danced around the hearth, intoning chants about fire and sacrifice.

When this ceremony ended, the lords and noblemen came out to commemorate their own day, which, as we shall explain in *The [Ancient] Calendar*, was the day of the great lords. They appeared spendidly adorned, magnificent, with flowers in their hands, on their necks, and on their heads, together with many jewels, other finery, and feathers. With them came all the women and maidens, with their cropped hair hanging over their brows, wearing garlands of the large yellow flower called *cempoalxochitl*.[1] They were attired in their most splendid garb; their arms, with the most luxurious plumes; [they wore] gold and stone earrings in their ears and carried flowers in their hands. Alternating with the men, they

---

[1] Today the *cempoalxochitl* is known as *sempasuchil*, an orange marigold used in Indian Mexico on the Feast of the Dead and other ceremonial occasions. The name of the flower is derived from the words *cempoalli* ("twenty") and *xochitl* ("flower"). This appellation, rather strange to our ears, may be derived from the pre-Hispanic feasts celebrated every twenty days. Thus, *cempoalxochitl*, freely translated, may mean "ceremonial flower."

danced all day with the most extraordinary order, array, and dignity. When the dance ended, [the maidens] took all the flowery garlands and necklaces with which they and the men had danced and ascended to the summit of the Temple of Huitzilopochtli, where they offered [the garlands] to the statue of Huitzilopochtli as first fruits of the flowers of the season. This rite was called Xochipaina, which means First Flowers of the Season. It was also called Xochicalaquia, which means To Offer or Bring Flowers to the Temple as a Tithe or First Fruit. When these flowers had been presented, the boys who were cloistered in the house appeared. They placed themselves in a row next to the skull rack which stood in front of the doors of the temple; and as soon as they had been given the signal, they ascended swiftly, the strongest struggling to climb up and be the first. Thus some got there first, others second, others later, all seizing the flowers. Some snatched from others, and the struggle and persistence in snatching flowers was a merry thing to see.

Thus ended the feast, except that for ten days there was eating and banqueting in [the City of] Mexico. Each one of the nearby provinces was obliged to contribute and feed the lords. The Chalcas provided on the first day, the Tecpanecs on the second, others on the third. Thus each had its turn, providing splendid, rich foods and drinks: chocolate, pinole,[2] great quantities of pulque, all striving to give the best. On one day this was done for the princes, on another for the knights, on another for the Tequihuas, on another for the Cuachique Otomis.[3] In this way the ten days were spent—eating, drinking, and feasting, celebrating the octave of the goddess and her feast.

Before the chamber of the goddess Cihuacoatl was an outer

---

[2] *Pinolli* (pinole) is defined by Molina as "la harina de maiz y chía." Today pinole usually refers to a tortilla that is ground to a powder and occasionally mixed with sugar. It is a staple among certain groups in northern Mexico and some indigenous peoples in the southwestern United States.

[3] According to Molina, the term *cuachichictli* means "tonsure," and *cuachichiquilli*, "feathered crest." It is paradoxical that the Otomis, considered weak and timid in our own times, should have been the vanguard of the Aztec army and thus symbolized strength on this ceremonial occasion.

hall which contained the Divine Brazier I have described. Next to this room stood a great residence where dwelt the elders and priests of the temple and of the goddess. This was as can be seen in the illustration [Plate 22].

In this first hall sat two priests, taking turns, night and day. They tended the fire which was never to fail in the Divine Hearth. They never entered the sanctum sanctorum in the next chamber, with its multitude of idols, all concealed in the darkness. These priests did not do penance or draw blood from any part. Their sacrifice was that of scorching themselves once a year with the incense of myrrh. These ministers received all those who came to offer incense. Ordinarily women arrived with offerings for their children and husbands. Since offerings were presented there at all hours, someone had to receive them and present them to the goddess and to the other [deities]. The priests and ministers of this temple were called by the same name as the idols: Tecuacuiltin. They were always smeared with black. They followed the same order of rites as the others. In addition to offering incense to the idols four times day and night, sweeping, sprinkling, and setting up ornaments of branches, they were especially careful to satisfy the hunger of the goddess. They went once a week to visit the sovereigns and warn them that the goddess was famished. Then the rulers provided the repasts: a captive taken in war, to be eaten by the goddess. He was led to the temple and delivered to the priests, who took the prisoner and thrust him into the chamber of Cihuacoatl. He was slain in the usual way: his heart was extracted and offered up. They also ripped off a part of his thigh, casting it outside, crying out loudly, "Take this for it has been gnawed on!" feigning that the goddess had spoken.

The priests outside lifted the dead body, considering it to be the "leftovers" of the goddess. It was given back to the owner [as a reward] for having fed the goddess. [The piece of thigh] was carried away and eaten, each one receiving his part, the number depending upon the number of those who had captured him—never more than four. If there were three captors, it was divided among three; if four, it was distributed among four. This ceremony was performed every eight days. I explained that in pictures the goddess was always shown with a large, open mouth. She was always famished, and thus in this temple and in honor of this goddess more men were slain than in any other.

The site of the temple was the place the boys used to call the "House of the Devil," as I believe it is still called today. This is contiguous [to the house] of Acevedo at the intersection of [the house of] Don Luis de Castilla.[4] This was named the "House of the Devil" because of the many idols and stone images of different shapes which stood there. As I say, we boys used to go look at them as if [the place] were haunted, never daring to enter because of the name they had given it: the "House of The Devil." In truth the name fits it well, for it was a house where the demon was attended and honored. Countless idols and effigies stood there against the walls, as I have said, attending the goddess in that gloomy place. Today the natives call that house Tlillan. Thus we should stop calling it the "House of the Devil"; it should be called the House of Gloom, according to its ancient name.

The deity Cihuacoatl was called the sister of Huitzilopochtli, the great god of Mexico. Therefore she was served by the same cloistered nuns who attended her divine brother. They lived in the cloister I have described under his feast. They prepared the daily food of this goddess, carried it, and set it before her. Her food consisted of small breads like buns in the form of feet, hands, and faces; [she was also served] porridge in gourds. All this food was carried there every day to be eaten by the priests in the name of the stone [goddess] under whose favor they were sustained and honored. [By the way], I have noticed something about the natives: there are no people on earth capable of eating more and better at the expense of their neighbors; yet there are no people who manage to survive with less food, when it is at their own expense.

The temple of this divinity adjoined that of her brother Huitzilopochtli and was treated with the same honors. Therefore,

---

[4] Modern archaeologists seeking the "House of the Devil" in modern-day Mexico City would probably find it at the corner of República de Brasil and Justo Sierra streets.

all who served in the Great Temple came to sweep, sprinkle, and beautify it with branches, and also performing the personal services of carrying fire, wood, and water. The priests of this temple were not penitents or fasters, because of their privilege of not having to bleed their ears, tongues, or shins as did those of the other temples. Their title has already been given, that is, Tecuacuiltin, which means Gods.

This feast and its rites were remarkable since they were not at all typical. [It was an occasion] on which, year after year, Satan carried away countless human beings at the hands of his ministers, who served him with their fiery and bloody sacrifice. His hunger will last till doomsday, and he will never be filled; he is the bloody enemy from whom David begged deliverance by our Savior. May He spare us through His mercy and kindness! May He tear the veil from the blind hearts of these poor people—if such [a veil] exists! May He remove their numerous rites which served the devil!

If we examine these things, we find that not all the rites are the same, though there was no great disparity or difference in the ceremonies, depending on the imagination of the priests and the persuasions of the devil. [Considering that] these people were so ceremonious, superstitious, and watchful of omens, few miracles were necessary to make them believe that something had been ordained by the gods or proved by revelations.

Since I am not speaking idly, I wish to narrate what I heard an old man tell regarding the revelations of the ancient priests which led them to be reputed or held as saints. As an example, I once asked an old man why they had a god of the maguey plant and why they depicted the maguey with a face and hands surrounded by maguey leaves. He answered that in olden times one of the dignitaries or satraps had dreamed of a maguey with face and hands. Amazed by such a dream, he made it known that the god of the maguey had appeared to him and that he had ordered him depicted as in his dream and worshiped. Ceremonies and rites were invented then, and he was adored as a god. Thus it went with all the things these people worshiped. Sometimes they confess things they believe to have seen in dreams. Let the father confessors of the Indians take note that in ancient times these things were thought to be divine revelations. If they dreamed that their teeth fell out, they believed that their children would die soon. If they dreamed that they ate meat, they feared that their husbands or wives would die. If they dreamed that they were being carried off by water, they were afraid that their properties would be stolen from them. If they dreamed that they flew, they were afraid of death.

Consequently, now that we are dealing with dreams, [the natives] should be examined [in confession] regarding what they dream; in all of this there may be reminiscences of pagan times. In dealing with these things, it would be good to ask them [in confession], "What did you dream?" and not try to skim over it like a cat walking on hot coals. Our preaching should be dedicated to condemning and abominating all this. The Indians themselves do not understand these things, and [the preachers] have scarcely a notion of them. They should preach about the One True God, the Universal Lord of All Created Things. As soon as the Indians forget their ancient idolatry and rites, let them be persuaded that God has sent famines and plagues because of the just wrath He feels against them—unless they serve Him without this mixture of heathenism and idolatry—as His [Divine] Majesty desires to be served. This is what they need most—much more than hearing [the ministers preach]:

> . . . the sun shone upon the golden shields
> and its splendor filled the mountains.

I say these things because one day I went to hear a preacher who was fair in the native language. When he saw me, realizing that I understood the tongue, he tried to show himself at his best, using as his theme "Refulsit sol in clipeos aureos, etc. ["The sun shone upon the golden shields"]. Then he began to deal with the "Divine Splendor" and the "Divine Persons." He had no idea of what he was talking about, leaving his hearers in the dark and me extremely disappointed. How little we, the preachers, have grasped the real needs of the Indians. For the preacher who wishes to rise one step above the low mental stage of the Indian becomes dissonant and will reap few fruits. Once the Indian has lost the track [of the sermon], he hears the voice of Jacob and touches the hands of Esau.[5] He begins to scratch lines on the floor, to count pebbles, not heeding in the slightest, desiring that the sermon end and [the preacher] be gone, since he has understood nothing whatsoever.

[5] Durán, quoting from the account in Genesis 27:1–46, compares the Indian who whiled away the time during mass playing *patolli* with the aged Isaac, who paid no attention to the voice of his first-born, Esau, and let himself be deceived by his sense of touch as he felt Jacob's hands.

CHAPTER XIV

¶Which treats of the goddess Chicomecoatl, also known
as Chalchiuhcihuatl, which means Precious Stone. She
was also called Xilonen.

As I continue to write this ancient history, I always find new
things to tell. This should be an incentive to the reader to continue
reading the history. The more he reads, the more new things he
discovers, and his appetite is whetted by the desire for knowledge—
desire to reach the end of what I promise and intend to tell. Seldom
will he drop his reading, become weary, especially if the account is
novel. If he is of poor and dull judgment, when he sees the light, he
may choose to ignore it, shutting his eyes so as not to see it, imitating
the dumb beasts.

In our present chapter we shall deal with many remarkable
things which will bring joy, interest, and even wonder [to the
reader] when he becomes aware of the manner of this celebration
and the accompanying festivities and ritual. Therefore, I request
the attention our story merits in order to consider the consistency,
awe, and reverence with which the laws and rites of the false religion were obeyed. [Let us also consider] our frailty, negligence,
want of awe and reverence in holding and making others obey the
divine and true [laws and rites of Christianity]. These were put

together not by human invention or through dreams or the imagination but by the Holy Spirit, under whose protection the Catholic Church lives and commands.

The first thing to be said about this goddess is that she was the deity of the harvest and of all the grains and plants of this nation. She was known as the goddess Chicomecoatl or Chalchiuhcihuatl. The first name, Chicomecoatl, which means Serpent of Seven Heads, was applied because of the harm she did in barren years, when the seeds froze, when there was want and famine. Thus it is common, when the cornfields have frozen, to hear the natives say that ice has eaten up the crops. Others say that the Tecuani ate them. To explain a Tecuani, it should be remarked that anything that stings or bites (whether or not poisonous) is called a Tecuani. Thus this goddess was called the Seven-Headed Serpent to indicate the harm she caused when the cornfields and the plants were spoiled by frost.

Her second name was Chalchiuhcihuatl, which means Woman of Precious Stone. This name was applied to her when she granted an abundant and fertile year. In such a year was celebrated her feast, filled with rejoicing and offerings—a wondrous thing. The feast of this goddess was commemorated on the fifteenth of September, and the festivity was common through the land, with such devotion and ritual that it was a marvelous sight.

Nevertheless, before we begin with the feast, I shall describe the way in which the statue was fashioned. It was made of wood, carved in the form of a young woman, a maiden some twelve years of age, modeled in the best carving in the land. She was garbed in the native womanly garments, all red, the most splendid obtainable. On her head she wore a tiara of red paper upon her cropped hair, which fell to her shoulders. In her ears were incrusted golden earrings. On her neck she wore a necklace of golden ears of corn, carved like real ears of corn, tied with a blue ribbon. In her hands she held ears of corn, imitated in featherwork and garnished with gold. She held her arms open, like a woman dancing. Her cheeks were colored like those of a woman wearing rouge [Plate 23]. This was the usual garb and form of this goddess, who stood in a chamber on the summit of the temple next to the chamber of the great Huitzilopochtli, all to her greater glory and honor. This hall was not large but was decorated richly, magnificently, with cloths, featherwork, golden jewels, and stones, which were continually offered there.

A week before the celebration of the feast, on the seventh of September, a great festival was held, something like our carnival. Because of the fasting expected in the near future, the people drank and ate meat dishes, together with other things, until they were filled. On this same day of banqueting and gorging, a woman was purified and dedicated to honor the goddess known as Atlatonan. She was the divinity of lepers and of those born with physical defects or who suffer from sores. She was thought to be the cause and giver of these ailments. On the next day, on the eighth of September, the time of fasting, or "little Lent," began. This lasted seven days in a row, during which no one ate anything but leftovers, scraps of old, dry tortillas without salt, or anything except water. This feast was common throughout the entire land, inviolable, similar to Lent in Christendom. This fast was kept with a great deal more rigor and care than Lent and fast days are kept.

When the sacrifice had ended, another slave was dressed and purified to represent the goddess Chicomecoatl. She was given ornaments, a tiara upon her head, ears of corn on her neck and hands. She was forced to make merry and dance and was taken from the home of one nobleman to another who had been in sadness, penance, and fasting. To the hair on the crown of this woman's head was tied a vertical green feather, which represented the tassels of the stalks of corn. It was tied with a red ribbon, indicating that at the time of this feast the maize was almost ripe but still green. A girl twelve or thirteen years old, the most comely to be found, was chosen to represent this goddess. And the poor little one went about all day with the splendid feather stuck on her head.

At dusk on this day the people came to the temple and filled the courtyards with lights and bonfires. Each ward stayed awake all night around its bonfire. When midnight arrived, the conch shells, flutes, and trumpets sounded. And to their sound a litter was brought forth. This was finely decorated with strings of ears of corn, chili, replete with all types of grains. It was set down at the door of the chamber which contained the image of the goddess. Inside and out, this chamber had been decorated and made green with numerous strings of ears of corn, chili peppers, squash, flowers, and all kinds of seeds. It was a most remarkable, a most ornate thing to see. The entire floor was garnished in this way. Instead of rushes it was covered with all these offerings to the height of about one yard.

When the music finished, to the solemn company of dignitaries and priests, [to the light] of the fires and incense burners, the girl representing the goddess was brought forth and placed upon the litter. She stood in the center, on top of the ears of corn, chili, squash, and amaranth seeds which lay on the floor. Her hands were bound to two rods which were attached to the litter and firmly fixed so that, bound, she might not fall. While she stood there, the priests offered her incense. When the incensing had ended, the instruments began to sound, the trumpets and conch shells which I have described. At the sound of these one of the high priests of the temple appeared. Suddenly, from behind, with a blade he cut off the feather which bound her hair, close to the scalp. He held it up in one hand and presented it to the wooden goddess who stood in the room, together with the tuft of hair belonging to the bound girl. It was offered up with great solemnity, ceremonies, and tears. Thanks were given for the fruits, for the abundant year granted to the people, all of whom stood there, devout and tearful. The ceremony having ended, the girl was again removed from the litter. She was brought down and, surrounded by a great crowd, was placed upon a special seat. All the people remained watching by the light of the fire, as they had done the night before. It almost seemed Christmas Eve. Thus the wake was called Ixtozoztli, which means the Watchful Wake, and thus they watched till sunrise.

When dawn arrived, no one having dared leave the temple (for that was considered a sacrilege), the priests brought the young girl out of the chamber. She was adorned and garbed like the goddess, with her red dress, the red tiara on her head, with the ears of corn hanging from her neck. Again she was made to stand in the litter, holding on to the rods to which she was tied. Then [the litter] was lifted from the floor and placed upon the shoulders of the elders of the temple. The rest [went along], offering incense with their burners, others playing instruments and singing. Thus she was carried in a procession into the great courtyard of the serpent wall. She was passed through the end of the hall where Huitzilopochtli stood. Her passing through this room was the essence of the ceremony. Then she was carried to the chamber of the wooden goddess whom she represented, where she was untied from the litter. She was made to stand on the ears of corn and vegetables which had been offered up in the room. While she stood there, the lords and nobles came in; forming a line, and one by one, they approached her. They squatted on their knees and removed the dry blood they had preserved on their temples and ears during the seven days. They scratched this off with their hands and flung it in front of the girl consecrated as a goddess. Thus they entered, one by one, and when they had finished, the women came in to perform the same ceremony. They presented that blood as an expiation for their sins and as a thanksgiving for the benefits they had received in foodstuffs. According to my information from the natives, these people suffered terrible famines, barren years, and plagues sent by God in olden times. Thus they were afraid of certain years and their numbers, prophesying wars, plagues, or famines, just as we do. There are people who can foretell the year in which there will be war, hunger, and so on, just as these people used to prophesy in ancient times.

When the blood offering ended (with the exception of no one, young or old—and it lasted long because of the great crowds), everyone went to wash himself. When they had washed, they went home to eat freely of meat and all the other types of food which had been prohibited during those days. Let the reader imagine the contentment and joy today on Easter morning, after the people have flagellated themselves during Holy Week, after they have fasted for a long Lent, abstaining from meat. With what pleasure they go to eat freely of meats, pies, and fried bacon! Thus these people went to feast after having fasted eight days (a very rigorous fast) and after having bled their ears, the equivalent of scourging and doing penance. I have been assured that they became so weak because of the terrible eight-day fast that for another eight days they were not themselves, nor were they satisfied by eating. Many became gravely ill, and the lives of many pregnant women were in danger. Such a fast which included everyone I consider brutal.

Once they had eaten, all returned to the feast which had commenced, to see its end. Some say, however, that it was not so, that it was suspended for the entire day owing to the poor night they had spent, and that they slept and rested all day, coming to the temple on the morrow. When the people had gathered, the girl was offered incense again, no less solemnly than on the previous day. Then she was cast upon the piles of ears of corn and seeds and decapitated. Her blood was gathered in a small bowl, and the wooden goddess was sprinkled with it. All the chamber was sprinkled, and so were the offerings of ears of corn, chili and squash, seeds and vegetables which lay there. After her death she was flayed, and one of the priests donned her skin. On it were placed all the garments the girl had worn—her tiara on his head, her ears of corn on his neck and hands. He was presented to the public while the drums sounded and all danced, led by the man dressed in the skin of the young girl and the robes of the goddess. She had been honored only to be slain to the glory and honor of the deity.

After having danced and enjoyed the feast, as has been described, all entered a spacious chamber called Zacapan, which means On the Grass. And truly the entire floor was covered with dry grass, resembling the way in which floors are covered today to receive guests and envoys. All the lords and noblemen entered, each taking his place and seat [according to his rank], and the sovereign of the land came in carrying splendid gifts: feathers, gems, gold, stones, arms and insignia, shields, and other fine and precious things, such as earplugs, labrets of gold and silver, bracelets, and so forth, presenting a gift to each of the lords. He showered them with presents; he offered them magnificent gifts; he garbed them with many kinds of mantles, breechcloths, sashes, and sandals, all richly and beautifully worked. The same was done to all the captains and braves of the armies and forces. When the favors and presents which the king distributed on that day had been given, the shooters or archers took up their arms and donned the costumes of the gods Tlacahuepan, Huitzilopochtli, Titlacahuan, the Sun, Ixcozauhqui, and the Four Dawns. Then they gathered their bows and arrows. Prisoners and captives of war then appeared who were crucified upon a high scaffolding which stood there for that purpose. Their arms and legs extended, they were all bound to one board or another. Then the archers dressed in the divine garb shot them with great fury. This was the sacrifice of the goddess; it was performed in her honor like the fire sacrifice of the other goddess.

Once the wretches had been slain by the arrows, they were cast down. Their chests were opened, their hearts were extracted, and their bodies were delivered to their owners, together with [the body of] the young woman who had been skinned—all for feasts and banquets of human flesh! As I have stated, this was not held [to be cannibalism]. Many a time have I asked the natives why they were not satisfied with the offerings of quail, turtledoves, and other birds which were sacrificed. They answered sarcastically and indifferently that those were offerings of low and poor men and that the sacrifice of human beings—captives, prisoners, and slaves—was the honored oblation of the great lords and noblemen. They remember these things, treasure them, and tell of them as if they had been great deeds.

Furthermore—to finish our description of the manner in which men were slain in sacrifice—it is to be remarked that not one died or was sacrificed unless he was offered up by the wealthy class, unless he was a man of valor. Some were obtained in war, others in the markets (markets existing especially for that purpose). When many traders in men were around, many men were killed; and when there were few, few were slain. Thus in those times the sacrifice of a man was like the presentation today of a couple of hens to the church, depending upon one's devotion to a special feast. This is what I have been able to gather regarding the goddess of the breads and cornfields.

We shall now deal with the goddess Toci, Mother of the Gods, who was honored on the day after [the feast of] this goddess, on the sixteenth of September. If we examine it closely, we shall find that it was like a Pasch, a holy day, lasting three days in a row. As we have seen in this chapter, on the first day they sacrificed to Atlatonan, goddess of the leprous and maimed; on the second, to the goddess Chicomecoatl; on the third, to this divinity, Mother of the Gods, whom we shall describe in the following chapter. It must be noted that the offerings of strings of ears of corn and flowers on the Day of Our Lady in September and during the festivities in that month are a survival of the [pagan] custom.[1] But I believe they have been turned into an offering to His Divine Majesty. I pray He may receive it in Her name! Praise be to Him *in saecula seculorum!* Amen.

---

[1] The "Day of Our Lady" is undoubtedly the Feast of the Nativity of the Virgin Mary (September 8) in the Roman Catholic calendar.

CHAPTER XV

¶Which treats of the goddess known as Toci [Our Grandmother], Mother of the Gods and Heart of the Earth, and of her most solemn feast.

Tᴴɪs deals with the pagan feast and commemoration which, in their blind religion, the Mexicas celebrated in honor of the goddess Toci, also called Mother of the Gods and Heart of the Earth. It was one of the most solemn, and the diversity of rites and sacrifices clearly demonstrated their veneration for her. Her feast fell immediately after the Feast of Chicomecoatl, with whom we dealt in the last chapter. It fell on the sixteenth of September; and, though it was the feast day of this goddess, it was also a festive day in the calendar. It was called Ochpaniztli, which means Sweeping of the Roads. We may call it the Feast of Sweeping. Thus, since two festivals came together, the Indians prayed a "double rite" (as it is called), commemorating both feasts. Therefore we shall deal with both of them together, but first discuss that of the goddess.

It should be remarked that at the gates of the City of Mexico (where the first cross now stands) there was a shrine called Cihuateocalli, which means the Temple, or Shrine, of the Women. This shrine stood at one side of the road which left the city, on the left; as one entered, it stood on the right side.

In front of this stood four poles, driven into the ground in the form of a square. Each measured about thirteen feet in height, so thick that two men could not embrace them. At the top of the four poles was attached a platform which held a hut covered with straw. We shall tell of its use later. This place was called Tocititlan, and it is so called today. It means Next to the Place of the Goddess Toci.[1]

Eyewitnesses tell a noteworthy thing regarding the shrine: how the Marqués del Valle lodged and set up his camp there. This was after he had secretly fled from Mexico City. A frightful rainstorm had just begun. The bonfires the sentinels kept had gone out, and it was believed that the guards had gone to sleep. But [Cortés] was unable to depart in secret, without being seen or heard. The [Mexica] sentinels sounded the alarm, and [the Spaniards] were attacked, and all the bridges were raised. Seven hundred Spaniards perished, though the captain managed to escape with five hundred men. When they reached [what is now the shrine of] Our Lady of los Remedios,[2] they were so fatigued and mangled that many of them wanted to die there, because of the weariness and anguish in their hearts. [They were revived] by their leader, who urged them on and gave them spirit from beginning to end with his unconquerable courage. From there he journeyed to Tlaxcala, rebuilt and

[1] The shrine of Tocititlan, Place of the Goddess Toci, has traditionally been situated at the corner of Pino Suárez and República del Salvador streets. An inscription on the east wall of the Church of Jesús Nazareno at that corner reminds the visitor that Cortés and Moteczoma II first met at this spot in November, 1519. The conqueror's tomb lies within the epistle side of the nave of the church. Early in March, 1968, while workmen were excavating a tunnel for Mexico's first subway, a pre-Hispanic structure was uncovered and identified by archaeologists as the Temple of Toci. This partly destroyed platform stands two blocks south of Jesús Nazareno, at a corner of San Miguel Square. The building is supported by wooden piles driven into the earth. The structure is about 150 feet long and about 65 feet tall. Since Tocititlan lies under a busy thoroughfare, it was decided to cover it again with a view to future exploration.

[2] The shrine of Our Lady of los Remedios is still one of the most popular shrines in Mexico. It stands upon a hill a few miles west of Mexico City. The small image of the Virgin Mary at the shrine is said to have been dropped by one of Cortés's soldiers during the flight on the *noche triste* in 1520. Like Mayahuel, the pre-Hispanic goddess of pulque, Our Lady of los Remedios used to stand upon a maguey, or century plant and also is the patroness of the brewers of pulque, a drink fermented from the maguey.

strengthened his army, and returned to Mexico. The Indians say that he stayed at the shrine [of Toci], maintaining his camp [there] until the land had been conquered.[3] The dikes extended to that place, to the very boundaries of Mexico City. They served as a wall to the city, together with the surrounding canals. All were reopened and made narrow for fear of the return of the Spaniards. It was something to see: behind each canal there was a wall which was useful in filling up the canals. As soon as the Spaniards took one of these walls, their Tlaxcalan allies tore it to pieces and filled the canal, and thus the army advanced.

In the room which served as a shrine at the gates of Mexico City and which (as I have stated) was called the Shrine of the Women stood a wooden idol representing an old woman. Above the nose the face was white, and from the nose down it was black. Her hair was dressed in the fashion of a native woman, and locks of cotton were attached in the form of a crown. On both sides of the hair were stuck spindle whorls with their bunches of spun cotton. From the end of these spindle whorls hung bundles of carded cotton. In one hand she held a shield; in the other, a broom. On the nape of her neck she wore plumage of yellow feathers. Her short blouse was adorned with a fringe of unspun cotton, and [below it she wore a] skirt. All her attire was white. This idol always stood in that room on an altar, without a priestly guard or other keepers. Those who occasionally came to sweep and adorn the shrine were from that same ward. There were no priests there because her image stood in the city temple in the dark chamber, as we have said, where special services were offered to her and to all [the other gods], for it was a sort of Temple of All Saints, where all were jointly honored, where their days and feasts were remembered, each having its special ministers for its cult.

A woman, not too old and not too young—about forty or forty-five years of age—was sacrificed forty days before the occa-

[3] In his description of the flight of the Spaniards westward on the *noche triste* in 1520, Durán unintentionally misleads the reader in implying that the Spaniards fled from Mexico City southward, toward Tocititlan. The shrine of Toci described here stood about one mile south of the Great Temple. As Durán says, it was used by Cortés as a strategic point in the siege of Mexico a year later.

sion of this festivity. This woman was purified and washed like the other slaves who represented deities. On her purification she was given the name of the goddess Toci, Mother of the Gods, Heart of the Earth. Behold why she was called Heart of the Earth: it is said that, when she so desired, she made the earth tremble. This woman, hallowed as a goddess, consecrated to avoid all sin or transgression, was locked up and kept carefully in a cage from that day on. After having been kept there twenty days, she was brought forth and garbed exactly as the goddess is shown in the illustration [Plate 24]. She was presented to the public so that all could see her and worship her as a divinity. And she was made to dance and rejoice.

From that time the people held her to be the Mother of the Gods and revered her, respected and honored her as if she had been the goddess herself. Daily she was brought out to dance and sing in public; then she was returned to the captivity of her cage. Seven days before the feast she was taken out of her prison and delivered to seven midwives or witch doctors, who served her and attended her wants with great care and lifted her spirits. They amused her, narrating stories and gossip. They filled her heart with gladness and merriment, inducing her to laughter. As I have stated, if those who represented the gods and goddesses alive became downcast, remembering that they were to die, it was an ill omen. To prevent them from becoming sad, an attempt was made to give them joy and good cheer from that day, the seventh before the sacrifice.

[The victim] was delivered to the old women, who brought her a bundle of maguey fiber. They made her comb it, wash it, spin it, and weave a cloth of it. At a certain hour she was led out of the temple to a place where she was to perform the act [of weaving]. While she was busy at this, youths and maidens, holding each other by the hands, danced before her. The music was played by old men who wore white tunics reaching to their feet, their backs adorned with small gourds filled with tobacco and other magic objects. These were hung from red, cordlike strips of skin.

When the eve of the feast arrived, the woman, who had finished her weaving (which was a skirt and a blouse of maguey fiber), was led by the old women to the market place. They made her sit there and sell the things she had spun and woven, thus indicating that the Mother of the Gods [also] had been engaged in that occupation in her time to make a living, spinning and weaving garments of maguey fiber, going to the markets to sell them, thus providing for herself and her children.

When [this woman] was led to the market place, she was accompanied by men disguised as Huaxtecs, together with other attendants who served her when she was alive. They were called Iztactlamacazcauh, which means White Servants. Another was called Itlilpotoncauh, which means Her Servant Feathered with Black Plumes. These carried her merchandise to the market place, and, though she went to the market, she did not sell the skirt or the blouse. This was performed only as a ceremony, and the things were returned from the market.[4]

At dawn on the same day of the feast the woman was slain in the manner I shall describe. When all the people had gathered in the temple, which had been closed for [some] hours before daybreak, this woman consecrated as a divinity was brought forth. A priest took her on his back, carrying her face upward. And so, as she was held thus by the arms on the man's back, the sacrificer appeared. He took her by the hair and beheaded her so that the man holding her was drenched with blood from head to foot. Once she was dead, she was skinned from the middle of the thigh upward as far as the elbows. A man appointed for this purpose was made to don the skin so as to represent the goddess again. Over that skin he was clothed with the blouse and skirt which the woman had spun and woven of maguey fiber, and on his head [he displayed] the cotton garland with her spindle whorls and carded cotton. In

[4] Durán either is unaware of or chooses to ignore the phallic symbolism of the fertility rite described in the last passages of this chapter. The brooms, poles, human skin (symbolizing a renewal of vegetation), and blood play important roles in the ceremony. The phrase "disguised as Huaxtecs" may mean that the four men were naked. In this connection Sahagún made the following observation: "The defects of the Huaxtecs: the men did not provide themselves with breechclouts, although there were many large capes. They perforated their noses with palm leaves. And when they were enlarged, they inserted there a gold palm leaf stem, or a reed from which emerged a red *arara* [feather]. They filed their teeth; they darkened them with red or with the *tlamiaualli* herb" (Sahagún, 1961, X:186).

his nose he wore a silver jewel and in his ears earrings or earplugs of silver. On his chest he bore an ornament of shining silver. Thus arrayed, this man was taken out before the people, appearing before the Huaxtecs and her other servants, all armed for war. While these departed through the chamber door, all the nobles and knights of the city entered in good order by the courtyard gates. They carried their swords and shields; they were well armed with their helmets and devices of rich feathers in different patterns, decorated with gold, silver, gems and feathers, the pride of those who bore them. Some descended from the summit of the temple; others came in from the other side. When they were inside, they feigned skirmish or combat which looked like the real thing. This farce of war was called *moyohual i calli.* Today we say "to make a last remembrance," and thus a last remembrance was made. Her captain and defender against the Huaxtecs and servants was the man who wore the skin and dress of the woman. When the combat ended, everyone danced, following the man with the skin as their guide, singing songs in her honor. Having finished the song, those to be sacrificed in honor of the goddess appeared, and this sacrifice was a strange one—very different from the rest.

This took place in the following way: four heavy poles, about a hundred and eighty feet high (made for that purpose) were set up in the temple in the form of a square. On all four sides, steps were set up between one pole and the next, reaching to the top of the poles. Up those steps went the two sacrificers, with their miters on their heads and with their eyes, lips, fleshy parts, and thighs smeared with chalk, carrying chalked banners on their bodies. These climbed to the top of the scaffolding and, seated there on the summit, tied their bodies to the poles with ropes so as not to fall. Then four sacrificers brought out the victim, forcing him to ascend the pole. He wore a paper hood on his head. The four men went behind him, ascending, and if by any chance he hesitated through fear of death, they pricked his buttocks with maguey thorns. When they reached the spot where the two stood at the summit, those who had ascended with him stood to one side while those on top pushed him. He fell from the poles with a mighty crash and was shattered to bits.

Once he had fallen, others came to behead him, and his blood was caught in a small bowl. All the other victims were sacrificed in the same manner. When the sacrifice had ended, the blood of the victims was carried out in a bowl. This container was plumed with red feathers and was set before the Mother of the Gods, who had stopped dancing and had been watching, accompanied by all her Huaxtecs and attendants. Instead of the swords they had carried, brooms were now placed in their hands—as I have said, this was the day of Ochpaniztli, which means the Feast of Sweeping. As these stood to one side lifting their brooms on high as insignia of the goddess, just as kings bear their scepters, the man who impersonated the goddess descended. He wet his finger with that human blood and licked his finger with his mouth. Thus bent over [the body], having finished his licking in the most frightful way, he moaned eerily. And everyone shuddered and was filled with fear at his moans. And it is said that the earth moved and quaked at that moment. I tried to investigate this and attempted to laugh off and mock this absurd belief. But I was assured that this part, this area of the temple, trembled and shook at that moment. Imagination may have served them well in this case, and the devil, always present, undoubtedly aided the imagination. When the rite performed by the man—that of licking the blood—ended, everyone went to place his finger on the ground, sucking it, eating the earth which had stuck to it. This rite was called Nitizapaloa, which means the Tasting of Chalk. This ceremony of the "eating of the earth" was very common at solemn rites and, when one approached the idols, a special sign of reverence and humility before the gods. In certain villages I found this ceremony performed in the presence of the saints' images and at the little altars set up in the homes with offerings of food, incense, candles, as if they had been idols! This occurred [in certain villages] neglected, forgotten, by God!

When all had eaten of that earth with their fingers, one of the warriors—the highest in spirit and valor, he who had fought and danced—approached the bowl of blood swiftly, before the others. He placed his finger within the bowl and performed the same ceremony which the man representing the goddess had performed. Then he turned against all those who stood there, armed, facing them with the courage of a Caesar. He defended himself from those who were leaving the temple, some attempting to wound him, others to defend him. A bloody fray then took place among them. With sticks and stones countless men came to the combat and fight, something awesome to see, all armed with their quivers, swords, and shields. Fighting all the way, they went to the shrine of the goddess (which I have described) which stood at the entrance of the city, called the Shrine of the Women. The man wearing the skin and maguey-fiber clothes of the woman went behind, among the Huaxtecs. One of these was dressed in white, another in red, another in yellow, yet another in green, each holding his broom high in his hands. Many of those who took part in this combat were sorely wounded by the stones and sticks. This battle raged from the gates of the Temple of Huitzilopochtli (from the ruins of what was the house of Alonso de Ávila—may he rest in peace—to the first cross beyond San Antonio [Abad], which lies half a league onward); the skirmish ended there. The flower of the knights, captains, and soldiers of the land had been present. I believe this [skirmish] was a kind of ceremonial self-sacrifice which they performed instead of bleeding their tongues or ears, as was usual on other feasts.

When they reached the shrine, or home, of the goddess, the fight ended. [This structure] was splendidly adorned and decorated with branches, together with the four tall pales which served as a scaffolding, as I have said. On top was a straw hut. These poles had their steps tied from pole to pole on all four sides. The man who represented the goddess, together with the Huaxtecs and attendants, climbed the pole to the platform. On the platform he stripped himself of his garments and finery, together with the woman's skin he had worn. He placed the latter upon a straw figure which stood on the platform, covering it with the rest of his finery so that the straw image seemed a representation of the goddess. Those who had impersonated the Huaxtecs and the others now took off their disguises, hanging them on the corners of the platform, leaving them as trophies. Then they descended, removing the ladder made of poles; in this way no one could ascend it again. When they came down, the festivities ended—both of the goddess and of the feast day.

Truly it has been worthwhile to describe the way, the manner, in which the Mother of the Gods, the Heart of the Earth, was honored. The Romans had this feast; they celebrated it to solemnize their own Mother of the Gods, [Berecinta], also called Cybele. The entire feast of this goddess was held within the majestic Temple of Huitzilopochtli, since [Toci] possessed no temple of her own—only the shrine we have described. On this day everyone swept his house and properties, the streets and the baths, the [four] corners of the homes. Nothing was left unswept, and this is what the four Huaxtecs symbolized when they held their brooms in the presence of the goddess or her impersonator. This custom of sweeping has survived to the present day among some people. Daily they sweep the streets though the house remains filled with dirt. But I believe that in our times this is no longer a heathen custom.

CHAPTER XVI

¶Which treats of the goddess named Xochiquetzal.

AMONG the most solemn feasts the natives celebrated there was one called Farewell to the Flowers, which meant that frost was coming and that [flowers] would wither and dry up. A solemn festivity, filled with rejoicing and merrymaking, was held to bid them farewell. On that same day [the people] commemorated a goddess named Xochiquetzalli, which means Flowery Plumage.

On this day they were as happy as could be, [filled with] the same happiness and delight they feel today on smelling any kind of flower, whether it have an agreeable or a displeasing scent, as long as it is a flower. They become the happiest people in the world smelling them, for these natives in general are most sensuous and pleasure-loving. They find gladness and joy in spending the entire day smelling a little flower or a bouquet made of different kinds of flowers; their gifts are accompanied by them; they relieve the tediousness of journeys with flowers. To sum up, they find the smelling of flowers so comforting that they even stave off and manage to survive hunger by smelling them.

Thus they passed their lives among flowers in such blindness

238

and darkness, since they had been deceived and persuaded by the devil, who had observed their love for blossoms and flowers.

The [people] celebrated a most solemn feast in honor of the flowers, which took place when they were about to wither, since frost was coming, and they were going to be absent for some time. The people celebrated a sort of carnival, just as during our carnival gluttons stuff themselves with meat without measure or control, for Lent is coming, and (as if the satisfaction of this could last the forty days) the same can be said of these blind and ignorant people [with their flowers].

On this day their persons, temples, houses, and streets were adorned with flowers, similar to the custom of the Christians early on Saint John's Day. Thus decorated with flowers, they engaged in different dances, merrymaking, festivities, and farces, all filled with gladness and good cheer. All this was in honor of and reverence for flowers. This day was called Xochilhuitl, which means Feast of the Flowers, and no other finery—gold, silver, stones, feathers—was worn on this day—only flowers. Besides being the day of the flowers it was the day of a goddess, who, as I have said, was called Xochiquetzal. This goddess was the patroness of painters, embroiderers, weavers, silversmiths, sculptors, and all those whose profession it was to imitate nature in crafts and in drawing. All held this goddess to be their patroness, and her feast was specially solemnized by them.

The image of the divinity Xochiquetzal was of wood in the form of a young woman, with a man's queue hanging to the shoulders and bangs over the forehead. She wore golden earplugs and in her nose a golden ornament which hung over her mouth. She was crowned with a garland of red leather woven like a braid. From its sides emerged splendid green feather ornaments that were round and looked like horns. She wore a finely worked blue tunic decorated with beautifully woven flowers formed of feathers with many little plaques of gold pendants all over them. She was represented with her arms open like a woman who is dancing [Plate 25].

The feast of this deity took place on October 6, two days after the feast on which we honor our Glorious Father Saint Francis;

and though the festivities began on this day, they did not end until twenty days later, when they came to an end with the usual sacrifices. I have become extremely aware of the reluctance that the natives feel in revealing and explaining these things, and I have easily become convinced of this because I have suspected that in some towns where I have lived (although it could be that I am deceived) they celebrate this Feast of the Flowers. It may be, however, that owing to the mercy of God it is not performed with an idolatrous intention. It would be a frightful thing if today reminiscences or ancient idolatrous objects still existed. Therefore, I do not find it amiss that our priests are warned so that if they should discover or hear about any of this they will investigate what the intention is, so that there is no secret evil, no deceit. I would not be surprised if in some place [heathen customs] exist because our Adversary is subtle and tricky, and the elders who have survived tell the noble youths about the lives and customs of their parents, grandparents, and ancestors and how the things of their cursed ancient religion were kept and fulfilled—a religion so old, so rooted, so solidly based that it has been impossible to obliterate it in fifty-seven years.

This goddess stood in a small temple next to that of Huitzilopochtli. Though small, it was a fine building, and, besides being well constructed, it possessed handsome ornaments of cloth, feathers, jewels, and other costly things. The idol was placed upon a tall altar, with as much reverence as the rest. It was celebrated with the same diurnal and nocturnal ceremonies, receiving incense four times a day like the others. This was done by the priests and ministers of Huitzilopochtli because in the temple where the goddess stood no special priests were designated. Thus those who served Huitzilopochtli were charged with performing the rites of the goddesses to be described. First [we shall deal with] this goddess [Xochiquetzal].

Her feast fell on the sixth of October and was called Pachtontli, which is the diminutive of Hueypachtli, since the celebration began on that day and ended twenty days later, [the latter] being the second Feast of Hueypachtli. *Pachtli* means "Spanish moss," a weed that grows in trees and hangs from them, gray owing to the moisture of the water. It thrives especially well on oaks and evergreen oaks. I do not know why these two feasts are both called by the name of that moss. It seems natural though, since—in that season—the trees in the woods were filled with Spanish moss. All their superstitious feasts and rites were always founded on nonsense and childlike things [which revealed] a remarkable blindness and ignorance.

But, to return to the minor Feast of Pachtontli and of the goddess Xochiquetzalli: it is to be remarked that on this day at dawn the cloistered nuns of the Temple of Huitzilopochtli began to grind corn and then made a great lump of dough which they pressed firmly into a large and beautifully decorated tub. The high priests carried this to the top of the temple with awe and reverence. At dusk [this tub] was placed before the image of Huitzilopochtli so that he would give a sign of his coming to earth from heaven and of his birth. The tub, filled with dough, was left there, and [the priests] went to their cloister, leaving their guards and wonderworkers to watch for the coming of their god. Their task was to go back and forth [watching] the tub, to see whether he had come. At midnight they approached the tub with their torches to see the sign which they so desired, coming and going, not stopping until they saw the footprint of a newborn babe impressed in the dough and the dough crumbling. On discovering that sign of the child, the trumpets, conch shells, and flutes resounded, and a great shout went up, announcing the arrival and birth of the warrior, who in their language is called Yaotzin.[1] The impression on the dough, the footprint of the child, occasionally a woman's hair, perhaps some straw—these were shown to all [the people]. It is said that often next to the footprint were found one or two hairs belonging to the mother of the child and a few dry grasses which came from her abode.[2]

[1] A more literal translation of Yaotzin is Small Enemy in War, identified as Huitzilopochtli-Tezcatlipoca.

[2] The "mother of the child" undoubtedly refers to Coatlicue, mother of Huitzilopochtli. In his *History* Fray Diego relates that Moteczoma I (who ruled from 1440 to 1469) sent messengers north from Mexico-Tenochtitlan to seek the

When all these things had been seen, [and] when the trumpets, conch shells, and drums had sounded, the people of the city came in great haste to see the miracle, the arrival of the god. When the courtyard was filled with people, all the dignitaries, priests, and ministers of the temples came out, offering incense to the dough, performing great ceremonies, homage, and obeisance with such an overwhelming number of lights and torches that the night turned into day. When the offering of incense had ended, they took up their sacrificial blades, and, as a recompense and thanksgiving for the boon they had been granted by his coming and birth, they bled their tongues, ears, chests, the fleshy parts of their arms and legs. Some perforated their ears by passing small straws through them. Others pierced their tongues and passed straws through them.

Thus ended the feast of that night, and all the people were advised that the Yacateuctin—for thus they were called—were due to arrive and be awaited three days later. These were three lords. One was called Yacatecutli, the second Cuachtlapuhcacoyaotzin, and the third Titlacahuan, He Whose Slaves We Are. These were expected with great eagerness for the third day when they were awaited, to accompany him who had already arrived—the War Lord!

After the twenty days of this Feast of Hueypachtli had been completed, it being the twenty-sixth of October, the solemn festivity ended. On the morning of this day two young maidens were brought forth, one older than the other, noblewomen of the royal lineage and generation of a great prince whose name was Tezcacoatl.[3] When these girls (the comeliest to be found in that lineage) were brought out, all the lords and temple dignitaries came to dance before them, wearing a special disguise consisting of brief shirts

---

abode of the mother of Huitzilopochtli, who lived on an island surrounded by rushes and grasses (Durán, 1964, 133–38).

[3] According to García Granados, the Tezcacoatl mentioned by Durán could have been one of the "god carriers" who took part in the Aztec pilgrimage which ended in Mexico-Tenochtitlan. Another Tezcacoatl, described by Tezozomoc, was a great Mexica warrior who perished in a war against Huexotzinco and Cholula (García Granados, 1952–53, III:251–52).

reaching to the waist and short skirts or aprons decorated with numerous hearts and hands. They carried in their hands and on their backs large gourds, some green, some red, others finely decorated. The two girls, handsomely dressed and attired in new clothing, with jewels at the neck, appeared behind the dancers. Their faces were made up with color on their cheeks and lips, while on their heads they wore elaborate tiaras.

One after the other, as if in procession, all proceeded to a round stone which, as we have said, was called the Cuauhxicalli (and let us remember that today it stands at the Door of Pardon, at the cathedral, near the Altar of Indulgences). The younger and, behind her, the older girl ascended to the flat surface of the stone. Then the four priests also climbed upon the stone, carrying in their hands four gourds of maize. [One] contained white corn, another black corn, another bright-yellow corn, and yet another purple. Then the one who carried the black corn stood in front [of the girls], who reached into the gourds with their hands and, like one who sows, having turned to the mountains, scattered it. When the gourd of black corn was empty, the white was brought forth. Turning toward the maize fields on the open land, they did the same. The yellow corn was scattered in the direction of the lake, and the fourth, or purple, in the direction which is called *amilpan*.[4]

[4] In Aztec cosmogony each cardinal direction was connected with a god, a color, a bird, a heavenly body, a year sign, and an associated idea, such as heat, cold, fertility, or war (Soustelle, 86–87). The corn used in these rites to Xochiquetzal was no doubt symbolic of the cardinal points, probably invoking the protection of the god represented by each color in his respective direction.

White was the west, represented by Quetzalcoatl and by earthly goddesses, associated with femininity (and, according to Durán, with cultivated fields). Black was the north, represented by Tezcatlipoca and by Mixcoatl, the Hunting God, associated with the night and darkness and war (according to Durán, with woods and hills). Yellow (in this case interchangeable with red) was the east, represented by Quetzalcoatl (as Tlahuizcalpantecuhtli, Morning Star), by Tlaloc, and by Xipe Totec, associated with fertility (and, according to Durán, with the lake). Blue (interchangeable with green, but purple in this case) was the south, represented by Huitzilopochtli (by Macuilxochitl in the Borgia Codex [Seler, 1963]), associated with fire and heat (and with the *amilpan* or *chinampas*—the floating gardens of Xochimilco—according to Durán, "watery fields"). The colors assigned to the directions varied with the culture. For example, among the Mayas black was west, white was north, red was east, and yellow was south (Thompson, 211).

After the four kinds of corn had been scattered, the people hastened to gather as much of it as they could, and even though one picked up only two grains, he took them, kept them carefully, and sowed them in order to obtain the seed of this blessed maize.[5]

While this ceremony lasted, the dance of the gourds (which I mentioned) was performed, while in the center one [priest] who did not dance stood with a large sacrificial blade in his hand, holding it on high in a cloth so that all could see it. This blade was used only on these noble maidens; it never served for another sacrifice, and was held up this way all day. When the hour came, the two girls were slain. Their breasts were opened and their hearts taken out. Four ministers held them down by the hands and feet. When the priest killed these two noblewomen, as an exception [to the usual custom], to indicate that they died virgins, their legs were crossed one upon the other and their hands extended as was usual. They were sent rolling down the steps and were picked up by the other ministers, who carried them to a place called Ayauhcalli [the House of Mist], and were cast into that place, which was like a cellar, made especially for that purpose.

After these rites ended, which the men of the temple and the lords celebrated for the coming of their god, the silversmiths, painters, sculptors, embroiderers, and weavers presented a woman dressed in the guise which we have described as that of the goddess Xochiquetzalli. She represented the goddess alive, as the others did. Thus she was sacrificed and flayed; then one of the men donned her skin and all her finery. This man was made to sit next to the steps of the temple, where a woman's loom was placed in his hands. They made him weave as the Indian women weave; thus the man pretended to be weaving. While he feigned to be weaving, all the master craftsmen—disguised as monkeys, ocelots, dogs, coyotes, mountain lions, jaguars—reveled in a jubilant dance. Each carried in his hands the insignia of his craft: the metalworker carried his tools; the painter his brushes and paint pots. On that day they ate their food in this way: the bread was formed in different figures,

5 An almost identical practice is followed today in Indian Mexico, on Candlemas, when seeds to be sown in the spring are taken to the church to be blessed by the priest.

such as dolls, brushes, flowers, or birds. By strict rule nothing else could be eaten.

On that day before dawn all went to the rivers to bathe, children and adults, elders and youths, according to a precept obliging all to wash on that day. This served to cleanse the sins and lesser, venial transgressions which had been committed throughout the year. I mention this because of the admonition that the ministers had given the people on the preceding eve: all, children and adults, should wash and purify themselves, warning and predicting that those who did not would suffer ills and contagious diseases, such as pustules, leprosy, and malformed hands. It was thought that these ills appeared because of sin and that the gods sent them as a vengeance. Through fear [of these ills] everyone, whether a child or a grown man, went to bathe at dawn. The ceremony of the washing having ended, everyone, believing he had received a pardon and remission of his sins, went to eat *tzoalli*, which, as I have said before, was always held to be bones of God. The priests then spoke thus:

"Those of you who have washed go forth to eat *tzoalli*!"

I do not wish to be repetitious, but, since our subject requires it, I must explain this term in case someone has forgotten what *tzoalli* is. It is a bread made by the natives from amaranth seed and corn grains, kneaded with dark honey, a thing highly esteemed by them. Today it is eaten as candy. In olden times [*tzoalli*] was held in great reverence and was the material with which the [images] of the gods were made. After these had been worshiped and sacrifices and ceremonies had been performed before them, [the bread], in pieces, was distributed and was partaken of as the flesh of God, and all received communion with it, having first washed by order of the priests.

Purification by washing was a most common thing when ordered by the priests. If a person went to tell the priests about his own illness or that of his child or spouse, the following prescription was given to him: he was to grind that seed, knead it with corn, and mix it with honey; but first he must wash, purify himself of his sins, and then go eat [*tzoalli*]. This sounds somewhat like advice from

Christian physicians on the first day they see their patient. Before beginning the treatment, they ask that he confess and receive communion. So it was that on this day [the natives] confessed and received communion, as I have said.

We have noted that this purification was valid only for minor faults and venial sins. However, for those who had committed crimes and grave transgressions there was, on this same day, another type of penitence very similar to that of the Scriptures. [The people] confessed their sins outwardly but not specifically; that is, he who had sinned proclaimed his unrighteousness in general and made an offering. Thus on this day the natives made a public confession, recognizing themselves guilty, manifesting the number of their sins, but the enumeration of each kind of sin was confessed in secret. Though obeying what the law and its precepts commanded of them as occult sinners, no one knew the nature of the wrongs committed.

When I order a penitent to scourge himself, to fast on bread and water, [all the people see the penance], but no one knows the nature of the sin or even suspects it. The same occurred among these people: he who had stolen, fornicated, or killed another or had broken any one of the commandments of laws, the law ordained that he examine his conscience on that day. And in accordance with the number of grave sins he had committed, he gathered the same number of straws the length of the palm of a hand, such as those used for brooms. After having counted his sins with those straws, he went to the temple at the hour when the others had gone to bathe. He squatted before that goddess; he took a pointed instrument and passed it through his tongue. When the piercing of the tongue had been accomplished, he picked up the straws and one by one passed them through the hole; and as he pulled each through, he cast it, full of blood, before the idol. All those present knew that if he cast down ten straws he had committed ten sins, and if twenty, twenty; but they did not know the nature of these sins. In this way they confessed their sins before the gods and the priests and then went to bathe like the rest and to eat of the food we have described. These penitents who confessed were numerous, both men and women.

When the sinners had finished their penance and confession, the priests gathered the bloody straws, went to the Divine Hearth, and burned them there. With this, everyone felt he was cleansed and pardoned for his transgressions and sins, having the same faith that we hold for the Divine Sacrament of Penance.

This was the type of confession practiced by these people. It was not oral, as some have claimed. Though it was intolerably blind, mistaken, unseeing, and ignorant, as was the amazing deceit in which the devil kept them, these things should not be buried in oblivion; yet other things, worthy of oblivion, are not forgotten. It would be better that Christian religion ignore [these customs], since they lead more to evil than to good, though those who write them use them as a shield for their hypocrisy. "Omnia munda mundis, et cetera."[6]

In many cases the Christian religion and the heathen ways found a common ground. And though I am convinced (owing to many arguments I have discovered which give me reason to believe thus) that in this land there were preachers [of Christianity], [my arguments] are not well enough established to permit us to use them as definite proofs. Nevertheless, we have already spoken of that man—a penitent, faster, and preacher [Topiltzin]. He and his disciples were called Teachers. He became angry with them; he and his followers fled from the persecution. One cannot give a definite opinion. On the other hand, one can say that the devil had persuaded and instructed them, stealing from and imitating the Divine Cult so that *he* would be honored as a god; for everything was a mixture of a thousand heathen beliefs, deceits, and imperfections; all was filled with stinking and abominable human blood, all consistent with [the ways of the devil] who had prevailed upon them!

---

[6] "All things seem good to people who are good." The Latin quotation is undoubtedly sarcastic; the second "good" might be translated "simple-minded." One can only speculate about Durán's comments on ancient pagan customs he believed worthy of oblivion. Durán himself was giving a detailed analysis of all the most objectionable aspects of the ancient religious practices. He implies that others were also recording heathen traditions at the time. This curious passage may someday be explained by the discovery of manuscripts still hidden from the world.

CHAPTER XVII

¶Which tells of the goddess Iztaccihuatl, meaning White
Woman.

THE feast with which these blind people honored the goddess
Iztaccihuatl, White Woman, took place on the Snowy Mountain.[1]
Besides considering her a goddess and adoring her as such, because
of their foolishness, great crudeness, blindness, and brutish ignorance, [they built] temples and shrines for her in their cities.
They were lavishly adorned and highly respected; in each was kept
the statue of this deity. And it was kept not only in the temples but
also in a cave on the same White Mountain. There she stood,
greatly adored and revered—no less than she was revered in the
city. There the natives often went with offerings and sacrifices.

There were numerous other idols within that cave. They
represented the names of the hills which surrounded the White
Mountain, such as that of the idol called Tlaloc. We refer the
reader to the description of his feast which is found in this work

[1] This great snow-covered mountain east of Mexico City has been called
Iztaccihuatl (White Woman), Iztactepetl (White Mountain), and Sierra Nevada.
Modern inhabitants of the Valley of Mexico often erroneously refer to it as Sleeping
Woman or Dead Woman.

248

[Chapter VIII]. The same ceremonies performed on the White Mountain were observed on the Hill of Tlaloc. In case we have forgotten about this name Tlaloc, let us remember that he was the God of Lightning and Rain. And the lords would go there to make offerings. Since we have described in such detail the ceremonies and rites which were performed, there is no reason to tell it again here. I shall say only that in the City of Mexico this goddess was a wooden statue dressed in blue. On her head she wore a tiara of white paper painted black. Behind it was a silver medallion to which were attached white and black feathers, and from this medallion hung many streamers of black paper which fell down her back. The face of this statue was like that of a young woman wearing clipped man's hair on the forehead and hanging down to the shoulders on the sides. Her cheeks were always painted with color [Plate 26]. She stood upon an altar like the other images within a small room which was embellished with precious cloth and other fine decorations. Night and day this divinity was served by the priests of the temple with the usual ceremonial; all was done with the greatest of care and orderliness, as befitting one of the main gods.

These wretched people never worshiped a god except with the greatest fear, reverence, and care. They were watchful of obeying the laws and ceremonies which had been disposed for each and feared that if something was lacking in their cult the gods' wrath and fury would fall upon them. In order to placate them, they would utter long lamentations, elegant orations, and prayers, accompanied by abundant offerings, sacrifices, and the deaths of many men. We know of the long and polished speech, accompanied by offerings and sacrifices, with which Moteczoma tried to placate the gods when the Spaniards were about to arrive in this land. I [shall] tell of this in more detail in my *History*, when I deal with this king and great lord. So that the gods would not become angry, the Indians were cautious and prudent and never failed in any way to serve and honor them with the rites and ceremonies corresponding to each one.

But let us return to the deity with which I am dealing. On the same day of the feast of this goddess an Indian slave was dressed all in green and was purified in the name of the idol. A white crown with black lines painted upon it was placed upon her head. This crown showed that the White Mountain is green where the trees grow and [that] above was the snow-covered peak. This Indian woman was slain in the City of Mexico in front of the idol. Two small boys and two small girls were carried on litters decorated with rich cloth up to the White Mountain. The children were dressed in an elaborate fashion. Upon this White Mountain they were sacrificed, in the second place [the cave] where the goddess was kept.[2] And the lords and noblemen carried another present of feather headdresses, women's blouses and skirts, jewelry and precious stones, and much food, just as they did on Mount Tlaloc, as I have described. They left guards to protect the presents which were placed there so that all that wealth would not be stolen, but [it] rotted away in a profitless manner, owing to rain and moisture. The lords remained on the heights of the White Mountain for two days. There they performed the ceremonies in honor of this goddess with solemn prayers and sacrifices, everyone enduring a rigid and severe fast on the great day.

It should be noted here that these people kept the strictest and most rigorous fasts under their old religion. There were no dispensations, not even for the sick or for children. Yet now how unpleasant it seems to them to have to forgo food on a single obligatory fast day during Lent! It seems so disagreeable to them that very few, perhaps none, fast on these days of precept. I believe this is caused by our laxity since we do not encourage them or insist in this. Their own priests, however, fostered this precept among them in the ceremonies of the cursed and tyrannical law, so

[2] Like many other mountains, Iztaccihuatl, White Woman, and Popocatepetl, Smoking Mountain, are covered with ancient ceremonial shrines. The archaeologist José Luis Lorenzo has described at least ten sites on the slopes of these mountains. Among them are Nexpayantla, Tenenepanco, Barranca de Nexpayantla, Milpulco, Cueva de Alcalican, Nahualac, El Estanque, El Caracol, El Solitario, and Llano Chico el Alto. All these shrines are about twelve thousand feet above sea level, not far from the snow line. At Alcalican the sacred site is still in use, and on May 3 a great nocturnal ceremony is held here, attended by people from distant villages who seek to discover the identity of their *nahual*—alter ego or animal guardian (Lorenzo, 16–20).

full of mystery and fear. Our own religious practices are different from the old, since they are light and tender. It is also true that we are moved by pity and mercy on seeing their poor food and their meager nourishment and sustenance; therefore, we pretend not to notice [that they do not fast]. We know that in those times they ate the same amount of food as they do today and did not die of hunger. Therefore, it would be just that they be informed regarding their obligations in obeying the things of our Holy Christian Religion. There have been friars who have stated that it is not necessary to force the people to observe the feasts that fall within the week, but I consider this improper and wrong, since they are Christians and should know better. If they wish to keep a holy day and go to mass, let them do it as Christians. And if they wish to take advantage of their privilege, let them do so, but let it be explained to them what this privilege has exempted them from. But, above all, let them be taught their obligations as Christians, since the same strictness applies to them as to us. If any recollection of the ancient religion exists among the natives, it is necessary that it be uprooted. Therefore, our own friars should incite them to observe our divine law with devout and frequent persuasion and should take pride in having listened carefully to the confession of one Indian instead of many in a careless and routine manner.

Some priests are content to hear a few trivial babblings from an Indian, though [they know] that many of his people, because of foolish fears and for no reason, shorten their confessions and hide their sins, sometimes because of an unfounded shame. Often [the Indians] tell things which are not even venial sins. This could be corrected if the confessor would only make a moderate examination, together with an exhortation. He should endeavor to remove fear with a kind and gentle warning at the beginning. Finally, [the friars] would perhaps discover deceiving ways and evils which are an important obstacle to the aid and salvation of the Indians, as some friars may have done during the terrible plague which God sent to them because of our sins. I understand that, desirous to save their souls, many of them were saved by revealing grave sins of the past. Therefore, I understand that our God has already swept clean the past so that no memory or reminder is left of it. May His will and mercy enlighten those who carry the dough of the Faith in their hands so that He may open their eyes regarding His divine honor! May they take pride in their labors and ministry for which God chose them, just as the shoemaker takes pride in his work.

I could say much regarding all these things, but I do not wish to condemn confessors from all the orders. They condemn themselves by hearing the confession of many Indians every day, and although many of them are learned men, they are not as familiar with the native language as others who confess fewer Indians. Some of the friars are content to allow the Indian to make the sign of the cross, and after that *per signum crucis* the native utters a few puerile things under the outward appearance and ceremony of confession. Therefore, I believe that many sacrilegious and incomplete confessions take place. Often they lack the parts which the Sacrament demands: sorrow, repentance, purpose of amendment, penance, and a true declaration of all one's sins. Very seldom does the Indian even show signs of attrition unless the confessor moves, awakens, warns, and enlightens him to not imitate what he sees, the way monkeys do, but to carry out his obligations in order to obtain the remission of his sins. The confessor should tell him that he must not come from habit or by force, or be compelled by fear of his superiors, as some come to confession. Let the Indian consider it a principal act for his salvation and a necessary remedy.

With this I terminate the feast of Iztaccihuatl, known as the White Mountain, referring the reader to the rites which are described under the Feast of Tlaloc.

CHAPTER XVIII

¶Which treats of the solemn feast with which the natives honored the volcano called Popocatzin [Popocatepetl], which means Smoker, and many other mountains.

THE Mountain of Popocatzin, which in our tongue means Smoking Mountain, is known to us all as the volcano which gives forth smoke two and three times a day (and often flames at the same time), especially at an early hour of the morning, as many have observed. Both Spaniards and Indians affirm that this flaming is very common, as do the villages contiguous to this mountain, which is visible from many leagues away because of its height.[1] Many people—both friars and laymen—attempted to climb it, curious to see the cone from which the smoke escapes, but they failed, defeated by the difficulties which they found, and had to return without having accomplished their purpose. A venerable old friar of our order told me these things. Wishing to see the cone, he and two laymen who had the same desire reached the [level of] ashes, from which they tried more than once to ascend. But the more they climbed, the more they fell behind, slipping upon the moving, enormous mass of ashes. Besides the great labors they suffered,

[1] Today Indian villagers believe that Popocatepetl was once a man and that the nearby Iztaccihuatl was his wife.

they also thought that they would be poisoned or die from the delicate, subtle air which blows there.

Thus I have been amazed by and have considered an exaggeration [the story told by] those who affirm that a conqueror named Montaño made the ascent. I have heard this said, and his children hold it as a trustworthy testimony. When sulphur stone was lacking for gunpowder, this conqueror went up and extracted sulphur rock from [the mountain]. This would be, in my estimation, one of God's miracles. What makes it most incredible to me is that, according to native history, Moteczoma, who rose to great and courageous feats, capable of attempting the impossible, desirous of discovering the origin of the smoke, appointed certain men to investigate. Thus ten were appointed who, more from force than from choice, fearing the punishment of the Angry King if his commandment was not fulfilled, ascended. Two were unable to reach the summit, having died on the way. The rest, with great difficulties, succeeded and saw the place from which the smoke emerged. On the third day they descended, and on the fourth six of them died. Lest the surviving two perished, they were taken in haste to the Great Lord so that he would be informed. King Moteczoma was careful to see that they were cured; and when they were well, they related the following:

> The place from which the smoke proceeds is not a great mouth, as we had imagined. That place, the summit or the peak of that mountain, is filled with enormous clefts like the mesh of a net, or like a grating, or like latticework. Clefts, one next to the other, rugged crags! Between one abyss and another two men can walk abreast. And that smoke, thick and evil, escapes from those clefts.

These men never recovered their good health to the time of their deaths. They told strange tales about the roughness of the summit and the network through which the smoke escapes. [They told] of the land which can be seen from there, and of the sea. They affirmed that everything seems close, as if the sea were at the foot of the mountain.

An old settler told me that he did everything in his power to ascend this volcano, a thing he was eager, desirous, to accomplish. I have heard of a man, whose last name was Martínez, who, in order to accomplish this and to satisfy his passion (for I consider it to be that), climbed up, and as he was reaching the top, [the mountain] began to smoke with such fury that the whole place shook, and the roar seemed to make the entire place tremble. This poor man, believing his end was near with the shock he had received, tried to turn back to flee from the smoke but did not manage it quickly enough to avoid smoke getting in his eyes. The injury was so severe that a few days later he became blind.

Another man was stubborn in his desire [to climb the mountain]: he was a carver of holy images and lived in La Trinidad, within the very church. His name was Petijuan, and he aspired to see this volcano. He made three or four attempts and never succeeded, and I have heard that he died owing to this. Because of these things I am willing to die without seeing it. I am also convinced that few have seen it or will see it, or perhaps none, unless it is some witch or sorcerer.

In olden times this mountain was hallowed by the natives as the most important among the mountains, especially by those who lived in its vicinity or on its slopes. In both climate and other desirable things it is the best part of the land. Even though its slopes are rough with cliffs and hills and the land most rugged, the hills and cliffs are thickly populated and always were so, owing to the splendid waters which come from this volcano and to the great abundance of maize and European produce which are harvested around it. The closer they are [to the volcano], the earlier [the fruit and grain] ripen and the tastier they are. I should not forget the beautiful and abundant wheat which ripens on its heights and its slopes. For these reasons the people revered [the mountain] and held it in high esteem. They offered it the usual and continued sacrifices and presents, aside from the special feast offered yearly. This feast was called Tepeilhuitl, which means Feast of the Mountains, and was celebrated as I shall describe.

It should be known that when the solemn day of the feast of this hill arrived a great multitude of people from the locality dedicated themselves to the grinding of amaranth seed and maize kernels, and with that dough they formed a hill representing the volcano. They gave him his eyes, his mouth, and they placed him in an honored spot in the home. And around him were set many smaller hills of the same amaranth-seed dough, each with its eyes and mouth, each one possessing its own name: one, Tlaloc; another, Chicomecoatl, or Iztactepetl; Matlalcueye; together with Cihua-coatl and Chalchiuhtlicue, the latter the goddess of rivers and springs which flowed from this volcano. On this day all these hills were placed around the [dough] volcano, each made of dough with its face. [They were] thus placed in order and left for two days, [and] offerings and ceremonies were made to them. On the second day they were crowned with paper miters and sleeveless tunics of painted paper. After the dough had been dressed with the same solemnity customary in slaying and sacrificing the men who represented the gods, the dough representing the hills was sacrificed in the same way. The ceremony concluded, this dough was eaten as a sacred thing.

On this day the priests went to the woods to seek the most distorted and gnarled branches they could find, carrying them to the temple and covering them with the dough. These were called Coatzintli, which means a Twisted Thing like a Snake. They were adorned with eyes and mouth and were honored with the same rites and offerings. After pretending to kill them, [the priests] distributed them among the lame, one-armed, and maimed, among those who suffered from pustules or paralysis. These people were obliged to contribute for a year hence the seed to make the dough for the images of the mountains. This repast was called Nicteocua, which means I Eat God. Children were also sacrificed on this day, together with a few slaves—offered up in the temples and in the presence of the dough (which symbolized the mountain and its neighboring hills), and also many ears of tender corn, food, and incense. [The people] climbed to the tops of the hills to light fires, to offer and burn incense, and to perform some of the usual ceremonies which have been described. On the same day the feast of this volcano and the hills was celebrated in Mexico and in the entire land, in Tlaxcala a solemn feast was made to the two principal mountains which exist today, lofty and fair; one is called Matlalcueye [Malinche] and the other Tlapaltecatl. Amatlalcueye means She of the Skirt of Blue Paper.[2]

Aside from the people of Tlaxcala all [those of] the neighboring towns—such as Tepeaca, Atlixco, Cuauhquecholan, and others —came to burn incense and offer rubber, foods, paper, and feathers and to sacrifice human beings. The second mountain was then and is now called Tlapaltecatl, Things of Many Colors or Lord [of Many Colors] (according to our translation). It was held in great reverence by those of Tlaxcala and propitiated with generous offerings and the usual sacrifices.

In Cholula there was a man-made hill called Tlachihualtepetl. Today it is called Man-made Mountain. It was called thus because it is said that the Giants built it in order to climb to the heavens; today it stands in ruins. This hill was much hallowed; there were the usual and unceasing adoration, the prayers, the great sacrifices, offerings, and slaying of men. On the southern side of the volcano, in the region of Tetelan, Ocuituco, Temoac, Tzacualpan, and other towns, there is a hill to which the entire country journeyed with its offerings, sacrifices, and prayers. This [hill] was called Teocuicani, which means Divine Singer. It lies so near the volcano that there is barely a league between them. It is so tall and rugged that it is a remarkable sight. It was called Divine Singer because usually when clouds gather about it (which are those frozen by the volcano), it gives forth terrible thunder and lightning, so resonant and echoing that it is awesome to hear its thunder and hoarse voice. All the [people of the] region journeyed to this mountain to sacrifice and offer incense, food, rubber, paper, feathers, jars, plates, bowls, gourds, and other kinds of vessels and toys—and to slay men.

---

[2] Durán's second spelling of the name of the mountain known today as Malinche is a variant form. The *A* as the first letter of this spelling may refer to *amatl* ("paper"). Durán's translation of the name as She of the Skirt of Blue Paper therefore makes sense. The particles would be *amatl* ("paper"), *matlalli* ("blue"), *cueitl* ("skirt"), and *ye* (a possessive).

On this mountain stood the best-constructed building in the entire area. This was called Ayauhcalli, which means Mansion of Rest and Shade of the Gods.[3] Within this house was kept a large green idol made of jade, as tall as an eight-year-old boy, so fine, so precious, that attempts to remove it precipitated great wars between the people of this province and Huexotzinco, Cuauhquecholan, and Atlixco, all the latter losing lives and disbanding without having attained what they desired. It is said that this idol disappeared when the Faith was introduced into this land. Thus the natives concealed it, burying it in the same mountain. There it lies with many other rich things, such as those hidden in all these hills: gold, silver, and stones of high value. Aside from these, there were many other mountains, and if I paused here to tell of them, it would be necessary to write another and voluminous book. It is enough, however, to mention the main and the most important.

Among them we could speak of [the hill] that is at Culhuacan, no less feared and venerated [than the one we have just described]. All the people of the area went there to worship, sacrifice, and fulfill their usual vows. These vows were continuous and standing. It did not give them a headache to promise something to the idols they were most devoted to. The offerings presented were in accordance with the [importance of the] gods. They were so insignificant that they were no larger than a small gourd for the gods to drink from, tiny bowls, plates, pots, little beads, incense, rubber, and feathers.

Thus those afflicted with tumors and the mange who ate the "flesh" of the hills made vows to contribute a year later all the seeds for the making of this "flesh." They furnished the seed in proportion to what they had been given to eat: if they had been given a large piece, they contributed a large quantity of seed; if they had been given little, they contributed little. The manner in which they complied with their vows in these days was so mean and base that everything the common people offered up was insignifi-

---

[3] Durán's translation of Ayauhcalli is a free one owing to the metaphoric character of the Nahuatl language. The word is derived from *ayahuitl* ("mist") and *calli* ("house").

cant. The nobles offered things of value, but their gifts consisted mainly of slaves who were killed and later eaten.

The principal aim in honoring these hills, in praying and pleading, was [not to honor] the hill itself. Nor should it be considered that [hills] were held to be gods or worshiped as such. The aim was another: to pray from that high place to the Almighty, the Lord of Created Things, the Lord by Whom They Lived. These are the three epithets used by the Indians on pleading and crying out for peace in their time, because in pagan times, according to what is well known, they commonly suffered plagues, famines, and other afflictions. Weeping, those who narrated all of this to me admitted the good our God has done for them, His mercy in having separated them from the great aberrations in which their ancestors had lived, thus recognizing that the Most Just God and Redemptor, the Righteous Lord, was punishing them justly since He was aware of their low, vile, bestial, and ignorant religion, deceived as they were by the devil.

This is the account which I have been able to gather regarding the Feast of the Hills celebrated throughout the entire land, where there was not a hill, nor is there today, which did not have its own name. Today all, small or large, have their names. If the feast was held on one [hill] one year, it had to be celebrated on another the next and another the following. Thus they managed to hold a feast on each hill by rotating, so that every hill might be revered and the divine food (in the form of dough mountains) [which had been eaten] on one hill might be eaten the next year on another. It was within the commandments; it was prohibited that the same solemnity be repeated the same year on the same hill.

This feast fell in August, but I have not been able to verify the exact date. I paid scant attention since it meant little to me. There are tares among the wheat [owing to] some superstitious or evil persons who wish to take advantage of weaknesses and ancient heathen customs (as I believe there are). It is necessary to bring these things into the open so that the good [believers] may be known. [These heathens] will soon show themselves for what they are if we take a small amount of care and interest in uprooting and destroying these things [of pagan times]. Let us plead, let us use persuasion, let us insist, let us admonish, for they are capable of recognizing error and being convinced of good, of exposing iniquity. Hence I would like to see more and better [ministers with knowledge of] the native languages among the people and less pretentious about their knowledge of them, for they are unaware of the important things, while they understand the petty ones.

CHAPTER XIX

¶Which treats of the universally revered Chalchiuhcueye, Goddess of the Springs and Rivers.

AFTER fire there was no element of the four so hallowed by the
Mexica people as water. All [four elements] were venerated with
all awe, attention, and reverence, some more highly than others,
depending upon the virtues and qualities which [the people] saw
in them and the benefits received from them.

Great was the honor and respect paid to the Earth under the
hallowed and glorious name of Tlaltecutli. This name is composed
of two terms, *tlali*, [which means "earth"], and *tecutli*, which
means "great lord"—thus Great Lord Earth. This element was
worshiped with impressive sacrifices and offerings. The highest
honor paid to him was to place one's finger on the earth, carry it to
one's mouth, and lick the earth. I have already explained under
the Feast of Toci that this element was the Mother of the Gods
and the Heart of the Earth. On the latter feast the earth was glorified with special offerings and sacrifices; shedding of blood; impressive ceremonies involving the use of incense, feathers, foods,
and the spilling on the ground of pulque; and the eating of the
flesh of sacrificed men, such as has been described.

On two occasions we have dealt with the element of Fire: the splendid, great feast where men were sacrificed and [the fire] was sprinkled with the human blood of those who, half-roasted, had been pulled out, their breasts cut open, their blood gathered in a small tub, and the fire sprinkled with it. The latter was adored and paid homage under the name of Xiuhtecutli. At the solemn Feast of Xocotl and Cihuacoatl the fire priests, in a group and as individuals, spattered themselves with torches of burning incense (a frightful, a dreadful thing) without the usual sacrifices and offerings. Every day [Xiuhtecutli] was presented with offerings of bread, pulque, viands of meat, and porridge. At some times these were offered from devotion, [at] others because of a vow, at others for one's health, and [at] others in search of prosperity or for the sake of one's children—for a thousand superstitions regarding the crackling of fire, the creaking of the embers, the leaping of sparks, the smoking [of the fire]. Thus it was sprinkled with pulque and was fed incense or tobacco (which is a type of plant with which the Indians deaden the flesh so as not to feel bodily fatigue). These beliefs, superstitious inventions, and lies had been made up by the deceivers and were held as trustworthy and true. Indeed, it has been an effort to uproot [these beliefs]. May it please the Almighty Lord that they now be torn up, [at least] in part!

A feast to the Air was also celebrated, under the name of Ehecatl. The Air and its virtues were attributed to the divinity of the people of Cholula: Quetzalcoatl, God of the Merchants and the Jewelers, the most highly reputed and saintly in all Cholula. Great virtues are attributed to him, heroic deeds regarding merchandise and marketing, the cutting of gems and stones. This Ehecatl was given huge offerings and sacrifices, especially on one day of the week, which was called Ehecatl, meaning Wind. When this fell on the number one—just as today we say Monday—(and, as I shall tell in *The Book of the Calendar*) since [these people] had weeks of thirteen days, when they reached thirteen, they began to count again, associating the day with the sign which fell on number one.

This was solemnized with great magnificence in special offerings and sacrifices, aside from the ordinary ones. [The people] never ceased fulfilling their vows, making their personal devotions, honoring and revering these false gods. This was due to an exaggerated subjection to religious matters and to the great credit they gave to the liars, the inventors of omens and superstitions, and to a great fear that ill fortune would fall upon their persons and their property. They could be pulled by the weakest thread; they feared the humming of the trees, the whispering of the wind in the woods and rocky places. Even we say, "It is such a strong wind that it seems to be talking." Thus they believed that it [really] talked.

[When these things happened], the people immediately made offerings and sacrifices, together with fasts and prayers, to Ehecatl to placate him, beseeching him to hold back his anger, because of the blood which was continually shed. Some [bled] their ears, some their tongues, others their chests, others their fleshy parts, others their shins or thighs, according to the rites of their temples and their rules. I say "according to their rules," because these people had ordinances and laws to bleed their tongues, those of one town to bleed their ears, those of another their fleshy parts, those of another their shins, and [those of] another their thighs. In a certain Mixtec province even the bleeding of the genital organ was practiced by passing cords as long as fifteen to twenty yards through it. Others, in order to become impotent, not to sin, slit it in two (something that makes the flesh crawl), so as to be considered servants of the devil, holy, penitent, chaste, and virtuous men, things which were highly extolled.

The fourth element, Water, was named Chalchiuhcueye, which means She of the Jade Skirt [Plate 28]. [This name] is composed of *cueitl*, which means "skirt," and *chalchihuitl*, which means "emerald."[1] In ancient times the Indians esteemed the

---

[1] Although Durán translates *chalchihuitl* as "emerald," he is referring to jade, symbol of water, "that which is precious," the heart of life itself. About Mexican jade Foshag has written: "*Jade* is a generic term used to designate several distinct mineral species widely used in primitive cultures for such simple utilitarian objects as celts or knives, and in more advanced civilizations for such decorative pieces as jewels, ceremonial objects and carvings.

"The word jade was derived from the Spanish term *piedra de ijada*, or 'stone of the loin,' in allusion to the virtue imputed to it of relieving pains of the side or of the

element [water] to such an extent that this fondness was truly a remarkable thing. Their priests, who persuaded and taught them, insisted ardently on their debt to water, just as we insist upon our great debt to our God and Lord for having created us and to Jesus Christ His only Son who redeemed us with His precious blood. Thus [the priests] preached and extolled the wonderful things owed to the gods, telling of the great gifts which each one of these offered. They extolled the water—for they were born in it, lived with it, washed their sins with it, and died with it. "Being born in water" means washing newborn babes four days in a row, the nobles in special basins made for that purpose; those of a lower class and condition [were washed] in small springs [or streams]. At these washing places were offered great quantities of jewels; they were carved in the shapes of fish, frogs, ducks, crabs, turtles, and golden jewels, all cast [into the water] by the principal lords whose children were washed there. They were washed by priests

---

kidneys. From the word jade was derived the specific name jadeite, applied to the pyroxenic mineral that constitutes one form of jade. The Spanish term, when translated into Latin, became *lapis nephriticus*, from which was derived the name *nephrite*, now used to designate a second mineralogical variety of jade. Thus, two distinct mineral species became associated with the term jade: jadeite (and its congeners diopside-jadeite and chloromelanite) and nephrite.

"*Jadeite* was used by all the advanced cultures of Meso-America. Among the Aztec it was known as *chalchihuitl* and was considered the most precious of stones. An indication of the great value put upon it by them was expressed by Montezuma, who, in presenting several jade ornaments to Cortés, told him: 'I will give you some very valuable stones, which you will send to him in my name; they are chalchihuitls and are not to be given to anyone else but to him, your great Prince. Each stone is worth two loads of gold.'

"Although Meso-American jadeite is similar to the Asiatic mineral that we know so well today, it shows significant chemical differences and a much wider variety in color and texture. In addition to the pure species, jadeite, two varieties, diopside-jadeite and chloromelanite, not found in oriental forms, are represented in the American material.

"The finest quality of oriental jadeite is known to the Chinese as *fei-t'sui*, or kingfisher jade, in allusion to its rich green color, not unlike the color of that Chinese bird. Its color is emerald green; its dense body texture yields a diaphaneity almost crystalline; and its luster on a polished surface is pearly. This supreme variety of jade is also found among Meso-American objects, and, like the Chinese stone, only in small and rare pieces. It was known to the Aztec as *quetzalitzli*, its rich color suggesting the vivid green of the plumage of the quetzal" (Foshag, 53–54).

and priestesses, both delegated, chosen, for that task. For (as I have stated) all ceremonies, no matter how nonsensical, were performed by special ministers. This was because the number of rites was so great that it was not possible for a single minister to attend to all. Thus for each ceremony certain priests had been appointed, each with his hierarch, who governed and ruled as a pontiff, just as in all other things. These ministers of each ceremony had their special names which indicated their rank, and, in order to comply with their tasks and as a badge for their persons, on the feasts they wore special insignia and decorations.

When I say that they lived [with water], I mean that water helped them to grow the cornfields and seeds which they ate. Therefore, on all the feasts of the calendar (which were eighteen) the entire aim in celebrating them—with so many men's deaths, with so many fasts and shedding of blood of their own bodies—everything was directed toward the procuring of food, of prosperous seasons, of the prolonging of human life. In all these they remembered and commemorated the water, the wind, the earth, the fire, and the sun, [not forgetting] to beseech all the other gods' favor, but especially water.

There was a feast called Etzalcualiztli, which fell when the rains had begun, when the corn was half-grown and already bearing ears. On this day the priests of the wards, in honor of water and the benefits it brought them, and in honor of the cornfields, broke the maize stalks two or three knots below the ear of corn. They gathered from each cornfield an armful of cornstalks with their ears. This the priests did in all the wards. They took the stalks and carried them to the point where the streets crossed and placed them on both sides of the road. They formed a sort of cross, leaving in the center a shrine which at these crossings was known as Momoztli, which in our language means Daily Place. The word is taken from *momoztlaye*, meaning "every day." When the maize stalks with their ears had been set up in the way which has been described, the women of all the wards came out and offered to that Daily Place called Momoztli tortillas made of *xilotl*. *Xilotl* is the name that ears are given before the kernels have dried. At this time both the corn and the cob were soft as milk, and bread was made and offered as first fruit in thanks to Chalchiuhcueye, the water. The offering having been made, [the people] of their own will gave the priests some of that bread to eat, since what was placed on the Momoztli was not touched by anyone. This was the usual custom regarding everything which was offered to the gods at these places: bread, pulque, seeds, chili, squash—it had to rot there [at the shrine]; no one was to touch it. Having done this, they danced and sang with good cheer; they drank their wines and ate their repast of fowl and other meats. All [was consumed] with the *xilotl* bread or with a cooked corn [dish] called *etzalli* because it was boiled together with beans, or *etl*. Corn boiled by itself was called *pozolli*, but since this was mixed with beans, it was known as *etzalli*. It was eaten in honor of the day named Etzalcualiztli, which will be described in the calendar in the celebration of that day.

[The natives] stated thirdly that they owed much to water since it washed away their sins and taints. For, as we have said, on the feast of the said Mecoatl, after having fasted a terrible fast, all the people, old and young, went to wash at dawn and then to eat the flesh of God, which was the *tzoalli*. The washing, together with the piercing of the tongue with straws, the ears with little reeds, and the fleshy parts with the same, served as a confession and purification of sin for those who had committed grave transgressions. After this ridiculous sacrifice they went to the water and washed themselves. They believed that their souls were cleansed and became free of the sins committed up to that time. This was called the Washing after the Penance. It was a common thing to wash the children and the sick since they believed that disease came as a result of sin. Therefore, they held great veneration for water and offered it rich things and sacrifices, as has been described under the Feast of Tlaloc, the God of Thunder and Lightning, who was like Jupiter among the Romans.

On the feast of this god there were also a commemoration and prayers to water. [This rite reminds us] of what has been said about that little girl dressed in blue whose throat was slit in the great lake, in honor and reverence of Chalchiuhcueye. [This girl] was placed under an awning while songs to the water were sung to her. These served as prayers to the gods. Thus the water was held to be the purifier of sin. In this the Indians were not too far from the truth, since in the substance of the water God placed the Sacrament of Baptism with which we are cleansed of original sin. In these things one may note that these nations had some information regarding the things of our Holy Faith, even though the great confusion of their ceremonies prevents us from reaching a firm conclusion.

There was a fourth thing that the men of the temple preached to the people so as to move them to a greater devotion to water: they were to die in it, since dead bodies are washed in it. The ceremony was thus: as soon as someone died, whether a man, a woman, or a child, whether or not a great nobleman, whether a rich man or a pauper, the first thing that was done after his death was to strip him naked and wash him carefully. After he was washed, he was again dressed in all his clothes, to be buried or incinerated. They said, therefore, that water served them for death.

In order to keep [water] happy and joyous, [the people] performed such nonsensical ceremonies that the Indians themselves laugh and are amazed at the comedy and foolishness which their ancestors had taken so seriously. These rites, however, had been planned in such a coherent manner that they gained great prestige and became essential.

The springs most hallowed were those which sprang from the roots of the trees we call sabinas [savins], which in the language is called *ahuehuetl*. This word is made up of two, that is, of *atl*, meaning "water," and *huehuetl*, meaning "a water drum." We call these trees sabinas. They are large and leafy, and the Indians once revered them greatly because they were always to be found at the foot of a spring, all of which was a cause of superstition and mystery.[2] Once I asked why the tree was called "water drum," and I

[2] The *ahuehuetl* (ahuehuete), of the genus *Taxodium*, is related to the redwood of California and the bald cypress of the southern United States. It is a huge coniferous tree, sometimes over one hundred feet tall, many specimens of which can be found in Chapultepec Park, in Mexico City, and in El Contador, Nazahualcoyotl's

was told that, since the water passes through its roots and its leaves and branches make a soft noise in the air, [it is called thus].

[The people] also revered the rivers which emerged from the volcano [Popocatepetl]. In these streams, ravines, and springs he who hungers for riches can find many precious things: gold, rich stones which have been offered up, cast in, by the Indians. These things were offered not only by the people of the local villages but by those from afar, from distant provinces, who came seeking, offering splendid gifts, precious jewels and stones. Even if in their own lands there existed springs, streams, and sources of water, they came in pilgrimage to the waters, to faraway hills, to strange caves, which contained idols. They came to fulfill their vows and promises and pilgrimages as we fulfill ours to Saint James, to [Our Lady of] Guadalupe, and Jerusalem.³

There are a thousand other nonsensical things I could describe under the superstitions they observed regarding water, and I would do so if I did not think that these [superstitions] have disappeared from the hearts of the natives. For my entire purpose was and is that of warning our priests of the mysteries and idolatrous practices of these people, so that they may be aware of and watchful for some survivals of ancient heathen beliefs which might still linger. I believed and still believe that I am honoring God and am relieving my conscience [by doing this], for, even though it is true that the Indians know God and are Christians, who can deny that among a thousand good men there are one hundred evil ones who still cling to their old ways, like poorly tamed foals? It might be better not to dwell on the details [of heathenish things], but even so, in order that the entire dough will not be contaminated, let our priests be aware that there were many superstitions about the

---

Garden near Tetzcoco. Other famous trees of this genus are the intertwined ahuehuetes on the road to the Shrine of Chalma, and the ancient Tule tree near Oaxaca. These trees live for hundreds and even thousands of years.

³ As a Spaniard from Andalusia, Durán does not fail to mention the great Shrine of Our Lady of Guadalupe, not far from Cortés's birthplace in Estremadura. Connections between the dark Spanish Virgin and the dark Mexican Lady of Guadalupe have not been exhaustively studied.

springs and rivers, about one's crossing of these, one's bathing in them, one's beholding his reflection in them as if he were looking into a mirror, the casting of lots in the water, the conjuring, the diagnosis of ailments in the water, the fortunetelling by use [of water], the swinging of children four or five times over water without touching it, the fear that if they crossed two rivers their lives would be diminished by one hour, or that if the Lady of the Waters became angered they would meet with misfortune.

The imagination which engulfed them was such that, these things held to be true, they often became reality, with the intervention of the devil. And since these natives were not saints, being men of flesh and blood, subject to good and evil (though more inclined to evil than to good, like myself and all others) perhaps, forgetting God, some of them relapsed into their ancient superstitions, wretchedness, and nonsense. Our priest, a servant of God, should be warned to fulfill his duty because, once my book is published, no one will be able to feign ignorance.

I could also tell of how women, new mothers who had given birth and also the sick, threw into streams and springs jars, little pots, dishes, clay bowls, clay dolls, together with countless baubles made of beads.

But since all this has been forgotten and left behind, there is no need to refer to it or tell about it in detail. Indeed, it would be a terrible thing if one had to give warning about these things now; it would have to pass as a story about ancient customs. There would be so many details to narrate and tell that they would fill a volume; it would be a lengthy project to set down all these things exhaustively and would perhaps bore the reader. It will be better, therefore, to terminate here the account of the goddess Chalchiuhcueye, She Who Was the Water.

Now that the foregoing theme is finished, it is time to deal with the baths which the natives of this land took—and take today. The bathhouse was called a *temazcal*, which means "bath house with fire," made up of *tletl*, "fire," and *mozcoa*, "to bathe" [and calli, "house"]. These bathhouses are heated with fire and are like small, low huts. Each one can hold ten persons in a squatting position; standing is impossible, and sitting is barely possible. The entrance is very low and narrow. People enter one by one and on all fours. In the back part there is a small furnace which heats the place. The heat is such that it is almost unbearable. It is like a dry bath. People sweat there only because of the heat of the bath and its steam, not through any other exercise or medicine meant for perspiring. [The *temazcal*] is used commonly by the Indians, both healthy and ill. After having perspired thoroughly there, they wash themselves with cold water outside the bathhouse so that the fiery bath will not remain in their bones. It frightens one to see someone with an exposed body, having sweated for one hour, abandon the bathhouse, be bathed, receive the splash of ten or twelve pitchers of water, without fear of any harm. Truly this seems brutal, but I understand that the body becomes inured and that he who was brought up in this system finds it natural. If a Spaniard were to go through this, he would go into shock or become paralyzed, and it would profit him little. It has been opportune to deal with these baths here and to forewarn regarding their ancient significance.

In the first place, it is to be remarked that there was a god of the baths. When a bathhouse was to be built, after this deity had been consulted, offered sacrifices, and presented with many gifts, all the people of the ward where the bathhouse was to be erected took the small stone idol and buried it in the same site where the building was to be constructed. The latter was built there, the idol remaining underground. [This idol] was usually given sacrifices, offerings, and incense, especially before people entered to bathe. There existed a diabolical superstition and belief about this: when women went to bathe, if they were not accompanied by a man or two, they dared not enter, considering it ill fortune. In the same way, in our own times, a man dares not enter if a woman does not accompany him. The same can be applied to a sick person: if it was a man who wished to bathe in the *temazcal*, he brought a woman fanner so that she could fan the flesh of that sick man; and if it was a woman, they brought a man to fan her. There were male and female fanners in the wards as bringers of health. The people were convinced that with that fanning they blew away illness, strengthened the flesh, and gave health and strength to the sick. The [fanners] were so highly honored, esteemed, and revered that they were held as saints and whenever it was necessary to call them were showered with gifts: plentiful food, pulque, and ears of corn, depending upon the quality of each [fanner].

I believe that all these things have been forgotten, but to demonstrate clearly the faith which the natives had in this heathenish custom of mixed bathing, I wish to tell what occurred to me in a certain village where this evil custom or way existed. I insisted and demanded both from the pulpit and outside [the church] that males bathe by themselves and females by themselves, speaking sternly and threatening them with punishment. Then [the people] played a droll trick on me: in order not to break their heathen law and tradition, when the women went to bathe, they carried with them one or two of their male children, and the men a little girl or two. This was a feint so that if they were reprimanded they could answer that these were their own children and therefore were taken in. Actually, this is what they did answer, and it was all due to their remembrance of ancient paganism. If someone should suspect or discover that the ugly and torpid custom of males and females bathing together still exists, he would do well to prevent and punish it so as not to revive an evil of the forgotten past. I myself have torn down some bathhouses in order to cause fear, especially because these were bathhouses built in the ancient times. For my own satisfaction I wanted to find, seek out, the idol which they claimed was buried there below, to find it for myself. It turned out to be an ugly and monstrous stone face.

Certain persons were appointed to heat these bathhouses; they performed special rites and spoke certain words on heating them. And so that the bath would be beneficial to those who took it, all who bathed contributed to those who heated [the bath] a certain number of ears of corn, chocolate, or seeds.

The noblemen possessed appointed people according to their category. These men and women accompanied them to the bathhouse to wash them. Most of those who carried out this task of bathing the lords and ladies were dwarfs or male and female hunchbacks. Bathing them consisted of taking cornhusks and flogging the entire body with those leaves, just as they flog each other there today with those leaves. I would not hold all this to be so unchaste and immodest if the husband entered with his wife, but at times there is so much confusion and laxity that, mingled and naked as they are, there cannot fail to be great affronts and offenses to our Lord. As a warning to those who are concerned with these matters, [I explain] that, while I am not referring to the ancient, pagan, heathen superstition, I am dealing with the evil that can come of [men and women] being mixed up in this way.

CHAPTER XX

¶Which treats of the Tianguiz, which means Market Place, and of the slaves who were bought there to impersonate gods and to be sacrificed.

W<small>E</small> have already dealt with all the main deities to whom men were sacrificed, with all the rites and ceremonies performed in their honor. Though briefly, in order not to be tiring, it is now timely and correct to tell something about the people who died as offerings to the gods, who were sacrificed and slain. Before we deal with this subject, though, first it will be necessary to say that in olden times there was a god of markets and fairs. This deity had his place upon a *momoztli*, which is like a roadside shrine or a pillory block. These were used in ancient times, and later we boys called them places of idle gossip. Many of these stood along the roads, on street corners, and in the market.

In the shrines at the market places were fixed round carved stones as large as shields, each one bearing a round figure like that of the sun with flowers and circles carved around it [Plate 29]. Some were carved with other images, depending upon the feeling of the priests and the importance of the market place and the town. The gods of these market places threatened terrible ills and made evil omens and auguries to the neighboring villages which did not attend their market places. There were clearly set limits regarding how many leagues could be traveled to attend the markets to honor their gods. Also a law and commandment forced the people to attend unless excused by some just impediment. [This obligation existed] not only through respect for the gods but also so that provisions would be on hand for the villages. What most awed them, what most forced them into obedience, was the ire and wrath of the gods.

Thus they came from all parts, from two, from three, from four and more leagues away, to the market places. From all of this has survived the strange custom of attending the market before going to mass. Since the ancient custom of holding the market every five days still exists, occasionally this falls on Sunday, and no one hears mass in the area of the town where the market is held. [I would like] all the markets to be held on specific days once a week, a custom which was introduced at the beginning in many places, where it has continued. In some towns it falls on every Monday, in others it falls on Tuesday, in others on Wednesday, and thus on the other days. Those who instituted this [system] made a wise decision, in this way removing the ancient custom of the *macuil-tianquiztli* (which means "market of five," because it is made up of the term *macuil*, meaning "five," and *tianguiz*, meaning "market"). On the other hand, when it falls on a Sunday, most of those who attend the market do not hear mass [since] they bear heavy loads. Furthermore: I would like to see all ancient customs disappear and fall into oblivion.[1]

The markets were so inviting, pleasurable, appealing, and gratifying to these people that great crowds attended, and still attend, them, especially during the big fairs, as is well known to all.

[1] In this rather confusing passage Durán is explaining that the pre-Conquest markets were held every fifth day, which meant that there were four market days within each twenty-day month. The early missionaries changed this system to one in which market day was held on every seventh day. By that system, of course, market day sometimes fell on Sunday, which Durán disapproved of because the people, preoccupied with buying and selling, did not attend mass. His idea of keeping Sunday sacred was probably not practical in the more remote villages, where Sunday was considered an ideal day for market, drawing the people to town and also to services. Even today in many Indian towns Sunday is always market day.

I suspect that if I said to a market woman accustomed to going from market to market: "Look, today is market day in such and such a town. What would you rather do, go from here right to Heaven or to that market?" I believe this would be her answer: "Allow me to go to the market first, and then I will go to Heaven." She would be happier to lose those minutes of glory to visit the market place and walk about hither and thither without any gain or profit, to satisfy her hunger and whim to see the *tianguiz*.

Regarding these opinions of mine, I wish to tell an anecdote which confirms my beliefs. While I was living in a town not too far from the City of Mexico, an old woman dwelt there, ninety or more years of age, who was accused more than once by the catechists of not attending mass. She constantly gave her advanced age as an excuse for her absence, and was brought to confession by force. She never missed a market day, however, or those held in the entire region. It so happened that on a Friday she walked two leagues from her house to a market place, and on the way back, as she was carrying a small bundle of scrawny ears of corn, she fainted because of the burning sun, her strength failed her, and she fell dead on the path. Her children and grandchildren, frightened by the sudden death, brought her body to the church. There they lost their fear, and all confessed that she had never missed a *tianguiz* [but that] there had been no way of getting her to mass. It was then agreed that she would be buried in the market place so that the place which had served her well in life and which she so loved, in death would not be denied her. How can anyone deny that this is a vice? It would be nonsensical [to deny] this because, after all, these people are Christians and know God, but, owing to this vice (as I have stated), many go [to the *tianguiz*], doing nothing but walking around, gaping, their mouths open, strolling from one end [of the market] to the other, perfectly contented with the world, as long as many go to buy and to sell and to trade according to ways and customs. Their manner of trading was to barter some things for others, just as is common today in many places.

The markets in this land were all enclosed by walls and stood either in front of the temples of the gods or to one side. Market day in each town was considered a main feast in that town or city. And thus in that small shrine where the idol of the market stood were offered ears of corn, chili, tomatoes, fruit, and other vegetables, seeds, and breads—in sum, everything sold in the *tianguiz*. Some say that [these offerings] were left there until they spoiled; others deny this, saying that all was gathered up by the priests and ministers of the temples.

But, to return to what I said about the market day being a feast day, the following is the truth. One day I was informed in a personal way, and now I shall tell what took place between me and a lord of a certain village.[2] When I begged him to finish a part of the church that was under construction, he answered: "Father, do you not know that tomorrow is a great feast in this town? How can you expect them to work? Leave it for another day." Then, very carefully, I looked at the calendar to see which saint's day it was, and I found none. Laughing at me, [the lord] said: "Do you not know that tomorrow is the feast of the *tianguiz* of this town? [Do you not know] that not a man or a woman will fail to pay it its due honor?" From these words I realized [how important] a feast and solemnity the market is for them. This was even more true in ancient times, because then there were heathen customs, superstitions, and idolatry, and now nothing remains except the habit or the vice of those who go to market [just for the pleasure of it], although they have nothing to buy or sell.

Furthermore, a law was established by the republic prohibiting the selling of goods outside the market place. Not only were there laws and penalties connected with this, but there was a fear of the supernatural, of misfortune, and of the ire and wrath of the god of the market. No one ventured, therefore, to trade outside [the market limits], and the custom has survived until these days. Many a time have I seen a native carry two or three hens or a load of fruit for sale in the market. On the road he meets a Spaniard who wants to buy them from him. The Spaniard offers the price which

2 By "lord of a certain village" Durán means one of the native *tlatoque*, descendants of the *tlatoani*, or local rulers, who had been permitted to continue to rule the townships after the Conquest.

he would have received in the market. The native refuses and is unwilling to sell, even though he would save himself a league or two of walking. He begs the Spaniard to go to the market place to buy them there.

Let me tell what occurred to me once. Early one morning I left my monastery on my way to the City of Mexico, and, since it was November, a bitter frost had fallen. On leaving the village, I encountered a naked Indian with his load of firewood. He was carrying it to sell at the market place. I felt such compassion on seeing him walking along, trembling with the cold, that, filled with pity, I asked him how much he could get for the firewood in the market place. He answered, "One real." I took out a one-real coin and gave it to him, telling him to go home and warm himself with the same firewood, which he was to consider a gift from me. With this I continued my journey, believing he had gone home. Somewhat more than an hour later I saw him coming behind me with his load of wood. I scolded him because he had not done what I had ordered.

"When I left my house," he answered me, "I was set in my heart to carry that firewood to the *tianguiz*. If you wish the real back, I have it with me." I refused the real and reprimanded the man for his ancient beliefs and superstitions and for his meager awe of God. He accepted this [scolding] with great humility and swore to me that this practice was not due to ancient belief but was simply their way of doing things, since he already believed in God and in the creed of the Holy Mother Roman Church. I tell these things because of the rigor with which the people kept their rules and laws. Even today, though they are Christians, the awe and fear of their ancient law is still strong. It must also be said that the planting of this awe and nonsense in these people brought a certain income from all that which was sold in the markets [in the form of taxes], which was divided between the lord and the community.

In this land the sovereigns had set up a regulation regarding the markets: they were to take the form of fairs or markets specializing in the selling of certain things. Some markets, therefore, became famous and popular for these reasons: it was commanded

277

that slaves were to be sold at the fair in Azcapotzalco and that all the people of the land who had slaves for sale must go there and to no other place to sell. The same can be said of Itzocan. Slaves could be sold in these two places only. It was at these two fairs that slaves were sold so that those who needed them would go there and to no other place to buy. In other places, such as Cholula, it was ordered that the merchandise must consist of jewels, precious stones, and fine featherwork. At others, such as Tetzcoco, cloth and fine gourds were sold, together with exquisitely worked ceramics, splendidly done in the native way.

It was established that dogs were to be sold in the periodic market at Acolman and that all those desirous of selling or buying were to go there. Most of the produce, then, which went to this *tianguiz* consisted of small- and medium-sized dogs of all types, and everyone in the land went to buy dogs there—as they do today, because at this time the same trade is carried on. One day I went to observe the market day there, just to be an eyewitness and discover the truth. I found more than four hundred large and small dogs tied up in crates, some already sold, others still for sale. And there were such piles of ordure that I was overwhelmed. When a Spaniard who was totally familiar with that region saw [my amazement], he asked, "Why are you astonished? I have never seen such a meager sale of dogs as today! There was a tremendous shortage of them!"

When I asked the buyers what they wanted [the dogs] for, they answered, "For fiestas, weddings, and baptisms." I was deeply distressed, for I knew that in olden times the little dogs had been a special sacrifice to the gods and that they were eaten afterward. I was even more distressed on seeing that in each village beef and mutton were being sold and that for a real one may buy more beef than [the meat of] two dogs, and yet [the latter] are still eaten. I do not understand why this should be permitted, and I am eager to believe that these people are now baptized Christians; that they believe in the Catholic Faith, in a True God, and in His Only Son Jesus Christ; and that they keep the law of God. Therefore, why should we allow them to eat these unclean things which formerly were kept as offerings to the gods and for sacrifice? And even though they no longer eat filthy things, such as dogs, skunks, moles, weasels, and mice, because of heathen custom or idolatry but as a vicious and a dirty thing, it would be praiseworthy for confessors and preachers to reproach [the people] so that they will finally become civilized.[3]

Having expressed [my opinion, I would like to say] some things regarding the slaves sold in the two markets I have mentioned, Azcapotzalco and Itzocan. Some things worthy of remembering can be said about these slaves. In the first place, it should be known that in honor of the gods (as has been noted) men and women were slain on all the feast days. Some of these were slaves bought in the market place for the special purpose of representing gods. When they had performed the representation, when those slaves had been purified and washed—some for an entire year, others for forty days, others for nine, others for seven—after having been honored and served in the name of the god they impersonated, at the end they were sacrificed by those who owned them.

Captives of another type were those taken as prisoners in war. These served exclusively as sacrifices for the man who had impersonated the god whose feast was being celebrated. Thus these were called the "delicious food of the gods." I do not have to deal with all of these, but only with the slaves who were sold in the market place for having broken the law or for the reasons I shall describe later. These were bought by rich merchants and by important chieftains, some to glorify their own names and others to fulfill their customary vows.

The masters took the slaves to the *tianguiz*: some took men, others women, others boys or girls, so that there would be variety from which to choose. So that they would be identified as slaves, they wore on their necks wooden or metal collars with small rings through which passed rods about one yard long. In its place I shall

[3] Like many other early-day missionaries, Fray Diego Durán regularly confused custom with religious and moral practice. Thus to him the practice of eating dogs, moles, weasels, and so on, was not only abominable but idolatrous.

explain the reason for putting these collars on them. At the site where these slaves were sold (which stood at one side of the *tianguiz*, according to market regulations) the owners kept [the slaves] dancing and singing so that merchants would be attracted by the charm of their voices and their [dance] steps and buy them quickly. If one possessed this facility, therefore, he found a master immediately. This was not the case for those who lacked grace and were inept in these things. Thus they were presented many times at market places without anyone paying attention to them, though [occasionally] some bought them to make use of them [in some way], since they were unfit to represent the gods. Singers and dancers were in demand because when they were garbed in the raiment of the gods they went about singing and dancing in the streets and the houses during the time of their impersonation. They entered [the houses] and the temples and [climbed to] the flat roofs of the royal houses and those of their masters. They were given all the pleasures and joys of the world—foods, drink, feasts—as if they had been the gods themselves. So it was that the merchants wished that, aside from being good dancers and singers, they were healthy, without blemish or deformity. They were not to be afflicted with any contagious sickness, such as pustules, leprosy, mange, arthritis, heart trouble, insanity, or feeblemindedness, or marked by nature—cross-eyed, with one eye larger than the other, or with uneven teeth or lacking teeth or one-eyed or bleary-eyed or lacking a hand or a foot or stained by scabs or scrofulous. [These slaves] were therefore made to strip, and were examined from head to foot, member by member. They were forced to extend their hands and lift their feet [as is done today with] Negro [slaves], to determine whether they were crippled. If one was found healthy, he was bought; otherwise, no. For it was desired that the slaves to be purified to represent the gods (this ceremony belonging to their rites, religion, and precepts) were healthy and without blemish, just as we read in the Holy Writ about the sacrifices of the Old Testament which were to be without blemish. These slaves were not strangers or foreigners or prisoners of war, as some have declared, but were natives of the same town.

There were many ways of becoming a slave within the law of the Indian nations, and I wish to enumerate them in their proper order. Just as in these republics there existed laws and ordinances established by the kings or by their councils and ministers, thus there was great rigor in their enforcement. For their execution there were supreme authorities, other lesser [authorities], others still lower, and boards where disputes were settled, some for criminal and others for civil cases. It was not possible to appeal from the civil to the criminal board or from the criminal to the civil board. [They could only appeal] to the supreme lord whom the king appointed to a place in his court to right injustices for those who felt they had been wronged. But since this does not belong here but in the history which I plan to write about the kings, I shall pass on to the way in which one became a slave.

First, he who stole the number of pieces of cloth or ears of corn, jewels, or turkeys which the laws of the republic had determined and set a penalty for was himself sold for the same amount in order to satisfy the owner of the purloined goods. And it should be remarked that the sale of a man, his enslavement, was like a death sentence. For it was a well-known fact that on his second sale he would be sacrificed unless he managed to earn his freedom through the laws which permitted him to recover it. Thieves or those who had committed frightful crimes seldom managed to attain their freedom.

Second, another way in which a native could become a slave was that of the gambler who risked all his possessions on the dice or in any other game which the natives played. After having lost, if he gave his word as a guarantee with the idea of regaining his losses, if he then won but did not pay within the period set by law, he was sold for the same amount. These [men] could become free by paying the price for which they had been sold.

Third, if the father of a family had many sons and daughters and among them was one [who was] incorrigible, disobedient, shameless, dissolute, incapable of receiving counsel or advice, the law (with the license of judges and justices) permitted [the father] to sell him in the public market place as an example and lesson to bad sons and daughters. Once he had been sold for his wrongdoing, he could not be ransomed.

Fourth, one became a slave if he borrowed valuable things, such as cloth, jewels, featherwork, and did not return them on the appointed date. By a law of the republic the creditors could sell him for the same amount; but if a second sale had taken place, the [debtor] could regain his freedom by giving the same quantity. If after a second sale the amount was not returned, his fate was sealed.

Fifth, he who had sold his son for the above reasons of disobedience and dissoluteness gave a banquet for all his relatives with the equivalent of the ransom of the son. This man was obliged to advise his servants not to eat that food because it [had been bought] with the money received for his son. If [in spite of this warning] some manservant or woman servant ate this food, and everyone was convinced that he had eaten it, he became the slave of [the father of the boy], for the law stated that only the father, the mother, the brothers and sisters, and close relatives could participate in that banquet.

If one killed another and the deceased had a wife and children, even though the law disposed that he was to die for that crime, if the widow pardoned him, he became a slave to serve her and her children.

In times of famine a man and wife could agree to a way of satisfying their needs and rise from their wretched state. They could sell one another, and thus husband sold wife and wife sold husband, or they sold one of their children if they had more than four or five. These could be redeemed later by returning their price to those who had bought them.

These people enslaved one another for many other reasons and were sold in the public market according to the laws and statutes of the republic. For those who protested against being sold, [for] those who had committed one of these crimes, and for other delinquents there was a jail. This was known by two names: one was *cuauhcalli* which means cage or wooden house. The second was *petlacalli*, which means house of mats. This building stood where today the House of the Convalescents of San Hipólito is found. This jail was a large, long, and wide hall lined on both sides with cages of thick wooden bars covered with thick boards [Plate 30]. When a trap door at the top was opened, the prisoner could be lowered into [the cage]. It was closed again, and a large stone slab was placed upon it. There began his misfortunes in regard to both food and drink. For these were people of cruel hearts, even among themselves—the cruelest in the world. Thus [the prisoners] were caged there until their cases had been studied.

Some people say that the natives made use of the gallows on which they hanged delinquents. I have investigated and inquired about this as deeply as possible and have not been able to find more than four types of execution with which these people punished criminal acts. One was by stoning of adulterers [and] casting them out of the city to the dogs and the vultures. Those guilty of ordinary fornication, of fornication with a virgin consecrated to the temple, or [of fornication] with the daughter or kinswoman from a good family were clubbed to death, burned, and their ashes thrown into the air. Another mode of death was that of dragging the delinquents with a rope about the throat, casting them into the lakes; these were sacrilegious people who had stolen sacred things from the temples. The fourth was the sacrifice in which the slaves ended their lives. Some died [with their chests] cut open; others were beheaded, others burned, others crucified, others killed with arrows, others cast over cliffs, others impaled, others flayed—all with the most cruel and inhuman sacrifices (invented by Satan to take yet more revenge on mankind in this world). It was worse than that which any human mind can imagine or think. For they were the most atrocious, devilish things which men have ever invented in this world to serve and revere false gods!

These sentences had been established by the law according to the crime. The judges listened to the case and investigated it and, once decided, sent the information to the royal representative. The latter relayed it to the king himself, who then approved the decision and ordered it to be applied to the accused. The sentence was then carried out impartially, even though it was one's own son. This

could set for us a salutary example, coming from the native kings
and great lords whom we have held to be barbarians. Yet they did
not pardon their own sons, nor did they allow the laws to be
broken if it could be avoided. Not even sons of sovereigns or noblemen were to set a bad example, a scandal to the republic. By allowing execution according to their crimes, [the lords] showed themselves to be freed from the stain of having produced ill-bred and
unworthy children, for which the parents were often blamed. The
latter were highly offended when anyone told them they should
chastise their sons for being shameless and bold.

Those authorized to arrest [criminals] were men who had
been appointed by the wards, and they were called by different
titles. I must explain that every city called [these policemen] by
a different name. In some parts they were called Tepixque, which
means Keeper of the People; in others, Calpixque meaning Keeper
of Many Houses. In other places they are called Calpuleque, which
means Lords or Guards of the Wards. [They were referred to] in
a thousand other ways, which need not be explained here. It is
enough to know that in the City of Mexico today those who hold
the post are called "royal superintendents." These offices, as in
ancient times, are passed on from father to son. They have been
inherited until the present day, and these men are awarded the
staffs of constable by election in the new year. Those who leave
office are charged with gathering people for mass and children for
catechism, still bearing their ancient name of Tepixque.

We have digressed from our theme (but not too far, because
what we have told is related to the slaves and is worthy of note).
Now that the way in which one became a slave has been described,
it would be interesting to note how one was freed. It should be
known that there was a law in this land of New Spain: whenever
the masters of slaves took them out for sale, they were weighed
down with collars and with rods one yard long across their backs.
One reason [for these collars and rods] was so that these [slaves]
might be easily recognized; furthermore, if they tried to escape, the
rod was an obstacle and hindrance to fleeing in a crowd. For it was
decreed that if the slave could escape from his master in the

tianguiz after having entered it and could pass the limits of the market before his master caught him, having passed these limits, he could step upon human excrement and in this way become free. Thus soiled, he went to the purifiers of slaves, showed himself to them, and said: "O lords, I was a slave, and, according to what your laws decree, I fled today from the market place, from the hands of my master! I escaped like a bird from a cage and stepped upon the offal as is the law. And so I have come to you to purify me and to free me from my servitude." The authorities removed the fetters, stripped him, and washed him from head to foot. Having washed him, they garbed him in new clothing and presented him to the lord; they told him that [this man] had been a slave but had been liberated according to law. The law praised him for his skill and enterprise and gave him complete freedom. Thenceforth he was to be honored and given insignia as a free and spirited man. Often he was kept in the palace as a lackey of the house.

There was another way to become free from slavery. If the master fell in love with his slave or the mistress with her slave, when this was confirmed by the birth of children or for some other reason, the slaves automatically became free. The masters held [the children] in high regard, married them off, gave them honors, kept them in their houses, and gave them lands, homes, and an inheritance to maintain them. In this land I have met bastards born of slaves, sons of noblemen, who later became lords and their fathers' heirs because they were good and patriotic. This nation held these things to be great virtues. The heir (whether a son or a brother—in most cases it was the brother who inherited) had to be a good patriot, spirited, well beloved, devout, and skillful in war.[4]

I have already described a third way of becoming free: that of returning to one's owner the price for which one was sold.

A highly amusing way for a man to become a slave still remains to be told. If in the market place a slave was in flight from

---

[4] A noteworthy example of Aztec social mobility was Itzcoatl, the first of the great Mexica emperors (1427–40), who was the illegitimate son of Acamapichtli and a slave girl of Azcapotzalco.

his master and the master after him, should anyone get in the way [of this slave], grab him, obstruct his way, the man became a slave, and the slave was freed. Through fear of this, all the people in the market—on seeing a slave fleeing from his master—made way for him, for this was a law and privilege of markets. The more the master cried out, "Hold him!" or, "Block his way!" the more space people gave him. In this way many became free, and those who stood in the way became slaves. But this was so well known that the event took place no more than once a year. The slaves, therefore, were watchful of any carelessness on the part of their masters [to seize an opportunity] to flee, and the masters were careful not to relax their vigil for even a moment.

Slaves were exchanged for cloths, which were called *cuachtli*, jewels of gold and stones, and rich feathers. Some [slaves], depending upon their disposition and quality, were worth more than others.

Regarding the second [type of slaves], men captured in war, no more can be added to what has been said. It was certain and sure that such captives were to serve as victims in sacrifice (unless they escaped), because they had been brought exclusively to be sacrificed to the gods.

CHAPTER XXI

¶Which treats of the God of Dance and the schools of the dance which existed in the temples of Mexico in the service of the gods.

MANY times I have argued with people from our Spanish country who have attempted to set this Indian nation in a low and inferior place. All they lack is to deny that [the natives] possess the use of reason. [These natives] have already been considered bestial and brutish and have been treated as such. Not only have they been held in this false opinion but some people have insisted that they had no good social system but lived as beasts without any concert or discipline. It is obvious that those [who believe thus] are deceived; no matter how brutish and incapable, [the Indians] possessed more [order] than can be imagined today. We can affirm that for people so remote and lacking contact with polished Spanish lands there has been no people, no nation on earth, who lived in their paganism with such harmony, good organization, and social order as this nation. I speak of the illustrious and noble people because I must confess that there was a coarse lower class, rude, dirty, bestial people—such as exist also in Spain, [who are] as brutish as these Indians or more so. It is my opinion that, no matter how beastly, they practiced their religion and its precepts well, though not with the refinements of the noblemen and lords.

Which nation on earth has sustained so many ordinances and laws for the common welfare, so just, so well codified, as those the natives had in this land? Where were sovereigns so feared, so well obeyed, together with their laws and commandments, as in this country? Where were great men, knights, and lords so respected, so revered? Where were their feats and deeds so richly rewarded as in this nation?

In which country in the world, where but in this land, has there existed such a great number of knights, nobles, so many brave warriors who with such zeal and spirit set out to show their personal qualities in the service of their king, to lift on high their names in war, solely to be honored by their sovereign?

In which country on earth was there, and is there still, such reverence, esteem, and awe shown to priests and ministers of the gods (coming not only from the common man but from kings, princes, and great lords), who prostrated and humbled themselves at their feet, obeyed and looked up to them as ministers of the false gods, almost to the point of adoration?

For [even] if we lower ourselves to observe their false religion, which people on earth has so jealously kept its laws, commandments, rites, and ceremonies?

I cannot be sure that another such people has existed on earth, nor can I prove that what I have said is true. I do not seek proof of these things because those who express their opinions are ignorant of the basic principles regarding the fine order in which these people lived under their old religion. This is well known to those who understand them and deal with them, even though everything has been turned upside down and lost regarding the ancient religion and customs. For these people no more than a shadow has remained of that admirable good order. [It was marvelous to see them] counting, registering, accounting for the people and natives of the village who were to go forth to any type of affair and business to which they were sent! Each [village] had its leaders, guides, and chiefs: one for the old, one for the youths, one for married people—all with such good control and order that not even newborn babes were forgotten! With what discipline did they assist at public works! And so methodically: he who has attended this week will not attend the next. The whole wheel turns with such harmony and order that no one feels weighed down.

Though I could now extol that which the elders tell about the education of youth [in ancient times], it is also true that I would lack words to insist upon the [bitter] feelings shown by those who were fortunate enough to see a little of this. When they see the young people today, eighteen and twenty years old—living in perdition, utterly shameless, drunkards, thieves, murderers, bandits, disobedient, rude, cocky, gluttons, loaded with girls—they affirm that under the old law there was not the dissoluteness or insolence they observe in the unruly youth of today. No one used to dare drink pulque or become drunk unless he was an old man, for warmth and comfort in his old age (and this applied as much to the ruling class as to the rest of the people). So I have heard it affirmed that if a noble was caught in a drunken state (outside of the occasions when he was permitted to drink—that is, on certain appointed feast days) he was deprived of his position and could even be executed if he went too far. This law was kept with a terrible vigor and was also applied to fornicators and adulterers, as I have described. The things I mention are not at all divorced from my theme but well describe the refinement of these courtly and polished people. Not only did this refinement exist, but it was the law of the state of a people who are not barbarous, as some pretend.

In each of the cities, next to the temples, there stood some large houses which were the residences of teachers who taught dancing and singing. These houses were called Cuicacalli, which means House of Song. Nothing was taught there to youths and maidens but singing, dancing, and the playing of musical instruments. Attendance at these schools was so important and the law [in regard to attendance] was kept so rigorously that any absence was considered almost a crime of lese majesty. Special punishments were inflicted upon those who failed to attend, and, besides these penalties, in some places there stood the God of Dance whom absentees feared to offend. I did not find that this God of the Dance was revered in the cities of Mexico or Tetzcoco or in the kingdom of Tlacopan but only in the province of Tlalhuic, which we call the Marquesado.

In that place I heard something about the existence of the God of the Dance, of whom the people asked permission before beginning the dance. First, they adorned the idol in the native way, bringing out its costume and placing flowers in its hands and around its neck and feathers down its back like those the natives wore in their dances. Occasionally they pretended that the idol was angry and that he did not wish them to dance. To placate him, they composed new chants in his praise, glory, and honor, making sacrifices and offerings to him. This idol was made of stone, with his arms open like a man who dances. In his hands were holes in which flowers or feathers were placed. He was kept in a chamber in front of the courtyard where the usual dances were held. It is said that during some feasts he was brought out into the courtyard and was set down next to the drum which is called *teponaztli*. In Mexico, in Tetzcoco, and in many other places of the land [the *teponaztli*] was honored as a god, given offerings and made ceremonies as a divine thing. And it does not surprise me that this instrument was honored thus since even the bark of resinous trees was revered so that it would create a good fire. The ancient blindness was such that even large and small animals, fish, and tadpoles were adored and revered.

Let us return to our subject. Those who came to learn to dance were many boys and girls anywhere from twelve to fourteen years of age. It is to be noted that they did not go to the dancing schools like our Spaniards here, who come and go in complete liberty. For these natives possessed a remarkably patterned life: certain elders were appointed to pick up and lead the children to their classes. They were elected exclusively for this task in all the wards and were known as *teaanque*, which means "men who conduct boys." Old women appointed by the wards went to fetch the girls; these were called *cihuatepixque*, which means "keepers of maidens," or duennas.

When the boys of each barrio had been gathered together, the elders placed them in front and walked behind them to the House of Song. The same was done by the old duennas; each one came with her girls before her. These old men were extremely careful to return boys to their schools and cloisters where they served and were educated or to the houses of their parents. The old women were equally cautious about guarding and caring for the girls. All were extremely watchful to see that there was no immodesty, no mockery, or any indication of these things. For the punishment was dreadful if such was suspected of any of these boys or girls.

In the cities of Mexico, Tetzcoco, and Tlacopan (and we are most interested in dealing with these, for they are the kingdoms which possessed the greatest refinement and breedings of the land) the Houses of the Dance were splendidly built and handsomely decorated, containing many large, spacious chambers around a great, ample, and beautiful courtyard, for the common dance. In [the City of] Mexico this house stood in the place where today are found the Portales de Mercaderes next to the great wall which enclosed the temples.[1] As I believe I have stated, ten or twelve of the lordly main temples of Mexico stood inside the great crenelated wall, which resembled a city wall. At one corner of this wall stood the House of Song and Dance.

The system of attendance was as follows. One hour before sunset the old men appeared at one end [of the wall] and the old women at the other, and they gathered the boys and girls as I have described. The latter accompanied them to that house, where the youths were placed in their own chambers and the girls in separate ones. Afterward the teachers of the schools of dance and song appeared, placing their musical instruments in the middle of the courtyard. Then the boys came out and took by the hands the girls they knew from their own wards, as we see in the illustration [Plate 31]. While the teachers stood in the middle, the dance and the song began, and he who could not dance the steps to the sound

[1] Today, after almost four hundred years, the Portales de Mercaderes, Merchants' Arcade, still stands on the western side of Constitution Plaza, between Madero and Dieciséis de Septiembre streets.

and the rhythm was then instructed with great care. They danced until the evening was well advanced; and after having sung and danced with great contentment and joy, the boys returned to their places and the girls to theirs. Again the duennas led the girls back to their homes, and the elders did the same with the boys, where they were left in their houses, delivered to their fathers and mothers, as has been said, without harm or bad example.

Wishing to find out the truth of these things, however, to know if perchance, holding hands as they did on that occasion, whether there was any misbehavior or instigation to evil, I was told this: it is true that there were agreements among them and that if a boy became fond of one of the girls (whether or not she was of his ward) while holding her hand at the feast, he promised her that when the time came he would marry her. And I say "when the time came to marry," because there was an appointed time for youths to marry. Those in charge of arranging the marriages, those who were the old matchmakers, arranged their marriage. This was their only occupation: that of marrying and asking the parents for the hand of their daughters, representing the youths who were ready to marry, and these marriage brokers still exist. They were and are still called *tecihuatlanque*, which means "petitioners of women," which in our own terms would mean go-betweens or matchmakers. They saw to it that when a young man reached the age of twenty or twenty-one he was to marry soon, unless he wished to become a priest or had made a vow of chastity, such as some did and kept, though not too many.

The promise made there [between the boy and girl] was to marry in due time, and thus, every time he came to that place, [the boy] sought her out and made it a point to hold her, and no other, by the hand, and she felt the same way about him. In this way they went along and suffered until their time came. This was when he had reached the proper age or had performed some notable feat.[2]

---

[2] A sample of the treatment girls accorded Aztec youths who had performed no great feat in war is found in Sahagún. If a novice was so bold as to approach a maiden, her reply was quick and cutting: " 'Verily, he with the long [tangled] hair of

We have already described the rigorous punishments which were applied to those who had committed immoral acts. Thus all the youths went about with their eyes to the ground, and all those who served in the temples did not venture to raise their heads to gaze upon women, especially priests whose lot was not that of marriage. He who was careless in these things suffered the pain of death. We have mentioned this above in the chapter dealing with the youths and maidens who attended the temples of Huitzilopochtli and Tezcatlipoca [Chapters II and V]. Extreme care was taken to see that the youths were brought up in great chastity, filled with awe, well-bred, well disciplined in all ways of virtue. For this reason there were different houses, some for boys from the ages of eight to nine; and others [for boys] from eighteen to twenty. There both had their masters and preceptors, who taught and made them practice all kinds of arts: military, religious, mechanical, and astrological, which gave them knowledge of the stars.

For this they possessed large, beautiful books, painted in hieroglyphs, dealing with all these arts, [and these books] were used for teaching. There were also native books of law and theology for didactic purposes. [The boys] did not leave this [house of learning] until they were men, wise and skillful, when their vocation had been perceived [and] they were married and directed toward their lifework. When [a young man] departed from [this school], he was charged to remain faithful to the things they had learned there: fidelity and religion [and] to be satisfied with the woman who had been destined for him, so that the gods would protect and favor him.[3]

a youth also speaketh! Dost thou indeed speak? Be thou concerned over how may be removed thy tuft of hair, thou with the long hair! Thou with evil-smelling, stinking forelock, art thou not only a woman like me?'" Shamed by such grave insults, the boy would reply with such choice expressions as: "'Anoint thy stomach with mud; scratch thy stomach; twist one leg about the other and fall to the earth; drop upon the dust. There is a stone, a rough one; strike thy face therewith, that blood may spurt forth; scratch thy nose with the stone; or bore a hole with a fire drill into thy windpipe, that thou mayest spit through it.'" Sahagún adds that ". . . thus the women would torment [young men] into war; thus they moved and provoked; thus the women prodded them into battle" (Sahagún, II: 61–62).

[3] As the chosen people of God, as the People of the Sun, as the inhabitants of the

Since these people were weak, vacillating, and of evil inclinations, however, and since the doing and fulfilling of good deeds has to be forced upon them through fear, there was always one who, guided by his evil inclinations, left the rest [of the students] asleep after the dance and sneaked out. He then went to the house of the girl who had caught his eye; but since the care of the masters and tutors was remarkable, if he was careless enough to return after they had noticed his absence, they spied upon him and, realizing where he had gone, after having reproached him for his baseness, applied the due punishment. With sticks and stones he was thrown out of the house, out of the company of the good [youths]. He was told that he had stained the homes and dwelling places of the gods with his evil life and was left half-dead at the doorway of the house of his father and mother, who were reprehended as careless and lax in educating and chastising their children, [branded as] people of base life since their son had turned out to be so wicked. This was considered a frightful offense, worse than death. In this way [the youth] was cast out of the company of the others as an incorrigible apostate. This was done once, for there could be no second time. He was held to be sacrilegious and was excommunicated, and some were mistreated to such an extent that they died because of the ill treatment, drubbed mercilessly with sticks, kicks, and stones. Those who survived lived in perpetual shame, like those among us who are given a hundred lashes or who are forced to wear a penitential scapular. They were known as violators, transgressors of the statutes and ordinances of the gods and of the schools. And even though the parents were distressed because of the ill treatment of their sons, whom these people loved dearly, they did not dare complain but acknowledged that the punishment had been just and good.

---

city whose destiny it was to form a great religious-military empire, the Aztecs of Mexico-Tenochtitlan were always a numerical minority. Hence one of the main necessities of their society was to develop a "heart of stone" (*yolotetl*) in each individual, thus exploiting his ability as a priest or a warrior. Small wonder, then, that no deviations or exhibitions of weakness or sentimentality had any place in that society.

Young people took great pride in their ability to dance, sing, and guide the others in the dances. They were proud of being able to move their feet to the rhythm and of following the time with their bodies in the movements the natives used, and with their voices the tempo. The dances of these people are governed not only by the rhythm but by the high and the low notes in the chant, singing and dancing at the same time. These songs were composed by poets who created them, giving each song and dance a different rhythm, just as we do with our songs, giving each sonnet, each eight-line stanza, each tercet, and other forms a different tune when sung.

Thus these differences in songs and dances existed: some were sung slowly and seriously; these were sung and danced by the lords on solemn and important occasions and were intoned, some with moderation and calm, [while] others [were] less sober and more lively. These were dances and songs of pleasure known as "dances of youth," during which they sang songs of love and flirtation, similar to those sung today on joyful occasions. There was also another dance so roguish that it can almost be compared to our own Spanish dance the saraband, with all its wriggling and grimacing and immodest mimicry. It is not difficult to see that it was the dance of immoral women and of fickle men. It was called the *cuecuechcuicatl*, which means "tickling dance" or "dance of the itch." I have seen this performed in some villages, and it is permitted by our friars as a recreation, but I do not consider this wise because it is highly improper. Men dressed as women appear there.

There were many other forms of dancing and merrymaking among the Indians on the feasts of their gods, when different chants were composed for each deity, depending upon his qualities and importance. Thus, many days before the arrival of the feast there were long rehearsals of dancing and singing. With the new songs out came different costumes and ornaments of cloth and feathers, wigs, and masks, all conforming to the song which had been composed and to its theme, all in harmony with the solemnity and feast. Sometimes their costumes represented eagles, at others jaguars or lions[4] or soldiers or Huaxtecs,[5] at others times hunters, at others savages or monkeys, dogs, or a thousand other disguises.[6]

The dance they most enjoyed was one in which they crowned and adorned themselves with flowers. A house of flowers was erected for the dance on the main pyramid at the temple of the great divinity Huitzilopochtli. They also erected artificial trees covered with fragrant flowers where they seated the goddess Xochiquetzalli. During the dance some boys dressed up as birds, and others [dressed] as butterflies descended [from the trees]. They were richly decked with fine green, blue, red, and yellow feathers. These youths ascended the trees, climbing from limb to limb, sucking the dew of the flowers. Then the "gods" appeared, each wearing robes such as the idols wore on the altars—a man or a woman dressed in the guise of each. With their blowguns in their hands they went around shooting at the "birds" who were in the trees. Then the Goddess of the Flowers—Xochiquetzal—came out to receive [the gods], took them by the hand, making them sit next to her, treating them with great honor and respect, as such divinities deserved. There she presented them with flowers and gave them to smoke, and then she made her representatives come to amuse them.

---

[4] The "lions and tigers" often mentioned by Durán are the jaguar (*Felis onca*), ocelot (*F. pardalis*), and cougar (*F. concolor*). Of course, neither the lion nor the tiger is native to the Americas.

[5] In their rudimentary dramatic performances the Aztecs of Mexico-Tenochtitlan poked fun at the neighboring Huaxtec people, possibly in crude but comical skits of a phallic nature. According to a contemporary account, the Huaxtecs "worship the penis and have images of it in their temples and squares, together with carved figures showing different forms of pleasure between a man and a woman, plus figures of human beings with their legs lifted in diverse ways. . . . the men are great sodomites, cowards, and—bored with drinking wine with their mouths—lie down and, extending their legs, have the wine poured into their anus through a tube until the body is full" (*El Conquistador Anónimo*, 37). Sahagún reported that the Huaxtec men "do not wear loincloths to cover their privy parts, though these people have many articles of apparel." He added that the Huaxtecs did, however, wear gold nose plugs decorated with feathers (Sahagún, 1938, III:132). These views were undoubtedly misinterpretations resulting from prejudice on the part of the people of Tenochtitlan.

[6] Farces in which "hunters" or "savages" appeared undoubtedly ridiculed the Chichimecs or nonagricultural peoples of northern Mexico. These tribes were described by Sahagún (1938, X:116–20).

This was the most solemn dance in the land, and I rarely see another one danced today unless it is by exception.

Another dance was performed: that of the Old Humpbacks, who wore masks representing old men. It was extremely gay, merry, and funny in the native fashion.

Another performance with dance and song dealt with rogues. A simpleton appeared who pretended to understand all his master's words backward, turning around his words. With this dance came [a juggler who manipulated] a round log with his feet with such skill that the tricks and turns he performed with it caused astonishment, to such an extent that some [Spaniards] believed it to be done through diabolical arts. Considering it carefully, [I believe] it is no more than the sleight of hand played in Spain. Here we could call it "sleight of foot." I myself can be a witness. When I was a lad, I remember a school of this game in the San Pablo Ward, where there was an Indian who was most skillful in this art. There many young Indians from different provinces learned how to juggle the log with their feet. Therefore, I can affirm that this dance and its trickery was more trickery of the foot than art of the devil. In some places when the Indians heard that people were shocked by it, [considering it diabolical], they let it fall into disuse and do not dare to perform it, nor many other dances, gay and refined, with which they made merry and feted their gods.

They also used to dance around a tall flying pole. Dressed as birds and sometimes as monkeys, they flew down from it, letting themselves go with ropes which had been wrapped around the top of the pole. They let themselves go little by little from a platform which stood on top. While some remained on the platform, others sat on the point of the pole on a large circular wooden rim from which the four ropes were tied to the platform. The latter went round and round while the four descended in a seated position, executing feats of daring and deftness, without becoming faint and often playing the trumpet.

At other times the natives performed a dance in which they painted themselves black, sometimes white, sometimes green, feathering their heads and their feet. Certain women stood in the center, and both men and women pretended to be drunk. In their hands they held jars and cups, pretending to be drinking. All of this was invented to give pleasure and fun to the people, amusing them with a thousand types of games invented by those who lived in the cloisters—dances, farces, short comedies, and zestful songs.

Everything we have been describing refers to the way in which the youths learned countless dances and diversions. Let us now speak of the ordinary dance which the warriors and soldiers performed daily, during the daytime, in that same building and school of dance. They went there to dance as a pastime, coming to an agreement, betting among themselves that they would find someone who would desire them. For that courtyard became filled to bursting with harlots, for there were many of these, and extremely shameless.

These warriors, known as *tequihuaque,* went there and, dressed in their best, danced in fine style. Since they were fearless men and highly esteemed, they were permitted to keep mistresses, play with women, and woo publicly, all these things being permitted as a reward for their bravery. When one of these men saw a harlot looking at him with a certain amount of interest, he beckoned to her and, taking her by the hand, danced with her in that dance. Thus he spent the entire evening with that woman, holding her by the hand while they danced, giving her color for her lips and cheeks, feathers for her head, and jewels for her neck. Each one regaled the woman he had taken a fancy to as best he could. This round of pleasure lasted until it was time for the youths and maidens to come [to the school].[7]

[7] Prostitution among the Aztecs, a little-known aspect of pre-Conquest culture, is rarely mentioned by Durán. The fact that it existed in ancient Mexico-Tenochtitlan is further attested to by a number of ancient sources, including Sahagún (1938, III:47–48). Molina, in his *Vocabulario en lengua Castellana y Mexicana,* defines *ahuilnenqui* as a prostitute, "she who goes about giving pleasure or fragrance." Another term listed by Molina is *motzinnamacani,* "she who sells the lower half of her body." As a reward for risking his life for his people, a warrior was allowed a few hours of indulgence with a harlot—an exception to the generally "puritanical" Mexica code. A vivid portrait of an Aztec prostitute of ancient times appears in Diego Rivera's mural of the Tlatelolco market place on the walls of the National Palace. The portrait could have been inspired by a sixteenth-century text recorded by Sahagún from

It was common to dance in the temples, but on solemn occasions it was even more common in the royal or lordly dwelling places. All these had their singers who composed chants about their own glorious deeds and those of their ancestors, and especially of Moteczoma, the lord about whom we know most, and Nezahualpilzintli of Tetzcoco. In their kingdoms songs had been composed describing their feats, victories, conquests, genealogies, and their extraordinary wealth. I have heard these lays sung many a time at public dances, and even though they were in honor of their native lords, I was elated to hear such high praise and notable feats.

There were other composers who created divine chants about the grandeur of and praises to the gods. These [composers] lived in the temples, and both [kinds of] creators of songs received salaries. They were called *cuicapicque*, which means "composers of songs." Let these things be noted by those who look with contempt upon the way of life of these Indians and who doubt that they had civilization. What I have said is not contrary to what is stated about the King our Lord who has his own choir of singers; and the Archbishop of Toledo has another, another great lord another, and so on. We know the same to hold true in this land, and today the chiefs of the towns keep [singers] in the old way. I do not consider this improper since it is all done for a good reason and to prevent the lowering of the authority of their persons. For they too are sons of kings and great lords in their own way, like those who came before them.

All the native lays are interwoven with such obscure meta-

interviews with native informants: "You are a harlot, a harlot. You come out to catch men. You wander about alone. You are talkative and restless. You are afflicted with sores and the itch. You beckon to men with your gestures. You smile at men. You fish for men. You call men with your hissing. You call men with your hands. You are dissolute, a dissolute woman. You are perverse. You are burning with your lust. You paint your face with cochineal. You have been used too much. You belong in the gutter. You walk about gnawed with the itch. You offer your body as bait. Your head is always held on high, always on high. You walk about without peace or rest. You do not attend your home. You give potions to men in order to be loved. You pervert the hearts of men. With spells you call men to you. You spend your time laughing. You are always making merry with men. You are always wasting your time in the square" (Garibay, 1947, II:242–43).

phors that there is hardly a man who can understand them unless they are studied in a very special way and explained so as to penetrate their meaning. For this reason I have intentionally set myself to listen with much attention to what is sung; and while the words and terms of the metaphors seem nonsense to me, afterward, having discussed and conferred [with the natives, I can see that] they seem to be admirable sentences, both in the divine things composed today and in the worldly songs. I believe that in general there is nothing to reprehend in this case. I say "I believe" because there might be a slip here, and they might amuse themselves by remembering their ancient gods and singing the evil and idolatrous chants, and perhaps more. These songs were so sad that just the rhythm and dance saddens one. I have seen these danced occasionally with religious chants, and they are so sad that I was filled with melancholy and woe.

Thus I shall end here my description of native dances, for I have noted the essential things within the subject of dancing. I could add a few trifling details of little importance if I felt they could be useful as an admonition. In that case I would set them down as a warning [to our priests], but the problem [of paganism] has been solved, praised be our Lord.

CHAPTER XXII

¶Which treats of the games which the Indians had for entertainment and amusement on feast days. [These were] also used to gamble one's life away and become a slave forever.

E very country has and has had its games and its gamblers, who invented and engaged [in these contests] not only to lose their patrimony and wealth but in some cases to lose their lives or—what is worse—their souls, a pitiful thing. These Mexican people were not lacking in these games, for they had contests and ways of losing their treasure and their lives. After losing the former, they put themselves up as stake and became perpetual slaves of the winners, thus losing their lives, since it was clear that once they had ended bondage they would end as a sacrifice to the gods.

In former times those given to this vice were both many and greedy; their desire of winning was so great that the gamblers held the very instruments of the game they favored to be their special divinity. Thus, if their game was dice, the dice themselves were revered as a god, as well as the lines and pictures which were painted upon the mat, as we see in the illustration [Plate 32]. These [were served] with special offerings and ceremonies, were honored and revered, and it was not only this game but all the others they played in their desire to either win or lose. These games were many and varied, employing different instruments and rules. They played the game of *alquerque,* or checkers, similar to our own game of chess, first one casting the chips, then another. Pebbles served as chips, some white, the others black.[1]

Another game was played as follows. Small cavities were carved out of a stuccoed floor in the manner of a lottery board. Facing each other, one [player] took ten pebbles, and the other [also took] ten. The first placed his pebbles on his side, and the other on his. Then they cast split reeds on the ground. These jumped, and those that fell with the hollow side face upward indicated that a man could move his pebbles that many squares. Thus they played against one another, and as many as a player caught up with he won, until he left his opponent without chips. Occasionally it happened that, after five or six [pebbles] had been taken, with the four remaining ones the reeds were also bet, together with the others, and thus the game was won.

The "game of the mat" was the most arduous of all. This was similar to our *primera* or *presas,* which are "short" games, as they say. Many people could play together in this game, as many as wished. It was their most common game, and I wish to deal with it and to explain it inasmuch as the main object of this chapter is to describe it and to set down its rules. Thus it must be noted that this game, played upon a mat, was called *patolli,* which is the same word we now use for cards.[2] On this mat was painted a large X,

[1] Durán's diffusionism again becomes evident in his descriptions of the games of the ancient Mexicas. Though he also compares *alquerque* with chess, it was indeed probably more like checkers.

[2] *Patolli,* similar to pachisi or backgammon, is of special interest to modern anthropologists specializing in diffusionism and parallelism: "Are pachisi and patolli connected? The great British anthropologist, Tylor, in 1896, thought so: and for a very good reason. There are five or perhaps six specific features in which pachisi and patolli agree: flat dice, score board, cross-shape, several men, killing opponents, penalty or safety stations. The mathematical probability of two games invented separately agreeing by chance in so many quite specific features is very low. On a bet, long odds could be laid against so complex a coincidence, long odds for its not being a coincidence, hence an influence or a connection" (Kroeber, 551).

On the other hand, there were valid arguments against such diffusionist theories: "If pachisi was anciently imported from India to Mexico, as it was later carried from India to England and America, it is extremely unlikely that the people who brought

which reached from corner to corner. Within the arms of the X certain lines were marked which formed squares. The X and its squares were marked or striped with liquid rubber. I have already explained what rubber is. Twelve pebbles were used in these squares—six red and six blue. These pebbles were divided among those who played, each given his share. If two played, which was the usual form, each took six; and when many played, one played for all, [the others] abiding by his luck, just as the Spaniards play games of chance betting on whom [they hope to be] the winner. The same was done here. [Bets were made] on the one who best handled the dice. These were black beans, five or six, depending upon how one wanted to play. On each bean there was a small space painted with the number of the squares which it could advance at each play. If the painted number was five, it meant ten [squares]; and if it was ten, it meant twenty. If it was a one, it meant one; if two, two; if three, three; if four, four. But when the painted number was five, it meant ten, and ten meant twenty. Thus those small white dots were indicators and showed how many lines could be passed while moving the pebbles from one square to another. When this game was played, such a crowd of onlookers and gamblers came that they were pressed against each other around the mat, some waiting to play, and others to bet. It was a remarkable thing to see. When there was rubber to paint the lines on the mat (if the game was spontaneous), special herbs were used to draw the lines on that board of chance—squash leaves, the same small squash itself, an herb called *chichicpatli*, which means "bitter medicine"; or [they drew] with pine soot. Heathenism was involved here as always in their idolatry, since it had to be that herb [*chichicpatli*] and no other.

it would have brought that and nothing else; or that only pachisi survived as *patolli*, but practically everything else brought with it failed to be accepted in Mexico, or died out, or was so altered as to be unrecognizable. To be sure, just this *might* conceivably have happened: but it would admittedly be extraordinary; on the basis of chance, improbable. As a matter of fact, the same stream of influence that brought pachisi from India to the West also brought polo and curry and Paisley shawls and theosophy; and more ancient connections brought chess and position numerals. There are few such possible counterparts, and no unquestionable ones, in native Mexico. In short, the context probability is against connection" (Kroeber, 551).

The gamblers dedicated to this game always went about with the mats under their armpits and with the dice tied up in small cloths, like some gamblers today, who go from board to board carrying their cards inside their hose. Those dice, together with the pebbles used in the game, were carried in a small case. They were revered as gods, as it was believed that they were mighty; and thus when they played, [the people] spoke to them as if they possessed reason or intelligence regarding the request made to them. That they spoke to them and begged them to be favorable, to come to their aid in that game, does not surprise or astonish me. Though these were people who were less alert than our own people, [I must admit that] there are Spanish Christians who (though pretending refinement) when the cards are being dealt demand of the card a good number and good fortune; and if this is not obtained after having "worshiped the cards" (if thus it may be termed), with the cards in their hands they give voice to a thousand blasphemies against God and his saints. In this way the natives spoke to the beans and to the mat, uttering a thousand loving words, a thousand compliments, a thousand superstitions. After having spoken to them, they placed the painted mat and the small case containing the implements of the game in a place of worship. They brought fire, cast incense into the flames, and offered their sacrifice in the presence of the implements, placing food before them. When the ceremonial gift had been delivered, they went off to play in the most carefree manner.

At this point it seems to me that I should not continue without referring to something connected with this superstition which I discovered in a certain village, after having been a minister among the natives for many years. In this village there was a man who was a great player of pins, and his vice was such that he played not only on holidays but also on workdays. As soon as he had a moment of leisure, he brought out his pins and sought someone to play with him. One day when I had to examine him on things regarding the Faith, I discovered that his profession was that of a pin gambler. I asked him whether he was making out well with the game. He answered in the affirmative, saying that he seldom lost. I asked him what he did to the pins to make them so lucky, and I insisted and pestered him so much that he admitted that before he went out to play he placed the pins next to the image on a small domestic altar, that he knelt, joined his hands, and implored in the old style for luck in the game. He also offered incense, food, and so forth, to the pins.

Those who were players, given to this vice of gambling, whose profession and custom it was, were held to be infamous and knavish people, idle, dishonest, vicious, enemies of honest toil. Persons proud of their honor fled from any contact with them, and thus parents advised their children to keep away, to shun them and their presence as bad company. They were afraid that [their children] might become addicted, learn to gamble, and gamblers came to no good end. [Gambling] was considered a vice; and once one had begun to enjoy it, only a miracle freed one of it. These gamblers always went about indigent, in need; they staked jewels, stones, slaves, fine cloths, breechcloths, their homes, their wives' jewelry. They gambled their lands, their fields, their granaries filled with grain, their maguey fields, their trees and orchards; and finally, when there was nothing left to gamble, they staked themselves at a set price, with the agreement that if within a certain length of time they could not redeem themselves they would forever remain slaves of the winner. Occasionally some became free, though this was rare and came late. It happened once in a lifetime. That is why they say, "I am not worried about the game but about getting out of it."

There was another type of slave (besides those which we have described) who served as a sacrifice to the gods. These were sold in the market place (as I have told in its place) and could be sold by those who had won them, who had placed upon them the collars and signs of slavery undefied, with general approval.

The name of the god of dice was Macuilxochitl which means Five Flowers. He was invoked by the gamblers when they cast the beans from their hands. This was done in the manner I shall describe. The beans which served as dice are five, in honor of the god who bears the name Five Flowers. To cast their lots, [the players] rolled them a little in their hands, and, on throwing them on the mat (where the lottery pattern was drawn in native manner, resembling two clubs), they noisily called to Macuilxochitl and clapped loudly. Then they went to see the points that had come up. Macuilxochitl was the only [god] for this game of dice; however, there was another divinity who was customary for all these games. This is the one shown in the illustration [Plate 33]. His name was Ometochtli, which means Two Rabbit. Thus in this game (as in others), whenever they wished the number two to appear, they would cry out the same invocation on casting down the pebbles, clapping for Two Rabbit, "Ometochtli!"

It was also inevitable that the wine they drank was held as a god in ancient times. This [deity] was called Ometochtli, and all the men and women who sold wine celebrated his rites, ceremonies, and offerings with all the crude native solemnity and devotion.

It would not be amiss to describe this god here for he was the same as that of the gamblers. When they gambled, they placed a small jug of pulque next to the game, and, just as they always remembered the other gods when they made sacrifices and celebrated, they kept pulque like a god. The pulque makers, on casting in the roots and honey when the liquor began to ferment, put incense into the burners, offering [the pulque] food, other presents, and the same rites performed before other [deities]. At one time I was curious about why the god of wine was called Ometochtli, and I questioned an old man, believing that he might clarify this for me. After I had insisted a great deal, he answered, "Why do *you* invoke your wine when you toast?" And since I saw the question was turned on me, I decided to drop the subject so as not to have to explain what "to toast" is, since I would have to tell about the game of "Let's see who can drink more." They drink enough as it is without our [teaching them how]. This evil game is played because it belongs more to the Flemish taste than to the Spaniards', who are honorable men. I found out from the Indian that Ometochtli refers to the god Bacchus and is much celebrated among them today, more than he was solemnized in ancient times. Though he was worshiped and revered as a god, not everyone drank, nor were there the drunken brawls or the evils which this cursed wine brings and causes in our modern times. Today young and old go along with the norm which it seems that the devil has set up, so that once they begin to indulge they would rather lose their lives than pulque. The same can be observed among some Spanish drunkards who become fond of it and indulge as much as the Indians in this cursed and diabolical vice.

Abandoning this theme of drunkards, I shall return to the gamblers who invoked the god when they played, crying out, "Ometochtli! Give me luck!" to the god. And since the cursed devil is so evil, he was supposed to come immediately to help them in order to be better served and esteemed. I remember that the civil judges at one time tried to eliminate these games, to arrest and chastise the gamblers with harsh penalties, and the painted lottery mats were destroyed. All this rigor was applied to destroy the superstition and the ill fortune which were associated with this game, and also to uproot a vice so absorbing that one who gambled all day failed to sow, till, and care for his fields and land. Because of this, some—together with their children—went about poor and half-naked, while others died of hunger. The rigor applied [by the judges] to eradicate these things was such that the beans which served as dice in their hands were burned. Aside from the suffering brought upon them, their wives, and their children, [the gamblers] fled from personal services and communal activities, for they spent the entire day sitting around gambling. It was the will of our Lord that the severity and the fear instilled in them was of such efficacy that these things were extirpated, annihilated, in such a way that they have been forgotten. With them disappeared many other idolatrous customs and evils. If such was the will of our Lord (since He destroyed the name of the god Ometochtli through the game in which he was invoked), one prays that it would please Him to destroy the memory [of this god] by eliminating drunkenness. The memory [of Ometochtli] lives through the latter, and I state that there is no judge stern enough to prohibit it.

Also to be considered are the vested interests of the pulque makers, who, although they are fined twice a month, do not realize that until these wretched people abandon this abominable vice they will never find the True Faith or knowledge of God. No matter how much our priests preach and write, I claim that while this vice is prevalent and is protected and spared we are voices crying in the wilderness. The friars who have dealt with native men and women have had some experience in this. Once they have abandoned the vice, they draw nearer to God. They learn more about the things of our Holy Faith and about the mysteries of our Redemption. Let anyone say what he will, but he who is addicted to pulque and does not reform makes me doubtful regarding his faith, and I consider it stupid to administer the Sacraments to him until he has reformed. I am referring not only to Communion—the Most Holy Sacrament—against which an intolerable irreverence is committed, since it is given to a man who with his own hands and will has deprived himself of something as precious as his natural senses, which not even animals would do were they administered the Host. These men become like the beasts themselves or worse, very different [from an ailing person] who has lucid intervals: one is deprived of the senses God gave him by illness, and the other [is deprived] voluntarily. Thus not only do I believe that the latter should be denied Communion during all the time he remains addicted to this vice but, having been warned two or three times, if he does not reform, I do not see why he should be admitted to confession. If our priests were more strict (since the secular judges are so negligent in toiling for the honor of God) and if we did not have so much pernicious pity and imprudent compassion (the results of which are cruel regarding excessive drinking), on being denied absolution twice, [this man] would be filled with shame; he would become afraid of another fall. Through my own experience I have seen them suffer so because of the denial of absolution and an admonishment that not even [when] given permission to drink moderately would they become inebriated. On the contrary, they made vows never to drink again in their lives. Once this vice is eliminated, another mite would be added to the things of God and our Faith, and among the natives there would reign awe, truth, and dignity, bases and fundamentals of all human intercourse. Since this is lacking, they are not afraid to indulge in this unspeakable vice, the cause of such unheard-of and brutish sins as these drunkards commit.

Indulging in this vice was punished with severe prohibitions and penalties under the old law and was permitted only to those who already had grown children. [For this exception] an intelligent reason was given: if the father and the mother were invited to a feast and if they became tipsy with the wine, their sons and daughters (who could not drink under pain of death) were present. The latter then guided [their parents] and led them to their homes, covered them up, and kept them from committing excesses and transgressions such as are committed today. The sons and daughters watched over them, and there was an ancient law prohibiting anyone, under pain of death, to drink pulque unless he had children to restrain him and guide him if he became intoxicated so that he would not fall into a river or a hole or have a mortal accident.

There was another law typical not of savages but of polished, wise, and cultured people. He who did not obtain wine from his own crop was not allowed to drink excessively. Two reasons were given for this: one that all were thereby forced to sow and cultivate the maguey plant, the other that if [a man] did not have children to care for him in case he drank away from home, he would have it to drink in his own home and thus would avoid having difficulties in returning to his abode or falling on the road or killing himself or getting into a fight or committing a transgression which he would not have committed in his house. The republic took care to provide and pass a law or statute which prevented evildoing and the occurrence of disastrous cases. Thus everyone planted and cultivated magueys, from whose honey water comes the wine which they drank and still drink. Today what is called pulque, made by the Spaniards from black honey and water with the root in it, was never known to [the ancients]. Nor did they know how to concoct it until the Negroes and Spaniards invented it.[3] Thus the term *pulque*

[3] In pre-Conquest times only fermented beverages were known, such as *balché* in the Maya area, *nectli* in the central highlands, and *tesgüino* in the northwest. This passage is probably the earliest extant reference to tequila, mezcal, and other distilled spirits.

is not a Nahuatl word but comes from the Islands, like *maiz, naguas* ["skirt"], and other words brought from Hispaniola.

Native [Mexican] wine came from the honey water of the maguey plant with the root inside. This was used not only for feasts and orgies but also as a medicine. It is still in use today and truly has medicinal quality. [This drink] was called *iztacoctli*, which means "white wine." I believe that they have added the word "white" to differentiate it from the one made of black honey. The latter is diabolical, stinking, black, potent, rough, without flavor or taste—something which is admitted by [these people]. In spite of this they drink it readily, and it makes them more foolish and wild [than before]. Owing to its strength they take to it more than to their own native wine, which is lighter and medicinal.

As I have said, this *octli* ["wine"] was adored as a god and was called Ometochtli. Besides being considered a god, it was the oblation to the divinities, especially to that of fire. Sometimes it was offered [to the God of Fire] in vessels, at others sprinkled on the fire with a hyssop, at other times poured around the hearth. It was the usual offering at weddings and wakes, just as our own Spanish people celebrate festive and funeral occasions with bread and wine. It was a remedy for the sick because of its moderation and is not too harmful.

With this I bring to an end this chapter, beseeching His Majesty the Lord our God that He intervene with His divine mercy to reform these His creatures who are so rooted in this abominable vice. I fear, though I do not state this categorically, that, judging from the inclination that they have for it, even though they do not serve it or worship it as their ancestors did— and even though I may exaggerate, I venture to state that if an Indian, fond of this wine, saw on one side hell itself and on the other a jug of pulque and was told, "Do not drink the entire jug! If you do, hell will swallow you up!" If he so much as touched it with his mouth, his resistance would fail him. Faced with temptation he would find it easier to repress lust and not yield to it than to resist drink, even though there were a thousand hells. The accursed devil bequeathed them this snare so as to become their lord, for [otherwise], because of the Faith, he would lose the dominion and power he held over them.

CHAPTER XXIII

¶Which treats of the popular and solemn ball game, much played by the lords, in which some, after having lost their wealth, staked their own lives.

Many of the Indians' games were extremely subtle, clever, cunning, and highly refined. [It is a pity] that so much heathenism and idolatry was mixed up with them!

For who will not grant that it is a subtle and skillful thing for a man [on his back] to balance a thick log about nine feet long upon his feet as nimbly as another with his hands, playing so many tricks and turns with it, casting it hither and thither and on high, catching it with the soles of his feet with admirable deftness?

Who will not wonder on gazing upon a dance in which forty or fifty men appear around the drum, on stilts six or twelve feet tall, moving and turning with their bodies as if they were walking with their own feet?

Who will not consider it a skillful and mighty thing that three men walk about upon one another's shoulders, the lower one dancing with his arms outstretched and his hands filled with feathers or with flowers, and the one in the middle doing the same, and the third one doing the same—each without more support than his feet on the other's shoulders? It is true that this shows not only skill and dexterity but also an amazing strength in the feet.

Nor is it less wondrous to see an Indian standing on the top of the "flying pole" (for so they call it) anywhere between one hundred eighty and two hundred forty feet in height! He stands there with a trumpet in his hand, and, just watching him, those who observe become giddy. Yet he is so calm and firm that he seems completely at ease. He walks around at the summit of the pole—a space a few inches wide which barely accommodates his feet. And after having performed a thousand turns and tricks, he descends with an expression as serene as if he had done nothing!

What could be more entertaining than to see a man lying on the ground on his back with one foot lifted and other men climbing upon the sole of that foot, doing twenty turns upon it, then jumping down quickly, one after another, so lightly that I cannot understand how the man can tolerate such punishment to his leg, since [the others] jump and turn upon it, yet do not bend it or move it any more than they would a post.

I have presented this preamble so that we may describe the ball game, which I am going to deal with, as the chapter indicates and the illustration shows [Plate 34]. It was a highly entertaining game and amusement for the people, especially for those who held it to be a pastime or entertainment. Among them there were those who played it with such skill and cunning that in one hour the ball did not stop bouncing from one end to the other, without a miss, [the players] using only their buttocks [and knees], never touching it with the hand, foot, calf, or arm. Both teams were so alert in keeping the ball bouncing that it was amazing. If watching a hand-ball game among Spaniards gives us such pleasure and amazement on seeing the skill and lightness with which some play it, how much more are to be praised those who with such cunning, trickery, and nimbleness play it with their backsides or knees! It was considered a foul to touch [the ball] with the hand or any other part of the body except the parts I have mentioned—buttocks and knees. Through this demanding sport excellent players were formed, and, aside from being esteemed by the sovereigns, they were given notable dignities, were made intimates of the royal house and court, and were honored with special insignia.

Many a time have I seen this game played, and to find out why the elders still extol it [I asked them] to play it in the ancient way. But the most important [factor] was lacking, namely the enclosure where the contest took place, within which it was played, and the rings through which they cast and passed the ball. And it was a foolish insistence of mine to try to see today something which existed in ancient times, as different as the real thing from a picture. So that we can understand its form and begin to appreciate the skill and dexterity with which this game was played, it must be noted that ball courts existed in all the illustrious, civilized, and powerful cities and towns, in those ruled by either the community or the lords, the latter stressing [the game] inordinately. A regular competition existed between the two [types of communities]. [The ball courts] were enclosed with ornate and handsomely carved walls. The interior floor was of stucco, finely polished and decorated with figures of the god and demons to whom the game was dedicated and whom the players held to be their patrons in that sport. These ball courts were larger in some places than in others. They were built in the shape that can be seen in the illustration: narrow in the middle and wide at the ends. The corners were built on purpose so that if the player's ball fell into one it was lost and was considered a foul. The height of the wall was anywhere between eight and eleven feet high, running all around [the court]. Because of heathen custom, around [the wall] were planted wild palms or trees which give red seeds, whose wood is soft and light. Crucifixes and carved images are made of it today. The surrounding walls were adorned with merlons or stone statues, all spaced out. [These places] became filled to bursting when there was a game of all the lords, when warlike activities ceased, owing to truces or other causes, thus permitting [the games].

The ball courts were anywhere between one hundred, one hundred fifty, and two hundred feet long. In the square corners (which served as ends or goals) a great number of players stood on guard to see that the ball did not penetrate. The main players stood in the center facing the ball, and so did the opponents, since the game was carried out similarly to the way they fought in battle or in special contests. In the middle of the walls of this enclosure were fixed two stones facing one another, and each had a hole in the center. Each hole was surrounded by a carved image of the deity of the game. Its face was that of a monkey.

As we shall see under *The Calendar*, this feast was celebrated once a year, and to clarify the use of these stones it should be noted that one team put the ball through the hole of the stone on one side while the other side was used by the other team. The first to pass its ball through [the hole] won the prize. These stones also served as a division, for between them, on the floor, was a black or green stripe. This was done with a certain herb and no other, which is a sign of pagan belief. The ball always had to be passed across this line to win the game, because if the ball, projected by the backsides or by the knee, went bouncing along the floor and passed the stripe the width of two fingers, no fault was committed; but if it did not pass, it was considered a foul play. The man who sent the ball through the stone ring was surrounded by all. They honored him, sang songs of praise to him, and joined him in dancing. He was given a very special reward of feathers or mantles and breech-cloths, something highly prized. But what he most prized was the honor involved: that was his great wealth. For he was honored as a man who had vanquished many and had won a battle.

All those who played this game were stripped except for their usual breechcloths, on top of which they wore coverings of deer-skin to defend their thighs, which were continually being scratched on the floor. They wore gloves so as not to injure their hands, which they constantly set down firmly, supporting themselves against the floor. They bet jewels, slaves, precious stones, fine mantles, the trappings of war, and women's finery. Others staked their mistresses. It must be understood that this took place, as I have described, among the nobility, the lords, captains, braves, and important men. Countless lords and knights attended this game and played it with such pleasure and enjoyment, changing places

315

with one another occasionally, taking their turns so that everyone could take part in that pleasant sport, to the point that sometimes the sun set upon them while they enjoyed themselves.

Some of these men were taken out dead from that place for the following reason. Tired and without having rested, [they ran] after the ball from end to end, seeing it descending from above, in haste and hurry to reach it first, but the ball on the rebound hit them in the mouth or the stomach or the intestines, so that they fell to the floor instantly. Some died of that blow on the spot because they had been too eager to touch the ball before anyone else. Some took a special pride in this game and performed so many feats in it that it was truly amazing. There is one trick especially that I wish to describe. I saw it done many times by skillful Indians. They employed a bounce or curious hit. On seeing the ball come at them, at the moment that it was about to touch the floor, they were so quick in turning their knees or buttocks to the ball that they returned it with an extraordinary swiftness. With this bouncing back and forth they suffered terrible injuries on their knees or thighs so that the haunches of those who made use of these tricks were frequently so bruised that those spots had to be opened with a small blade, whereupon the blood which had clotted there because of the blows of the ball was squeezed out.

As some may have seen, this ball was as large as a small bowling ball. The material that the ball [was made of] was called *ollin*, which in our own Castilian tongue I have heard translated as *batel*, which is the resin of a certain tree. When cooked it becomes stringy. It is very much esteemed and prized by these people, both as a medicine for the ailing and for religious offerings. Jumping and bouncing are its qualities, upward and downward, to and fro. It can exhaust the pursuer running after it before he can catch up with it.

Having described the manner in which the noblemen played this ball game for recreation and sport, we shall now deal with those who played it for profit and as a vice, their endeavors and happiness depending upon not losing but winning, like professional gamblers, whose only occupation and job this was, and no other, who depended upon this for their food. Their wives and children (as I described in the last chapter) lived constantly on borrowed bread, asking alms of their neighbors, bothering this one and that one, such as some Spaniards do, sending here for bread today, there for vinegar tomorrow, another day for oil, and so on. In this way these men usually went about poor and ill-fortuned, without sowing or reaping, lacking instruction in anything else but ball-playing. It is rare [even today] to find one of these players prosperous, and they have nothing to show for their efforts. Thus moved and torn by greed and desire of gain, they performed a thousand ceremonies and superstitious acts, invented ways of fortunetelling and idolatrous beliefs which I shall explain here.

In the first place, it should be known that, when night had fallen, these players took the ball and placed it in a clean bowl, together with the protective leather breechcloth and gloves, and hung it all on a pole. Squatting before these accouterments of the game, they worshiped them and addressed to them certain superstitious words and magic spells; devotedly they besought the ball to be lucky on that day. During the incantation to the ball they invoked the hills, the water, the springs, the cliffs, the trees, the wild animals and snakes; the sun, the moon, and the stars; the clouds, the rainstorms—in sum, all created things, together with the gods which had been invented for each of these.

When that cursed heathen prayer terminated, [each player] took a handful of incense, cast it into a small incense burner which existed for this purpose, and offered sacrifice to the ball and to the leather gear. While the copal burned, [the player] went forth to bring food, consisting of bread, a humble stew, and wine, and offered these things in front of the paraphernalia, leaving them there until dawn. When day broke, he ate that simple fare which he had offered and went out to seek someone to play with. They went along, each so sure of winning that if anyone suggested to either that he was to lose his faith was such that he would come to mortal blows with [that person] and seven times over defend his heathen belief, something I doubt he would do today in defending our True Faith.

Someone might ask whether they always won with that magic incantation. The devil is subtle in permitting some to win occasionally, thus confirming their unholy beliefs. At other times, when they lost, they were persuaded to curse their own bad luck, which is what losers do. They blaspheme and put misfortunes in the hands of the devil.

These wretches played for stakes of little value or worth, and since the pauper loses quickly what he has, they were forced to gamble their homes, their fields, their corn granaries, their maguey plants. They sold their children in order to bet and even staked themselves and became slaves, to be sacrificed later if they were not ransomed in the manner which has been explained.

Their way of using themselves as stakes was this. Once they had lost their valuable articles, such as pieces of cloth, beads, feathers, they would give their word saying that at home they had certain valuable articles. If this was believed, it was well, but if not, the winner would accompany [the loser] to his house and take the articles which [the loser] had offered upon his word. But if he did not possess them or find a way to make payment, he was sent to jail; and if his wife or children did not ransom him, he became a slave of the creditor. The laws of the republic permitted that he could be sold for the sum he owed and not for more. In case he wished to become free and if he discovered that he was unable to gather the sum for which he was enslaved, he lost [his liberty] if someone else could pay more. The same was applied to all the other games. This created fear and held back many who took warning in the example of others and did not bet that which they did not possess, in case the opponent took advantage of this and won [him]. As I have said, these were always people of the lower orders, because illustrious, noble people never lacked that with which to gamble. [The latter], however, played more for recreation and relief from their constant warfare and toil—not for profit.

This is an advantage of the rich: if they lose today, with what they have left they can win tomorrow. It is important that one who takes part in this sort of game have large wealth behind him.

With this we have now finished the theme of this chapter and [the account of] the way in which men became slaves to represent the gods alive. These came from among the serfs of the villages, from the natives who had been born and raised in them, from the children of villagers who, because of crimes or transgressions, theft, or gambling, or from other causes, came to be slaves.

We have also finished dealing with the games, tricks, and skills which these people performed with their feet, hands, and bodies. And I venture to say that there is not and never has been another nation in the world which has practiced greater and cleverer skills than these. If I were to describe each of them in detail, I could write a chapter [about each one], but the bit I have told is enough.

We are finished with what concerns the feasts of their gods and their rites. We have described, though briefly, the devotion, the rites, and religion with which they were honored. I wish to warn the priests and the friars to be watchful of all the ancient customs so that they may be ready to cast out and uproot every kind of heathenism and idolatry or any hint of these that might have survived. For these reasons I shall now continue and shall explain the calendar according to whose system the natives patterned their lives, governed themselves, and counted the course of time. May His Divine Blessedness grant that today these things are no longer in use, and, though I do not know for sure, nor can I affirm this, I fear [that the ancient calendar is still used].

Book of the Gods and Rites

Plate 1. Topiltzin-Quetzalcoatl, ruler of the Toltecs, seated on the type of serpent bench used by the war god Huitzilopochtli. Before him are six of the seven caves of Chicomoztoc, in Aztec tradition the place of origin of the tribes. (See Chapter I.)

Plate 2. Toltecs, followers of Topiltzin, dressed in tunics and shell-shaped headdresses. The seventh cave of Chicomoztoc is in the center. (See Chapter I.)

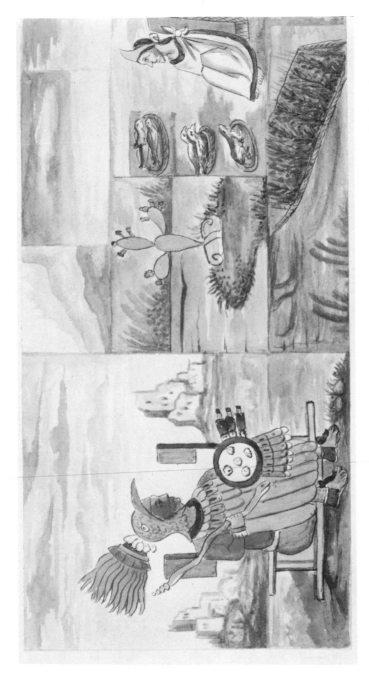

Plate 3. Huitzilopochtli, Aztec tribal deity and war god. He wears a hummingbird helmet and a feathered mantle. One gold flag tops his shield, and another is at his back. His staff is in the form of a serpent. On the right appear a prickly-pear cactus and examples of the fauna of Lake Tetzcoco. (See Chapter II.)

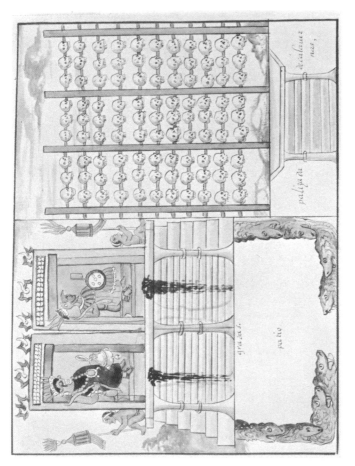

Plate 4. Surmounting the Great Temple of Tenochtitlan are the twin shrines of Tlaloc (left) and Huitzilopochtli (right). A serpent wall surrounds the courtyard, and next to it stands the *tzompantli*, or skull rack, where the skulls of sacrificial victims were placed. (See Chapter II.)

Plate 5. Youths in the service of the god Huitzilopochtli. Their tonsures indicate their religious status. On either side are Chichimec hunters. (See Chapter II.)

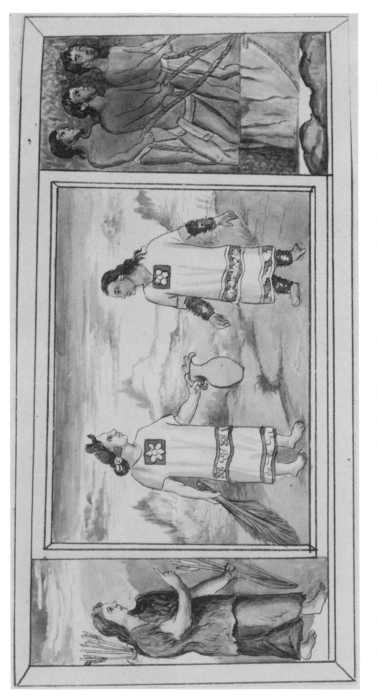

Plate 6. Aztec girls who spent a year in the religious school attached to the Temple of Huitzilopochtli. A Chichimec huntress appears on the left. The scene on the right probably represents men working at the lake. (See Chapter II.)

Plate 7. Five priests hold a sacrificial victim on a waist-high stone while the high priest cuts out his heart with a flint knife. (See Chapter III.)

Plate 8. The god Tezcatlipoca. He is painted black. In his left hand he carries a fan at the center of which is a gold mirror that reflects all that takes place in the world. The four arrows in his right hand symbolize punishment for sinners. The gold ear in his headdress is a sign that Tezcatlipoca hears the confessions of wrongdoers. (See Chapter IV.)

Plate 9. Tezcatlipoca in his temple in Mexico-Tenochtitlan. The tufts of cotton on his shield are "garments of the sky"; the quail feathers on his head are associated with sacrifice. His mantle is decorated with skulls and crossbones. (See Chapter V.)

Plate 10. Youths and maidens dedicated to the cult of Tezcatlipoca dancing during the Feast of Toxcatl. They are adorned with garlands of popcorn, symbolic of the dry season during which this feast took place. (See Chapter V.)

Plate 11. A priest of Tezcatlipoca offering incense to the figure of the god, while another does penance by letting blood from his shins. After the bloodletting the used maguey thorns were placed in the ball of hay in the upper right corner. (See Chapter V.)

Plate 12. Quetzalcoatl, in his role as Ehecatl, God of the Wind, wearing his typical bird beak, conical cap, gold breast pendant shaped like the cross section of a shell, and shield covered with marine-bird feathers. In his right hand he carries a sickle-shaped instrument. (See Chapter VI.)

Plate 13. Camaxtli, God of the Hunt, carrying the hunter's equipment—bow and arrows and net for the game. One of the distinctive decorations of this deity is the striped body paint. (See Chapter VII.)

Plate 14. Tota, Our Father, a tree placed in an artificial forest set up in the courtyard in front of Tlaloc's temple on the Feast of Huey Tozoztli. Tota is tied to four smaller trees, probably signifying the four cardinal directions and the center. (See Chapter VIII.)

Plate 15. Above, the god Xipe dressed in the skin of a flayed human victim. Below, a prisoner of war, armed with dummy weapons, one foot tied to a round stone, taking part in the gladiatorial combat. His opponent is a Jaguar knight using real arms. (See Chapter IX.)

Plate 16. A prisoner of war carrying a message to the Sun. Later he would be sacrificed on the top of a Sun stone. (See Chapter X.)

Plate 17. Knights of the Sun, warriors of high rank and noble birth, carrying razor-edged swords. The man on the left wears a stiff pony-tail headdress bound with red cord and feathers, signifying that he has taken prisoners in war. The net mantle worn by the man on the right is another sign of bravery. (See Chapter XI.)

Plate 18. The leader of a dance group of maidens and youths performing during the Feast of Xocotl Huetzi. The leader wears an animal and quetzal-feather headdress and bells on his ankles and carries a gold rattle. (See Chapter XII.)

Plate 19. During the Feast of Xocotl Huetzi, Aztec youths compete in climbing the Xocotl pole to win as a prize a bird of amaranth dough. (See Chapter XII.)

Plate 20. Cihuacoatl, one of the principal Aztec goddesses. Her open mouth symbolizes her ceaseless hunger for the flesh of sacrificed men. (See Chapter XIII.)

Plate 21. A fire sacrifice in honor of Cihuacoatl performed in the presence of a maiden representing the goddess. (See Chapter XIII.)

Plate 22. Two priests in the service of Cihuacoatl guarding the sacred fire in her temple day and night. (See Chapter XIII.)

Plate 23. Chicomecoatl, Seven Serpent, a corn goddess, carrying tasseled ears of corn and wearing a necklace of young maize. (See Chapter XIV.)

Plate 24. Above, Toci, Mother of the Gods, or Our Grandmother, sweeping the road for the coming of the gods. She wears a headdress of spindle whorls with cotton. On the right she sits on a wooden scaffold at the entrance to Mexico-Tenochtitlan. At the left is a mock battle between the Huaxtec leader of Toci's attendants, clad in a human skin, and an Aztec warrior. (See Chapter XV.)

Plate 25. Xochiquetzal, Goddess of Flowers and Love, protector of painters and artisans, represented as a young woman carrying flowers and wearing a gold nose ornament. (See Chapter XVI.)

Plate 26. Iztaccihuatl, White Woman, a mountain goddess, wearing a white paper headdress, which may signify the mountain's snowy peak. (See Chapter XVII.)

Plate 27. Popocatepetl, Smoking Mountain, surrounded by other hills, including Tlaloc and Matlalcueye. (See Chapter XVIII.)

Plate 28. Chalchiuhcueye, Goddess of the Waters, She of the Jade Skirt. The volutes around the skirt of this mountain goddess represent streams. (See Chapter XIX.)

Plate 29. An Aztec market. The round stone in the center is a *momoztli*, or altar. A number of men and women are engaged in trade, and two slaves, wearing wooden collars, are for sale. This illustration is one of the few in the collection with a pronounced pre-Conquest composition. (See Chapter XX.)

Plate 30. The *cuauhcalli*, "wooden house," a cagelike cell in which a transgressor was enclosed without food or drink until his case came to trial. (See Chapter XX.)

Plate 31. Youths and maidens in the dancing schools, alternating in a circle, dancing and singing, while two teacher-musicians play drums in the center. (See Chapter XXI.)

Plate 32. Men playing *patolli*, a game similar to pachisi or backgammon, using beans as dice and painted stones as chips on a cross-shaped board. They wagered their valuable possessions, such as the feathers and jade beads shown in the background, and even their own persons. (See Chapter XXII.)

Plate 33. Ometochtli, Two Rabbit, the god of games, wagers, and pulque. Like Xipe, he is dressed in the skin of a flayed victim. He carries a flower, probably associated with Macuilxochitl, Five Flower, patron of *patolli* players. (See Chapter XXII.)

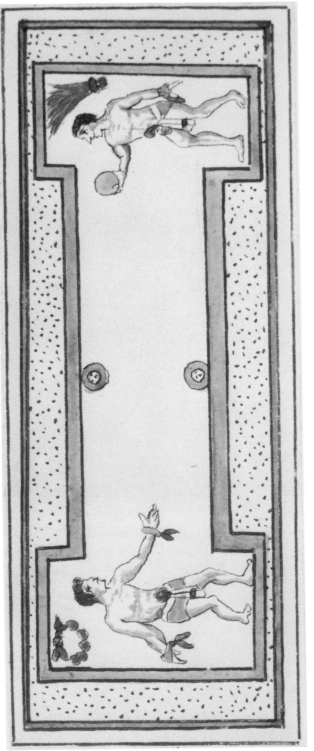

Plate 34. An Aztec ball court, with four corners representing the cardinal directions. The players must pass the rubber ball through the stone rings in the center, striking the ball only with their hips or knees. Jade and feathers, shown above, are wagered on the game. (See Chapter XXIII.)

The Ancient Calendar

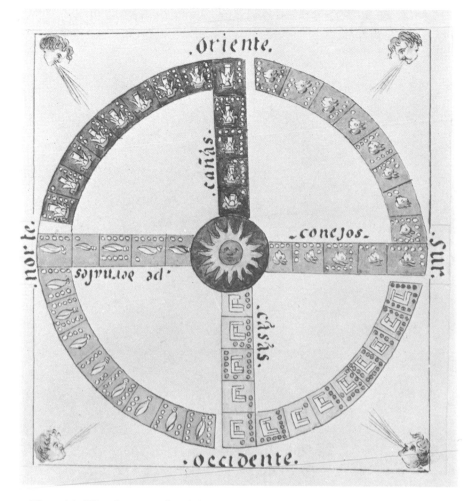

Plate 35. The Aztec cycle of fifty-two years, divided into four parts of thirteen years each, each part associated with a cardinal direction, in a juxtaposition of time and space. Unlike the European system, east appears to the north. (See *The Ancient Calendar*, Chapter I.)

Plate 36. The twenty days of the Aztec month (left to right): Alligator (which Durán calls Head of Serpent), Wind, House, Lizard, Serpent, Death, Deer, Rabbit, Water, Dog, Monkey, Wild Grass, Reed, Jaguar, Eagle, Buzzard, Motion, Flint Knife, Rain, Flower. (See Chapter II.)

Plate 37. Thirteen numbers combined with thirteen of the twenty day signs made up the Aztec "week." In the illustration above the week covers a period from One Alligator to Thirteen Reed. The next week will begin with One Jaguar. (See Chapter III.)

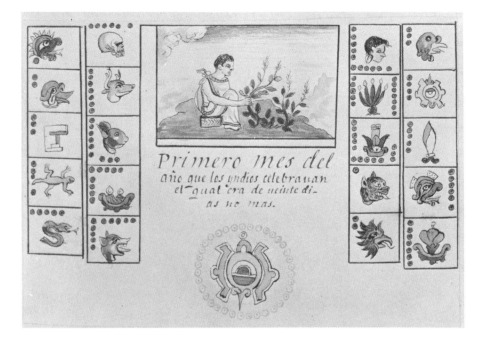

Plate 38. The first month of the Aztec year, Xiutzitzquilo, Cuahuitlehua, Atl Motzacuaya, or Xilomaniztli. The first month is symbolized by a "butterfly-motion" sign, which appears not in the sky but underneath the Spanish inscription. (See "The First Month of the Year.")

Segundo mes
del año que los naturales
çelebrauan el qual
era de ueinte dias
llamauan
A esta fiesta tlacaxipehualiz
tly.

Plate 39. The second month of the Aztec year, Tlacaxipehualiztli. The constellation for this month cannot be identified because the upper part of the illustration was lost when the manuscript was cut and bound. (See "The Second Month of the Year.")

Tercero mes de
el año que los yndios celebra
van antiguamente
debajo deste non.
bre, toçoz
tontly.

Plate 40. The third month of the Aztec year, Tozoztontli. The constellation is shown in the form of a bird pierced with a bone. According to Durán, it can be identified as Taurus and is made up of a number of stars. (See "The Third Month of the Year.")

Qvarto mes del
año que los yndios celebrauan
en su antigua ley, era de ue
ynte dias como los de
mas y celebra
uan en el la
fiesta,
llamada Ochpaniztly quiere de
zir dia de barrer y juntamente cele
brauan la fiesta de toçi madre de
los dioses.

Plate 41. The fourth month of the Aztec year, Huey Tozoztli (which Durán mistakenly calls Ochpaniztli). The constellation is the same as that of the third month. (See "The Fourth Month of the Year.")

Quinto mes en el
qual se çelebraua la fiesta del pri
mero dia del mes llamado
toxcatl que quiere
decir cosa seca
en el qual
dia celebrauan la solenidad del
ydolo llamado tezcatlypuca
fiesta principal de los
naturales
ect.

Plate 42. The fifth month of the Aztec year, Toxcatl. The upper half of the illustration is missing. (See "The Fifth Month of the Year.")

El sexto mes del año de
que uamos tratando tenia ue
ynte dias llamauan
a la figura que en
principio y,
dia pri
mero del se celebraua
etzalqualiztly que quiere dezir
dia de comer maiz
y frisol cocido.

Plate 43. The sixth month of the Aztec year, Etzalcualiztli. The constellation is represented by the figure of a man walking through water, carrying a cornstalk in one hand and a basket in the other and bearing a plumed device on his back. (See "The Sixth Month of the Year.")

El septimo mes que este
año tenia era de ueinte dias çele
brauan en el una fiesta que
llamauan tecuil
uitontly que
quiere
Dezir fiesta pequeña de Señores, ect.

Plate 44. The seventh month of the Aztec year, Tecuilhuitontli. This illustration was mutilated in binding. The remaining fragment of the constellation appears to be the fringe of a sovereign's diadem. (See "The Seventh Month of the Year.")

368

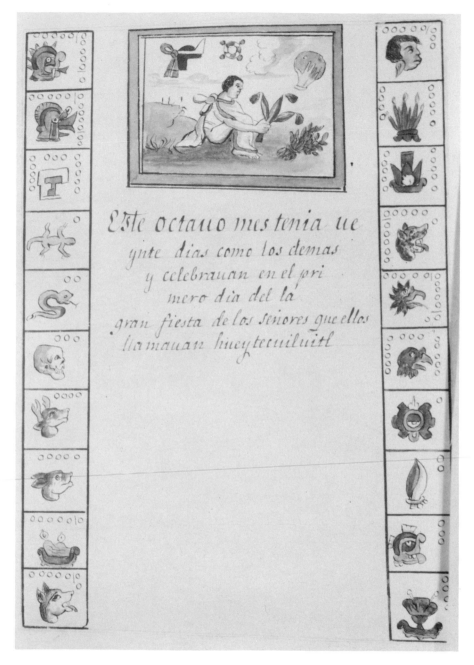

Este octauo mes tenia ue
ynte dias como los demas
y celebrauan en el pri
mero dia del la
gran fiesta de los señores que ellos
llamauan hueytecuilhuitl

Plate 45. The eighth month of the Aztec year, Huey Tecuilhuitl. The three signs, left to right, are a royal diadem; a jade disk, to which four small circles are attached, and a hand patting into shape a tortilla of young corn.

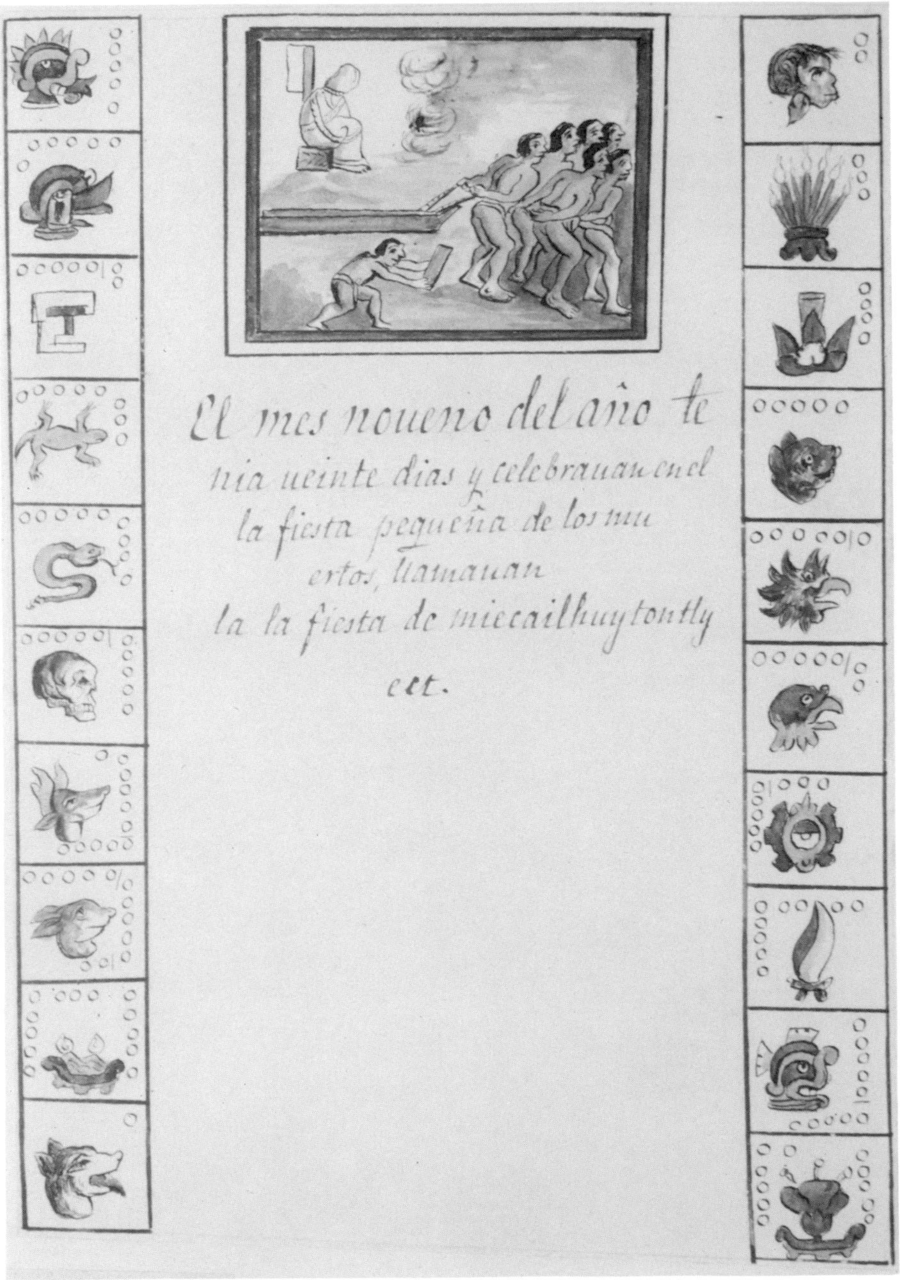

El mes noueno del año te
nia ueinte dias y celebrauan en el
la fiesta pequeña de los mu
ertos, llamauan
la la fiesta de miccailhuytontly
ect.

Plate 46. The ninth month of the Aztec year, Miccailhuitontli. A dead man is shown in his shroud, reclining upon a seat with a banner identical to the symbol for the number twenty protruding from his back. The symbol "was thought to be seen in the heavens at that time of the year." (See "The Ninth Month of the Year.")

El decimo mes del año te-
nia ueynte dias y celebra
van en el la fiesta
grande de los
muertos y juntamente la fiesta so
lenissima de jocotluetz si
esta de los tepane
cas ect.
Auia este dia un sacrificio de fue
go espantoso y de gran temor.

Plate 47. The tenth month of the Aztec year, Xocotl Huetzi. The constellation is the same as that for the ninth month. (See "The Tenth Month
of the Year.")

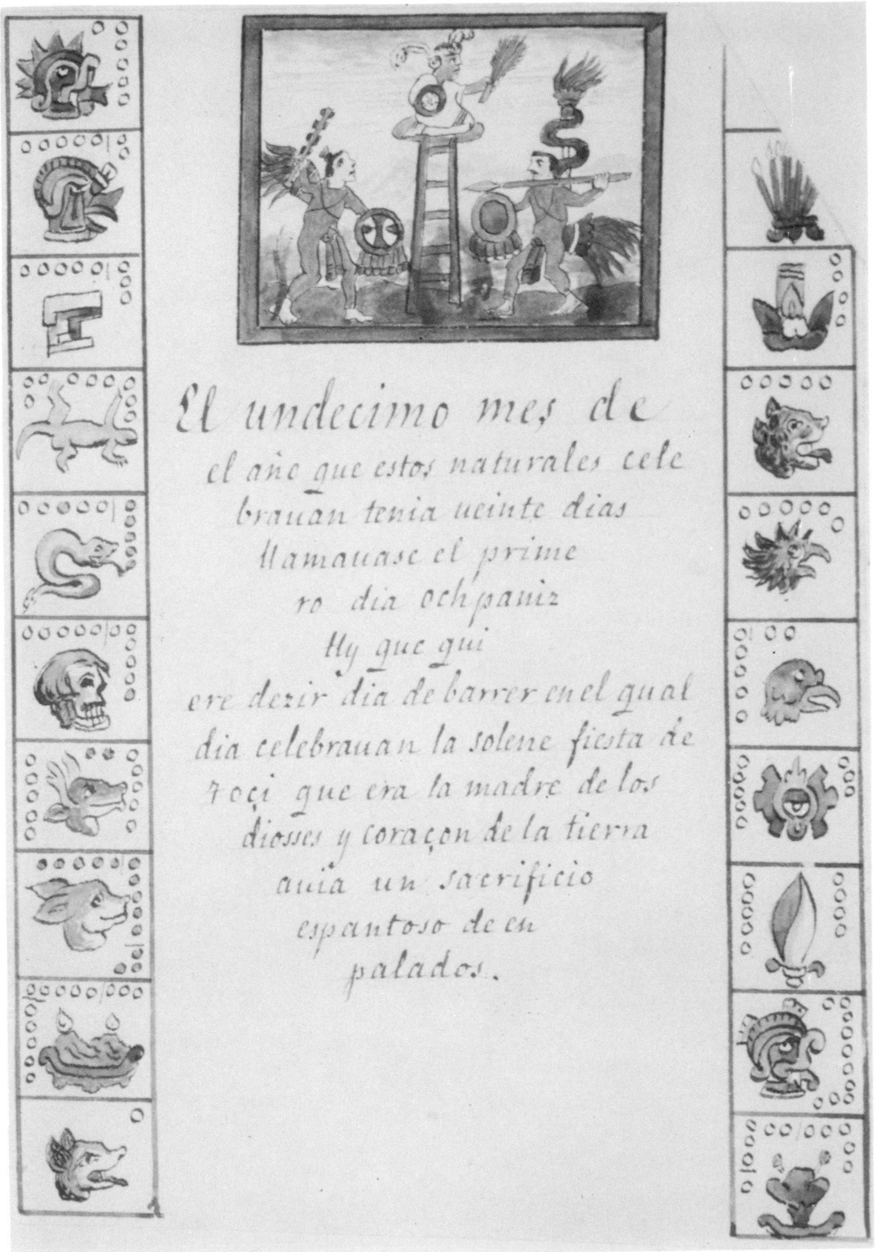

El undecimo mes de

el año que estos naturales cele

brauan tenia ueinte dias

llamauase el prime

ro dia ochpaniz

tly que qui

ere dezir dia de barrer en el qual

dia celebrauan la solene fiesta de

toçi que era la madre de los

diosses y coraçon de la tierra

auia un sacrificio

espantoso de en

palados.

Plate 48. The eleventh month of the Aztec year, Ochpaniztli. No constellation is shown. (See "The Eleventh Month of the Year.")

El duodecimo mes de
este año de que uamos tratando
tenia ueinte dias celebraua
se en su primero dia la fi
esta de pachtontli
que quiere dezir

mal hojuelo nonbre diminutiuo
en el qual dia celebrauan juntamen
te la fiesta solene del aduenimien
to de uitzilopochtly en el
qual dia auia un te
rrible y espanto
so sacrificio
de on
bres.

Plate 49. The twelfth month of the Aztec year, Pachtontli. The constellation is represented by garlands of Spanish moss. (See "The Twelfth Month of the Year.")

El trezeno mes deste
año tenia ueinte dias celebrauan
el primero dia del la fiesta de uey-
pachtli superlatiuo nonbre
que quiere decir el gran
mal hojo. llamauan
le por otro non
bre coaylhuitl que quiere dezir
fiesta general de toda la tierra don
de se celebraua la fiesta de los cerros
en particular la del bolcan
y sierra neuada
eet.

Plate 50. The thirteenth month of the Aztec year, Hueypachtli. The constellation is the same as that for the twelfth month. (See "The Thirteenth Month of the Year.")

El mes catorzeno de
este año tenia ueinte dias y ce
lebrauan en su primero dia la sole
nidad de el dios de la caça que
se llamaua camaxtle
por otro noubre ye-
maxtle que
g. d.
El de los tres bragueros. El noubre
propio del dia era quecholli que
quiere deçir uaras o fisgas arro
jadizas ect.

Plate 51. The fourteenth month of the Aztec year, Quecholli. No constellation is shown. Durán indicates that the people believed they saw the figure of a hunter in the sky. (See "The Fourteenth Month of the Year.")

El mes quinzeno des
te año de que hazemos mencion era
de veinte dias y la fiesta que
el primero dia del se celebraua
tenia por nonbre panquetza
liztly que quiere de
zir ençalçamiento
de vanderas
celebrauan juntamente la solene y
larga proceçion presurosa del gran
dios de los mexicanos llamado
vitzilopochtly.

Plate 52. The fifteenth month of the Aztec year, Panquetzaliztli. The month is symbolized by the figure of a man in a squatting position wearing a mantle and holding a feathered banner in his hands. (See "The Fifteenth Month of the Year.")

376

El mes diez y seis que
los naturales celebrauan era de
ueinte dias llamauase la solem
dad del primero dia del atemoz
tly que quiere decir decen
dimiento de agua.
era commemo
racion

Del aduenimiento de uitzilopochtly
dia muy solene y de gran fiesta
ect.

Plate 53. The sixteenth month of the Aztec year, Atemoztli. The illustration, severely mutilated, shows a child dressed in mantle and breech-cloth. (See "The Sixteenth Month of the Year.")

El mes diez y siete
tenia veinte dias celebrauase en
el la fiesta que llamauan tititl
juntamente celebrauan a la
commemoracion del Dios
de la caça llama
do Camaxtle.
ett.

Plate 54. The seventeenth month of the Aztec year, Tititl. The month is symbolized by two small boys dressed in mantles and breechcloths, their hair arranged in topknots. They are engaged in tugging at each other. Durán compares this sign to Gemini. (See "The Seventeenth Month of the Year.")

En este mes diez y ocho ce
lebrauan la solenidad de yzcalli
y xilomaniztly y la commemora
cion de tlaloc que era el dios
de las aguas y truenos
rraios y relanpa
gos eet.

y en el fin deste mes antes de los dias
sin prouecho y demasiados celebra
uan la commemoracion de gueuitleua.

Plate 55. The eighteenth month of the Aztec year, Xilomaniztli or Izcalli. The month is represented by two stellar signs. The first (above) is a man dressed in mantle and breechcloth, wearing a band about his head, seated upon a stool of woven reeds. What appears to be a bolt of lightning emerges from his back. The second sign (below) is a tree, apparently symbolizing the forests on Matlalcueye. (See "The Eighteenth Month of the Year.")

The Ancient Calendar

HERE BEGINS

THE ANCIENT CALENDAR

USED in antiquity by all the Indian nations in heathen times, both in their feasts and ceremonies and on other occasions during the year when they sowed and reaped [and] observed the days upon which children were born so as to understand the fates and destinies under which they were brought forth. This is described here in order to instruct the priesthood for the honor and glory of our God, for the dissemination of Holy Catholic Faith, and the extirpation of the ceremonies and rites of the past.

This work was terminated in the year 1579.

An Epistle
To the Gentle Reader

THERE has never been a nation or a generation since our first progenitor Adam that has not been moved in all its activities for interest and reward. So it was that Adam and Eve were enticed by the reward and promise of the serpent, which told them they would become as gods and know of good and evil. This is why they decided to break God's commandments. And when God took the children of Israel out of Egypt, He had already assured them the promised land which flowed with milk and honey. When the Romans pursued a thing and made an effort to attain it, they endeavored to gain worldly glory through the triumphal receptions they enjoyed. And lastly, I must say that man moves in his toil for a reward, which makes the peasant endure the labor he suffers under the sun, rain, and cold, desirous of the fruit of his work. Likewise the soldier is spurred into battle by the desire of the spoils he will take from the enemy.

The Holy Apostles themselves were to be rewarded for their sufferings in Christ and for His love. In Saint Luke we find that Christ himself said: "But you are they who have continued with me in my trials. And I appoint to you a kingdom, even as my Father has appointed to me, that you may eat and drink at my table in my kingdom; and you shall sit upon thrones judging the twelve tribes of Israel."[1] O Christian reader! These divine promises greatly console the missionaries in their endeavors, [which are] always at the cost of their well-being and their health. They are moved by the reward which they expect from a Divine Hand. For the moment they give up life, honor in exchange for insults, offenses, and, in the end, solitude, depriving themselves of all human consolation. They expose themselves in the mountains, hills, and valleys and deal with people who are strangers, contrary to their own ways and civilization. They do so in order to serve God. Their reward is infinite and will be shared by these gentile Indian nations when they are converted and instructed in the way of the truth.

The peasant receives his satisfaction (as I have said) when he reaps the fruit of his toil. The minister and servant of God receives no less satisfaction on seeing the fruits of this preaching. He has offered it to God with the greatest humility. He has worked like those who are moved by zeal and by profit and by the holy

[1] Luke 22:28–30.

desire of the salvation of these nations. Nevertheless, he is expecting a reward for his labor: God himself!

On the other hand, it would bring sadness to this spiritual worker to see the earth he has tilled so many years lost—ravished and frozen with the devilish frost of heathenism, even though it is only part of his crop. It is a terrible thing to see a people abandon the faith as quickly as they had accepted it as soon as it is convenient to them. Oh, what sorrow, woe, sadness, are felt in the hearts of those who love God! What sorrows, what emptiness must Saint Paul have felt when he was weary of preaching, of admonishing, when people mocked him and laughed at the word of God: "We shall listen to you again if you return to repeat these things." And thus he spoke: "O foolish, witless Galatians! Blind and unfortunate regarding your salvation!"[2]

Perhaps someone will tell me that something is higher and more lofty when it is more difficult to reach and needs to be taught not once but many times. Tell me then, I beg you, what people in the world has been preached to, indoctrinated, and taught more than this nation? What generation has lived in this world with so many ministers and preachers as this one has? None. It would be false to say that they have grown fainthearted and weak. On the contrary, with the greatest of fervor and enthusiasm, like true laborers of Christ with the penetrating instrument of doctrine, some have written books of instruction and sermons, others have preached, and others have heard confession. They have tried to cleanse [the land of idolatry]. They have roamed the hills and the precipices, saving men from the most dangerous places—men created in the divine image, like chips cut from knotty, rough, and unpolished wood, their low, earthy minds covered with bark so hard and rugged that in order to strip it off a special gift from the Holy Spirit is necessary.

Even though it is true that the memory of Huitzilopochtli, Tezcatlipoca, Quetzalcoatl, and the other countless gods that this

---

[2] Here Fray Diego compares his troubles with the Nahuatl-speaking peoples to the tribulations of Saint Paul with the Galatians. The text is freely paraphrased by Durán from Galatians 3:1–3.

nation worshiped has been forgotten, and even though it is true that bloodletting in honor of these deities, the slaying of men, the offering of sacrifices, and the eating of human flesh [are ended], I strongly suspect that a scent of superstition has remained. Not only today but in the past we have known of old men who were prose-lytizers, soothsayers, wise in the old law, who taught and still teach the young folk who are now being educated. They instruct them in the count of the days and of the years, and of the ceremonies and ancient rites; [they tell them] about the fabulous and false mir-acles of the old gods. Because of this suspicion I was encouraged to produce this work, moved only by the zeal of informing and illuminating our ministers so that their task may not be in vain, worthless. In some places their labor [has been in vain]. The ministers, workers in this divine task of the conversion of the natives, should know about these things, if their aim is to be effec-tive and fruitful in their doctrine. In all of this we are concerned with the salvation of the soul or the perdition of both the teacher and the disciple. To administer the Sacraments one needs more knowledge of the language, customs, and weaknesses of these people than most think.

Let not the servant of God who wishes to bring forth fruit in this vineyard of the Lord be content in saying that he can under-stand confession [in the native language] and that is enough. We need a great deal more than that to explain the mysteries of our Faith and the benefit and necessity of the Sacraments in which they abound. Let the minister beware lest he endeavor to preach the truth and preach falsehood and lies. For this will be to the detri-ment of our brethren and the detriment of the conscience of the man who, without knowing or understanding with certitude what he is saying or what is said to him, claims that the natives are not deceitful or insincere and are in dire need [of spiritual help]. This attitude was realistic for some time, but today it is false, for we now have many missionaries and an abundance of ministers who translate the many native languages.

What I shall deal with now is the count of the years, the days, the months, and weeks which governed these people in pagan times; the names and figures that designated the days to predict the fates, destinies, and inclinations of the newborn; the order of the calendar and the feasts, the common as well as the main ones, which were celebrated every twenty days; the leap year; the count that went round and round without conflicting with the season for sowing, reaping, putting away the harvest in cornbins. Regarding all of this there was careful computation, so that things had to take place on such and such a day or season and so that everything might be in its right time.

We beseech our Lord that this order and tradition may be forgotten in our times. I confess that I am extremely skeptical [about the practices of the Indians]. Or is it possible that I have seen too much? I beg our God (again this is my prayer) that I may be mistaken and someday He will allow me to do penance for this sin [of skepticism].

CHAPTER I

¶Regarding the count of the passing of the years used by the natives and the numbers [of days] in each week and the images with which they were represented.[1]

THE curious reader interested in discovering what this circular design means will understand and easily comprehend what the characters and symbols signify [Plate 35]. It simply teaches us to understand the way in which the years were counted by the natives in olden times. Within this circle, it must be understood, we shall find fifty-two squares, and each signifies a year. So it is that in

[1] *The Ancient Calendar* is a mine of information about Aztec astronomy, astrology, and calendrical symbolism and about the dating system, which was the product of several thousand years' observation of the sun, the moon, and other celestial bodies. This highly important compilation has seldom been consulted by scholars studying Indian astronomy and the incredibly complex calendars devised in Mesoamerica.

In this work Durán briefly describes the eighteen months of twenty days each, as well as the five useless days. Occasionally he refers to "figures in the sky," by which he obviously means constellations and which indicate that each period of days was associated with a group of heavenly bodies. The corresponding constellations are listed for some months but not for others. In some of the illustrations the astronomical symbols are shown above the main drawing, within a ring of clouds. In others the symbols are portrayed by the main figure itself. Unfortunately, many of the symbols were lost when the manuscript was cut during binding. The five useless days are not shown in the illustrations, evidently because they were never pictured by the Aztecs.

this circle are shown fifty-two years. These fifty-two years were called a hebdomadary by the natives.[2] At the end of the cycle a solemn feast was held. This was called Nexiuhilpiliztli, which means Completion, or Binding, of a Perfect Circle of Years. At this time this round circle reached the end of its cycle and returned to its starting point again, terminating the complete number of fifty-two years. As I have described, a great solemnity and feast was held—it was in many ways similar to the manner in which the Jews under the Old Law commemorated the year of the jubilee every fifty years.

The round circle was divided into four parts, each part containing thirteen years. The first part belonged to the East, the second to the North, the third to the West, and the fourth to the South. The first part, belonging to the East, was called the Thirteen Years of the Reeds, and so it was that each square of the thirteen contained a picture of a reed and the number of the year in the same way that we reckon the day of this present year, as in December, 1579, we say, "Such and such a thing happened in this year."

So it was that the natives said: "On the year One Reed or Two or Three Reeds a certain thing took place."[3]

The second part of the [circle] dealt with the North, which also contained thirteen squares, called the Thirteen Squares of the Flint Knife. In each was pictured a flint knife plus the day of the current year, and all of this was done in order to show the number of Flint Knife when "such and such a thing took place," just as in the eastern direction.

The third part lay to the West. It was called Thirteen Houses, and so we see a small house painted in each of the thirteen squares.

[2] In this context Durán uses "hebdomadary" to mean "cycle."

[3] Durán follows the custom of most sixteenth-century writers in sometimes giving native dates in the plural: Two Houses, Eleven Dogs, Five Reeds, and so on. Most modern scholars translate the dates as Two House, Eleven Dog, Five Reed. The form used by Durán is explained by the fact that he was referring to the passing of the house sign the second time (for example, the second Thursday in a month could be called "Two Thursdays"). Moreover, Classical Nahuatl seldom used plural forms; thus *macuilli calli* could be translated as either "Five Houses" or "Five House."

Next to it is the number of the year, following the same patterns I have described.

The fourth and last thirteen-year cycle was called the Thirteen Squares of the Rabbit, and thus in each square we may discern the head of a rabbit. Next [to each rabbit's head] is the number of the year, just as I have described in the other parts of the cycle. In this way through the years of the rabbit could be calculated the number of the current year.

We have now seen how they used the four parts of the cycle with their numbers as shown in the circle, but now it will be necessary to understand the way in which they were counted. Four symbols were used: Reed, Flint Knife, House, and Rabbit, and in this way the count continued: One Reed, Two Flint Knives, Three Houses, Four Rabbits. . . . The reader will find these numbers around the sun [in the illustration]. After that there followed Five Reeds, Six Flint Knives, Seven Rabbits, Eight Reeds, Nine Flint Knives, Ten Houses, Twelve Rabbits, Thirteen Reeds, the number thirteen following on "reed," just as it had begun, the count ending in the sign of Reed, just as it had commenced.[4]

Once the number Thirteen Reeds had terminated, there immediately commenced the number One Flint Knife, which is shown in the fourth square of the second part, which belongs to the North. Following the same order I have described, the natives counted One Flint Knife, Two Houses, Three Rabbits, Four Reeds, and so on, until they ended in Thirteen Flint Knives, whereupon the third part, that of the West, began with the number called One House. This number will be found in the seventh square of the third part, and they must be counted just as in the first and second parts, saying One House, Two Rabbits. . . . This number, that of Two Rabbits, can be found in the seventh square of the fourth part, which refers to the South. Three Reeds is the number found in the eighth square, belonging to the reeds; then follow Four Flint Knives, which are shown in the eighth square of the flint knives.

---

4 In giving us this example of combinations of numbers with symbols, the author mistakenly writes Seven Rabbits instead of Seven Houses, which throws off the sequence of the combinations to the end of the passage.

Thus the wheel turned until it terminated in Thirteen Houses, and the southern part, the fourth, indicated by the head of a rabbit, was shown as One Rabbit. This appeared in the tenth square of the fourth part. Then was shown Two Reeds, which lie within the eleventh square of the reeds; and after that Three Flint Knives, which lie in the eleventh square of the knives; and Four Houses, which lie in the eleventh square. And so it turned, round and round, until it had reached the number of Thirteen Rabbits, like the others. So ended the period of fifty-two years, and the cycle, as they said, was bound.[5]

I do not wish to omit anything or to leave confusion. Therefore, I wish to explain that these cycles were fixed and numbered so that the events and happenings which had taken place in each would be remembered. An example: "It happened that in the year Two Rabbits, during the eighth cycle, there was a great plague in the land which destroyed half the population." In olden times, in heathen times, this was written in their records and paintings. "In the year Two Rabbits many people perished in the Eighth Cycle," and so forth. Also: "In the year of the jubilee, which began on One Reed, the first year of the sixteenth cycle, there came to this land Don Hernán Cortés, Marqués del Valle." This was written in the native records: "In the year One Reed, at the beginning of the sixteenth cycle, the Spaniards arrived in this land." In this way was kept the record of all the events of importance which took place—wars, famines, plagues, comets, deaths of kings, princes, and lords, without any possible mistake in registering month, year, or day.

Now that I have explained these things, I shall describe something about the four above-mentioned parts of the circle—East, West, North, and South. In each of these were to be found, according to these people, great omens, signs, and the forecasting of events by astrologers. Some held that the thirteen squares in the

[5] The idea of "binding" or "tying up" a bundle of fifty-two years was basic to the Mesoamerican calendrical system. Perhaps the most dramatic sculptural representation of this theme is the carving on the Temple of the Plumed Serpent at Xochicalco, Morelos, which shows a hand stretching a taut rope pulling two dates together, thus indicating the completion of a fifty-two-year cycle.

eastern part, belonging to the Reeds, were good, foretelling fertile and abundant years, healthy, filled with fortunate happenings. Other men made predictions regarding the western years, which were the Houses. Others prognosticated about the northern ones. Still others [were soothsayers of] the southern years. And so it was that all were deceived, since the future is known only to God. Most of the time they erred; they failed in their auguries and omens. It is worth knowing, however, that the years most feared by the people were those of the North and of the West, since they remembered that the most unhappy events had taken place under those signs. The southern direction, that of the Rabbits, was not held to be favorable either.

This is what was believed regarding the North: in that direction lay the underworld. It was called Mictlampa, which means the Infernal Region. A Flint Knife symbolized these years, and it stood for the cold, the ice, and the thin airs of those parts, and it indicated that the barren, fruitless, dry, hungry years belonged to the Flint Knife. And so it was that when an evil man died he was wrapped in old, thick cloth made of maguey fiber and was buried with his face toward the North. This was done because the people said he had gone to hell because of his wicked life; and, because of the terrible cold there, they wrapped him in those thick blankets to give him warmth. With him was buried food for him to eat, since the place was sterile.

The western direction was considered evil and was symbolized by a house to indicate that during those years the sun would hide himself within that house and never help the land to give fruit. These were cloudy years, rainy, filled with mist; all one's day was spent in idleness. The region was called Imiquian Tonatiuh, which means Place of the Death of the Sun. It was also called Icalaquian Tonatiuh, Where the Sun Goes Down, or Hides Himself. The natives believed this since they knew that the sun was the second cause of life on earth.[6]

6 This passage, which Durán obviously heard directly from a *tlamatini*, one of the ancient "wise men," or from someone who had received lessons in the old cosmogony, appears to indicate that the sun was believed to be a second cause of

The third part of the figure and circle of the years was the South. Like the rest, it contained thirteen squares, marked with the figure of a rabbit. It was considered neither bad nor good, for in some years things went well and in others badly. These years were depicted in the form of a rabbit because he leaps to and fro and never stays in one place.

The most important area, the East, was shown with a green reed. This [direction] was always thought of as the best, the most fertile, fruitful, and abundant; thus they loved the reed years, and were happy when these years came. Nevertheless, as I have stated, these men often erred and predicted wrongly on many occasions. As proof of this we can point out that it was in the year One Reed that Spaniards arrived in this land. The benefit for the souls of the natives, however, was a great and blissful thing because they received our Faith, which has multiplied and continued to multiply. [But] when did the natives suffer more than in that year? Their sufferings, afflictions, and toil reached their climax on the third year of the square [of the Reed], when the Spaniards slew innumerable people, and the pox and a famine ravished the land. I have heard old men tell how a handful of corn was exchanged for another of gold or of stones. I could tell about many other things and set down in my writings other occurrences which before and after have taken place. But the one I have narrated set the seal upon all the misery of the Indians. In this manner ends this chapter.

This briefly, is what the circular figure contains. From here on we shall describe the months, which contained twenty days, and then the years, which we have just described. Presently we shall see that [the year] contained eighteen months.

creation. It can be assumed that the first cause was Ometeotl, the Divine Couple, the Two whose abode was at the top of the nine heavens above the earth.

CHAPTER II

¶Which treats of the months of the year and of the symbols by which the days of the month were known.

I N ancient times the year was composed of eighteen months, and thus it was observed by these Indian people. Since their months were made up of no more than twenty days, these were all the days contained in a month, because they were not guided by the moon but by the days; therefore, the year had eighteen months. The days of the year were counted twenty by twenty.

Each of the twenty days of the month had its name and symbol to designate each day. This is similar to the way in which we name the days of the week: Monday, Tuesday, Wednesday, and so forth. In this same manner the people indicated the twenty days of their month, in the order which is shown in our illustration [Plate 36]. It is well to give the names of these symbols. They are: Cipactli, which was the first figure and which means Head of Serpent. And when [the people] called it a head, I think that they understood it to be the beginning of the month, or its first day. The second day was called Wind; the third, House; the fourth, Lizard; the fifth, Serpent; the sixth, Death; the seventh, Deer; the eighth, Rabbit; the ninth, Water; the tenth, Dog; the eleventh, Monkey;

394

the twelfth, Wild Grass; the thirteenth, Reed; the fourteenth, Jaguar; the fifteenth, Eagle; the sixteenth, Buzzard; the seventeenth, Motion; the eighteenth, Flint Knife; the nineteenth, Rain; and the twentieth and last, Flower.

At the beginning of each month, on the day which we have called Head of Serpent, a most solemn feast was held, as we shall see later in the description of the calendar. This day was observed and celebrated in such a manner that one was not even permitted to sweep the house or prepare food. All victuals had to be cooked and left ready on the previous day. This first day was like a Sunday to them in all the land, and was kept with a great deal more rigor than the way we observe Sunday, with the same zeal that the Jews kept and observed the Sabbath.

Everyone knows that the year is made up of three hundred sixty-five days. But the number of these days divided into twenties makes up eighteen scores. These were the months of the year, but the five days which were left over were held by this nation to be unlucky, nameless, and profitless. Thus they remained as blanks; there were no symbols for them, or number[s]. And so they were called *nemontemi*, which means "days left over and profitless." These fell at the end of February, on the twenty-fourth, the day of the glorious Saint Matthias, in the month when we ourselves adjust the year. The natives also observed this day, and thus the year ended and a new year began. Later I shall tell of the things that were done during those five days.

Aside from giving names to the days of the month, these twenty symbols, or characters, were used for telling the fortune of those born on them. The soothsayers and astrologers predicted these things with their false and deceitful astrology. Perhaps it would be better to call it witchcraft. They foretold good or unfortunate fates to befall people, a long or a short life, one of wealth or of poverty.

The symbols representing each day of the month functioned as letters. In general, these painted characters were used as picture writing, describing native history and lore, memorable events in war, victories, famines and plagues, prosperous and adverse times.

395

All was written down, painted in books and on long papers, indicating the year, month, and date on which each event had occurred. Also recorded in these painted documents were the laws and ordinances, the census, and so forth. All this was set down painstakingly and carefully by the most competent historians, who by means of these paintings recorded extensive chronicles regarding the men of the past. These writings would have enlightened us considerably had not ignorant zeal destroyed them. Ignorant men ordered them burned, believing them idols, while actually they were history books worthy of being preserved instead of being buried in oblivion, as was to occur. Even for the ministry we profess, that of the salvation of souls and aid to the natives, they left us in darkness.

These characters also taught the Indian nations the days on which they were to sow, reap, till the land, cultivate corn, weed, harvest, store, shell the ears of corn, sow beans and flaxseed. They always took into account that it had to be in such and such a month, after such and such a feast, on such and such a day, under such and such a sign. All this was done with superstitious order and care. If chili was not sown on a certain day, squash on another, maize on another, and so forth, in disregard of the orderly count of the days, the people felt there would be great damage and loss of any crop sown outside the established order of days. The reason for all this was that some signs were held to be good, others evil, and others indifferent, just as our almanacs record the signs of the zodiac, where we are told that some influences are good, others bad, and others indifferent regarding the sowing of crops and even the health of our bodies. Wise and experienced doctors wait, consider, and know when bloodletting or a cathartic is beneficial or harmful.

[Spanish] farmers observe the rules of the almanac and are governed by them when they sow. They observe the date, and through experience they know whether there will be drought or barrenness. But this Indian nation observed different rules. Our own people fight the ravages of frost, drought, excessive rainfall, or other catastrophes, trusting only in God. They place all their hope in Him, but each does his share and all the necessary work. But these Indians awaited a specific date to the exact day and moment, and then to a man they would sow first on the slopes and then on the flatlands. It is understood that all of this was done with idolatry, superstition, and irreverence, as in everything these people used superstitions, sorcery, and idolatry.

"Did you not say," someone might ask, "that among these painted characters there were good, evil, and indifferent signs?"

So it was; but when they feigned that this or that sign was bad and that or the other was good and still another indifferent, it is clear that the system was evil, since these signs were common not only in agriculture but also in trade and commerce, in buying and selling, in marriage, and in bathing. The same was the case in the eating of certain foods: except on specified days and times certain foodstuffs could not be eaten. I believe this superstition to be difficult to uproot, and I fear that in certain places these ancient rules and rites have not disappeared.[1] I see that they are still kept strictly, and I base my opinion upon the fact that one day I asked an old man why he was sowing a certain type of small bean so late in the year, considering that they are usually frostbitten at that time. He answered that everything has a count, a reason, and a special day.

I shall give another example. Let us suppose that the maize of a certain field is already dry, ripe, and ready to be harvested. It will deteriorate if it is not reaped. Here and in many other places they will not harvest it, even though it is lost entirely, until the elders decide that it is time to reap. I dare to swear to these things because in church I myself have heard the public announcement, all the people being present, that the time of the harvest has come. They all rush off to the fields with such haste that neither young nor old remain behind. They could have gathered the crop earlier, at their leisure; but since the old sorcerer found in his book or almanac that the day had come, he proclaimed it to the people, and they went off in great speed.

Finally, I suspect that regarding these things the natives still follow the ancient laws and that they await the correct time ac-

---

[1] In his eagerness to uproot native superstition, Durán failed to see the similarities to the superstitions of his own people and most other Europeans of his time.

cording to the calendrical symbols. There are few places where the ancient calendars are not kept in hiding, consulted often, and taught to the new generation so that this system will not fall into oblivion *in aeternum*.[2]

We have described how the symbols of the months and the days were used to foretell the good or bad fates of those who were born. Thus, when a boy or girl was born, the father or relatives of the babe immediately went to visit the astrologers, sorcerers, or soothsayers, who were plentiful, begging them to state the destiny of the newborn boy or girl. The inquirer always carried with him offerings of food and drink. The astrologer and sorcerer-fortune-teller brought out the Book of the Horoscope, together with the calendar. Once the character of the day had been seen, prophecies were uttered, lots were cast, and a propitious or evil fate for the babe was determined by the consultation of a paper painted with all the gods they adored, each idol drawn in the square reserved for him. I wish to explain this. The God of the Harvest was in his square, the Divinity of Wealth in another, that of Poverty in another, that of Penance in another, that of Lust in another, the Deity of Drunkenness in another, that of War in another, and the Divinity of the Cult of the Gods in still another, and so forth. Next to these gods were painted the characters of the days of the month in the native calendar. Lots were cast upon this paper, and the future could be foretold according to the way each lot fell. If it fell upon the God of Life, it was said that the child would live long. If it fell upon Death, they said he would live but a short time. And so it went for all the rest. So as to be brief, I shall not explain each one in detail. It is enough to know that one could find out whether the child was to be rich or poor, brave or courageous or cowardly, or a priest or a married man, a thief or a drunkard, abstemious or

---

[2] The fate of the powerful pagan priests in the years during and after the Conquest was one of determined, though doomed, resistance. While a large number of priests probably died during the years of consolidation of Spanish political and religious rule, it appears certain that strong elements of the ancient, well-organized hierarchy survived for many years to oppose the conquerors and their socioreligious order. The representatives of the ancient religion may have been more powerful in keeping alive Aztec traditions than even Durán suspected.

lustful—all these things could be found in those prophetic pictures. The parents or kinsmen were told about these things, having first listened to assurances and then to long, flowery speeches. After this the soothsayers told two dozen lies and fables, prophesying what even the devil, their adviser, does not know, since only God is aware of things to come.

To explain further what I have described, it should be known that the twenty figures used for the days of the month had their symbols. Some of them were good, of happy fortune, others were evil, and some of them were indifferent.

The good symbols were these: Head of Serpent, House, Lizard, Deer, Buzzard. All these signs were good and meant success for those who had been born under them. The neutral ones were Rabbit, Monkey, Reed, Jaguar, Eagle, Flower, Motion. These were called indifferent signs because those born under them participated in both good and evil. At times they lived in prosperity; at others, in poverty, subjected to both fortunate and unfortunate occurrences. The evil, ill-omened signs were Wind, Serpent, Death, Water, Wild Grass, Flint Knife, and Rain. These seven signs, or figures, were considered evil for those born under them. To see this more clearly, even though this may take a little longer, I wish to set down all of this and give examples. I shall explain the system figure by figure, according to the way I found it, painted on an old paper of ancient times, so filled with hideous pictures of demons that it filled me with terror.

I have explained and made known which were the good, neutral, and evil symbols. Let us go on to speak now of the effects which these signs caused upon those born under them and of the false beliefs concerning them. To begin with, the first sign, Ce Cipactli, as we have seen, means Head of Serpent. It is painted thus, and the etymology of the word described the child in this way. First of all, they said, he will be a man of outstanding courage and strength, a hard worker, a great tiller of the soil, a famous warrior, a merchant, a man who is a good keeper of his wealth, desirous of increasing it, an enemy of idleness, addicted to constant activity, never wasteful, never prodigal, never tricky or unscrupulous.

399

The second sign, known as Ehecatl, meaning Wind, was considered evil. Those who were born under this sign were prophesied the following. They were to be fickle, inconsistent, negligent, lazy, enemies of toil, addicted to merrymaking, gluttons, parasites, rovers who have neither roots nor rest.

Those born under the sign of Calli, which means House and which is the third sign, were to meet the following fate. They were inclined toward seclusion and a cloistered life, peaceable, calm, respectful of their parents, beloved by their kinsmen, disinclined to roaming and to long journeys. They were to die peacefully and in bed.

Those born under the sign of Cuetzpallin, which means Lizard, a good sign, were said to be fortunate. Whether he was the youngest or the oldest or born between these, he was to be outstanding within his family and to prosper vastly. He was destined to possess wealth and never be hungry. All of this was based upon the characteristics of the lizard, who calmly rests on the wall, never lacking flies or mosquitoes, all of them coming naturally to his mouth. And so it was omened that the man born under the sign was to be prosperous without great toil.

The fifth sign was the Serpent, which in the native language is Coatl. It was predicted that those born under this sign were to be paupers, bare, unclad, ragged beggers with no home of their own. They were to live always on loans, depending on others, and to be menials all their lives. In this they imitated the snake that goes about homeless and naked, exposed to the sun and the wind, living today in one hole and tomorrow in another. This sign was considered evil.

The sixth sign was Miquiztli, which means Death. This symbol was also held to be an evil one, melancholy and sad. And thus those brought into this world under this sign were held to be timorous, faint, craven, weak-hearted, forgetful, lax, sickly, of poor appetite, ill of heart.

Those born under the sign of Mazatl, Deer, were to be woodsmen, fond of the forest and of hunting. They were to be woodcutters, runners, walkers, not overfond of the homeland, desirous of visiting strange lands and of dwelling in them, unloving toward their fathers and their mothers, abandoning them with ease.

Those born under the sign of Rabbit, which, as we have said, was called Tochtli, were considered to fall within the same category of destiny as those born under the last-mentioned sign, Deer.

The ninth sign was called Atl, which means Water. This sign was evil. Men born under it were apathetic, of a short life. They lived in illness, and few reached old age, suffering long and troublesome sicknesses, never to be cured. They were grumblers, dissatisfied, always unhappy and angry-looking.

The tenth sign, which belonged to the tenth day of the month, was Itzcuintli, which means Dog. This sign was held to be fortunate and happy. Those born under it were omened bliss and felicity. They were to be courageous, generous, likely to ascend in the world, men with many children, overflowing with plenty, lavish, prodigal, fond of having enough to give away, enemies of poverty, friends to those who asked favors, always willing to comply.

The eleventh sign which this nation used to name a day of the month for its special functions, and discover the fate of a man when he was born, was Ozomatli, meaning Monkey. Those born under this sign were held to be gay, like actors, roguish, filled with charm, clever, making their living because of these attributes. They were to have many friends; they were to be found among kings and nobles. If the child was a female, she was to be a merry singer, graceful, not too modest or chaste, pleasant, easy to persuade in any matter.

The twelfth sign is called Wild Grass, Malinalli in the native language. Those born under this sign were augured a grave illness every year, which was to reach its crisis and then disappear completely. The disease was like wild grass, which dries up every year and then grows green again. Thus the child born under the sign of Wild Grass yearly became ill and then got well. He did not die of the illness. No other predictions were attached to this sign.

Another sign was that of Reed, called Acatl. This symbol was held to be neutral, even though the characteristics attributed to it were not especially good. It was said that the man born under it was to be like the reed, hollow and without a heart. Therefore, those born under this sign were men without heart, incompetent, unwise, empty, insignificant; and even though they had wealth and goods, they were fond of telling about their poverty, of begging. They were to be fond of sweetmeats, gluttons, addicted to idleness. They were to spend their entire day lying naked in the sun.

After this sign came another, called Ocelotl, which means Jaguar. Those born under this sign were destined to be like the jaguar—courageous, daring, haughty, presumptuous, proud, conceited, grave. Eager for honor, public positions, they were to obtain them by tyranny, by force, or by gifts and were to gain what they sought. This person was prodigal, lowered himself to servile things. He gave himself to sowing and reaping by his own hand. He was addicted to farming, and he never fled from toil. Going to war was a satisfaction to him, in order to show himself off and his courage. He had a smile for everything; his heart was always ready to fight for any good undertaking. If the babe born under this sign was a female, she was to be independent, proud, presumptuous, contemptuous of other women, restless, openhearted, mocking everyone, filled with haughty thoughts.

The next sign is Cuauhtli, meaning Eagle. It has the same nature as the sign of Jaguar, of which we have spoken. But it is added that those born under the sign, besides having the characteristics of the jaguar, were to possess others. They were to be addicted to theft, coveting their neighbor's wealth, miserly, hiding their goods like the eagle, which is a bird of prey.

Cozcacuauhtli is the next sign, and it means Buzzard. To those born under it, it signified and predicted a long life. They were vigorous, free of disease, tall, robust, muscular, inclined to be bald, prudent, men of good advice, authoritative. They were wise, grave, calm, discreet, eloquent, and given to teaching and good counsel. They were fond of giving good advice and of censuring evil, eager to gather disciples and instruct them.

Sign seventeen was called Ollin. This word means something that moves or goes about, Motion, and is identified with the sun. All the males born under the sign were thought to be men who would shine like the sun. They were held to be blessed, fortunate, of good fate, blissful. It was considered desirous, well omened, and fortunate to be born under this sign. Principalities and kingdoms were promised to all those born under this sign. Just as the sun is king and supreme among the other planets, so it was promised to those born under this symbol that they would enjoy a high station on this earth. And this was promised, as I have said, to the males, because the sign affected women in a different way. It was predicted that the women would be stupid, foolish, stubborn, limited in their intelligence, obtuse, and confused. But they were to be rich, prosperous, and as powerful as the men. Thus this sign was held in part to be good, in part neutral.

The eighteenth sign, Tecpatl, means Flint Knife. It was considered to be the worst of all signs, harmful to the republic and to the multiplication of mankind. It was said that this sign was as hard as the flint knife, and harsh. It caused sterility in men and in women born under it. Thus it was believed that the person born under it would never engender children, which is the greatest sorrow and calamity felt by these natives. It is also their greatest shame. One can say nothing worse than to call someone "sterile" or "barren." In this way those who were incapable of bearing children live in shame. And in place of having children they do much evil and commit sins. Those born under the sign of Flint Knife were held to be fortunate [in many things] except in being fertile and in engendering children.

The next to last sign, the nineteenth, was that of Quiahuitl, which means Rain, or Rainstorm. All those born under it, men and women, were augured very bad luck. They were to be blind, lame, maimed, pimply, leprous, claw-handed, mangy, bleary-eyed, lunatic, insane, with all the ills and sicknesses associated with the above calamities.

The last sign, the twentieth, called Xochitl, means Flower. This was the last day of the month and was a sign which was associated with masters and craftsmen. Thus it was said that those born under it were to be painters, metalworkers, weavers, sculptors, carvers—that is to say, [workers in] all the arts that imitate nature.

Women were to become laundresses, fine weavers. They were to be skilled in decorating breads, fond of beautifying and adorning themselves, loving embroidered blouses and finely decorated mantles. These people were cleanly, diligent, hard-working in order to fulfill their needs, each toiling with his own hands at his own skill.

With this we have ended that which refers to the months and the names and the figures with which the latter were pictured. We have stated and narrated how the Indians thought they could discover the fate of man through them: by the day in which the child was born, by the symbol under which he was born. And I believe that there was no science here; all was sorcery and superstition. I have questioned certain elders regarding the origin of their knowledge of human fate and destiny, and [the old men] answered that the ancient ones bequeathed it to them, taught it to them, and that is all they know. I have also tried to question some of the old men, and I have found them wanting in the ancient knowledge, though they still teach youth and foretell the fate of children and earn their daily bread in this way. They tell me that such and such a picture or sign is evil, but it is clear that they have not acquired this knowledge from their own investigations. All this knowledge comes rather from the falseness of their imaginations regarding a certain sign or picture bequeathed to them by their ancestors.

¶Which treats of the number and the count of the weeks and the manner in which each individual observed the day of his birth.

Now that we have described and spoken of the months and days and of their signs, it now behooves us to deal with the weeks and to explain their order. Regarding our first theme, it must be noted that the native "week" was composed of thirteen days, just as ours is made up of seven. And it was counted from one to thirteen. The year contained exactly, precisely, twenty-eight weeks, because, in order to adjust their years and weeks with precision (as we saw in Chapter I), the years were counted thirteen by thirteen. And so it was that the months and the weeks were adjusted so well and in such good order that the calendrical count these people used was admirable and highly ingenious.

The reasons for dividing the week into thirteen days were based on the supernatural, since the aim was the celebration and commemoration of each of the symbols of the twenty days of the month. And so that none would remain unhonored and unheeded, it was ordered that the first day of every week was to be regarded as a solemn feast. Thus the sign under which the first day of the week fell was always a solemn day, just as we observe and keep the Lord's Day and the Jews the Sabbath.

There was yet another reason given, and this was that, after each sign had been commemorated, all those born under said figure or sign made merry and rejoiced. So a custom existed whereby all those born under a certain sign were honored on that day. The calendar was governed and ordered in such a way by these signs that one of the twenty signs fell on the first of each of these thirteen-day periods. This was the beginning of the week and at the same time was a "Sunday." On this day were celebrated jointly the feast of the sign itself and that of all those born under it. In order to understand this more clearly and with greater ease, it should be noted that the first day of the month was called Cipactli, Head of Serpent, and this day was a "Sunday." Starting with this day, the count was One Cipactli, Two Wind, Three House, Four Lizard, Five Snake, Six Death, Seven Deer, Eight Rabbit, Nine Water, Ten Dog, Eleven Monkey, Twelve Wild Grass, and Thirteen Reed. The week ended on the last sign. Immediately another week began, and the count commenced with One Jaguar, which was a Sunday, the Feast of the Jaguar and of all those who had been born under it. In this order, thirteen by thirteen, the natives counted all the days of the year, commemorating all the signs of the month [Plate 37].

The natives celebrated each other's birth dates in a way different from our own. Around the neck of the honored one we place a rosary or a jewel, perhaps a golden chain. These people did not observe these customs. Instead, they seized the individual whom they expected to hold a feast because of his birthday. Some took him by the feet, others by the head. They tossed him into the water and immersed him. When he came out [of the water], he was bound and obliged to provide festivities for his day. If he did not do so in that year, he would not again be honored, because it was said (with a great deal of scorn and contempt) that he was still bound and there was no reason to celebrate his birthday any more. This feast was called Apantlazaliztli, which means To Go Through the Water, and it is still in use today, and I have seen it observed in certain places. Once the day of the saint whose name a person bears arrives, he is cast into the water, just as was done in ancient times. In some places, however, the natives are becoming more like us.

Regarding the weeks I have discussed, I find little more to say. Nor do I believe that this count of days fulfilled any other purpose than that of honoring and solemnizing the twenty symbols, assigning one day of the year to each. I mention this as a yearly happening because, even though the number one could occur twice during the turn of the year, the first time it was celebrated and commemorated, but on the second it was not. It was true, however, that the latter was a holiday, kept like a Sunday at the beginning of the week. These people were so enamored of feasts that they never let one pass without some celebration. So it was that the natives spent the entire year in festivities. There were the feasts of the principal gods and goddesses, the feasts at the beginning of each month, every twenty days, then the feasts on the first day of each week, every thirteen days. These were fiestas so continuous and intertwined that they overlapped.

From all of this it may be understood and gathered that these people were so slothful, so lazy, so idle, so fond of festivals and banquets and merrymaking that today we can observe that the priests who work among them are most careful and solicitous to see that the saints which have been placed in the shrines of the wards and farms are feasted and celebrated. I heartily believe that all of this merrymaking is not in honor of God or of the saint but in honor of the natives' sensuality, their bellies. Their aim is simply to eat, to drink, and to get drunk. This, in sum, was the ultimate aim of the ancient feasts.

And if anyone says that I am exaggerating, that I am stressing this point too much, let him ask himself why a ward of ten or twelve houses spends as much on a splendid banquet as if it possessed two hundred houses. It invites all the other wards and the neighboring people and lacks and spares nothing regarding food and drink. Plenty is left over, plenty. And on the next day the people will be idle, and those who served the guests on the first day will then eat

407

the leftovers. By all of this I mean that the custom of eating, drinking, and being idle comes to us from ancient times. According to the ancient and demoniacal law, each ward had its shrine and special god which served as a patron of the ward, and on the feast day of the idol persons would invite one another to celebrate it. The people of the ward spent all they had so that nothing would be lacking. This [custom] is practiced religiously today on the solemnities of the saints.

Some have criticized me because I condemn something evil which has lost its pagan significance and has been turned toward the honor of God and His saints. Let them prove to me that it is proper for our God and His saints to allow themselves to be honored with orgies, gluttony, and a thousand other unspeakable and abominable acts which take place during such feasts. Then I shall beg pardon of them and recognize that I am filled with malice. But while I see the law of God mixed with the ancient idolatrous customs, I say that all of this is an offense to God and His saints since they are not properly venerated, as we can see by the fact that the people of the ward do not even hear mass. If there are five hundred persons in a community, all five hundred happen to be busy—the women in grinding corn and making bread, others in preparing chocolate; the men in carrying water and firewood, in blowing and caring for the fire and in poking at it, at roasting turkeys, sweeping, in working with branches, adorning the rooms, collecting from house to house the food which has been prepared. All of this is done to avoid working on that particular day. They live in drunkenness, and if I were to tell the things I have seen and heard, I feel that my story would never end.

I desire to be brief but do not wish to omit what I feel about this changing about and prolonging of the feasts. I think it an evil custom to be changing festival occasions from one Sunday to another. Let the Christian servant of God consider that I speak from the experience of my own eyes and not from hearsay. There may be a great deal of deceit, malice, and diabolical superstition when the Indians feign that in order to make a celebration more solemn they wish to postpone it to the following Sunday. We must understand, however, that this is done only because the idol of that particular ward or the sign of the birth date of the chieftain falls upon that day, and therefore he wishes that his saint's day and that of the idol may be commemorated together and that the whole arrangement may appear legitimate.

I can only imagine how many times the following has happened to our priests. Three or four months have gone by since a holy day, and now the Indians come to ask for [a priest's] services out of time and tune, when the feast has already been forgotten. And if our priests question the natives regarding this great delay, they answer that the ramada was not ready, that the altar had not been whitewashed, that they had been busy working on the fence, and so on. Three thousand excuses and lies are offered, but when one looks into the native calendar, one finds that the feast of the idol which the ward solemnized falls on that day. So it is that saint and idol are celebrated together. Rest assured that I am not lying. On such days I have heard chants in honor of God and of the saint during the festivities, mixed with ancient metaphors which only the devil, their teacher, understands.

Since we have decided to give advice to our ministers, let nothing be omitted. Let the reverend fathers know that, together with the Christian name, the Indians use the name of the ancient sign under which the person was born, and it is a second name. An example: If a man was born under the sign of Snake and at baptism he was christened Peter, his name is Peter Coatl, which is the name of the sign under which he came in to this world. And if he was born under the sign of Lizard, his name is John Cuetzpal, one name joined to the other. And so it goes with the rest. May God our Lord give light to His ministers against the evil enemy and adversary, the devil! May He give us understanding regarding all superstition so that we may destroy the demon! God help us to understand this salad, this mixture which they have made of their ancient superstitions and of our Divine Law and ritual. And so that no one say I speak without experience, I wish to tell a story.

At one time I lived with a most honest priest, a man who was zealous of the glory of God and of His doctrines. At the time I

409

dwelt with him he gave orders that crosses were to be set up in all the wards so that prayers could be said there. The Indians then placed crosses everywhere except in a ward where the people were so devout that they wished to be superior and therefore asked permission to build a shrine. This was granted. When they were told that the saint was to be Saint Paul or Saint Augustine, the people said that they would discuss this. After two weeks had gone by, the natives returned, saying that they wished neither Saint Paul nor Saint Augustine. When they were asked which saint they desired, they named Saint Luke. I took note of their petition and the insistence of their request and suspected that something might be wrong. Therefore, I went to the pagan calendar and looked up the feast and sign under which Saint Luke fell. Having done this, I took myself to the chieftain of that ward and asked him his name, whereupon he answered that it was John. I asked him to tell me his birth and day name under the old law, and he responded that it was the sign of Calli, which means House. It was then that I saw clearly that he had asked for the Feast of Saint Luke because it falls on the day and sign of House. Furthermore, two days before this feast came one of the greatest and most solemn festivals of ancient times. I scolded him for his deceitfulness and evil intentions, and I told him that he had been moved more by superstition than by the sorrows of Christ when He carried the cross or by the devotion that the chieftain had for the cross.

Once I questioned an Indian regarding certain things. In particular I asked him why he had gone about begging, spending bad nights and worse days, and why, after having gathered so much money with such trouble, he offered a fiesta, invited the entire town, and spent everything. Thus I reprehended him for the foolish thing he had done, and he answered, "Father, do not be astonished; we are still *nepantla*." Although I understood what that metaphorical word means, that is to say, "in the middle," I insisted that he tell me which "in the middle" he referred to. The native told me that, since the people were not yet well rooted in the Faith, I should not marvel at the fact that they were neither fish nor fowl; they were governed by neither one religion nor the other. Or, better said, they believed in God and also followed their ancient heathen rites and customs. And this is what the Indian meant in his despicable excuse when he stated that the people still were "in the middle" and were "neither fish nor fowl."

Some persons (and they are not few) say that my work will revive the ancient customs and rites among the Indians. Would that in His kindness the Lord our God might erase all these things from the memory and understanding of the natives! I would be the first to cast these things into the fire so that such an abominable religion would fall into oblivion. But how can one be silent, how can one refrain from suffering on seeing that many men in many places are still filled with the ancient idolatry, superstition, and wretchedness! Though not all the people follow these customs, it is enough that there is a single man with the ancient ideas in a village to do much harm. For this one alone it is worthwhile for the minister to seek him out, examine him, and deprive him of his influence. It is a thing which involves the honor of God and so that the sweat and toil and past affliction of the missionaries for the conversion of souls will not be in vain. These men labor, walk much and hurriedly through the woods and cliffs; they live exiled from all comfort; they live as solitary as hermits; they have become beasts with the beasts, Indians with the Indians, barbarians with the barbarians, men estranged from our own ways, nation, and order.

Those who speak as outsiders, those who have never wished to take part in these affairs, understand little about these things. Thus I swear that my intention is not to instruct the Indians regarding these [pagan] things, because they are already well informed. They are so careful in hiding their papers and ancient traditions, so secretive and so deceitful that they do not need an instructor!

THE FIRST MONTH OF THE YEAR

¶As celebrated by the Indians; it contained only twenty days.

O N the first day of March this nation formerly celebrated its new year, just as today we commemorate January 1. The first of March was then celebrated with such diverse ceremonies that it was a marvelous thing. These rites are worthy of our remembrance, and it would be a pity to abbreviate our description. And though long-windedness is the enemy of any history book, I shall tell something regarding the new year without boring the reader.[1]

The day of the new year had four names, since four solemn feasts coincided at this time. The first was known as Xiutzitzquilo, which means Taking of the Year in One's Hand. A more literal translation of the term would be Taking a Bouquet in One's Hand. We must understand that *xihuitl* means two things, "year" or "bouquet." The word signifies both things. If one understands it to mean "year," [Xiutzitzquilo] signifies Taking the Year in One's

---

[1] Durán places the beginning of the Mexica year on March 1, whereas Sahagún states that it is February 2. According to Durán's calculation the Aztec year would end on February 28, and on February 29 in leap years. It is curious that Fray Diego accepted February 28 as the final day of the Aztec year, a calculation that adjusts neatly to the European system of regular and leap years.

Hand, and if one understands "bouquet," it means Taking the Bouquet in One's Hand. The native painting of the feast shows an Indian with a bouquet in his hand, [Plate 38], and it could be that the second interpretation of the word is correct: Taking a Bouquet in One's Hand. Considering that the natives thought of the year as a series of many months and days, composed, like a bouquet, of many branches and leaves, it would be a proper metaphor to speak of Taking the Year in One's Hand. We say, "to begin the year," or, "I took to the road," meaning "I began to walk." In a similar manner the Indians used this metaphor to indicate that it was the beginning of the year and that they took or started the course of the year. This was the first name of the new year.

The second name was Cuahuitlehua, which means When the Trees Begin to Walk or When the Trees Begin to Rise. This meant that the trees, which were drooping and had withered with the frost of winter, now rose, budded, and gave forth flowers and leaves. And in truth that is when trees become green again and become covered with flowers and life. This was the second name given to this day.

The third name applied to the new year was called Atlmotzacuaya, which means Shutting Off of the Water. This is my interpretation of this term, though the natives were unable to explain satisfactorily why New Year's Day is also called Shutting Off of the Water. It is because in March a few showers began to fall and the cornfields, which had been irrigated up to that point, no longer needed the water.

For the same reason the fourth name of this day was Xilomaniztli, which means The Corn Is Green and Tender.

The above tells what I have been able to learn regarding the four names of the new year and why they were so named.

We have stated that the first name was Xiutzitzquilo, which, as we said above, means To Touch Bouquets. This term goes well with the ceremony performed on that day. Old and young men and women would sally forth to the country, to the cornfields and orchards, to touch with their hands the herbs and plants born on the new year. Men and women did this, as is shown in the illustration. Some tell the story differently and say that besides touching the plants the people pulled out some of them and carried them in their hands to the temple, just as we carry palms in our hands to the church on Palm Sunday. Some old Indians have marveled at this, saying that Palm Sunday often falls around the time in which this feast of plants and the new year fell.

On this day special offerings were made to the gods: foods, feathers, jewels, and other things. Petitions were made to the deities, begging for a good, fruitful year full of fortunate events. New foods were eaten, different from everyday fare. This custom of eating different foods on feast days was a ceremonial rite. The people made distinctions among the dishes, and for every feast a new food was prepared—that which was permissible on said festivity.

On the seventeenth day of this month the Feast of the Sun took place—a most solemn occasion for the natives. This day fell on the symbol called Ollin, which means Motion, on the number four after the thirteen days had passed. It was called the Feast of Four Motion. Warriors and Knights of the Sun celebrated it, as the reader has seen in Chapter XI [of the *Book of the Gods and Rites*], where I dealt with the Feast of the Sun and his knights. On the seventeenth day of the month which we are describing, the symbol venerated was shown in the form of a butterfly. This feast was special; it was not counted among the eighteen contained in the year. It was celebrated twice a year, the second time on the second of December, because the sign for Motion, according to the count of thirteen days, fell again on that date.

On this day another ceremony, of a superstitious nature, took place. Once the rites with the greenery terminated, before the children breakfasted, their mothers and fathers took hold of them and stretched all their members—hands, fingers, arms, legs, feet, necks, noses, ears. All their members were stretched, omitting none. They believed that if this was not done the child would not grow naturally during the year unless the ceremony was performed. Stretching him helped him grow for that year. In this way we conclude all that must be said regarding this month.

THE SECOND MONTH OF THE YEAR

¶Which was celebrated by the natives, contained twenty days, and was called Tlacaxipehualiztli.

The second month began, according to our own calendar, on the twenty-first of March. On the first day of this second month was commemorated the first of the eighteen feasts which fell at the beginning of each month. This feast was called Tlacaxipehualiztli, which means Skinning of Men [Plate 39]. In a chapter of my previous book [Chapter IX] I have already dealt with this solemn occasion, its cruel, terrible sacrifices, frightful slaying of men. I explained how the dead were skinned and others, commissioned for the event, donned the skins. Then they begged alms from door to door, frightened children, and danced from house to house until the skins cracked.

Likewise, in the last chapter [of this book] I explained how each of the feasts of the calendar had a different type of food, to differentiate it and its sacrifices from others. On this day a certain type of twisted, honeyed tortilla was eaten. It was made of a special corn. The Indians hang this corn with its leaves from the ceiling in bunches called *ocholli*. Today these bunches of ears of corn are kept in the same way. Tortillas made from this corn and never

415

from another and eaten on this day were called *cocolli*, which means "twisted bread."[1] Chains were made of these tortillas. People made chains of these; they adorned and girded themselves with them to dance all day. Large quantities of these small tortillas were offered on that day. Those who were clad in the skins of the dead also offered up bunches of ears of corn which had been kept all year for that superstitious ceremony. This is still in use today; it is and was founded on superstition. I realized this after hearing a description of the ancient feast.

Today it is common to hang bunches of ears of corn from the ceiling, and one cannot enter any home, humble as it may be, without finding two or three bunches hanging. This corn is kept solely with the idea of eating it at this [ritual] time. Based on this evil superstition, the people believe that the food must be made from the corn hanging in bunches and not from other corn, even though the bin is full. The evil lies in the fact that from the hour the corn is hung up in bunches it is dedicated and offered to the devil. For such ceremonies this is the corn that must be sown and no other. It may be that in our times the original intentions have been forgotten, since the people are now Christians. But it lies heavy upon my heart when I see the corn hanging from the beams, because I am reminded of ancient usage. I leave all of this to the judgment of God and shall say no more, because it is fruitless. There are men who impose silence, who order that these things are not to be discussed, and thus many things will remain secret and hidden until the will of God decides that they are to be exposed.

The things offered on this day were paper, rubber, and incense. All of this had been stored by the priests, who now melted the rubber and painted stripes with it upon the paper. Once the stripes had been painted, the papers were taken to the hills, where the caves, shrines, places of sacrifice, and temples were filled with little stone and clay idols. These were then dressed in the striped paper, which was placed upon them like a scapular, and before them was placed all the paper, incense, and rubber that was left over. The

[1] The word *cocolli* has survived in modern Mexican Spanish as *cocol*, designating a sweet bun made of wheat flour.

416

word for rubber means "bounce." It is like a nerve, and it is extracted from trees. It possesses the quality of leaping into the air, and it is swift. Out of it were made large balls for the ball game. Once it is placed upon the fire, it melts easily. It was a special yet common offering to the gods, and the Indian physicians used and still use it to cure certain illnesses.

All the seats which were used on this day had to be made of the leaves of the white sapote. The sapote is a fruit about the size of a quince, green outside and white inside. From its leaves were made the seats to be used on this feast—never from other materials, which is another diabolical superstition. These heathen customs lasted until the next feast twenty days later, and during all these twenty days the offering continued. Thus large quantities of paper, rubber, and incense were gathered.

This feast was most solemn and ostentatious, as important as, or perhaps more so than, Easter is among the Christians. It causes great harm and is offensive to the most holy Paschal Feast of the Resurrection of Christ, our Beloved. The fact that the Indians hold this feast so near, so close, to the day of Jesus Christ's commemoration makes it impossible for our feast to be without contamination of ancient superstition. But what can be done about this? Let those in power find a solution!

Once an old Indian woman, wise in the ancient ways, perhaps a former priestess, was brought to me. She told me that in ancient times the natives had an Easter, Christmas, and Corpus Christi, just as we do, and on the same dates, and she pointed out other very important native feasts which coincide with our celebrations. "Evil old woman," I said, "the devil has plotted and has sown tares with the wheat so that you will never learn the truth!"

This paschal feast had a twenty-day period of postcelebration, during which a thousand rites, dances, and games were performed in the public square each day.

THE THIRD MONTH OF THE YEAR

¶Which the Indians formerly called Tozoztontli.

According to the count of the natives, the third month of the year had twenty days, like the others. Its feast took place on the first day, like the rest. The image venerated at this time was a beautiful bird with a bone piercing its body. This figure was called Tozoztontli. This term means Small Perforation in the diminutive. To speak in our own fashion, it signifies Something Bored from One Side to the Other. The symbol used to represent it shows a flying bird pierced through the middle with a bone. The diminutive form was used in naming this figure because the Great Perforation was twenty days later, at the beginning of the next month.

In order to make clear this barbaric thing (even though I must confess that I do not find words to explain it in Spanish), it must be known (though confusedly) that I understood it to refer to a star formation that appears in the heavens like a bird pierced with a bone. The imagination of the natives may be compared with that of the poets and the astrologers, who imagined they saw the sign of Taurus, made up of many stars. Thus these people imagined this sign in the sky and called it, in a diminutive form, Small Perforation. This occurred for two reasons, the first, because it was beginning to rain a little at this time of the year, and during these twenty days the rains increased until the Big Perforation was reached, and then the rains really came. This day was celebrated on April 10 in our calendar. Everyone went out to sow his fields and properties, even though some were left to be planted in the following month, the Great Perforation.

The second reason why this feast was called Small Perforation was that ten days later (in the middle of the month) all children under twelve were bled, even breast-fed babes. Their ears were pierced—their tongues, their shins. All this bloodletting was in honor of the coming feast, which involved a general purification of the mothers, almost according to the ancient Hebrew ways and law. We shall discuss this later.

On this day another heathen custom was practiced which I have seen done in our times. In most places ropes were strung from tree to tree in the cornfields. From these cords hung at even distances a number of small effigies, cloth images, or some such object. Those who know nothing, understanding little about these things, will believe that they are scarecrows or the playthings of children, but in reality all of this is pagan superstition!

They also made bouquets with flower buds in order to revel in them on that day. People ate, drank, and danced on this festive day and improvised a thousand ways of carousing. This ceremony constituted the offering of the first flowers to the gods. The reader will see in the illustration a seated Indian, arranging flowers in the ancient manner [Plate 40]. There were and still are great masters in this craft.

Another custom: All children under twelve years of age who were obliged to let blood (as I have described) were fed on bread and water. And so that everyone would observe this rite without violating it, early in the morning all the food was put away. This removed temptation from them. Everything was hidden—chili, corn, bread, all vegetables—until the hour of midday. At this time they ate copiously, and after this nothing was prohibited to them. A couple of hours before they had been eating only bread and water.

Certain heathen old men, the soothsayers of each town, went from home to home this day, inquiring about the children who had fasted and done penance by pricking their ears and other parts. If they had fasted and had accomplished what was required of them according to the pagan law, red, green, blue, black, or yellow threads (any color which the soothsayers liked, in fact) were tied to their necks. To the thread these men tied a small snake bone, a string of stone beads, or perhaps a little figurine.[1] The same was attached to little girls' wrists, not just for adornment but because of heathen ideas.[2] Mothers and fathers, in accordance with their position, gave alms to the soothsayers in recognition of the good act performed upon their children. With this they were made to believe that they could avoid illness and that no evil would befall them. Today in every region there are many of these soothsayers, who with a thousand deceits cause people to believe in two thousand omens and falsehoods. They try to persuade the people to have faith and hope in the clipping of the hair: "Let the hair be cut thus," or, "Let it be this way," or, "Let it be the other way." The ancient priests used to cut the hair of some in crowns, others in circles or crosses, others with locks left in front or behind, others on the sides. The priests adorned people with necklaces of snake bones, pendants, and stones. They gave them potions to drink, mixed with the shavings from idols, telling the people that these things would cure illnesses such as diarrhea or fever. In this way they deceived these

[1] Durán's description of these necklaces, strung with bones, stone beads, and small figures of clay or stone, offers a solution to a problem frequently encountered by the archaeologist in Mexico seeking to explain the function of the thousands of small clay figurines found in excavations and in the farmers' cornfields. These small images—often representing the Mother Goddess, Tonantzin, or the Rain God, Tlaloc— are usually perforated, as though meant to be strung on necklaces. Others undoubtedly served magical functions as fetishes or were used in funerary rites, while still others served as lares and penates. Some of the diminutive clay figures may have been designed to exert a baleful influence on the enemy in the practice of black magic, and they were undoubtedly used in medical practice as well.

[2] The Spanish text reads, "Lo mesmo hacían a las muñecas de las niñas, poniéndoles zarcillos en las orejas . . ." (Durán, 1967, I:248). Since *muñeca* means both "wrist" and "doll," it is possible that the passage refers to adorning little girls' dolls. We have chosen to translate *muñeca* as "wrist," however, because of the ancient custom of wearing magical protective emblems or adornments in this fashion.

simple, wretched people, who believed these things as one should believe in the Creed—though they do not believe in the Creed and hold on firmly to those things. To try to persuade them is to preach in the wilderness, and if a zealous missionary tries to crop the hair of a child and to remove the crosses and hairs, the Indian looks as if he were about to die, is as terrified as if his son, dead, were lying before him.

The farmers used to go out on this day to sanctify the fields. They journeyed thither with incense burners in their hands, going about all the fields, incensing them. Then they went to the place of the idol, god of the planted field, to offer him incense, rubber, food, and pulque.

With this ended the Small Feast of Tozoztontli.

THE FOURTH MONTH OF THE YEAR

¶Celebrated by the Indians under the old religion; was composed of twenty days like all the rest. It solemnized the feast known as Ochpaniztli [Huey Tozoztli], which means Day of Sweeping; a feast to Toci, Mother of the Gods, was celebrated at the same time.

THIS great feast celebrated by the natives fell at the beginning of the fourth month, and according to our own calendrical count it took place on the thirtieth of April [Plate 41]. The occasion was called Huey Tozoztli, meaning Great Perforation, which, as we have said, is connected with the small feast held in preparation for this.

This was the feast of the purification of women who had given birth to children and of an act similar to the circumcision of little boys. This was similar to our Purification, performed for the sake of both the mother and the child. On this day offerings were made in the fashion of the old Hebrew law, which prescribed gifts of lambs, turtle doves, and young pigeons. In this land quail, turkeys, bread, cloth, and other things were offered. All women who had given birth during the previous year took part in this ceremony, and it was performed in the following manner.

In those times immense quantities of pine splinters were bought, and a great thick torch was made of them. Care was also taken in the preparing of the food offering. A small quantity of

422

coarsely ground corn was prepared, and this was mixed with toasted amaranth seeds. A dough of these two flours was kneaded, and it was mixed with honey instead of water, and a sort of bread was made. In the native language this bread was called tamales, and because of its type it was called Tzocoyotl. In a similar way we refer to this bread by using a diminutive term, *bollitos*, "little loaves." This kind of bread was not only prepared as an offering but was also eaten on this day. According to ancient ceremony it was the only bread eaten this day.

The mothers who were to be purified in the temple and who were to present their children devoted themselves to the weaving of mantles, blouses, loincloths, and skirts. These were worn by all the relatives and friends who accompanied them to the ceremony. The cost of the latter was covered by each one according to his means: the rich spent more, the poor less; each one spent according to his wealth. At sunset on the day before the feast the priests of the temple blew the conch shells and horns and beat the drum which sounded on the great feasts. When this had been done, those who were to appear adorned themselves. A man and a woman who had been hired for this occasion were also dressed up. The man was given a lighted pine torch, and the woman was made to carry a child on her back. Each mother carried her offerings in her hands and on her back. Preceded by the man who went along giving light with his torch, the mothers abandoned their homes and went to visit all the shrines of the city wards, just as we do on Holy Thursday. At each shrine they left an offering, and in this way went all the women who had given birth, and the city was so filled with men carrying torches that it was something to see. The streets were so full of people that they found it difficult to pass one another. Once they had finished visiting the shrines of the wards, the women came to the great temple where the principal offering took place. They came before the priests, who purified them with certain rites and words, and they were cleansed of their childbearing.

We have already stated that the ceremony on this day can be compared to the circumcision of boys, and I shall explain why. On reaching the Great Temple of Huitzilopochtli, the women took the child, no matter how small, and delivered it to the priest, who took the child and with a stone blade brought by the mother made an incision in his ear and the bud of his virile member. Thus on the ear and on the other place a slight cut was made, so delicate that blood barely came to the surface. The little girls were incised only on the ear. Once the priest had finished cutting with the blade, he cast it down at the feet of the idol, and the mother requested a name for her offering. If he was a nobleman, he might be given a fine-sounding name, such as Moteczoma, which means Angry Lord. And this was the reason that Moteczoma received such a name: the priest looked upon the child's face and saw that it was scowling, somber, and disdainful. Or is it possible that Moteczoma was born on a sad, melancholy day and that he was named because of this?

The same was done with other members of the nobility. If the child was a peasant, a person of low birth, he received the name of the day on which he had been born and no other. Once her child had been named, the woman presented her offering, great or small, and returned to her home, as hallowed and purified as before—or worse [because of the diabolical ceremony]. She offered a banquet or dinner to those who had honored her, regaling them with clothing and thanking them for their attention. Then everyone returned to his home.

It remains now to describe the ceremony performed by the children's fathers, who had been anything but idle on this day. The great noblemen seldom took part in these rites, excusing themselves because of their position and high station, always buying their way out through compensations of offerings and alms. Those who complied with the custom were lowly peasants. The ceremony consisted of the following. Men went to the same fields which had been visited on the previous feast, a preparation for this one, the Small Perforation, where they had sanctified the fields and plots of land. Early in the morning they went in groups and broke into these fields with great shouting and yelling, ripping out small or large branches of the cornstalk, taking one or two. Carrying these in their hands, some men went to the temple and cast them there. Others cast them in the shrines which we have mentioned; others, in the streets. Each one deposited the cornstalks where his devotion and inclination demanded. Then they returned home to prick their ears, fleshy parts, and shins. Every one of them did this penance on that day, piercing himself on the parts of the body which have been mentioned. This is why the feast was called the Great Perforation, because of the bloodletting performed by adults and children.

On this day was celebrated a great, solemn Feast of Tlaloc, God of the Rain, with whom we have dealt in Chapter XII [VIII] of the book treating of the gods. We also dealt with the lake in Chapter XXIII [XVII], where it was explained that on the hill where this god dwelt children were slain, just as a little girl was sacrificed to the goddess of the waters in the middle of the lake. This was such a solemn feast and such numerous ceremonies were performed that inasmuch as I have already described them (though briefly) there is no reason to deal with them again. Nevertheless, I wish to refer to a pagan rite carried out by the Indians in olden times. The people tore out stalks of corn, calling them *centeotlana*, which means "to tear out the god of the ears of corn." When these plants had been ripped out, they were offered as first fruits of the fields. And the women cried out in loud voices, "O my lady, come quickly!" They said this to the cornfields so that they would ripen soon, before the frost could fall upon them. Then the men took up their flutes and went about playing in the fields.

THE FIFTH MONTH OF THE YEAR

¶On which was celebrated the feast of the first day of the month called Toxcatl, which means Dry Thing. On this day was commemorated the solemnity of the god called Tezcatlipoca; it was one of the main feasts held by the natives.

THE fifth month of the Mexica year fell upon May 20 according to our own calendar [Plate 42]. On this first day of the month, just as on the first days of the other months, was held a solemn feast called Toxcatl, one of the most ostentatious and imposing known to the Indians. I have dealt with this festivity in Chapter VIII [IV], when I referred to the solemnization of Tezcatlipoca, one of the most revered of all the native gods. The day was held to be so important that it excelled even that of Huitzilopochtli, as I have narrated in the above-mentioned chapter. There I explained that the festival, merrymaking, dance, farces, and representations can be compared to those of Corpus Christi, which usually falls around this time. Cursed be the Evil Adversary who planned it thus and brought this water to the mill so that his wheel would keep turning! And his mill grinds out the ceremonies, rites, and hellish sacrifices we have described.

Aside from being the day of the feast we have mentioned, this was one of the festivities counted by twenties, one of those which

426

occurred at the beginning of the month. It was called Toxcatl. Though I had studied this name at length, I had been unable to decipher it because of the obscurity of the term. At long last I realized that it meant Dry Thing and that it symbolized drought. I finally understood it through a word uttered by a native informant. He told me that around this time of the year rain was scarce and was greatly desired. The people begged it of the god whose feast they were keeping, similar to the way we say "as welcome as rain in May." The Indians also had a proverb, *titotoxcahuia*, which means "to dry up with thirst," and so it is that Toxcatl means Drought and Lack of Rain. I am going to refer to some of the things which took place upon this day other than what I have said regarding the solemnization of this idol.

The priests performed a superstitious ceremony in every part of each town. Early in the morning the minor priests from the wards went from home to home with incense burners in their hands, and even though the master of the house was most humble, [the priest] would incense the entire house all the way from the threshold to the last corner. Having done this, he then went on to the furnishings of the home; he incensed the hearth, then the grinding stone, then the tortilla griddle, the pots, small vessels and jugs, the plates, bowls, weaving instruments, the agricultural implements, storage bins, and the artisans' tools. In this way everything received incense—even the little baskets in which were kept spinning and weaving instruments and those used for tortillas. The house owners were obliged to give alms to these priests. This was done in return for having performed the ceremony and having favored the house by incensing and blessing it. The ministers were given as many ears of corn as objects they had blessed. These priests went about in this way because of the alms which were given to them, since, as I have said, they lived on alms and in poverty. It was like Spain, where the acolytes go from door to door to sprinkle holy water with the hope that they will be given alms in the form of flour or firewood. Thus these priests ate nothing but that which was given to them as alms. They begged for it, and it was offered to them in the doorways, just as the fathers of Saint Francis do today. Because of this I think the Indians are especially fond of them.

On this day a great and solemn dance took place. All crowned themselves with headdresses or miters made up of small painted wreaths, beautifully adorned like latticework. In the small spaces between reed and reed hung little figures of gold or stone or many other finely worked things, for all those who danced were lords or chieftains. This feast was called Toxcanetotiliztli, which means Dance of Toxcatl. These crowns of headdresses were called tzatzaztli, which means "something wrought like a lattice." Since it was a great feast, the usual foods on this day were birds of different types and human flesh; this was the flesh of the numerous sacrificial victims on this occasion.

The purpose of this feast was to pray for rain. The people invoked the clouds when the water had ceased to fall in May, so that that which they requested would be granted. On this day there was a general invocation of the main gods: Huitzilopochtli and Tezcatlipoca, the Sun, and the goddess Cihuacoatl. All of these were remembered on that day. When the people of each town heard the piping of the flutes which were played on that day, everyone ate earth and prostrated himself on the ground.

Owing to their heathen customs, the natives of all this land ate toasted burst corn on this day. These grains of corn were like sweets. Besides eating them, the people made necklaces of the corn to adorn their idols and wore them around their necks while dancing. At this time men and women took part in the same dance, and each woman had to be a maiden. These maidens adorned their legs with red feathers up to the knee and on their arms as far down as the elbow. This superstition was usual at weddings: all those who were marriageable, as long as they were unwed maidens, were feathered on their legs and arms with red plumes. On this feast they were the singers who began the chanting, and the lords, who formed a circle about them, responded while the maidens danced around the drum.

I could tell of many other diversions, farces and mockery, and

428

jesting games and representations of those people. But this is not the purpose of my account, since I am only desirous of exposing the evil that existed then so that today, if some of it is suspected or felt, it may be remedied and pulled out by the roots, as it should be.

THE SIXTH MONTH OF THE YEAR

¶Which contained twenty days. The sign of the first day celebrated at the beginning of this month was called Etzalcualiztli, which means Day of Eating Cooked Corn and Beans.

I am aghast at the silly and childish customs of these people under their heathen law! On what lowly things they based their solemnities and their great variety of feasts! So that the reader may perceive the foundation of this feast, I wish to explain its name, and in this way we shall understand its low character. This first day of the sixth month [is] Etzalcualiztli, which means Day on Which *Etzalli* is Allowed to be Eaten. Since during my childhood I ate [*etzalli*] often, I can explain that is a sort of bean stew containing whole kernels of corn. It is considered very tasty, so coveted, so greatly desired, that it is small wonder it had its own special day and feast on which it was honored.

This day or festival was held for many reasons. In the first place, it was at this time that rain began to fall copiously and that corn and other plants were growing and were beginning to bear fruit. Thus the sign of this day was shown, proud and handsome, as a hand holding a cornstalk in the water [Plate 43]. This denoted fertility and predicted a good season, since the water had come at the proper time. Another hand held a small pot, which meant that

430

the people could eat without fear of that food of beans and corn. There was to be no famine, since the year was proceeding in a satisfactory way. It also meant that there was general permission to eat corn and beans in the same plate as one dish. This is considered costly, and not all can afford it. In times of famine the eating of a handful of beans is comparable to the plucking of a handful of eyelashes. If they ate corn, they abstained from beans, and if they ate beans, they abstained from corn, adjusting themselves to the season. But once this day arrived, if it was not a barren but a fertile year, indulgence was given to eat this combination, thus indicating abundance. These feasts fell upon the ninth of June, when there are native cherries and other small fruits to eat. Many people who suffer a lack of corn live off these fruits, like people in Spain who sustain themselves throughout the summer with lima beans and cherries. Thus when the Indians are able to get the *capulin* (which is the name of the native cherry), though there may be a corn famine, they fill their bellies with native cherries and a thousand other edible plants, until the corn is ripe.

It was a precept or law (I believe) that under pain of death no one could eat of this food [etzalli] except at this time. This was obeyed, because the laws of the Indians (especially those of divine nature) were kept with such rigor that the death penalty was certain for the transgressor. These people considered it a small thing to slay a man. It was as natural in those times as the killing of a hen or a chicken to us, without fear of punishment.

On this day there was a ceremony, a heathen rite, which our confessors and ministers should be warned of, since they may find this knowledge useful. All the native farmers and common people performed a ceremony with their agricultural implements: hoes; sharp sticks for sowing; spades with which the earth is dug; tumplines with which they carried things; *cacaxtles*, consisting of some small crossed boards placed within a wooden framework where the load is tied; the cord with which the load is carried; and the basket within which the load is placed. On the day of the feast all these things were placed by the Indians upon a small platform in their homes, and the objects were revered and thanked for their help in the fields and on the road. Food and pulque were offered to them, together with the dish eaten on this day, already described. Incense was offered before them and a thousand salaams, salutations, and speeches. This rite was called Repose of the Servile Implements. Oh, strange brutishness of people who in many ways possessed good discipline, social order, keen intelligence, ability, and breeding! In other things, however, they displayed a strange bestiality and blindness—greater even than what we have described. Let me give warning: In our own times I have beheld some iron implements attached to digging sticks used in tilling the soil, and at the end of them were carved faces of monkeys, dogs, or devils. This did not seem good to me, though it is such a common custom that there is not an Indian who does not use these effigies, especially in the area of Chalco and in the nearby mountain range. I asked certain friars to look into this, but they claimed that these images were just decorative. I shall do the same; it is better to give the benefit of the doubt.

At the temples, in front of the large idols, offerings were made of that coarse heathen food which I described, corn and beans. To it were added pieces of fowl, turkey, and human flesh. This was done especially when a man wished to honor the gods—and occasions were never lacking. One of his slaves was killed, part of the flesh was offered up, and the rest was eaten. After having eaten, everybody, children and adults, young and old, without exception, went to wash in the rivers or springs. He who did not wash was held to be addicted to the god of famine, known as Apizteotl, which means Hungry God. At the same time the people washed their agricultural implements and all the tools used for sowing. After everyone had bathed, the noblemen came out to dance in the courtyards of the temple and in the market place. All these men were adorned in the manner which can be seen in the illustration at the beginning of the account of this month. They held their cornstalks in one hand and in the other some small pots, such as have been described. This solemn dance lasted almost all day.

While the lords and noblemen were dancing, the common people took part in another solemn dance. They carried some of the branches with which the temple was adorned, and from the leaves they made wreaths or hoops which they placed around their eyes, tying them behind with strings. Without exaggeration they looked like blinders for a donkey. Wearing these things on their eyes, with a staff in one hand and an empty pot in the other, they went from house to house. They stopped in the courtyard of each house and cried out, "Give me to eat of your *etzalli*!" This was the dish of corn and beans we have described.

With this we finish our description of the feast falling in the sixth month and of the servile and ridiculous heathen ceremonies which these people practiced, indulged in. These rites lacked a sound basis, were such products of the imagination to the extent that today the Indians laugh at and mock them. In spite of this, they are abandoning their ceremonies with great difficulty. This is especially true in things having to do with food, because these people are worse than Epicureans and more sensual!

THE SEVENTH MONTH OF THE YEAR

¶Of twenty days, which commemorated a festival called
Tecuilhuitontli, which means Little Feast of the Lords.

THIS fell upon the seventh month of the calendar, on the first
day, commemorating the feast called Tecuilhuitontli, which means
Little Feast of the Lords. On our calendar it occurs on the twenty-
ninth of June. It was an unimportant festivity, with little ceremony,
few special foods, and no human sacrifice. Thus it was only a
preparation for the coming feast of the next, or eighth, month. This
period of twenty days was to be similar to the Great Perforation
and Small Perforation of which we have spoken—one being preliminary to the other. This feast was also called Tlaxochimaco,
which means Distribution of Flowers.

The fact that it was called Feast of the Lords or Little Feast
means that the celebrations performed on the Great Feast did not
take place at this time. It was also known as "Little" because the
sign or planet of this day did not possess great significance or importance. It was just an occasion for enjoying the flowers which
abounded in that season. And so we shall see in the illustration of
the feast a picture of a man arranging flowers [Plate 44]. That is
why it is called by its second name, Distribution of Flowers. Thus

434

the most notable rite was the exchange of flowers among the people, mutual invitations, and festivities which included finely prepared dishes and costly banquets. Mantles, breechcloths, and jewels were exchanged, and this custom has lingered to our own times. None of the lords abandoned their homes on this day, nor did they take part in any of these things. They remained reclining upon their seats, surrounded by flowers, picking up one and laying it down, taking another and abandoning it, all this time exhibiting their high dignity and lordliness. Sovereigns also donned their crowns on that day and thus showed their stately and exalted position.[1]

On this day all the concubines of the great lords emerged from their homes and places of seclusion and were permitted to walk about in the streets, with garlands of flowers upon their heads and around their necks, on their way to the pleasure gardens. There the paramours of one lord would meet with those of another. They were all dressed in their most luxurious ornaments and elaborately embroidered huipils. As they went along, many of the courtiers and noblemen flattered them and directed jovial remarks to them, though the guardians and duennas of the women were with them, watching over their every act.

Most men were not permitted to keep many women or mistresses, contrary to what is thought by some today. This privilege was reserved for the highest and most esteemed noblemen and braves, [who] were not allowed to keep more [women] than they could provide for in food and dress. When these ladies had finished the promenade, they rejoiced in song, dance, and feasting, together with their admirers. Once this had terminated, each one of the women returned to the palace where she was kept.

[1] This passage, like many others, points up the highly stratified society of the ancient Mexicas. The pre-Hispanic Mixtec codices, which deal largely with genealogies and royal weddings, make it clear that marriage alliances among members of the ruling classes were as important in the Aztec world as in Medieval and Renaissance Europe and that aristocratic blood was to be kept pure.

THE EIGHTH MONTH OF THE YEAR

¶Of twenty days like all the rest, on the first day of which was celebrated the Great Feast of the Lords, called Huey Tecuilhuitl.

THE present feast was known as the Solemnization of Huey Tecuilhuitl and fell upon the eighth month of the Indian year. The name of this feast means Great Feast of the Lords, during which terminated the splendid festivity which had begun on the Little Feast of the previous month. When I asked why it was called the Great Feast of the Lords, I was told that on the feast of the previous month the idol which represented the lords had been small, while on the present occasion it was large and highly adorned. It was decorated with a golden diadem on its head and sat upon the sort of throne that the lords and kings used. On this day the natives imagined they could see celestial signs similar to the royal insignia which they carried.

As a pictorial representation of this feast a man was shown with ears of corn in one hand and a maize cake in the other [Plate 45]. The latter sign indicated that on the arrival of this feast the ears of corn were ripe. Therefore, they ate tortillas of young fresh corn and greens such as amaranth and sorrel. Bread was made

436

from the latter two; they were ground up, mixed, and cooked with corn flour. The tamales made of these things were called *quilta-malli*, which means "corn with greens." This dish was eaten on this day, and part of it was offered to the gods in the temples, together with many strings of green chili and strings of fresh ears of corn. These were offered as first fruits.

The god Ehecatl was commemorated on this same feast. He is also the one known as Quetzalcoatl, and we have dealt with him in Chapter X [VI] [of the *Book of the Gods and Rites*]. Ehecatl means Wind. A man was sacrificed on this day, and this sacrifice was performed in the name of the Wind and in the honor of this deity. And even though only one man died for the above-mentioned god, many others were slain in observance of the Feast of the Lords, which was grave, dignified, yet joyous.

This feast took place in the Temple of Tezcatlipoca, honoring the latter in this manner, [but] the ceremony honored Quetzalcoatl, God of the Wind, and the manner in which he had been persecuted, plus the victory which had been achieved over this holy man when he lived in this land. If we are not mistaken, we dealt with this subject in Chapter V [I] of our first book. [The enemies of Quetzalcoatl] triumphed and remained in power. That is why this solemn feast was called the Great Feast of the Lords.

On this same day, the Great Feast of the Lords, another diabolical rite took place, involving fresh ears of corn. As we have stated, *xilotl*, "tender corn," was in season in some parts at the time of this feast. [The Indians] paid homage to these new, tender ears of corn by sacrificing a woman in the name of the goddess Xilonen, which in Spanish means She Who Always Walked and Remained as Fresh and Tender as a Young Ear of Corn. To explain this further, the name means She Who Remained a Maiden Without Sin.

This goddess had three names. One was Chicomecoatl, which means Seven Snake, because the natives believed that she had prevailed against seven serpents, or sins. Another name was Chalchiuhcihuatl, which means Precious Stone or Emerald, because

437

she was chosen from among all women. Her third name was Xilonen, which means She Who Was and Lived as Delicate and Tender as a Fresh Ear of Corn.

Together with this virgin four men were slain in sacrifice. These formed a sort of platform for her, and she was killed upon their bodies. All of this was in remembrance of her lifelong contempt for carnal things and for human frailty. We have dealt with this goddess in Chapter XVIII [XIV], especially in the place where we showed an illustration of her with her small ears of corn in hand, just as she appeared in the hours after midnight [Plate 23].[1]

On this day there was a dance in which the lords and the maidens took part. All of them were adorned with large yellow flowers, and after the dancing and reveling the flowers were offered to the gods. After the girls had presented their garlands, the young men vied with one another in a race up the steps of the temple to pick up the garlands. The first four to arrive—whether one alone or all together—were the winners in that contest. It was thought that the girls who had deposited the four garlands which the youths picked up were truly maidens. This was another evil and foolish superstition of the natives.

This feast began with a ceremony that lasted ten days in a row, and though it was an ancient ritual, it seemed more like an extravagance and a despotic practice. All the wards, singly or

---

[1] It is apparent that the girl representing the goddess, like many other sacrificial victims, knew what her fate was to be. According to Durán and other early scholars, some of the victims walked willingly to their deaths. It is doubtful that they were lured by thoughts of a glorious and blissful afterlife comparable to the Christian heaven, though it was believed that after death sacrificial victims went to the Home of the Warriors in the north. It appears likely that the individual who gave up his life did so because of tenets which had controlled his entire existence since birth and which placed the welfare of the society far above that of the individual. The "divine" victim went to his fate with the certainty that his blood was to keep his society alive and prosperous and that the world—even the sun itself—profited by his death.

As in many other societies, there were lukewarm individuals who had to be coaxed into the supreme act by drugs or intoxicants. It is also significant that most of the victims described by Durán were very young, at an age when human beings are easy prey to highly emotional situations and eager to perform heroic deeds.

together, were obliged to provide food and drink to all the braves, captains, and old soldiers of the army as payment or reward for their good deeds in waging war and defending the country from its enemies. Sometimes those who sponsored this ceremony were strangers—men from Chalco, the Tecpanecs, or the Xochimilcas.

On this festive day of the eighth month was held the sacrificial ceremony of the midwives and healers who dwelt in the cities. There were many of them at that time, just as there are today; they are deceitful, superstitious and so harmful to the republic that it would be better if they did not exist. These women sought out a young maiden, dressed her in a fine and elegant manner, covered her with flowers in the guise of the goddess whose feast was celebrated on this day. They led her out of the City of Mexico. She walked in the middle, greatly honored by all. The midwives walked in this procession, and all others were excluded. The girl was taken to Chapultepec and was led to the summit of the hill.[2] Once she was there, the women exclaimed, "Oh, daughter, let us make haste, since we must return to the place from which we came." They turned round and hurried swiftly down the hill with the maiden. All of them returned to the City of Mexico at the swift pace and were breathless by the time they arrived. The girl went straight to the temple and ascended the steps with the mob of hags behind her. Once she was at the summit, she was forced to dance and sing for half an hour, and if it was noticed that she did not comply with good will, the women made her intoxicated with a certain potion,

[2] Chapultepec Hill, a few miles west of the ceremonial center of Mexico-Tenochtitlan, was hallowed by ancient traditions. There, at the end of the twelfth century, Hueymac, the last ruler of Tula, hanged himself in a cave. Revered images of heroic Aztec emperors were carved in the rock of the hill. At the top stood a temple in honor of Tlaloc, God of Rain. Soon after the Conquest the temple was transformed into a church dedicated to Saint Michael the Archangel. The church was later destroyed, and in the eighteenth century Viceroy Bernardo de Gálvez built his rural Versailles on the summit of the hill. A military academy was established there, and in 1864, Maximilian transformed the ruins of the academy into a palace which was subsequently rebuilt by President Porfirio Díaz. Today this castle houses the National Museum of History. The only visible pre-Hispanic remains lie at the foot of the hill, where a number of badly damaged relief carvings are all that survive of the Aztec emperors' desire for eternal fame. Nearby lie the ruins of the Bath of Moteczoma.

439

and she became gay. After the maiden had danced and sung, she was turned over to the butchers, who opened her chest, ripped out her heart, [and] offered it to the sun, and the idols and the threshold were smeared with her blood.

THE NINTH MONTH OF THE YEAR

¶Contained twenty days, and during this time was celebrated the feast of Micailhuitontli, or Little Feast of the Dead.

IT was on the eighth of August by our calendar that these people observed the ninth month of the year of twenty days, like all the rest. The festival celebrated at the beginning of this month was performed with great rejoicing. It was called Micailhuitontli, which is a diminutive and means Feast of the Little Dead.[1] According to my information, it was the commemoration of innocent dead children, and that is why the diminutive was used. In the solemn ceremonies of this day offerings and sacrifices were made to honor and venerate these children.

The second reason this feast was named in the diminutive is the same [as that] used for the name of the previous feast. That is to say, it was a preparation or anticipation of the coming festivity, called the Great Feast of the Dead, when adults were to be remembered. There was another reason (and this was the main one), founded on omens and superstition. This feast fell on the eighth of

[1] Today in Mexico the Feast for Dead Children takes place on October 31–November 1, when altars are set up in the homes, with candy, toys, and other special treats.

441

August (and just as our own Spaniards say, "Of August beware: there'll be frost in the air!"), and so these people feared the loss of their crops owing to frost at the beginning of August. Thus the natives prepared their offerings, oblations, and sacrifices for this feast and for that of the following month.

I have already mentioned that the first reason for the name Feast of the Little Dead was due to the offerings made for deceased children. I wish to refer to something I have seen take place on the Day of Allhallows and on the Day of the Faithful Departed. In some towns offerings are made on Allhallows, and further offerings take place on the Day of the Faithful Departed. When I asked why offerings were made on the Day of Allhallows, I was told that this was in honor of the children, it being an ancient custom which had survived. I inquired whether offerings were also made on the Day of the Faithful Departed, and the answer was, "yes, in honor of adults." I was sorry to hear these things because I saw clearly that the Feast of the Little Dead and [the Feast] of the Adults were still being celebrated. On the first I saw people offering chocolate, candles, fowl, fruit, great quantities of seed, and food. On the next day I saw the same being done. Though this feast fell in August, I suspect that if it is an evil simulation (which I do not dare affirm) the pagan festival has been passed to the Feast of Allhallows in order to cover up the ancient ceremony.

The figure representing the sign of this day was a dead man in his shroud, just as these people prepared their dead. He was shown reclining upon a seat which was thought to be seen in the heavens at that time of the year, and it is shown in the native pictures as the planet of that season, in the midst of the clouds [Plate 46]. This was the principal feast of the Tecpanecs, who were the nation and land of Tlacopan, Coyoacan, Azcapotzalco. This main festivity of theirs lasted the entire month until the beginning of the Great Feast of the Dead. On this day an enormous thick tree trunk was cut—the largest that the woods could produce. The bark was stripped off and smoothed. Once this had been done, it was brought and set up at the entrance of the city or town. Upon its arrival the priests came out of the temples with trumpets, singing and dancing. The common men appeared with conch shells, offerings, food, incense burners filled with copal, and other types of incense. The pole was called Xocotl and lay there for twenty days, venerated by all with the same honors and reverence which we show to the cross of our Redeemer. This pole was blessed and hallowed each day with splendid ceremonies, singing and dancing, incense, the letting of blood, fasting, flagellation, and many other forms of penance practiced while the tree trunk lay there. We have dealt with these things in more detail in Chapter XVI [XII]. All these offerings were placed upon the wood, and it was addressed as though it were a rational being. On this Day of the Little Dead no one was sacrificed because of their respect for the pole, but—since the natives were solemnizing the first day of their month, and in order to honor the corresponding planet—there was always someone to offer up a slave to solemnize the feast.

On this day the elders performed numerous rites upon the children of a superstitious and magical nature. They convinced mothers that if they offered up such and such a thing their children would not die during the year. A thousand diabolical inventions were used: hair cropping, sacrifices, anointings, baths, tarring, feathering, covering with soot, beads, and little bones. All of this has lasted until the present day, and mothers still observe these practices with fascination, happy, satisfied, desirous of offering gifts to the cursed and deceitful sorcerer or witch.

THE TENTH MONTH OF THE YEAR

¶Made up of twenty days, during which was celebrated the Great Feast of the Dead, together with the most solemn commemoration of Xocotl Huetzi, festival of the Tecpanecs. On this day a frightful, fearsome fire sacrifice took place.

THE Great Feast of the Dead, which we are going to deal with now, fell in this tenth month and, according to our own calendar, on the twenty-eighth of August [Plate 47]. It was a great and most solemn day and included the sacrifice of many men. Mass sacrifices always indicated that a feast was of the highest rank. If there were no [sacrifices], as in certain feasts which involved only offerings, ceremonies, and merrymaking, the festivals did not show the pomp, display, or grandeur of those involving human sacrifice. The eating of human flesh made a feast double of the first class. The rest of the days were simple or at best double.

On the major solemnities the high priests donned their pontifical vestments; they placed their richly feathered, gold, and jeweled tiaras upon their heads. The priests covered themselves with their wide tunics and sacerdotal dress, the deacons wore surplices and dalmatics, and the ministers of the temples all adorned themselves with the jewels and vestments kept in the temples. All of this signifies the magnitude and importance of this day, upon which they were to butcher men and make stew of their flesh. Thus

444

they were to serve as victims for the false and deceitful gods. It is remarkable to note how this feast was celebrated without any trace of the presence of our God, and not founded upon reason. Their celebration of such a base thing shows us how blind they were, how deceived by the devil, as blind as those in whom the roots of these things still survive!

We have already described how last month's feast was a preliminary of this one. The natives cut down the great pole, left it lying on the ground at the entrance to the city, hallowed and blessed it with diabolical ceremonies, calling it Xocotl. Now on this day, with grave reverence, the priests and ministers of the temple lifted the pole from the ground at dawn. Then they raised it in the temple courtyard. On its top was placed a bird made of dough of same type described in Chapter XVI [XII]. Once this ritual had ended, men tried to climb [the pole] to cast down the image. When this had been accomplished, the pole was also knocked down. On this day a new word was added to the name of the idol and pole. This was Xocotl Huetzi, which means Fall of Xocotl.

Before the pole was thrown down, an amazing amount of food and pulque was placed around it. This is especially true of the town of Coyoacan, where the pole was the deity and advocate, just as now it is the glorious Saint John the Baptist. There this pole was adorned in a splendid and artful manner with jewelry, featherwork, and flowers.

Young men and women who lived in the schools, all of them offspring of highborn men, danced a solemn dance on this day. Covered with feathers and jewels, [youths and maidens] attended. [The girls'] faces were covered with cosmetics, [they wore] paint on their cheeks, [and] their arms and legs [were] heavily adorned with red plumes. This dance took place around the pole, a circle formed by the dancing lords, all of them richly bedecked. Instead of flowers, the dancers carried in their hands little images made of dough and balls of the same dough. Food was plentiful on this feast, and drink was even more abundant. It was a day of drunkenness, a day of indulgence, a day of drinking—including everyone

445

except the youths and maidens, who were never permitted [this excess]. I should remark that abstinence from drink and the prohibition against drunkenness existed for the following reason. These people held the century plant to be something divine, celestial; this maguey was known to be extremely useful, and, therefore, it was highly revered. The same may be said of its juice, which, fermented into wine, was held to be no less than a god who bore the name of Ometochtli, which means Two Rabbit. And, just as we now prohibit communion to children who have not reached the age of reason because they do not know what they receive, so these people prohibited pulque to the young. No one could drink it, not even mature men, unless they were nobles feeling reverence for this accursed wine, which not only was an inebriating drink but also was a god to be revered. Therefore, it was held to be a divine thing, considering its effects and power to intoxicate.[1]

This accursed beverage was a special offering to the gods. Thus I have heard of sacrifices and offerings where, besides food, feathers, incense, foolish and childish things such as bones and little clay dishes and beads, tiny pots filled with pulque were used. I am afraid that even today—to judge by the love the natives feel for pulque, craving it as they do—there may be some supernatural intent. Today, as far as I can see, all of them drink it—old men, youths, women, men, boys, girls. Even newborn sucklings are given pulque by their mothers with their fingers when the mothers are imbibing. And the mothers say they allow the child to lick their finger so that he will not be weakened by the desire he feels on watching others drink. If someone wishes to abstain from drinking, the old men and women tell him that he will become hoarse, sores will appear in his throat, together with a thousand diabolical inventions. In this way they provoke him to drink. The great lords are proud, consider it a superior thing, to be drunk, while the boys do it for fun.

[1] As Durán indicates, to the Aztecs, pulque, or *nectli*, had a sacred and restricted purpose. The wine of the Mexicas lost its holy character soon after the Spanish invasion and became as prosaic a drink as beer, mezcal, or tequila.

THE ELEVENTH MONTH OF THE YEAR

¶Which in the native calendar contained twenty days. The first was called Ochpaniztli, meaning Day of Sweeping. On this day was solemnized the feast of Toci, who was the Mother of the Gods and Heart of the Earth. A horrendous sacrifice of impaled men took place.

THE reader will remember the solemn feast that was described in Chapter XV, in honor of the Mother, or Grandmother, of the Gods, known as Toci, Our Grandmother or Heart of the Earth. This goddess and her feast were glorified on the first day of the eleventh month [Plate 48]. This day was called Ochpaniztli, which means Day of Sweeping. This celebration, according to our system, fell on the seventeenth of September. As I have described, the feast was so filled with ceremonial that it would be sufficient to read it without returning to it here. There we described how she was the Heart of the Earth, how she made it tremble and shake in rites filled with the shedding of human blood.

We have also described the way and manner in which squadrons simulated combat until they reached the place where stood a scaffold bearing the insignia of the goddess. These consisted of a broom, bones, and the garments which she wore. All these ceremonies were performed in honor of the goddess Toci. It now remains for us to deal in detail with the rites which took place on the first day of the month, even though they overlapped with those of

447

the feast. The main feast was on the first day of the month, called Ochpaniztli. This was the festival of sweeping, on which the natives celebrated the feast with the signs and ceremonies peculiar to rules and rites established by the order of the months.

This was the first act of the day: everyone had to sweep his possessions, his house, and all its corners, leaving nothing without diligent sweeping and cleaning. Besides this, all the streets of the town were swept before dawn. This custom has remained in the country. The people sweep the lots and the streets [daily], but they leave the inside of the home so dirty and filled with rubbish that it looks like a stable. I believe that they do not sweep the inside of the house except on this day, [and this practice is followed] because it is such an ancient rite. I consider this to be evil; I have fought against it; I have opposed it in some places. I have explained that it is a superstition, a pagan custom, but I do not know whether this has done any good.

On this day the baths were also swept and washed. There is a great deal of paganism here, since it is true that never did men bathe without women or women without men. It was considered an evil thing for men or women to bathe alone. Even today it is considered so, and I am afraid that this custom has not disappeared, owing to heathen beliefs. And what fills me with fear is the following. Once when I censured the abominable habit of mixed bathing, some natives, afraid of my threats and perhaps my punishment, abandoned the custom. Since adult men no longer entered the bath then, women took a small male child with them, and the men one or two small girls. All of this was due to fear of ill fortune, ancient idolatry, and ill omens of which the elders had spoken. It would be necessary to saw the people apart before we could eliminate their bathing together. Women would rather spend their entire lives without bathing unless a man enters with them, and the same may be said of the men. The same may be applied to the bathing of the sick. If the patient is a woman, a male doctor must go in to bathe her; and, if a man, the doctor must be a female.[1] In all of this I

---

[1] The igloo-shaped *temazcalli*, or bathhouse, is still a prominent feature in the back yards of rural homes. A fire is built outside the mud-and-stone structure, and

have found much evil, ill omens, superstition, abomination, and sin. I not only imagine but hold it for a truth that our priests are not ignorant of these things. I do not know why they feign ignorance, since this custom is so extended throughout the land that no one can possibly ignore it. Perhaps they do not believe that superstition and heathenism are connected with the habit; but they are, in a very pronounced way. All of this is filled with evil inclinations and a strong smell of idolatry.

At this same time the ditches, streams, and springs were cleaned. People bathed and washed in them on these days, just as some do today on the morning of Saint John the Baptist.[2]

Roads and highways were also adorned and swept on this day, especially the one that goes to Coyoacan, paying homage at the shrine of the goddess whose day it was. This stood on the road and was associated with the combat which had taken place on that day.

the bather within splashes water upon the hot stone wall, causing steam to fill the bathhouse. It is used for ordinary bathing, medicinal purposes, and purification of women who have given birth.

[2] Ritual bathing on the Feast of Saint John the Baptist, June 24, is still customary in Mexico. In the villages people usually bathe in a nearby stream or pond at dawn, and in the larger cities the swimming pools teem with bathers.

THE TWELFTH MONTH OF THE YEAR

¶Contained twenty days. This was the celebration of the Feast of Pachtontli, which means Moss, a diminutive name. On this day was kept the solemn feast of the coming of Huitzilopochtli, on which occasion a terrible, frightful human sacrifice took place.

W~E~ shall deal now with the twelfth month [Plate 49]. A most solemn feast, which involved the killing of many people, took place on the first day. This first day of the month was called Pachtontli, a diminutive term like the others I have explained (because this small feast was to be followed twenty days later by the great feast). Pachtontli means Moss. This moss is a plant that grows on trees and hangs on branches. The great festivity was based on this plant, since the sign of the moss plant was thought to be among the clouds or in the heavens or in the stars, similar to the other signs that we have already described.

Aside from being one of the feasts at the beginning of the months, it was also the special festival of the god called Huitzilopochtli, commemorating his coming, which I have described elsewhere.

At seven o'clock in the evening the natives placed a gourd filled with dough in the upper part of the temple and watched over it. Carefully, vigilantly they visited it from time to time until they found a child's footprint or a hair on the dough. Then the trumpets and conch shells sounded, and there was great rejoicing over the advent of the divine Huitzilopochtli.

In the midst of all the merrymaking and rejoicing, and as a grateful recompense for the great favor their god had bestowed upon them in coming, the people made frightful wounds upon their own bodies. They bled their own chests, tongues, ears, fleshy parts, and shins and passed cords, reeds, and straws through their fierce wounds, each one according to his devotion. Thus they were bathed in blood through their cruel penances and bloody sacrifices. This blood was offered to the devil by that traitor Abimelech, the devil, so fond of human blood that he licked it during the sacrificial occasions of these blind, unfortunate natives. For an instant, with blood, these people placated the ire of their wrathful gods, who could not be pleased except with the blood of mankind.

When the bloody penance had terminated, when the blood-letting had ended, each striving to do the utmost, the ministers appeared with incense burners in their hands. They incensed the gourd of dough, together with the idols; they cast great fistfuls of copal incense, which clouded all the temples with smoke. On this day a certain bread was eaten, and it was identical to the dough that was placed in the gourds where Huitzilopochtli had left his sign. Thus ended this feast, which was simply a preparation for the next.

THE THIRTEENTH MONTH OF THE YEAR

¶Which contained twenty days. The Feast of Hueypachtli was celebrated on the first day. This superlative name
means Great Moss. It was also called Coailhuitl, which
means General Feast for All the Land. At this time was
celebrated the festivity of the hills, especially the Popocatepetl and Iztaccihuatl.

T<small>HE</small> thirteenth month of the Indian year was made up of twenty
days like all the rest [Plate 50]. The feast celebrated on the first
day, called Hueypachtli, meaning Great Moss (a superlative of
the Small Moss, which had passed), now took place. The preparation had lasted twenty days, and its name now appears in the
superlative. It was a most solemn occasion, a most magnificent
affair in which the mountains and hills were honored. I have already
described this celebration in Chapters XII [XVII] and XXII
[XVIII]. Besides commemorating Tlaloc, God of Lightning and
Thunder, and the Goddess of the Waters and Springs, the feast was
also held in honor of the Popocatepetl and the Iztaccihuatl and the
other principal mountains of the land. Thus it was called Tepeilhuitl, Feast of the Hills. This fell on the twenty-ninth of October.

I have already described the honor paid to these hills in
Chapter XXII [XVIII]. People made little hills of amaranth
dough within their homes [and placed them] in shrines or special
niches where the idols were kept, just as today they keep the
[Christian] images.[1]

452

In these small sanctuaries the following rite was performed. Images were made of each one of the principal mountains of the land. In the center were placed the Popocatepetl and Iztaccihuatl and the rest of the surrounding hills. Eyes and faces decorated these hills of dough. They were dressed in a native paper which was similar to cheap tan paper, *estraza*, with designs in black rubber paint. Small trees were also placed there, and from them hung the plants (I do not know how to say this in Spanish) called moss—in the native language [called] *pachtli.* As I have explained, this is a dark-gray plant which grows and hangs from the branches of evergreens and oaks, like strings attached to each other.[2] This plant was hung on the walls of the temples on that day, and the floors were covered with it instead of sedge. A joyous feast took place in each home. No expense was spared to honor these models of the hills. They were offered fine things, incense, and numerous rites and obeisance. When these things had ended, the little dough hills were decapitated with a flint knife as if they were alive. The heads having been chopped off, in the name of sacrifice, the dough which had represented the hills was eaten. It was believed to have medicinal qualities for those afflicted with tumors or paralysis. Thus the maimed and the crippled twisted snakes out of this dough, "killing" them afterward, much as the others had "slain" the hills, believing them to be gods. These things were eaten in the belief that they could cure lameness and imperfections.

[1] One can picture the little room, space, or niche in which the household gods and ceremonial objects were kept. Upon an altar or shelf stood holy figurines made of clay, wood, and stone, dressed in their appropriate costumes of cloth or paper. Before them lay humble offerings of food, drink, flowers, and at certain times rubber, herbs, tobacco, drugs, and other medicinal elements. During worship, native incense smoldered in a small tripod vessel, and slivers of resinous wood gave off a flickering light at night. Today in Indian Mexico the household shrine is rarely a room or building set apart from the home, except among certain groups such as the Otomis and the Mazahuas. In the typical Indian home, consisting of but one room, stands a small wooden table or shelf containing the images and colored prints of the Trinity, the Virgin in any of a number of intercessory roles, and other saints, as well as candles, flowers, incense, paper streamers, and souvenirs from famous Mexican religious shrines. The household shrine is such a widespread institution that even the bus or truck driver sets up a small altar in his vehicle, complete with saint, an electric light (as a substitute for a candle), curtains, and paper flowers.

[2] The parasite Spanish moss, also called *malhojo.*

453

Another ceremony was performed on this day. Grains of corn were cast toward the four cardinal points associated with the native year. To the east lay Reed, to the west lay House, to the north lay Flint Knife, and to the south lay Rabbit. These were represented by four types of corn: black, white, yellow, and spotted.

And a magnificent dance was danced; everyone was dressed in decorated tunics which fell to the feet, finely ornamented and adorned with hearts and with the palms of open hands. This meant that they besought a good crop with their hands and their hearts, since the harvest was upon them. All the dancers carried wooden trays and finely decorated large gourds, and with these they implored the favor of the gods. Short skirts worn by the women dancers were painted with twisted entrails, which represented either the famine or the plenty which might come.

On that day's sacrifice two young sisters, representing famine and plenty, died.

THE FOURTEENTH MONTH OF THE YEAR

¶Made up of twenty days, on the first of which was celebrated the God of the Hunt, Camaxtli, also called
Yemaxtli, which means He of the Three Breechcloths.
The actual name of the day was Quecholli, which refers
to spears or propelled points.

WE have now reached the feast of the hunters. This was held in
the fourteenth month with the many and varied ceremonies which
have been described in Chapter XI [VII] in dealing with the idol
Camaxtli, Divinity of the Hunt. The reader who has forgotten
these things may go back to read [them] again, since it would be
tedious to repeat them needlessly. The first day of this fourteenth
month was known as Quecholli, in Spanish [meaning] Flying
Spear. Thus we see in the hieroglyphic painting and sign of this
day a man with bow and arrows in one hand and a basket of rushes
in the other, together with a deer at his feet [Plate 51]. The Indians
imagined that they could see this figure in the heavens representing
the sign of this month. According to our own monthly calendar,
this feast fell on the sixteenth of November.

Besides being the Day of Quecholli, it was also the solemn
festival of Camaxtli, who was remembered and venerated in the
most lavish manner. Game, not men, were sacrificed on this day. In
this way the beasts served as victims for the gods. Thus those who
had caught game that day—whether little or much—were honored

and dressed in new ornaments and finery. A path was made [for the hunters] all the way from the woods to the city. No one was allowed to pass along this way unless he had killed game. The road was covered with dry grass from the woods instead of the usual rushes. Thus the successful hunters came in a procession toward the city, all walking in order, merry and glad.

These hunters had their eyes painted with circles of soot, and their mouths were feathered with eagle plumes. Their heads were also feathered, and so were their ears. Their legs were smeared with white chalk. Thus they went along, proud and boisterous, since the honor they had received was the highest a hunter could obtain.

Over all the land a great festival was held on the mountains on this day. Rich offerings were made to the God of the Chase, especially by those who were desirous of hunting. Because of this fine offerings were made, superstitious prayers and supplications were uttered, together with magic spells and circles and soothsaying. They invoked the clouds, winds, earth, water, heavens, sun, moon, stars, trees, plants, shrubs, mountains, cliffs, hills, plains, snakes, lizards, jaguars, mountain lions, and all the beasts. These things were petitioned so that the beast would fall into the hand of the hunter, for, if a hunter was successful, he rose to the rank of a senator, knight, or chieftain. Their titles became Amiztlatoque and Amiztequihuaque, which mean Chieftains, Lords, and Captains of the Chase.

THE FIFTEENTH MONTH OF THE YEAR

¶Which consisted of twenty days and began with the feast celebrated on the first day. This was called Panquetzaliztli, which means Raising of Banners. At this time occurred the magnificent, long, and rapid procession of the supreme god of the Mexicas, Huitzilopochtli.

I N this fifteenth month, on the first day, was held the commemorative feast of the great idol known as Huitzilopochtli, the supreme god of the Mexicas in whose succor and favor the people placed all their trust. So it was in strife (since he waged war for them) as in all their other needs. He was remembered in festivals, celebrations, commemorations, octaves, and a thousand other occasions, the most important of which took place after the one described in Chapter VI [II]. Even though in that chapter I told about the procession and haste of Huitzilopochtli, all of this did not take place until the first day of the present month. In that chapter I referred to it as part of the celebrations of this day.

This day was called Panquetzaliztli, which means Raising of Banners. This name went well with the ceremony performed then, as I shall tell after I have finished my description of the long, solemn procession which was carried out at this time.

Aside from being the first day of the month, the Feast of Panquetzaliztli (in itself a solemn occasion), a commemoration of the great idol Huitzilopochtli took place. An image of dough was

457

fashioned. It was about as large as a man could carry in his arms while fleeing so swiftly that others could not catch up with him. Let us not forget that this race was called Ipaina Huitzilopochtli, the Haste, Velocity, or Swiftness of Huitzilopochtli. Thus was named this commemorative celebration because while the god was alive he was never caught, never taken prisoner in war, was always triumphant over his enemies, and, no matter how swift his foes, none ever caught up with him. He was the one who caught them. Therefore, this feast honored his speed.

A swift runner burst out of the Temple of Huitzilopochtli with the greatest speed, carrying in his arms the dough idol. He ran along what is now the Street of Tlacopan; he turned at the orchard now called the Orchard of the Marqués. He reached Tacubaya and from Tacubaya set out for Coyoacan; from Coyoacan he ran toward Huitzilopochco; and from that place he turned back toward Mexico, without having paused a moment along the way.[1]

Behind him ran a great multitude, men and women, who chased after him with all the speed in the world. It is said that some of them sought to catch up with the man who carried the idol in order to snatch it from him; and if anyone accomplished this (which was very seldom), the latter was held to be a courageous and fortunate man upon whom the deity had showered his favors, since he had permitted that encounter. All along the way stood

[1] The route of this ceremonial race began at the Temple of Huitzilopochtli, the ceremonial center where the Cathedral of Mexico stands today, ran westward along what are now Tacuba, Hidalgo, Puente de Alvarado, and San Cosme streets. The route then turned southward at La Tlaxpana, at the present-day British Cemetery, and continued along what is now Melchor Ocampo Avenue, where traces of an ancient causeway are still visible. Skirting the hill of Chapultepec, the runner reached the modern suburb of Tacubaya, hastened on to Coyoacan and to Churubusco, and then returned northward to the center of Mexico-Tenochtitlan. Thus he covered an oval-shaped route of fifteen to twenty miles, completing the race in a little more than two hours. That there were expert runners among the Mexicans is indicated not only by this ceremonial race but also by the chroniclers' descriptions of the rapid communications maintained between the Aztec capital and the Gulf Coast—at the very moment of the arrival of the Spanish conquerors in Veracruz, Cortés and Moteczoma exchanged messages. Some modern Indian groups, such as the Tarahumares, have kept up the tradition and are capable of running a hundred miles with little fatigue.

triumphal arches embellished with flowers and featherwork, lavish-ly adorned with banners of many types—some of gold, some of cloth, all in honor of the Day of the Raising of the Banners. At each arch men sounded drums, trumpets, and conch shells, which made an abominable, dismal sound.

When the runner returned to Mexico, a little more than two hours later, depending upon his swiftness, all the dignitaries of the temples appeared solemnly, to the sound of drums [and] trumpets, and in the midst of dancing received their god of dough. These priests picked up the idol and carried it into the temple. Later they performed the rite of exhibiting the effigy to all those who were to be sacrificed. As we have explained before, the latter stood in line next to the skull rack.

Four days before the Feast of Panquetzaliztli there was a voluntary fast to prepare for this four-day occasion. At midnight sharp those who fasted ate some honeyed amaranth cakes and drank a small amount of water; they ate nothing more during the day, nor did they drink until twenty-four hours later. This fast was called *netenhuatzaliztli*, which means "drying up or removing of moisture from the mouth." Those who kept this fast had to keep it strictly, because they feared the wrath of the god and his chastise-ment. All of this involved many omens and superstitions. There was another heathen belief. Even today I have seen it practiced in some places, though not everywhere, except among a few super-stitious people. These rites and low, baseless practices have not been erased totally from the people's minds. The ceremony was this. On the day of Panquetzaliztli small banners were placed upon fruit trees and plants. These flags were hung from the native cherry trees, the different types of sapotas, the avocado trees, the guavas, the plums, the prickly-pear cacti, the century plants, and so forth. Little flags were placed upon all these trees. This rite was especially common in the Marquesado and in the provinces of Cholula and Tlaxcala. But it was most prominent in the Marquesado. The people there were the most superstitious and the greatest fortune-tellers, sorcerers, that ever existed in the entire land. The most remarkable were the people of Malinalco, where sorcerers were taught their craft. Even today they are considered infamous because of these things.

Returning to our subject, let us remember that the natives placed little flags on all the trees, because of their superstitions, on this day. Let the Christian reader remember this so that when he sees it practiced he will fight against it as something smacking of idolatry. After the banners were placed upon the trees, offerings were made of bread, pulque, incense, and a thousand other things. What I have described is sufficient for [the reader] to be wary.

THE SIXTEENTH MONTH OF THE YEAR

¶Which was celebrated by the natives. It consisted of twenty days, and the feast on the first day was called Atemoztli, which means Coming Down of the Waters. It commemorated the advent of Huitzilopochtli, a most solemn feast.

Up to now we have been dealing with the most important feasts held in the previous months to honor the false gods. Now in this sixteenth month, in the last, and in the two which are still to be described we shall see more about how the false gods were extolled and new festivities held in their honor. These fell every eighty days after the real celebration had been solemnized. Thus the feast at the beginning of the sixteenth month commemorated the descent of Huitzilopochtli to the world; it refers to the abominable descent we described under the tenth month of the year. At the beginning of this month, then, lavish rites and ceremonies took place because of his coming. According to our calendar this fell upon the twenty-sixth of December, on the day of the glorious Saint Stephen, one day after the birth of our Redeemer Jesus Christ.

The hieroglyphic painting of that day is the one shown here at the beginning of the month [Plate 53]. It was believed that a child came down from heaven. This infant was called Water, as can be understood from the Nahuatl name for it. Let us remember that Atemoztli means Coming Down of the Waters. *Atl* means "water,"

461

temo signifies "to descend," and thus is composed the term *atemoz-tli*, which we have explained. Thus the natives indicated that the purpose of this feast was a plea for water in the springtime. That is why it was called Coming Down of the Waters. All the ceremonies of the day were associated with this petition: the offering up of special foods, such as dough tamales, vegetables [and] blood-letting from the tongue, ear, genital organs, arms, shins, and breasts. Some of the people pulled long pieces of thin cord through the wounds in their fleshy parts or shins. Some passed these cords through their virile members, wreaking upon themselves a terrible butchery.

And on that day all were obliged to eat of that food without tasting any other. A most rigorous rule commanded that no one was to sleep on this night. Everyone was to remain watching in the temple courtyard, awaiting the "coming of the water." This vigil was called *ixtozoztli*, which means "to be on watch, or alert." Thus all the men and women waited in their vigil in the temple courtyard, with bonfires against the cold. All of this was similar to the way in which the people spend Christmas Eve today; people from the villages come to stay in the courtyard from evening on to observe this custom.

THE SEVENTEENTH MONTH OF THE YEAR

¶Of twenty days, in which was celebrated the feast called Tititl. Camaxtli, God of the Chase, was also remembered on this occasion.

ANOTHER commemoration took place at the beginning of this month. This was the Feast of the God of Hunting, Camaxtli. We have also mentioned him in Chapter XI [VII] and in "The Fourteenth Month" of this calendar. Eighty days before the feast we refer to, the god Camaxtli had already been honored in a way similar to that of the month Tititl (which means "to stretch"). Thus it is shown in our illustration, since the Indians placed or imagined in the heavens two children pulling at each other, very much as we picture the sign Gemini in certain stars [Plate 54]. Thus on the solemn feast of this day men and women joined hands, danced. On this feast a sour bread (called *xocotamalli*, "sour" or "bitter bread") was consumed. This bread and no other was eaten by everyone. [The people] also drank a bitter porridge made of purple corn. All this food and drink was offered up in the temples, and each person offered the same in his domestic shrine. The boys from the schools and monasteries amused themselves in a strange manner on this day. They fought a battle. Some made balls of the leaves of rushes; others made them of paper; and having attached

463

them to cords about a yard long, the two groups divided and fought until the balls had crumbled to pieces. Some say, however, that this combat took place in the previous month and not in this. It is of little importance, since we are dealing with childlike ceremonies, all the feasts being founded on foolishness.

The solemnity in honor of the divine Camaxtli was performed as has been described in Chapter XIV ["The Fourteenth Month"]. No men were sacrificed, only game from the hunt, which served as a victim on this month. Nevertheless, the natives did buy and dress up a slave for this day, and once he was clad in the garments of the God of the Chase, he was obliged to be a live representation of the divinity for this day. After he had played the role of the god, the slave was sacrificed. He was torn open, and when his heart had been offered to the devil, it was cast at the feet of the idol called Yemaxtli, He of the Three Breechcloths. With this the day was considered extremely solemn, and the false god was honored. The flesh of the man was eaten by those who had bought him for the occasion. According to our own day count this feast took place on the fifteenth of January, two days after the [octave of] Epiphany.

THE EIGHTEENTH MONTH OF THE YEAR

¶On which fell the solemn Feast of Izcalli and Xilomaniztli, together with a commemoration of Tlaloc, God
of the Waters, Thunder, Lightning, and Thunderbolts,
[the deity] presiding over the month. The Feast of
Cuahuitlehua took place at this time, before the coming
of the useless extra days.

THIS chapter deals with the eighteenth and last month of the
year and its ceremonies [Plate 55]. I have discovered that the first
day, the festive one, possessed two names: one was Xilomaniztli,
which means When the Ears of Corn Are Tender or When the Ear
of Maize Is Born. The other name was Izcalli, which means
Growth. The term comes from the verb *mozcaltia*, which, as I have
said, means "to grow." Both names are similar. When the ear of
corn is tender, this means that it is gradually growing. Thus the
rites on this day fit both names well: at the beginning of each year
the children's members had been stretched so that they would grow
well. Everything was stretched—necks, ears, noses, hands, feet,
and so on, so that the children would not fail to develop properly.
This ceremony was called *izcalaana*, meaning "to make grow by
stretching."

There was a special food for this day; it was made of boiled
amaranth leaves and corn mixed with the amaranth. No other food
could be eaten except this. It must be noted that there were diverse
types of food at each of the ancient feasts so as to revere the gods in

a ritual or ceremonial manner. The regulations could not be trespassed, nor could one eat anything on these special days except that which had been prescribed. As I have explained, all the native feasts included the eating of certain dishes as a basic part of the ritual. All was performed to obtain victuals and [to beg] more food of the false gods. I believe that the special food eaten on each feast was consumed in order to assure that this type of food [would not] be wanting at any time. Throughout the festal year all the foods appeared: breads, special dishes, and vegetables.

The second feast was in honor of Tlaloc and Matlalcueye. These were two majestic mountains which lie in this country; rainstorms are born there. One of [these mountains] is in Tlaxcala, and on the other lived the God of Thunderbolts and Tempests, as we have said. The one in Tlaxcala is called Matlalcueye, which the Spaniards have nicknamed Doña Mencia.[1] This territory breeds great storms, many of which cause much harm to the City of the Angels.[2] The mountain was called Matlalcueye, which means She of the Olive-Green Skirt. Others say it means She of the Net Skirt, since *matlatl* means "net"; but they are mistaken, since *matlalin* means "olive green." I myself believe that the latter meaning is correct because of the fresh greenness and green woods that cover the slopes of this mountain.

On this feast the natives slew a little boy and a girl in honor of the two mountains. Sacrifices, offerings of food, and the blood of

---

[1] Matlalcueye, She of the Green Skirt, or She of the Net Skirt, today known as Malinche, is a rocky mountain soaring some twelve thousand feet above sea level in the State of Tlaxcala. It has been almost totally neglected by archaeologists. John Hobgood, of the University of Chicago, reports that halfway up the hill there is a flat terrace called Tlalocan, Paradise of Tlaloc, scattered with pre-Conquest potsherds (Hobgood, personal communication, 1954). Fittingly enough, Tlaloc, God of the Waters, whose mountain stands nearby, was the spouse of Matlalcueye, or Chalchiuhcueye, She of the Jade Skirt, the same goddess. In 1950, according to Miguel Barrios, of the National School of Anthropology of Mexico, a pre-Hispanic cult was still flourishing on the slopes of Malinche, where neophites were instructed in the chants and rites of the ancient deities. Barrios, though a Nahuatl-speaking Indian, was never admitted to any of the cave rituals, and he considered it dangerous to intrude on those secret gatherings (Barrios, personal communication, 1950.)

[2] The modern Puebla de los Angeles, or Puebla de Zaragoza.

their own bodies were the oblations on that day, in the woods, in the caves, in the rocky places.

The season for sowing began in this month—on slopes and hills. This was because in ancient times there was such a large population without any other way of earning a living that it had to sow on the hills and plains, slopes and cliffs, leaving nothing unsown. But now the Indians have a thousand trades and occupations, and they are unmindful of sowing, since they believe that with the profit of these trades they can buy corn whenever they wish.[3] Thus today the people are unwilling to sow, and a scarcity of maize has been the result.

This feast was designed to encourage sowing on the hills. This was done early because as they say, moisture begins on the hills, rainstorms being more common there before they appear on the flatlands.

This month was also remembered as Cuahuitlehua, a name it was given at the beginning of the year. As we have stated, the word means To Bud or When the Trees Grow Green. We have explained these things more fully on describing the celebration of the native new year, when this feast was celebrated but on this occasion it was only a commemoration. Trees were honored, set up; and therefore a ceremony was made to extol the festivity. Long branches with their twigs were stuck into the ground near the places of sacrifice and along the streets. This festivity took place on the last day on the month, on the twenty-third of January [February]. With this solemn feast ended the ceremonies of the year, and there began the five extra and useless days, which, as I shall explain later, were never taken into account.[4]

[3] In these few lines Durán describes an economic upheaval as dramatic as the religious clash between the two cultures: the introduction of money, which was unknown in pre-Hispanic Mexico. Though cacao beans and small copper axes had served as rudimentary forms of currency, the appearance of gold and silver coins had a cataclysmic effect on the native economy.

[4] According to Durán, the Aztec months began on the following dates, according to the European calendar: First month, March 1; second month, March 21; third month, April 10; fourth month, April 30; fifth month, May 20; sixth month, June 9; seventh month, June 29; eighth month, July 19; ninth month, August 8; tenth month, August 28; eleventh month, September 17; twelfth month, October 7; thirteenth

month, October 27; fourteenth month, November 16; fifteenth month, December 6; sixteenth month, December 26; seventeenth month, January 15; eighteenth month, February 4; Nemontemi (the Five Extra Days), February 24. In concluding his description of the eighteenth month, Durán mistakenly substituted January for February.

THE EXTRA DAYS

It is well known to all of us that the year is composed of three hundred sixty-five days. Yet the natives counted three hundred sixty days, and the five additional ones were called the Extra, or Useless, Days. Unlike the others, they were nameless; no hieroglyphs were used for them; they were left blank; they were considered unfortunate; they were called Nemontemi, which means Useless, or Profitless, Days. On these five days the people fasted and did great penance, including abstinence from bread and water. They dined no more than once a day, and even that meal consisted of dry tortillas. They endured flagellation, bloodletting, and sexual abstinence. Those born at this time were considered unfortunate.

These people observed the leap year much as we do. If we look closely at the illustration, we shall see that the dominical symbol is on top of a small hill, thus beginning the [new] month [Plate 55, bottom]. Even though the [last] day fell under the sign of Flower, this [other] sign was added in order to pass from Flower to Head of Serpent. It was similar to the way in which we change the *a* to *g* in our leap year.[1]

Thus we terminate our brief and condensed version of the calendar. I understand, I realize, that I could have enlarged the book and described more things in a detailed way, but my sole intention has been to give advice to my fellow men and to our priests regarding the necessity of destroying the heathen customs which they will encounter constantly, once they have received my warning. My desire is that no heathen way be concealed, hidden, because the wound will grow rot, and fester, with our feigned ignorance.

Paganism must be torn up by the roots from the hearts of these frail people!

Let this [book] be to the honor and glory of the One True God, our Lord, He Who Lives and Reigns, Father, Son, and Holy Ghost, *in saecula sempiterna*. Amen.

---

[1] In this rather involved passage Durán describes the following process for adding one day to the leap year: (1) the current year ends in the eighteenth month; (2) the last sign of the month and year is, as always, Flower; (3) immediately afterward occur the five extra days; (4) in order to add an extra day to the year about to begin, the nineteenth sign, Rain (the symbol for which appears on the hill in Plate 55, in the last illustration), becomes a "false" first day of the new year; (5) the following day, Head of Serpent, is the "real" first day of the new year.

Durán's reference to the change of *a* to *g* indicates the dominical letter system. In some religious calendars one of the first seven letters of the alphabet is used to designate all the Sundays of a particular year. In 1970, for example, Thursday, January 1, was *a*; Friday, January 2, was *b*; Saturday, January 3, was *c*; Sunday, January 4, was *d*. Thus the dominical letter for 1970 is *d*. In order to adjust the day count, leap years are indicated by two dominical letters.

Acolhuacan.—The kingdom of the Acolhuas, who migrated to the Valley of Mexico in the thirteenth century and settled in Coatlichan (*q.v.*). By Nezahualpilli's time the Tetzcocan kingdom had become known as Acolhuacan.

amilpan.—"Irrigated fields." See *Book of the Gods and Rites*, Chapter XVI, note 4.

Amiztlato or amiztlato-Tecuhtli.—Lord of the Hunt, a title given by the Aztec state as a reward for outstanding services.

Atlacuilhuayan.—Present-day Tacubaya, a section of Mexico City south of Chapultepec Park.

Atlatonan.—One of the names of the Mother Goddess. Other names were Toci, Teteoinnan, Tlazolteotl, Cihuacoatl, and Xochiquetzal.

Azcapotzalco.—Ant Hill, meaning Metropolis. An important center in pre-Conquest times, capital of the Tecpanec people. Today it is part of Mexico City.

Aztec.—From Aztecatl, Man of Aztlan, the legendary home of the Aztecs. A name applied to the Mexica people of Mexico-Tenochtitlan.

Calmecac.—A school attached to a temple, run by priests, which prepared its pupils to be priests, civil leaders, and scholars. Sons and

471

daughters of nobles attended the school, and merchants' children were also admitted.

Calmeca Teteuctin.—Lords or dignitaries of the Calmecac (*q.v.*).

calpuleque.—An official in charge of a *calpulli*, or ward.

Camaxtli.—God of the Hunt.

capulin.—Wild cherry, *Prunus capulli.*

Ce Cipactli.—In the Aztec calendar, the first day in the year, similar to January 1. Ce means One. Cipactli, Head of Serpent, is a day name.

Chachalmeca.—High-ranking priests in charge of sacrifice. Their name may have derived from a cult originating at Chalman, near the city of Chalco.

Chachalmecacihuatl.—See Chachalmeca.

Chalca.—A citizen of Chalco. (*q.v.*).

Chalchiuhcihuatl.—A goddess of the harvest. Although Durán translates the name as Precious Stone, it actually means Precious Woman.

chalchihuitl.—"Jade." The word also referred to anything precious, since jade (together with quetzal feathers), was considered the most precious of materials.

Chalco.—Capital of the Chalca people, part of the Aztec empire, southeast of present-day Mexico City.

Chapultepec.—Grasshopper Hill, a small hill at the western end of Mexico-Tenochtitlan, at the foot of which the Aztec sovereigns had their likenesses carved. Today Chapultepec Park in Mexico City.

Chichimec.—Lineage of Dogs, probably a clan name. In Aztec history, the Chichimecs were barbarians from the north who invaded the Valley of Mexico in the early part of the thirteenth century.

Chicomecoatl.—Seven Serpent, Goddess of Corn and Agriculture. Durán, possibly influenced by Green mythology and the seven-headed beast of Revelation, at times calls her Seven-Headed Serpent.

Chiconquiahuitl.—Seven Rain, the calendar name of a deity, represented by a slave during the Feast of Xocotl Huetzi.

Chililico.—According to Durán, an impersonator of Huitzilopochtli. According to Sahagún, one of the main pyramids within the Sacred Enclosure of the Temple of Mexico.

Cihuacoatl.—Serpent Woman, one of the names of the Mother Goddess. She was also patroness of *cihuateteo*, women who died in childbirth. Cihuacoatl was also a title given to the public official who was second in command, substituting for the sovereign on occasion.

Coatlichan.—A town near Tetzcoco (Texcoco), today called Coatlinchan. According to Jiménez Moreno, Coatlichan was the principal cultural and political center of the Valley of Tetzcoco in the fourteenth century, reaching its peak under the sovereigns Huetzin and Acolmiztli. After the conquest of the city by the Tecpanecs of Azcapotzalco in 1375, Coatlichan lost its importance.

Coatlinahual. The name given to a slave who represented the god Coatlinahual, Weresnake. See *Book of the Gods and Rites*, Chapter I, note 15.

Coatzacualco.—The modern port of Coatzacoalcos in the southern part of Veracruz. See *Book of the Gods and Rites*, Chapter I, note 16.

cocolli.—"Twisted (bread)." Although it was made of corn dough in pre-Conquest times, the name has endured, and today one can buy a *cocol,* now made of wheat flour, in Mexican bakeries.

cocotlaxcalli.—"Twisted tortilla." See *cocolli.*

Colhuacan or Culhuacan.—Place Where the People have Grandfathers (that is, Important Ancestors). The name could also refer to the twisted (*coltic*) form of the hill upon whose slopes the town lies.

Cuachtlapuhcacoyaotzin.—A title, derived from *cuachic,* from *cuachichictli* (a tonsure characteristic of a high rank of warriors); *puhca* ("smoke"); and *yaotzin,* the diminutive of *yaotl* ("enemy"). All indicate attributes of Tezcatlipoca and can be translated Tonsured and Smoking Enemy.

Cuauhtemoc.—Descending Eagle, the last Aztec ruler, so called because of his relationship with the Sun, symbolized by the eagle, *cuauhtli.* In ancient theocratic Mexico the rulers were believed to be descended from the Sun.

Cuauhtlaxayauh.—Eagle Face, the name of a deity, represented by a slave during the Feast of Xocotl Huetzi.

cuauhxicalli.—"Eagle vessel," a great stone bowl in which the hearts of sacrificial victims were deposited.

Ehecatl.—God of Wind, one of the names of Quetzalcoatl.

etzalcualiztli.—The eating of corn and beans at the same time.

huauhtli.—Amaranth seed. See *Book of the Gods and Rites*, Chapter II, note 12.

huehuetqui.—Elder; old man.

Huexotzinco.—A city-state in what is today the State of Puebla, traditional enemy of the Aztecs of Mexico-Tenochtitlan.

Hueymac.—Great Hand, one of the last rulers of the Toltecs. Durán
identifies him with Topiltzin. See *Book of the Gods and Rites*, Chapter I, note 13.

Huitzilopochtli.—Humming Bird on the Left, a deity associated with
Tezcatlipoca. An Aztec war god and tribal deity, also considered to
be the Sun at high noon.

igualaz?—"Is it coming?" In Nahuatl, *Ye huallaz?*

Itzocan.—The present-day town of Izúcar de Matamoros, south of the
City of Puebla.

Itzucan.—See Itzocan.

Ixcozauhqui.—One of the attributes of Xiuhtecuhtli, the Fire God.

Ixhuacan.—See Itzocan.

Ixtliltzin or Ixtlilton.—The Little Black-Faced One, one of the four
hundred divinities of wine and drunkenness.

Iztaccihuatl.—White Woman, from *iztac* ("white") and *cihuatl* ("woman"). Worshiped not only as the mountain which bears this name but
also as a representation of the Mother Goddess, who dressed in white.

macpal tlaxcalli.—A tortilla shaped like a hand.

macuiltianquiztli.—A market held every five days.

Macuilxochitl.—Five Flower, also known as Xochipilli, Flowery Prince.
A Dionysus-like deity. See *Book of the Gods and Rites*, Chapter IX,
note 3.

Matlalcueye.—She of the Olive-Green Skirt, a name given to a mountain
in the State of Tlaxcala, today called La Malinche.

Mayahuel.—Goddess of Pulque. See *Book of the Gods and Rites*, Chapter IX, note 3.

Mecoatl.—Possibly Mixcoatl (*q.v.*).

Mexica.—An Aztec or citizen of Mexico.

Mexicatecuhtli.—Lord of the Mexica People, a title given by the Aztec
state as a reward for outstanding services.

Mexico.—In the Navel or Center of the Moon (Metztli) or In the Navel
or Center of the Century Plant (Metl). The capital of the Aztec
empire; today, the Republic of Mexico.

Mimixcoa.—Youths in the service of the god Mixcoatl (*q.v.*).

Mixcoatl.—Cloud Serpent. God of the Hunt, another name for Camaxtli
(*q.v.*).

Mixcoatontli.—A diminutive of Mixcoatl (*q.v.*).

Mixtec.—One of the People of the Clouds, an ethnic and linguistic group
in what is now the State of Oaxaca.

474

Miztoncatl-Tecuhtli.—Lord of the Mountain Lions, a title given by the Aztec state as a reward for outstanding services.

Moteczoma II.—Angry Lord, ruler of the Aztec empire from 1502 to 1520. Also spelled Motecuhzoma, Moctezuma, Montezuma, and Motecuzomatzin (the diminutive *tzin* was often attached to the names of the rulers).

mozauhque.—"They who fast."

Nahuatl.—The language of the Aztecs of Mexico-Tenochtitlan and of other areas in Mexico.

nepantla.—"In between."

Nezahualpilli.—Fasting Lord, son of Nezahualcoyotl of Tetzcoco and sovereign of that city after his father's death.

Nezahualpiltzintli.—Diminutive of Nezahualpilli (*q.v.*).

papalocuachtli.—A white mantle with a butterfly design in black, worn by certain Aztec priests.

pilli.—"Lord" or "child."

Popocatepetl.—Smoking Mountain, a snow-capped volcano southeast of the Aztec capital of Mexico-Tenochtitlan (today Mexico City).

Quetzalcoatl.—Feathered Serpent, one of the gods of creation, inventor of the arts, of writing, and of the calendar; patron of Cholula. Also, a culture hero, sovereign of the Toltecs: Ce Acatl (One Reed). See *Book of the Gods and Rites*, Chapter I, note 1.

Quilaztli.—One of the names of the Mother Goddess.

uiltamalli.—Tamales or cornbread made with greens.

ramada.—A bower made of branches.

Tacubaya.—See Atlacuilhuayan.

Tecpanec.—An inhabitant of Azcapotzalco or of Coyoacan.

Tecpanecatl or Tepanecatl-Tecuhtli.—Lord of the Tecpanecs, a title given by the Aztec state as a reward for outstanding services.

Tecuani.—Literally, "man eater." Anything that stings or bites, especially the jaguar.

tecutli or *tecuhtli.*—"Lord."

Telpochcalli.—House of Youths, a school under the direction of lay officials. Children of all classes were educated in such a school, and boys were trained to become warriors.

telpochtlatoque.—Leaders of young men in Aztec society.

Tenochca.—An inhabitant of Tenochtitlan.

Tenochtitlan.—Place next to the Hard Prickly-Pear Cactus, from *tenochtli* ("hard prickly pear"), *ti* ("next to"), and *tlan* ("place"). Mexico-

Tenochtitlan, together with Mexico-Tlatelolco, was the capital of the Aztec empire.

Tepanec.—See Tecpanec.

teponaztli.—A horizontal wooden drum.

tequihua.—Singular of *tequihuaque* (*q.v.*).

tequihuaque.—Freely, "they who have important work to do," derived from *tequitl* ("work"), *hua* ("he who has"), and *que* (plural).

tetzacualco.—"Enclosed by stone."

Tezcatlipoca.—One of the gods of creation, associated with Huitzilopochtli, with the night sky and stellar deities, and with darkness and destruction. He was the patron of wizards but was also the eternally young god—as such called Telpochtli, who resided over the Telpochcalli (*q.v.*).

tianguiz.—"Market," from the Nahuatl *tianquiztli.*

Titlacahuan.—One of the many attributes of Tezcatlipoca (*q.v.*), He Whose Slaves We Are.

Tlacahuepan. A divine and semilegendary personage associated with Huitzilopochtli (*q.v.*). See *Book of the Gods and Rites*, Chapter IX, note 3.

Tlacatecuhtli.—Lord of Men, a high title given by the Aztec state as a reward for outstanding services.

tlachihualtepetl.—An artificial hill or pyramid.

Tlacochcalcatl-Tecuhtli.—Lord of the House of Darts, a title given by the Aztec state as a reward for outstanding services.

Tlahuic.—One of the Tlahuica people who settled what is today the Valley of Morelos.

Tlapaltecatl.—A mountain near Tlaxcala, from *tlapilli* ("color" or "paint") and *tecatl* ("man").

Tlatelolca.—An inhabitant of Tlatelolco (*q.v.*).

Tlatelolco.—The northern part of present-day Mexico City. It was a separate entity until 1473, when it was absorbed by Mexico-Tenochtitlan.

tlazoyotl.—According to Molina, "an admirable and highly valued thing," or "something priceless."

Tleitoca.—"How do you say this?"

tlemaitl.—"Hand of fire," an incense burner.

tlenamactli.—The ceremony of offering incense.

Toltec.—A member of a Nahuatl-speaking group whose civilization reached its peak in central Mexico around A.D. 1000. See *Book of the Gods and Rites*, Chapter I, note 2.

Topiltzin.—The Toltec priest-king and holy man also called Quetzal-coatl. See *Book of the Gods and Rites*, Chapter I, note 1.

tzoalli.—Dough of amaranth seed mixed with honey. See *Book of the Gods and Rites*, Chapter II, note 9.

Xilonen.—Goddess of Tender Corn, another name for Chicomecoatl (*q.v.*).

Xiutecuhtli.—God of Fire.

Xochiquetzal.—Goddess of Flowers and Love. She is identified with the Mother Goddess.

Yacatecutli.—He Who Leads, God of the Merchants.

Yecatl.—See Ehecatl.

Yemaxtli.—See Camaxtli.

yoztlamiyahual.—According to Garibay (1967), "tassel of the cave."

Zacapan.—"On the grass."

zapote.—The fruit of the *sapota achras*, from the Nahuatl *tzapotl.*

Zapotec.—A member of an indigenous group in what is today the State of Oaxaca.

BIBLIOGRAPHY

I. Manuscripts

Durán, Diego
    1581   "Historia de las Indias de Nueva España y Islas de Tierra Firme." Microfilm of the sixteenth-century manuscript in the National Library of Madrid. Microfilm in the collection of Raúl Noriega, Mexico City.

    1854   "Historia de las Indias de Nueva España y Islas de Tierra Firme." Handwritten copy, made for José F. Ramírez, of the original sixteenth-century manuscript in the National Library of Madrid. Copy in the Historical Archives of the National Museum of Anthropology, Mexico City.

II. Printed Works

Acosta, José de, S.J.
    1590   *De natura Novi Orbis*. Salamanca.

    1962   *Historia natural y moral de las Indias*. 2d ed. by Edmundo O'Gorman. Mexico City, Fondo de Cultura Económica. Originally published in 1591.

Aguilar, Francisco de
1938 *Historia de la Nueva España de Fray Francisco de Aguilar.* Mexico City, Ediciones Botas.
Alvarado Tezozómoc, Fernando
1949 *Crónica Mexicáyotl.* Mexico City, Universidad Nacional Autónoma de México and Instituto Nacional de Antropología e Historia.
Anonymous
1941 *El Conquistador Anónimo: Relación de algunas cosas de la Nueva España y de la gran ciudad de Temestitan México. Escrito por un compañero de Hernán Cortés.* Ed. by León Díaz Cárdenas. Mexico City, Editorial América.
1944 *Códice Ramírez: Relación del origen de los indios que habitan esta Nueva España, segun sus historias.* Mexico City, Editorial Leyenda.
1948 *Anales de Tlatelolco y Códice de Tlatelolco.* Mexico City, Antigua Librería Robredo de José Porrúa e Hijos.
Barlow, Robert
1945 "La Crónica 'X,'" *Revista Mexicana de Estudios Antropológicos,* Vol. VIII.
1963 "Remarks on a Nahuatl Hymn," *Tlalocan,* Vol. IV, No. 2.
———, and George Smisor
1942 "Introducing *Tlalocan*," *Tlalocan,* Vol. I, No. 1, pp. 1–2.
Beristáin y Souza, José Mariano
1816–21 *Biblioteca hispanoamericana septentrional.* 3 vols. Mexico City.
Bernal, Ignacio
1947 "Los calendarios de Durán," *Revista Mexicana de Estudios Antropológicos,* Vol. IX, Nos. 1–3.
1964 "Introduction," *The Aztecs: The History of the Indies of New Spain,* by Fray Diego Durán. Tr. by Doris Heyden and Fernando Horcasitas. New York, Orion Press.
Caso, Alfonso
1953 *El Pueblo del Sol.* Mexico City, Fondo de Cultura Económica.
1958 *The Aztecs: People of the Sun.* Tr. by Lowell Dunham. Norman, University of Oklahoma Press.

479

Clavijero, Francisco Javier, S.J.
1944   *Historia antigua de México*. 2 vols. Mexico City, Editorial Delfín.

Cortés, Hernán
1963   *Cartas y documentos*. Introduction by Mario Hernández de Sánchez-Barba. Mexico City, Editorial Porrúa.

Covarrubias, Miguel
1947   *Mexico South: The Isthmus of Tehuantepec*. New York, Alfred A. Knopf.

Dávila Padilla, Agustín
1955   *Historia de la fundación y discurso de la provincia de Santiago de México, de la Orden de Predicadores*. Facsimile of the first edition of 1625. Introduction by A. Millares Carlo. Mexico City, Academia Literaria.

Díaz del Castillo, Bernal
1928   *The Discovery and Conquest of Mexico: 1517–1521*. Tr. by A. P. Maudslay. Mexico City, Mexico Press.
1939   *Historia verdadera de la Conquista de la Nueva España*. 3 vols. Mexico City, Editorial Pedro Robredo.

Durán, Diego
1867–80 *Historia de las Indias de Nueva España y Islas de Tierra Firme*. 2 vols. and *Atlas*. Ed. by José F. Ramírez. Mexico City, J. M. Andrade and F. Escalante (Vol. I), I. Escalante (Vol. II).
1951   *Historia de las Indias de Nueva España y Islas de Tierra Firme*. Ed. by José Fernando Ramírez. 2 vols. Mexico City, Editora Nacional, S.A.
1964   *The Aztecs: The History of the Indies of New Spain*. Tr. by Doris Heyden and Fernando Horcasitas. Introduction by Ignacio Bernal. New York, Orion Press.
1967   *Historia de las Indias de Nueva España e Islas de la Tierra Firme*. 2 vols. Ed. by Angel María Garibay K. Mexico City, Editorial Porrúa.

Eguiara y Eguren, Juan José
1944   *Biblioteca mexicana*. Mexico City, Agustín Millares Carlo.

Fernández del Castillo, Francisco
1925   "Fray Diego de Durán," *Anales del Museo Nacional de Arqueología, Historia y Etnografía*, Vol. IX, p. 3.

Foshag, W. F.

1959   "Mineralogical Attributions," *Precolumbian Art: Robert Woods Bliss Collection*. London, Phaidon Press.

Franco, Alonso

1900   *Segunda parte de la historia de la provincia de Santiago de México*. Mexico City, Imprenta del Museo Nacional.

Gallo, Eduardo L., ed.

1873   *Hombres ilustres mexicanos: Biografías de los personajes notables desde antes de la conquista hasta nuestros días*. 3 vols. Mexico City, Ignacio Cumplido.

García Granados, Rafael

1952–53   *Diccionario biográfico de historia antigua de Méjico*. 3 vols. Mexico City, Instituto de Historia, Universidad Nacional de México.

García Martínez, Bernardo

1966   "La historia de Durán," *Historia Mexicana*, Vol. XVI, No. 1.

Garibay K., Angel María

1947   "Paralipómenos de Sahagún," *Tlalocan*, Vol. II, No. 2.

1952   "Poema de travesuras," *Tlalocan*, Vol. III, No. 2.

1953–54   *Historia de la literatura náhuatl*. 2 vols. Mexico City, Editorial Porrúa.

Gibson, Charles

1964   *The Aztecs Under Spanish Rule: A History of the Indians of the Valley of Mexico, 1519–1810*. Stanford, Stanford University Press.

González Obregón, Luis

1941   *Las calles de México*. Mexico City, Editorial Botas.

Icaza, Amelia Martínez del Río de

1963   "Costumbres y creencias de Tetelcingo," *Tlalocan*, Vol. IV, No. 2.

Jaeger, Edmund C.

1953   "Poorwill Sleeps Away the Winter," *National Geographic Magazine*, Vol. CIII, No. 2.

Jiménez Moreno, Wigberto

1956   *Historia antigua de México*. Mexico City, Ediciones SAENA.

Kroeber, A. L.

1948   *Anthropology*. New York, Harcourt, Brace and Company.

Kubler, George
   1948   *Mexican Architecture of the Sixteenth Century.* New Haven, Yale University Press.
Leal, Luis
   1953   "El Códice Ramírez," *Historia Mexicana*, Vol. III, No. 1.
León Pinelo, Antonio de
   1629   *Epítome de la biblioteca oriental i occidental náutica y geográfica.* Ed. by Juan González. Madrid.
Lorenzo, José Luis
   1957   *Las zonas arqueológicas de los volcanes Iztaccíhuatl y Popocatépetl.* Series Publication No. 3, *Dirección de prehistoria.* Mexico City, Instituto Nacional de Antropología e Historia.
Lowie, Robert
   1924   *Primitive Religion.* New York, Boni and Liveright.
McAndrew, John
   1965   *The Open-Air Churches of Sixteenth-Century Mexico.* Cambridge, Harvard University Press.
McGee, W. J.
   1898   *The Seri Indians.* Washington, D.C., Bureau of American Ethnology *Fifth Annual Report.*
Molina, Alonso de
   1944   *Vocabulario en lengua castellana y mexicana.* Facsimile of the 1571 edition, by Antonio de Spinola in Mexico. Madrid, Ediciones Cultura Hispánica.
Motolinía (Toribio de Benavente)
   1941   *Historia de los indios de la Nueva España.* Mexico City, Editorial Salvador Chávez Hayhoe.
Muñoz Camargo, Diego
   1948   *Historia de Tlaxcala.* Mexico City, Ateneo Nacional de Ciencias y Arte.
Nohl, Johannes
   1960   *The Black Death.* New York, Ballantine Books.
O'Gorman, Edmundo
   1962   "Introducción," *Historia natural y moral de las Indias*, by José de Acosta. Mexico City, Fondo de Cultura Económica.
Paso y Troncoso, Francisco del, ed.
   1905   *Papeles de Nueva España.* 7 vols. Madrid, Sucesores de Rivadeneyra.

Prescott, William H.
n.d.   *History of the Conquest of Mexico.* New York, Modern Library.

Radin, Paul
1920   *The Sources and Authenticity of the History of the Ancient Mexicans.* Partial translation of the Códice Ramírez. University of California *Publications in American Archaeology and Ethnology,* Vol. XVII, No. 1.

Ricard, Robert
1947   *La Conquista espiritual de México.* Mexico City, Editorial Jus, Editorial Polis.

Robertson, Donald
1968   "Paste-over Illustrations in the Durán Codex of Madrid," *Tlalocan,* Vol. V, No. 4.

Ruiz de Alarcón, Hernando
1892   "Tratado de las supersticiones y costumbres gentílicas que hoy viven entre los indios, naturales de esta Nueva España," *Anales del Museo Nacional de Arqueología y Etnografía,* Vols. I–VI. Mexico City.

Sahagún, Bernardino de
1938   *Historia general de las cosas de Nueva España.* Introduction by Wigberto Jiménez Moreno. Notes by Eduard Seler. 5 vols. Mexico City, Editorial Pedro Robredo.
1950–63 *Florentine Codex: General History of the Things of New Spain.* Tr. from Nahuatl by Arthur J. O. Anderson and Charles E. Dibble. 10 vols. Santa Fe, School of American Research and University of Utah.

Sandoval, Fernando B.
1945   "La relación de la Conquista de México en la *Historia* de Fray Diego Durán," *Estudios de Historiografía de la Nueva España.* Mexico City, El Colegio de México.

Seler, Eduard
1963   *Comentarios al Codice Borgia.* Tr. from German into Spanish by Mariana Frenk. 2 vols. and facsimile of codex. Mexico City, Fondo de Cultura Económica.

Soustelle, Jacques
1959   *Pensamiento cosmológico de los antiguos mexicanos.* Tr. from French into Spanish by María Elena Landa A. Puebla, Federación Estudiantil Poblana.

Spence, Lewis
1923   *The Gods of Mexico*. London.
Tapia, Andres de
1950   "Relación de algunas cosas," *Crónicas de la Conquista*. Mexico City, Biblioteca del Estudiante Universitario, Universidad Nacional Autónoma.
Taylor, Norman
1963   *Narcotics: Nature's Dangerous Gifts*. New York, Dell Publishing Company.
Thompson, J. Eric S.
1934   "Sky Bearers, Colors, and Directions in Maya and Mexican Religion," Carnegie Institute of Washington *Publication* No. 436, Contribution 10.
Toor, Frances
1947   *A Treasury of Mexican Folkways*. New York, Crown Publishers.
Weitlaner, Roberto J., and Carlo Antonio Castro
1954   *Papeles de la Chinantla Mayultianguis y Tlacoatzintepec*. Mexico City, Instituto Nacional de Antropología e Historia.
Wicke, Charles, and Fernando Horcasitas
1957   "Archaeological Investigations on Mount Tlaloc, Mexico," *Mesoamerican Notes*, No. 5. Mexico City, Mexico City College.

INDEX

485

494

San Antonio Abad, church of: 236
Sandals: 73, 86, 99, 130–31, 183, 198–201, 226
Sandoval, Fernando: 12, 13, 37
San Francisco, monastery of: 74
San Hipólito, church and hospital of: 7, 283
San Juan de Letrán, school of: 6
San Juan de Ulúa, Mexico: 69
San Juan Moyotlan (ward): 7
San Pablo Zoquipan (ward): 7, 297
San Sebastián Atzacualco (ward): 7
Santa María Cuepopoan (ward): 7
Santiago: *see* Saint James the Apostle
Santiago (Compostela), Spain: 268
Sapota: 176, 417, 459
Sayago, Spain: 52
Scorpions: 115
Sculpture and sculptors (Aztec): 59, 74, 111, 215, 255; in stone, 63, 76, 80, 98, 155, 156, 174, 177–81, 189–90, 210–11, 212, 217, 243, 258, 270, 273, 290, 314–15, 416, 428; in wood, 98, 103, 130, 143, 222, 231, 249, 432; in straw, 236; and goddess of sculptors, 239; in *tzoalli*, 245, 256, 445, 457–59; and day sign of sculptors, 403; in clay, 416, 420
Serpents: 115, 118, 147, 400, 420, 456
Seville, Spain: 3, 4
Shields (Aztec): 73, 74, 86, 109, 112, 124, 131, 174, 178–79, 188–90, 191, 192, 226, 231, 234, 236
Sierra Nevada: *see* Iztaccihuatl
Silver: 98, 122, 129, 130, 143, 152, 155, 195, 226, 234, 239, 249, 258
Skirts (Aztec): 210, 231, 250, 257, 423, 454
Skull racks: *xxii*, 40, 79, 215, 459
Skunks: 279
Slaves and slavery (Aztec): 96, 106, 122, 281–86, 301–305, 318–19; purchase and sale of, 133, 138; as sacrificial victims, 138, 175, 183, 191, 204–205, 212–14, 227, 250, 256, 259, 432, 443, 464; Negroes as, 180, 280; as impersonators of gods, 204–205; market of, 278–80; wooden collars of, 278–80, 305; as dancers and singers, 280; children of, 283–84; freeing of, 284–86
Smisor, George: 35
Sociopolitical organization (Aztec):

birth in, 55, 124–25, 424; marriage and sexual relations in, 55, 123–24, 148–51, 198, 199, 292, 397, 435; old age in, 96, 309; and social ranks, 96, 112, 137–39, 194–202, 256; and government, 109, 137–39, 194–202, 284, 287–89; and age grading, 113–14 & n., 428; and circumcision, 124, 423–24; and lineages, 242; *see also* laws
Songs and charts (Aztec): 55, 71, 207; to Huitzilopochtli, 94; to Tezcatlipoca, 107; to the dead, 122–23; of impersonator of Quetzalcoatl, 132; to Tota, 162; to Tlaloc, 164; to Xipe, 177, 183; about fire and sacrifice, 214; of impersonator of Toci, 232; at feast of Toci, 234; of slaves, 280; and school of song, 289–300; and poets, 295; about conquests, 299; about genealogies, 299; about gods, 299; about victories, 299; about wealth, 299; and incantations, 317–18; at Huey Tecuilhuitl feast, 438–40; at Xocotl feast, 442–43; *see also* rhetoric and metaphor
Soot: as body paint, 83, 91, 103, 110, 120, 138, 216, 456; in priest's gourd, 106; applied to children, 110, 125; of torch pine, 114; as "divine nourishment," 115, 116; as medicine, 117, 118; ritual use of, 118; on patolli mat, 303
Sorcerers (Aztec): 54, 118, 125, 150–53, 255, 459–60
Spain: 42, 43, 52; *see also* names of towns
Spears: 109, 112, 164
Spiders: 115
Squash: 182, 266
Squirrels: 147
Sun (in Aztec religion): creation of, 78; sacrifice to, 92, 106, 179, 440; prayers to, 101, 104; impersonator of, 175; image of, 180, 273; feast of, 185–93, 414; knights of, 194–202, 414; as god, 428
Superstition (Aztec): 54, 125, 134, 135, 150–53, 221–22, 263, 268–69, 319, 386, 414, 425, 431, 439, 441–43, 459–60, 470; about maize, 176, 416–17; about dreams, 218–19; about saints, 235; about hills, 259; about bathhouses, 270–72; about marketplaces, 277; about eating dogs, 279; about animals,